To

Rich

The Life and Histories of
EDWARD TULL-WARNOCK
(1886-1950)

Many thanks for your
kind and generous support

Best wishes

Phil

First published 2023
Rymour Books
with the Hog's Back Press
45 Needless Road,
PERTH
PH20LE

© Phil Vasili 2023
ISBN 978-1-7394801-9-6

A CIP record for this book is
available from the British Library
BIC Classification BG HBG

Cover and book design by Ian Spring
Typeset in Garamond
Printed and bound by
Imprint Digital
Seychelles Farm
Upton Pyne
Exeter

Rymour Books is committed to the sustainable use
of natural resources. The paper used in this book
is approved by the Forest Stewardship Council

The Life and Histories of

EDWARD TULL-WARNOCK
(1886-1950)

Phil Vasili

RYMOUR

Dedicated to the memory of my selfless father, Varnavas Vasili, who died 10 October 2017.

And to friends of colour from my childhood and youth, John Fraser and David Hector, consistently and destructively battered by endemic racism.

Contents

Chapter Eleven—Edward and Walter

Chapter Twelve—Edward, Paul and Politics

Chapter Thirteen—Changing Colour of Narratives

Preface

Why I chose a large canvas

Writing the biography Edward Tull-Warnock and his families was a mixture of pleasurable research and writing disciplined by successive lock-downs. Working on such a fulfilling, inspiring project was a privilege. It would not have happened without the support of his grandchildren, the Finlaysons and Justads. They were never too busy to respond to my frequent and numerous requests for help and guidance and allowed unlimited time and access to their uniquely valuable family history repository, the Finlayson Family Archive. As I got to know him I purposefully chose to go beyond the chronology of Edward's life. A character emerged moulded as much by his enslaved inheritance as by his professional and spiritual life. Needing sunlight, fresh air and exercise at the close of the keyboarding day I would walk on the heath near my flat. Despite passing it numerous times an inscripted bench always turned my head: I was born tomorrow, Today I live, yesterday killed me. These ten words capture the essence of Edward's life: a man of colour that embodied twenty-first century (BLM) demands of respect and equality; who enjoyed each day and improved the lives of others because of that; but was burdened by a predominant narrative that attempted to diminish him and people of similar pigmentation.

His life-long preoccupations of family, Christian socialism, sport and music remain sites of struggle. Children and families living in poverty has grown exponentially in Britain with the retraction of the Welfare State and declining per capita funding of the NHS. Council and social house building is virtually non-existent.

During spring 2021 the owners of six English Premier League clubs went public on their determination to play in a Europe Super League the following season. They and other founder clubs would be permanently protected from relegation. Expecting opposition from traditional fans, they dismissed them as 'legacy supporters' whose usefulness and necessity would fade over time. Misunderstanding completely the history and culture of football and its importance to working class communities, they were strategically outplayed by fans and forced to drop their idea of corporate-franchise football.

The All-Parliamentary Group for Music Education published their State of the Nation report in February 2019 revealing that music in schools was being acutely damaged by government policy. This was re-emphasised in the Incorporated Society of Musicians

December 2020 report, The Heart of the School is Missing. The last chapter attempts to provide a contemporary evaluation Edward's concern's, especially the struggle against racism and apartheid and the fight for a more peaceful, equitable and rational society based humane values. Discussions range across landscapes and architecture populated after his death, such as the Black Lives Matter movement and the renewed battle against fascism, an ideology that has White supremacy at its core.

It is a requirement of the empathetic biographer to, if not walk in the shoes of their subject, at least imagine stepping into them. Of mixed-European descent I will never be able to fully understand the lived experience of a person of colour. Growing up with a younger brother of African-American heritage did provide an insight into the different treatment and response each of us receive out of doors. I discuss the wild behavioural fluctuations Edward encountered along the cultural continuum of acceptance-indifference-hostility. Recently, just before I began writing up the research, I (was fortunate to have) encountered a milder, temporary yet very public manifestation of this socio-cultural phenomenon that seems to mirror in its unpredictability current weather patterns. Under the headline 'Suspended activists use fringe union to infiltrate Labour' the *Sunday Times*, 25 August 2019 attacked a number of trade unionists for supporting Jeremy Corbyn and Palestine. Then chair of Unite Community Camden I was labelled by their journalist Gabriel Pogrund a 9/11 conspiracy theorist. The article inferred we had been suspended as Labour members over alleged racism and bullying. He revealed that this amateur historian… has posted dozens of times that the CIA and Mossad masterminded 9/11. The *Jewish Chronicle* repeated the accusations. Nick Cohen, *Spectator,* 29 February, the following year repeated the assertions adding I saw Starmer as a right wing coup loser and neoliberal Blairite.

I had been pre-warned by my full-time union officer, Vic Paulino, that I should sit tight and say nothing. Reluctantly, I did.

In fact I had not been suspended by the Labour Party. That was to come some four months later for conduct which in the opinion of the National Executive Committee is prejudicial, or… grossly detrimental to the Party. I had been warned in a letter just a year earlier about posting tweets questioning the official narrative of 9/11 and reposting arguments by many that fundamental questions, not addressed by the 9/11 Commission, needed to be answered.

Pogrund has form: a year earlier he had smeared another political activist, Mike Sivier, with the tag of holocaust denier. An

Independent Press Standards Organisation ruling, 29 August 2018, found the journalist had breached the code pertaining to truthfulness and written material that was inaccurate, misleading and distorted.

The attacks were part of general smear campaign against those on the left of the Labour Party and supportive of the Corbyn leadership and rights for Palestine and Palestinians. Pogrund and Cohen had an audience of targets rather than a target audience.

Chaotic episodes that seek to demean, while momentary for me, were daily occurrences for Edward as a man of colour in an overwhelmingly White world. He never knew what was around the corner, whether he should duck and weave or respond with a smile. Often, he did both.

Introduction

Edward's home, Glasgow, has long been residence to people of colour. His life stands testament to this tradition. Glasgow University — its medical school in particular — has a proud history of hosting students of African, Caribbean and African American heritage such as James McCune Smith, the first man of colour in the United States to hold a medical degree. Grenadan-Scot Henry Wharton, Africa's first Caribbean-born Methodist missionary and father of world sprint champion and first professional footballer of colour, was schooled in the city. Queen's Park FC was the club of Andrew Watson when he became Scotland's first mixed-heritage captain in 1881, inspiring a 5-1 defeat of England, then their heaviest at home. The club signed the first footballer of colour Robert Walker in the eighteen seventies. Celtic FC signed Jamaican Gil Heron, whose son Gil Scott Heron became a world-famous jazz musician, just a year after Edward's death. Their first player of colour, Abdul Salim Bachi Khan, was signed two decades earlier.

Edward's brother Walter, when applying for officer training in 1916 was asked if he was of pure European descent, code for White. That question betrayed the ideological assumption that Europeans were naturally light-skinned. The conceptual zenith and most destructive manifestation of this ideology was Hitler's fascism.

Ahmed and Ibrahim Ali's discussion of brown-skinned Gaels, Black Celts, argue these were the first Indo-European people to reach the British Isles, arriving during the Iron Age. They suggest there is a link between the generic Celtic language and the Erythraic, which has its origin in Ethiopia. They draw upon written sources, folklore and tradition to argue brown-skinned people were the original inhabitants.

The authors cite ancient texts of history and mythology The Annals of Clonmacnoise and Lebor Gabala (Book of Invasions) recording the arrival of African pirates and invaders, Fomorians, as evidence of millennial presence. Geoffrey of Monmouth's twelfth century History of the Kings of Britain states

[Malgo] was succeeded by Kareticus, another lover of civil wars. He was too hateful to the sight of God and Britons alike. The Saxons took note of his instability and sent word to Gormund, the king of a group of Africans who had come to Ireland in great ships and had subdued the people of that land. And so this Gormund now sailed with 160,000 Africans to Britain, which was currently being ravaged by the Saxons on the one hand, and the horrible civil wars that the

Britons were fighting among themselves on the other. Making a pact with the Saxons, Gormund made war on King Kareticus.

The Ali's recount an Isle of Lewis legend claiming tall Black people erected Scotland's oldest man-made structure, the five thousand year-old, neolithic Calanais Stones. Locally named Fir Bhreig (false men), many folklore tales attempt explanation of their origin.

A story flooded mainstream news outlets during February 2018 claiming the earliest inhabitants of the British Isles probably had brown skin and blue eyes. It was the outcome of an analysis of bone powder taken from the skeleton of Cheddar Man, in a collaborative project between the Natural History Museum and University College London. The ten thousand year-old remains were discovered in 1903 in a cave in the west of England, hence the name. It is an interesting hypothesis and concurs with the general scientific consensus that our evolutionary origins began in Africa. The oldest bone belonging to the human family tree yet discovered is a cranium from Woranso-Mille, Ethiopia dated to 3.8 million years ago. In the Arctic region of northern Europe the indigenous brown-skinned Inuit have existed for millennia.

Reality or myth there has been an historical connection between people of colour, Scotland, Gaelic peoples and culture for thousands of years. There is indisputable evidence to support a consistent presence for at least five hundred years. And for over one hundred and twenty years Scotland has been the home Edward Tull-Warnock and descendants.

Abbreviations

ANC—African National Congress
ABH—Alexander Burnett Hutchison
BBC—British Broadcasting Corporation
BDA—British Dental Association
BLM—Black Lives Matter
BOSS—Bureau of State Security (South Africa)
BEF—British Expeditionary Force
BWIR—British West Indies Regiment
CHO—Children's Home and Orphanage
CIA—Central Intelligence Agency (USA)
CMA—Company of Merchants trading into Africa
CPGB—Communist Party of Great Britain
CLP—Constituency Labour Party
CPS—Crown Prosecution Service
EIC—East India Company
FBI—Federal Bureau of Investigation (USA)
GC—Guinea Company
GDP—Gross Domestic Product
GE—General Election
GHQ—General Headquarters
HQ—Headquarters
ILD—International Labour Defence
LBF—Lothian Black Forum
LCP—League of Coloured Peoples
LDS - Licensed Dental Surgeon
LFI—Labour Friends of Israel
LP—Labour Party (UK)
MoD—Ministry of Defence
MP—Member of Parliament
NA—National Archives (UK)
NATO—North Atlantic Treaty Organisation
NHS—National Health Service
NUM—National Union of Mineworkers
PCI—Communist Party of Italy
PTSD—Post Traumatic Stress Disorder
RA—Royal Adventurers into Africa
RAC—Royal Africa Company
RAF—Royal Air Force
SA—Senegal Adventurers
SIS—Secret Intelligence Service

Chapter One
The Barbados Tulls

Edward's paternal grandfather, born William Criss around 1808, was enslaved from birth on the Clifton Hall plantation, St. John, Barbados. Some seven years younger, it is not known on which plantation his paternal grandmother Anna Frances (nee) Lashly was born. William and Anna had at least five children: Sarah Elizabeth, born 30 April, 1842 at Clifton Hill, St. Thomas; William, 18 October, 1845, Olive Branch, St. Thomas; Samuel James, 14 February, 1848, Prinz Henry, 30 May, 1850 and Daniel, father of Edward, 7 April, 1856, all at Clifton Hill. These natalities suggest William lived in the Clifton Hill area of St. Thomas for at least two generations, a conclusion that cannot be made for Anna given the genealogical information available.

Post-emancipation Barbados was more structured by pigmentocracy – skin-colour as the primary influence upon life chances and social status – than virtually any other Caribbean island. In his *Short Journal*, begun 10 October 1877 soon after he arrived in England, Daniel writes of being educated by Moravian church missionaries when the family lived at My Lord's Hill, St Michael's parish in the early eighteen sixties. He states proudly that his cousin, Henry Simmons 'has the title of BA'.[1] His mother, Anna, could also read and write and from her letters it seems highly likely she had some form of education. This would not have been unusual for enslaved worshippers at Moravian chapels.

Education was important to the Tulls. Enslaved people and former enslaved people saw literacy as a gateway to personal and collective social and political progress. They believed their life chances could be improved if they could read and write.

Missionaries competed for indigenous hearts and minds in the colonies. Those souls consciously ignored by the elitist, planter-dominated Church of England were tempted by less established and smaller sects. Non-conformist Christian groups – notably Quakers, Methodists and Moravians – actively proselytised among the brown-skinned population. Although Barbados had more schools per square mile in 1834 than any other British colony, only five accepted pupils of colour. A visitor in the 1850s, the Reverend Edward Pinder, writing as

---

1 Daniel Tull, *A Short Journal*, Finlayson Family Archive, Strathpeffer, Scotland.

'Meliora', commented on the lack of education for children: from thirty-six thousand two hundred and eleven aged between six and fourteen only seven thousand five hundred were getting some kind of education. He felt this was a consequence of the colonial master being 'the most backward in the matter of education, of all the great European nations'.[2]

MORAVIANS

The Moravian church of the United Brethren had been active amongst the enslaved at Clifton Hill since at least the eighteen thirties. Their missionaries – *Brothers* and *Sisters* – had arrived in Barbados during the seventeen sixties intent on bringing the gospel to those who had been denied by law access to Christianity. Their first Synod of 1736 declared that the foremost objective of the church was 'the extension of the kingdom of God among Christians and the heathen'.[3]

A Protestant sect formed in the fifteenth century, they had been forced to leave their Moravian homeland in the seventeen twenties and for protection settle in Saxony, Germany. In the Caribbean they had originally been active on the Danish islands of St. Thomas and St. John, followed by Antigua. While they were progressive in wanting to work specifically amongst people of colour they did not publicly participate in political affairs or offer opinion. Their ministers tended to be German or English, a reflection of where they had the most adherents. They were meticulous record keepers and their archives are an invaluable and unique repository of documents that reveal details of the lives of a population that until 1817 was not formally registered or recorded.

As religious outsiders they relied on the goodwill of individual plantation owners, usually Quakers, to engage in missionary work. Beginning on Jackman's plantation, St Michael, in the spring of 1767 within a year they had baptised their first Bajan, Sarah. Brother Brookshaw's practice of visiting them in their homes[4] saw congregations grow slowly, more a consequence of a general reluctance by most Anglican planters and managers to facilitate meetings and services in fear of their enslaved becoming Christians. However, a perception developed

2 'Meliora', (Reverend Edward Pinder), *Letters on the Labouring Population of Barbados* (London, 1858), p. 22.
3 *Results of the Synod of the Brethren Church held in Herrnhut in 1836*, p. 63. ENG MS 1059, John Rylands Library, Manchester.
4 *Periodical Accounts XXV* p. 345, Moravian Archives, Muswell Hill, London.

amongst a very small minority of planters that church worship could accrue positive economic and political advantages. Near the close of the century 'there is [sic] 5 estates in which we can unmolestedly go on Sunday in the forenoon, the Negro hears the gospel with attention'.[5]

Reverend James Young Edghill suggested these friendly plantations were Lears, Exchange, Applethwaites, Friendly Hall and Yorkshire Hall/Vaucluse.[6] The last named in 1834 was owned, coincidentally, by Henry Simmons and had listed in the Slave Register, William Tull, aged four and ten months.[7]

Whites and people of colour initially attended Moravian services but the focus of the missionaries was upon the latter, engendering a cultural environment that became unpalatable to some Whites. This was gradually reflected in the ethnic composition of the congregation, a development not unwelcome to some brothers and sisters who found the 'vicious and immoral habits' of White worshippers a corrupting influence on their Negro flock.[8]

Enslavers had long denied Christianity to the enslaved whilst simultaneously and paradoxically justifying enslavement by reference to their non-Christian status. Most plantation owners were overwhelmingly hostile to the Moravians, seeing them as a disruptive radical cult that would foster in the minds of the enslaved dangerous ideas of equality and liberty. Some planters were proactively opposed, preventing their enslaved from going to Sunday chapel by threats and violence.

In practice the Moravian church was hierarchical, slave-owning and remained publicly silent on the abolition question. Nevertheless, its ethos and practice as a faith community was arguably less socially rigid than other faith groups, bar the Quakers. Its missionaries and services had space for active and meaningful participation by the congregation. The enslaved could acquire formal positions of responsibility through commitment and conformity – evidenced by consistent disciplined

5 Sharon, Barbados, 1 June 1796: letter from Brother Nicholas Hoffman to Christian Latrobe, London. *Barbados Letters from 1768-1813,* A Book, p. 141/2 Moravian Archives, Muswell Hill, London.

6 Reverend J Y Edghill *About Barbados* (London, 1890), p. 22.

7 T/71/561 N A London. Also the name of Daniel Tull's cousin, Henry Simmons had children with enslaved women.

8 G.G. Oliver Maynard *The History of the Moravian Church Eastern West Indies,* (Port of Spain, 1968), p. 62.

behaviour and action – as: 'Missionaries, Assistant Missionaries, Lay Readers, National Assistants/Helpers'.[9]

A procedural method of involvement was the unique activity of 'speaking'. Part of the preparation of being formally accepted into the church through Holy Communion, an individual would divulge to their congregation thoughts and motives pertaining to their faith. The 1836 Synod described 'the immediate object of this usage is to facilitate the duty of self-examination'.[10] The confessional was usually transcribed, retaining for posterity a unique insight into a neglected mental terrain. Unfortunately, no speaking transcripts have been discovered for the Tulls.

Music was also an important element to worship, the Moravians' enthusiasm contrasting with the planters' historical suppression of this enjoyment by the enslaved.

> A style of music and of musical performances, consistent with the true spirit of the congregation, tends in no degree to impress our religious services with a pleasing and harmonious character. The influences of music, upon the devotion and spiritual improvement of the congregation, ought therefore never to be lost sight of.[11]

The first purpose-built chapel was opened at Sharon, St. Thomas, in February, 1799. This was close to Clifton Hall plantation, in walking distance for William and Anna. Within twenty-five years, the success at Sharon had led to another mission station opening at Mount Tabor. At the end of the following decade, where emancipation had further boosted congregation numbers, a third site of worship was opened, Clifton Hill Chapel, on land donated by Henry Trotman, owner of Clifton plantation.

The increasing attraction of the church to both enslaved and planters was a combination of three juxtaposed and contradictory characteristics: 1) The missionaries willingness to respect people of colour as thinking, sentient human beings with a cultural history. This was illustrated by, for example, the practices of speaking; allocating positions of responsibility; visiting enslaved in their shacks; recording

9 *The Missionary Manual And Directory Of The Unitas Fratrum Or The Moravian Church* (Bethlehem, PA, 1875), p. 13

10 *Results of the Synod of the Brethren Church held in Herrnhut in 1836*, p. 30.

11 Ibid, p. 34.

both their indigenous ethnic origin – as opposed to continental origin – and their self-defined names, information unavailable elsewhere in the eighteenth century. 2) The church's unwillingness to involve itself in politics and make public comment. This apolitical public stance was official policy as outlined by the 1736 Synod. 3) Its preoccupation with congregational and communal discipline that demanded obedience to the teachings of the church. For example, Lewis (1985) identifies seven categories of membership of the church, one comprising 'excluded people' who had violated rules.

These practices were instrumental in nurturing a community of followers that were, by and large, literate, socially conservative and non-political.

A boast of the church in the vengeful and recriminatory atmosphere after the revolutionary 1816 Bussa uprising was that none of their congregations had been involved. This had noticeable appeal to planters, especially those with a residue of empathy towards the sufferings of their 'live' property. They recognised that a workforce that had absorbed the Moravian values of self-control and self-improvement was more efficient in the field and less rebellious in attitude and action. By the first quarter of the nineteenth century the United Brethren, now indisputably 'the Negro church', had offers of material help – land, time and finance – from numerous planters. However, ignoring the 1676 act forbidding the enslaved Christian status, did not sit well with most planters.

The success of the Moravian approach toward people of colour in the Danish and British Caribbean was noticed by the government in London. In January, 1788, one of the most influential members of the UK-wing of the church, London-based Christian Latrobe, was approached by slave-trade abolitionist William Wilberforce MP, a friend of prime minister William Pitt. He proposed that if the United Brethren was prepared to send missionaries to West Africa, the government would offer all necessary protection. The objective would be to convert to Christianity indigenous peoples in order to facilitate acquisition of their natural resources of cotton, indigo and gold. Wilberforce, member of Parliament for Yorkshire, confided to Latrobe that he was not against slavery as an institution.

The negroes in the West Indies will not be emancipated – for this would be unjust, but the impossibility of importing fresh slaves, will force the proprietors... to treat their slaves well and arrange marriages that the race may be continued and improved.[12]

He was also involved in the Sierra Leone project whereby the government would facilitate the settlement of formerly enslaved African-Americans who had fought with Crown forces in the American War of Independence. It is possible that these secret overtures to Latrobe came under the umbrella of this geo-political scheme by the government to both rid London of a proportion of its increasing Black population while using the apolitical Moravians to clear the way culturally for an enlarged political and economic presence in West Africa. Their trust in the church as a neutral body may also have been affirmed by its obstinate refusal to give evidence to the Privy Council in their ongoing investigation of slave trade.[13]

The London Association in aid of the Missions of the United Brethren was formed in 1817. It was a recognition by the metropolitan Brethren that its impoverished Caribbean congregations could not, over the long-term, sustain the principle that each mission have available education for enslaved of all ages. Within two decades it was raising hundreds of pounds annually for the building and upkeep of 'Negro Schools'. The funds helped subsidise learning at mission stations like Sharon where Edward's grandparents were introduced to the Moravian faith.

On land provided by Edmund Haynes, a day school was established in 1825. Its initial pupils included five children of the missionaries' domestic slave, Elizabeth. There was also evening classes twice a week, with between eighty and one hundred scholars for each session. The Taylors – Brother John had baptised William – had built the congregation to nine hundred and fifteen by the beginning of 1832 which suggests many were keen to become literate. The curriculum was based upon reading, writing, maths and studying the New Testament. Females had the additional choice to learn sewing. A Sharon Self-Improvement Society was formed to collectively share learning and focus ambition.

---

12 Christian L.G. Latrobe *Journal written in the year 1788 and beginning 1789,* entries for 25 January 1788. ENG MS 1244, John Rylands Library, Manchester.
13 Christian L.G. Latrobe *Journal...* entries for 7, 24, 25 January 1788. ENG MS 1244, John Rylands Library, Manchester; Kingsley Lewis, *The Moravian Mission in Barbados 1816-1886* (Frankfurt am Main,1985), p.137-8. The Moravians had attempted twice, in the 1730s and 60s, to establish a permanent mission on the Guinea coast without success.

Implementing the church's doctrine of self-reliance, missionaries would charge fees for classes with many scholars paying what they could. This money would have come from selling yams, bananas and plantain grown in minuscule gardens adjacent to their shack or provisions made inside the home, such as cakes and pickles. The Tulls would have been educated at Sharon until the Clifton Hill chapel had been built in 1839 whereupon six hundred and fifty worshippers transferred. The day school at Clifton Hill, which had daily between sixty and seventy students in 1840, received, on average, twelve shillings (sterling) per week in fees.

An ingredient of their success in growing their congregations had been the Moravian's unthreatening relationship with local planters who could prescribe and proscribe at will. In these anxious times contemplating the social and political ramifications of emancipation, many would have perceived the church as a force for stability and continuity. One of the plantocracy's most powerful figures, Sir Reynold Alleyne – compensated for over three hundred and seventy enslaved – invited the Taylors to preach on Turner's Hall estate comprising around one hundred and ninety enslaved, which he controlled on behalf of absentee, Sir Henry Fitzherbert.

It is highly probable the mission schools would have played some part in developing Anna's clear, fluent writing – discussed below – as it was church policy to employ people of colour to instruct. When the infant school began in 1834, the Taylors vowed to 'employ our former servant, Elizabeth, as the teacher.'[14] Latrobe described the school at Sharon 'as among the best conducted of their class in the country parts.'[15] From the eighteen fifties, with William and Anna creating a family – a natural right denied to their parents – they were fortunate to have as their resident missionary and teacher, James Young Edghill, editor of the *West Indian* newspaper. His second wife was a woman of colour and he talked publicly about the horrors of the Middle Passage learned from Sammy, a veteran of that hell. A pioneer of working class education he 'as much as anyone else in the nineteenth century Barbados... worked to promote the social advancement of the labouring classes through

14 *Periodical Accounts XIII*, pp.182. *Former servant* could refer to Elizabeth being an enslaved worker. The 1832 Slave Register records John Taylor of the United Brethren as owning twelve slaves. N.A. T71/552.
15 Quoted in Kingsley Lewis (1985) pp. 112.

education.'[16] Edghill's view of education as a means of collective and individual advancement, while characteristic of missionaries on the ground, was out of step with the thinking of the colonial authorities and the higher echelons of his church.

Schooling as a top-down method of inculcating obedience was the approach adopted by the British government. It established a Negro Education Grant in 1835 as part of its post-emancipation strategy. The finance would be used by the metropolitan and colonial ruling classes as an instrument in forging public tranquility and preventing social unrest. The priority of the local plantocracy was managing social change and expectations after the end of two hundred and eleven years of legalised slavery without undermining the economic status quo.

A related but more immediate and blunt administrative tool to engineer obedience was the despatch from the UK of six magistrate to Bajan parishes. They each controlled a station and a small gaol and were assisted by soldiers whose role was to enforce the compliance of the local population. An island police force was also created with the law and order budget accounting for over half of the Barbados government expenditure between 1838-50. They soon developed a reputation for casual brutality. Within a year of the end of the apprenticeship period most constables were men of colour yet ill-treatment of ex-slaves was far from unusual. Their violence against other people of colour on one particular occasion had so incensed a White political activist, Benjamin Goodridge, that he wrote a letter of complaint to the *Liberal* newspaper.[17]

With their values of education for all and non-involvement in public issues it is unsurprising Moravian were again approached to assist. The son of Christian Latrobe, Charles, was invited in 1837 by the government to report on the development of schooling for people of colour in the British Caribbean. In contrast to his father who declined open collaboration, he accepted. Making his findings known to the Barbados Assembly he commented

> I shall be inclined to doubt the wisdom or real kindness of any system or mode of instruction which would lead either the parent or the child to reason falsely on the subject, but not strongly impressing

16 Ibid., p.109.
17 *Liberal*, 13 March 1839 in Melanie Newton, *'The Children of Africa in the Colonies': Free People of Colour in Barbados During the Emancipation Era, 1816-1854*, Ph.D dissertation, University of Oxford, 2001, p.259.

the mind the necessity of submitting to labour.[18]

Considered a safe pair of hands for his emphasis that teaching should instruct the formerly enslaved how to be compliant wage labourers, he was later appointed superintendent of Port Phillip District, New South Wales, Australia.

'From our schools in Barbados men have gone forth to be good artisans [and] tradesmen', wrote Edghill proudly.[19] A comparison of letters within the Finlayson Family Archive provides an unscientific but nevertheless illuminating evaluation of the educational achievement of people of colour attending the Moravian church which supports this claim.[20] When Edward's father, Daniel, was betrothed to marry Alice Palmer, the daughter of a working-class couple from rural Kent, his future mother-in-law, Sarah-Ann Palmer, wrote a welcoming letter giving her blessing to their impending wedding. Unimportantly and understandably, it has grammatical errors. Dated January, 1880, it is illustrative of the limited access to formal education a woman from a family of agricultural labourers would have had in Britain prior to the introduction of compulsory elementary schooling a decade earlier. The majority of children of her generation would not have attended school. Around twenty-five per cent of women in the eighteen seventies were illiterate. In rural areas this would have been higher.

Post-emancipation there gradually developed a discernible educational route through the church to vocations and occupations that would have been closed-off to previous generations. Daniel Tull proudly proclaimed the BA status of his 'cousin' (though it is not known how Henry Simmons was related to Daniel); Henry Moore, whose work has been used in this study, was schooled by Edghill at Clifton Hill and became the first Moravian missionary of colour. Arguably the widest known graduate of Moravian schooling was Bermuda-born, Mary Prince.[21]

Henry Moore's progression within the church had entailed working as Assistant when, with Edghill, he may have tutored William and

18 Kingsley Lewis (1985), pp. 110-111.
19 Edghill (1890) p.28.
20 See Appendix 6 for both letters.
21 Mary Prince, *The History of Mary Prince, a West Indian Slave. Related by Herself. With a Supplement by the Editor. To Which is Added, the Narrative of Asa-Asa, Captured African*, (London, 1831).

Anna's children: Sarah Elizabeth, William, Samuel James, Prinz Henry and Daniel. Lewis (1985) states that two of Edghill's students became mariners and another a pastor abroad. Elizabeth and John Richard Tull, Mariner, are listed in the Moravian records as parents of John Richard Finlay (JRF) Tull, born in 1847 who died a Methodist minister in Antigua in Antigua, 19 August 1913. Was he the pastor? In the will of Sarah – who died in 23 April, 1897, the same year as her brother Daniel – JRF is mentioned as her nephew.[22] Unfortunately, because of the lack of corroborating genealogical details we cannot definitively state their kin relationship. At the 4 July, 1886 baptism of George Irving Tull, father Samuel James is also described as a pastor living at Station House Hill, St. Michael.

Baptism and marriage records suggest William (senior) – described as a labourer at the 1877 marriage of son Samuel to Elvira Nurse – and Anna had a network of friends built around their church.[23] It was an institution that had a number of functions: worship, education and social interaction. The chapel represented a site where the enslaved created a subcultural space devoid of the worst features of plantation life. The most obvious being the absence of gratuitous violence. It also allowed a limited degree of folkway expression by respecting and recording African names and ethnic identity. Moravian ministers did own enslaved people, thus the power relations and hierarchy of the plantation was still visible but this was mediated through the profound recognition that the enslaved had a natural right as human beings to become Christian. The social and cultural environment of the local chapel was a curious mix of discipline, obedience and self-empowerment.

The symbolic importance of baptisms for those born into enslavement was significant: participation in a ritual denied by law for centuries; the opportunity to replace a given name with a chosen one; and a chance to formally identify those people in the community you most trust by asking them to be sponsors (godparents). At the baptism of the William and Anna Tull's first child, Sarah Elizabeth, in 1842, performed by Brother William Humberstone at Clifton Hill, St. Thomas, the sponsors were W. Skeat, P. Simmons and D. Warner. Three years later, at the baptismal ceremony of their second child, William, at Olive Branch, St Thomas, presided over by Brother L.F. Oerter, the sponsors were Celia Pile, William Skeet and Samuel Warner. Patience Simons was also

22 Barbados Archives, Wills, Volume 91, p.510.
23 Barbados Archives, Moravian Marriages, RL 1/76 Vol.65 p.454.

a sponsor at the baptism – performed by C.W. Roentgen – of second son Samuel James at Clifton Hill, along with Christian Simons and Quinton Sandy. (The variations in spellings of the surnames are as recorded.)[24]

These baptismal registers indicate Christian and Patience Simmons (Simons) were parents of Daniel's cousin Henry Simmons, born October, 1840. Baptised at four weeks by Brother William Humberstone, one of the baptismal sponsors was William Skeate. The Simmons were also witnesses to the 1845 Clifton Hill baptism of Joseph Tull, son of Christopher Ford and Elizabeth Tull. It may be coincidence that William and Anna's daughter is Sarah Elizabeth Tull and that they worshipped at Clifton Hill and that the Simmons are also trusted friends of Christopher and Elizabeth. It is not uncommon for the same names to appear on different plantations at the same time. Four William Criss's are recorded in the 1834 Slave Register on plantations in St. Thomas and St. John alone. In her will Sarah Elizabeth, described as a 'spinster', bequeathed 'my piece of land' in Wellington Street, Bridgetown, to 'nephew' J.R.F. Tull after the death of her 'dear friend' Adelaide Montgomery Amery to whom she also left her annual dividend of eight shares in the Bridgetown Water Works Company. Baptism and other records indicate she had at least four children: Aubery Walter Tull, baptised 14 March 1873 (buried as George Awbridge Walter Tull, 17 December, 1874); Samuel Emmanuel Tull, born 21 March,1875; George Walter Tull, baptised 13 June, 1885 and Reginald Walter Tull, baptised 12 September 1885. George and Reginald may have been twins or siblings one of which was not baptised close to birth. In the 1878 and 1883 letters of Anna to William, the 'husband' of Sarah is referred to. It is likely, then, that no church/legal ceremony took place.

Moravian records indicate the Simmons, Warners and Skeets were part of Anna and William's faith and friendship group. William Skeete was witness at their wedding in 1838. A man of that name is listed on the Clifton Plantation, owned by Henry Trotman who provided land for the Clifton Hill Chapel school. The material speaks to an enslaved and post-emancipation community that forged family and friendship bonds despite economic, social and political obstacles and restrictions. First and middle names of kin were shared amongst relatives, friendships were often long-lasting. George Walter and Reginald Walter were

24 Barbados Archives, Moravian Baptism Records: G188, G194, G19.

baptised three years before Edward's brother Walter; eldest brother William is presumably named after his Bajan grandfather.

No provision was made for the economic welfare of the emancipated population in Barbados, whose poverty intensified with the decline of the sugar industry. Many rural labourers could not find work and migration to urban areas increased. It was a desperate throw of the dice that William and Anna took in the early eighteen sixties when they and the children moved to My Lords Hill, on the edge of Bridgetown. They joined the Roebuck Street chapel, with Daniel – and possibly his school-age brother Prinz Henry – being educated at the school.

BRIDGETOWN

Edward, looking back on the double consciousness existence of his nineteenth century kin, profoundly appreciated the core function religion played. The church was a refuge from the severity of everyday life, where reality could be momentarily pushed aside, the spirit invigorated and recharged with an imagined vision of an improved world.

The hard working Negroes saved their pennies for the collection plate on Sunday, the Church was the high note of their existence. Now religion became to a large extent their only physical, mental and emotional outlet. The church was the social centre. Here, after a long day of toil... they could dream of the pearly gates of heaven, and the streets paved with gold, and of the rest; after being quiet and meek throughout the week... they could raise their voices and sing loudly, Sunday mornings and evenings. These people who had so little time for fun and dancing, rocked their bodies in abandon to the powerful ritual of the Spiritual.[25]

It is not known if sons William and Prinz Henry relocated. They disappear from view after birth and baptism in 1845 and 1850 respectively. They may have migrated to another island as an adult or died as a child in the decimating cholera outbreak of May, 1854. The epidemic escalated from ten cases a week to around three hundred

25 Edward Tull-Warnock, *Paul Robeson*, (undated), Finlayson Family Archive, p.4.

and forty a day at its height. Edghill mentions both its devastation and the numerous and varied cures being offered by quack doctors. One precaution 'offered by many', that was ridiculed by the quacks, was 'that water was by no account to be given to the patient'.[26] By the close of the public health crisis in August, around twenty-thousand lives had been taken, more than one-seventh of the population. The cholera emergency that begun that month in London proved this 'common sense' advice to be correct.

The continued impoverishment of people of colour was an increasingly live issue in Moravian chapels of worship that could not continue to be ignored. The 1844 Poor Relief Committee report outlined how poverty and infant mortality were increasing in the wake of emancipation. The Negro Education Grant was terminated the following year, with the Church of England also decreasing its funding. Meanwhile, Edghill's active commitment to increase the provision of mass schooling was a sign that Moravian ministers were now more willing to involve themselves in politics. The 1863 Moravian Mission Conference discussed how economic reform was crucial to improving the lives of those who had been liberated in law only.

Almost every man or woman occupies a quarter of an acre of land on some property, for which he or she pays 10d per week, and is compelled to labour 5 days on the place, if called upon. On this land his 'shelter' is located, but he may be dismissed at 4 weeks notice, and must remove his shelter at the end of that time... the number that sleeps in one of these houses is almost incredible... and they will not have better houses until the land tenure is changed.[27]

These work and residence conditions were enshrined in the 1838 Master and Servant Act, a harsh piece of legislation designed to ensure power relations in the labour market remained firmly in favour of the buyer.

The move to My Lord's Hill did no harm to the Tull's educational progress. Unfortunately, this forward momentum was not matched by any economic progress. Life in the capital for the vast majority of people was extremely difficult. There were many more wanting work than jobs

---

26 Edghill, (London, 1890), pp.121-123.
27 Protocol of the Mission Conference in Barbados, minutes 26 May,1863, quoted in Kingsley Lewis (Frankfurt, 1985) p.83.

available. The countryside from which they had migrated was populated with a landless peasantry while urban areas such as Bridgetown and Speightstown were populated by an underemployed proletariat.

Once one of the three largest cities in British America, along with Boston, Massachusetts and Port Royal, Jamaica, Bridgetown was past its heyday. US citizen William Sewell visited in 1860. Sailing into Carlisle Bay he describes a vista dotted with ships from the northern ports of his home country. Anchoring offshore, his vessel was soon swarming with adolescents boys in small row boats offering to ferry ashore passengers and crew. While the streets of the capital were macadamised – compacted crushed stone – the buildings were shabby and rundown. Yet, the 'governing classes of Barbados are infinitely more prosperous now than she ever was in the palmiest days of slavery,'[28]assisted in great measure, no doubt, by the incredibly generous compensation payments and a further four years of free labour provided via the apprenticeship system. A total of £1,719,980 (£221,703,846)[29] was paid to Barbados planters and absentee owners for 83,150 enslaved people, an average of over £20 (£2,578) each.

An ecclesiastical visitor from the UK a few years before, in contrast, remarked upon the profound hardship of the many.

The sick, the aged, the infirm. This country makes no provision for them. I have seen repeatedly children wasting away from starvation, when sickness has prevented their parents from earning… in a wooden hut, not twenty feet by ten, with the bare unlevelled earth for a flooring, you not uncommonly find families of eight, ten, twelve in number, of every age and sex, crowded and herding together more like beasts.[30]

The life of the Tull's before and after emancipation was one of unceasing economic hardship. Anna laments the poor state of our

28 William G. Sewell *The Ordeal of Free Labour in the British West Indies* (London 1968 edition. Originally published 1861), p.15.
29 Using the Bank of England's inflation calculator (at 1.4% a year), 2019 values – to the nearest pound– will be in parenthesis. https://www.bankofengland.co.uk/monetary-policy/inflation/inflation-calculator accessed 27 April 2020.
30 'Meliora' (Reverend Edward Pinder), *Letters on the Labouring Population of Barbados,* (London, 1858). pp viii, 13.

'little hut' in her 1878 letter where she thanks Daniel for sending a 'gift' – money – for its much-needed 'repair'. Another communication, written five years later in her mid-sixties, informs him his family is 'still labouring with our usual passion until the master shall have come to take us to himself.'[31] Only death would deliver respite from poverty.

Monopoly ownership and commercial intensity was such that nearly every acre of the island – 100,000 of 106,000 – was cultivated, the vast majority given over to growing sugar cane yet the wealth produced did not go into public works. Barbados planters' reputation for being selfish and brutal slaveowners had not changed as post-emancipation employers and landlords.

> The planting interest of these islands may be characterised as one of unqualified selfishness... a narrow minded selfishness that pursued crooked paths to accumulate gain at the expense of the public weal.[32]

The long-term nineteenth-century decline in the island's share of the colonial sugar trade, coupled with the downturn in economic activity caused by the civil war in North America, contributed to the desperate famine of 1863. Planter indifference to hunger and anger led many to emigrate, Demerara, Guiana and St Lucia the most favoured destinations. Those that remained did what they had to do to feed themselves, including stealing from planters. A report into poverty in St. James Parish found 'many children are being convicted of petty theft – a circumstance which calls loudly for a reformatory school.'[33] The desperate residents of St Philip were starved into rebellion. Property was set on fire; they fought with police and mounted cavalry. Life for most people of colour had declined from barely tolerable to barely survivable.

> How many of this island still live, is a mystery to us. Hundreds have no ostensible means of getting a livelihood at all... thieves and vagabonds have been going about the country in gangs of from ten to twenty, robbing and plundering, and causing not a little alarm... adults and children have no clothes but rags, in which they can not

---

31 Letters dated 29 June, 1878 and 25 March 1883, Anna F. Tull to Daniel Tull. Finlayson Family Archive.
32 Sewell (London, 1968), p.38.
33 Beckles (Oxford, 2004) p.99

show themselves… The distress here is fearful… it is a crisis which…
I fear [will] entail severe suffering.[34]

DANIEL

In his *Short Journal,* Daniel writes that during the late 1860s, 'after I
left school', he was apprentice to journeyman carpenter, Mr Giddens.
Eight months later he changed masters, transferring to Joseph Massiah,
the husband of his cousin. 'Then did my trials commence', Daniel
comments with melancholy. Massiah was 'a good workman but a cruel
man to his apprentices,' suggesting he may have made a mistake in
leaving Giddens.

When a boy first goes to work or goes apprentice some master
generally ask the boy what are we going to make of you A Man, A
Mule or A Monkey. But he did not give me the chance to know the
Rabit [sic] plane from the jack plane before he had a flogging on me
they was scarcely a week pass over my head but for what I did not
have a thrashing from him.[35]

Nonetheless, he stuck with the cruel artisan, the beatings mercifully
decreasing in proportion to the increase in his skill and proficiency.
After three testing years, fed up with his pay of six pence per week,
Daniel left to work for 'one of his [Massiah's] mates'. Unfortunately,
his troubles continued, the new master often not paying when Saturday
came around.

Of course nothing left but for me to vindicate my right. I was only
a lad then but I went to his house with a determination to get my
money or else give him a thrashing man as he was. I called at his
house but could not see him & made several abuses. My father being
a Godly man was very much put out about this and so was I but he
sided with these oppressors… and never took my part but gave me a
thrashing one morning at 5 o'clock.[36]

34 Brother John Henry Buchner quoted in J. Taylor Hamilton, *A History of the
Church Known as the Moravian Church or the Unitas Fratrum or the Unity of the Brethren During the Eighteenth and Nineteenth Centuries*, (Bethlehem, P.A., 1900) p.455.
35 Daniel Tull, *A Short Journal.* Finlayson Family Archive.
36 Ibid.

Daniel's retelling of the story in his *Journal* suggests his father William was angry and frustrated at his son leaving his former apprentice master and taking employment with 'this villain'.

So from this time I vowed in my mind I would leave home or I told my mother I would because of my father [sic] mistake. I little thought then that it would come true afterward as it did so in course of time.[37]

He sailed away on 11 August, 1873 one hundred and seventy-four kilometres northwest to another Windward isle, St Lucia. The definitive reason(s) remain a mystery for this seventeen year old taking a course of action that he had threatened but not envisaged implementing. Undoubtedly, the Barbados economy was in decline, a context intensified by the scarce availability of land, both to rent and buy. The means to change this democratically was, in practice, non-existent with a property-based electorate of one thousand six hundred and sixty-four out of a population of around one hundred and fifty-thousand.

His actions reveal an acute intolerance of injustice alongside a fearless tenacity in righting wrong. It was a plantation-forged strength that would be transmitted, by will and osmosis, to his children.

For young Bajan men, migrating to find work was not uncommon, sixteen thousand leaving between 1838 and 1870. Wages were often higher on other islands, including St. Lucia, Trinidad, Demerara and British Guiana on the South American mainland, as much as four times the average Barbadian day rate. Daniel had portable skills, such as literacy and carpentry and a Moravian cultural network that could be utilised to deploy them. He left behind a rigid ethnic hierarchy, a pigmentocracy, more inflexible than other former enslaved societies where people of colour had more access to land.

Daniel's dissatisfaction embodied the collective feeling of his family and his class. Abolition had brought economic improvement to the enslavers through compensation but not their victims who were still deprived and dispossessed, economically and politically. It was a rationale that made no sense morally and could only be explained by the existing social relations of production. The plantocracy and their agents and trading partners in the City of London, represented

---

37 Ibid.

politically by the powerful and influential West India Committee who managed to secure an outcome better than the deal first proffered by the government where compensation was a loan. The enslaved were never asked what they felt would be a fair and just settlement. The vast majority of the population who were poor in Barbados in 1824 remained poor in 1834, 1844, 1854, 1864 and 1874. And, as if centuries of immiseration was not enough injustice, after the Abolition Act changes in the law had tended to more tightly control labour making their ability to assert themselves, individually and collectively, difficult.

The appointment by the Crown of governor John Pope Hennessy in 1875 had the primary objective of increasing the power of the metropole in order to push through a planned confederation of the Windward Isles. The ongoing expansion of the British Empire was also engendering a centralisation of power with the concomitant sacrifice of local governance.

Daniel left behind an island that within three years exploded into social unrest. The increased desperation of the hungry because of cuts in wages, increased taxes on imported food and widespread unemployment was a combustible mixture. Allied with the sense amongst workers that the imperial government had an agenda of direct colonial rule and was not interested in listening, a rebellion erupted on the anniversary of the Bussa revolt sixty years earlier. The aim of the revolutionaries was to overthrow the ruling class and create a more egalitarian society, one that operated for the many and not the few. Led by the Dottin brothers commanding over a thousand workers in regiments of one hundred, they 'went from estate to estate waving a red flag'. Their righteous fury lasted nine days, and 'was an attempt to restore the integrity of the emancipation promised, but compromised in the years after 1838.'[38]

ST. LUCIA 1873-76

St. Lucia, for much of the eighteenth century, was a French colony. During the seventeen nineties, inspired by the Haitian and French revolutions, the enslaved rose-up, defeated their captors and declared themselves free. However, the terror induced in the minds of the international ruling classes by both revolutions and the political necessity of quashing risings from below should they inspire others, led the British government – the biggest imperial power in the Caribbean – to invade and reverse the

38 Beckles (Oxford, 2004) pp136-7.

dangerous gains. As in Haiti, the military forces of the Crown were beaten on the battlefield and had to withdraw. It was not until 1803 that they managed to overcome the self-liberated people of colour and seize the island. On raising the Union Jack they immediately restored slavery and implemented direct rule from London via the governor and an appointed Legislative Council.

In his *Short Journal* began, October 10, 1877, Daniel writes that after 5 years working in St Lucia, he 'started to England on the 8 of June 76.' He implies he did not return to Barbados to say a final farewell to his parents. Given the October, '77 commencement of his *Journal* it is probable that the dates he gives for leaving both Barbados and St Lucia are accurate though he spent only three years working in the former French colony. He may have paid the standard fare and travelled as a passenger or worked his passage as a ship's carpenter to Folkestone, nearly seven thousand kilometres distant. It was soon after a rebellion on his home island had been brutally suppressed by the militia. Had the outcome of the tumultuous upheaval led him to believe change was not going to come? The journey across the Atlantic would have taken between a fortnight and seven weeks depending on whether the ship was powered by the new technology of steam or traditional sail. Research by Lynn Ewart raises the possibility that Daniel may have arrived on the *Netherton,* which docked at Deal, Kent on 5 July. Another possibility is the *Sarah* which arrived at Gravesend, Kent, 8 July.[39]

---

39 I am grateful to Lynne Ewart for providing this information on ships aboard which Daniel may have voyaged to England.

Chapter Two
Barbados Plantocracy and People of Colour

CLIFTON HALL PLANTATION

Clifton Hall plantation, on which Edward's grandfather was born enslaved in 1808, was owned by Abel Rous Dottin. It had been a Rous family possession since at least 1737, passing down to succeeding generations.[40] Dottin's mother and father's families were long-standing and influential plantation owners. Abel Rous acquired Clifton Hall two years before William's birth. For eighteen years prior to legal emancipation in 1834 he owned at least four plantations. An archetypal absentee owner, he spent most of his adult life in Britain – thirteen years as a Conservative MP and chair of London and Greenwich Railway – while delegating supervision of his Caribbean possessions to local managers. After the termination of slavery in most parts of the British Empire he received a total of £11,251 (£1,294,774) compensation for three hundred and seventy-two enslaved people he formerly possessed as property.

Within two years of inheriting Clifton Hall, which comprised three hundred and sixty-five acres and one hundred and fifty-one chattel slaves, Dottin sold it to (General) Robert Haynes, another of the island's plantocracy for £35,350 (£2,796,823). The new owner was shocked at its state of degradation. He thought it was 'in want of everything... The people on the estate had for many years been accustomed to no regular discipline, and only to do what they pleased.'[41]

Haynes was a prominent member of the militia, the island government and a former speaker of the Barbados Assembly, its parliament. In the middle years of his life, married to Anne Thomasine with whom he fathered ten children, he had owned or managed a total of at least seven plantations. In 1836, he collected more than £6,045 (£695,663) compensation for two hundred and seventy-one enslaved. Immediately

---

40 Legacies of British Slave Ownership https://www.ucl.ac.uk/lbs/estate/view/822 Accessed 4 May 2020. Clifton Hall House was built around 1656, belonging originally to Prince Ferdinand Paleologus (Paleolocus) who emigrated to Barbados after fighting for the Royalists in the Civil War. It is possible that Thomas Rous acquired the estate in 1662. See also John C. Street *The Genealogy of the Rouses of Devon,* (Wisconson, 2002) p.142.

41 Edmund C. Haynes et al *Notes by General Robert Haynes of New Castle and Clifton Hall Plantations, Barbados,* (1910) pp.18-19.

prior to Emancipation the Haynes family were the island's third biggest landowners with over two thousand acres.

Unlike most enslavers, Haynes kept a diary giving us 'a glimpse of the life and times of the Barbadian heyday, seen through the eyes of a typical owner-planter of Royalist stock.'[42] He refers to his Berkshire ancestors having been courtiers for Queen Elizabeth. As a supporter of the Crown during the Civil War the original migrant, Richard Haynes, sought safe refuge on the island in the early 1640s. The New Castle estate was bought jointly with Francis Dickinson in 1643.[43] Robert was born in 1769 on the estate to Richard Downs Haynes and Ann Elcock. His mother died twelve years later, his father remarrying widow Ann Walker. He laments that his stepmother

> almost ruined [the Haynes family] by her indolence and extravagance... allowing her favourite slaves to rob and plunder to an unlimited extent... she was also very benevolent to the poor.[44]

Planter indolence, on the other hand, was seen by some visitors and commentators as an inevitable outcome and common feature of life on an island built upon the dehumanisation of one group by the inhumanity of another. An unnatural endeavour that had but one purpose: wealth accumulation. Such a society, Frederick Douglas points out, little more was on offer other than unrestrained indulgence in base emotions and passions.

> The slaveholder as well as the slave, is the victim of the slave system. A man's character greatly takes it hue and shape from the norm and colour of things about him. Under the whole heavens there is no relation more unfavourable to the development of honourable character, than that sustained by the slave holders to the slave. Reason is imprisoned here, and passions run wild.[45]

---

42 Quote from the Foreword of M.W. Cracknell (ed.), *The Barbadian Diary of General Robert Haynes* (Medstead, Hampshire, 1934).
43 Henry Fraser and Ronnie Hughes *Historic Houses of Barbados* (Barbados, 1986).
44 Edmund C. Haynes et al (1910), p.9.
45 Frederick Douglas *My Bondage and My Freedom* (New York, 2003) in Andrea Stuart *Sugar in the Blood. A Family's Story of Slavery and Empire,*(London, 2012) p.226.

Andrea Stuart notes that one Barbadian planter boasted that he fathered seventy-four children with enslaved women.

Haynes' stepmother's generous relationship with the family's live 'property' stood in contrast to his. Slavery, he argued, was 'a most necessary institution', its reputation harmed by those who abuse it.[46] Haynes congratulated himself on the 'quick suppression of an uprising of slaves in 1805. It is much to be hoped that these over-zealous advocates of freedom may duly take this warning to hear before it is too late'.[47]

Proud of his Barbadian natality, 'my own dear country', he nevertheless sent his children to Scotland and England for schooling: five boys to Greenock; his daughter to Bath. At least one son, George Barrow, remained in the UK working for the family partnership of Thomas Lee, Haynes and Co of Liverpool and Barbados. It was a position that he might never have been able to occupy: on the children's 1805 voyage to the Lancashire city, the world's biggest slave port, twelve year old George fell overboard while their vessel was docking. He was saved from drowning by the heroics of their enslaved servant, Hamlet.

Owner of other estates and managing as attorney the Newton and Seawells plantations for absentee-owners John and Thomas Lane, Haynes handed over in 1816 Clifton Hall to his son, Robert Junior, calculating its worth at £50,000 (£4,910,776).

Two of the Lanes' enslaved complained about the brutal treatment at the hands of overseers, in particular Yard and Farrell. Thomas Lane cites an interview with enslaved John Thomas, who had escaped and paid his way to England. He complained that he rarely saw Haynes despite 'many people killed on the estate'. He also spoke of Farrell extorting what little money the enslaved had, charging a dollar a day not to be beaten. He 'treats all the people very ill, beating and breaking them down'. Thomas speaks of several being killed on the spot. He also relayed that Haynes took '10 working cattle from Sewells [sic] Estate to his place I don't know why'.[48] And that he, Thomas, had been used in the building of a house for him.

Karl Watson suggests that the former attorney for the Newton and Seawells plantations, Sampson Wood, attempted to improve the quality of life for the enslaved with medical care, providing tents for shelter

46 Cracknell (1934), p.23.
47 Ibid. p.24.
48 Newton Papers, University of London Senate House Library, MS 523/974.

in the field and appropriate, protective clothing. On taking over Wood wrote to the owner Lane complaining that

> the hospital or sick house where Negroes are put... is a horrid unhealthy hole, most ill-contrived, and men and women are most indecently mixed together, with other detestable circumstances... malnutrition seems to have been more widespread among the slaves.[49]

When Haynes succeeded him he discontinued many of Wood's innovations. John Thomas comments to Lane that Wood was much kinder than Haynes.[50]

The revealing encounter in London between Thomas and Lane is unusual because it provides an enslaved's view of a society in which their voices were rarely heard beyond the confines of their plantation. It is an alternative to the narrative constructed by plantation owners and managers about the world they had forcibly created. Haynes was a planter aristocrat, an elite member of Barbados society who, in his own words, headed a 'family... of high respectability'.[51] The implication in John Thomas's testimony was that he was lazy and dishonest, presiding over a regime of rape, extortion, beatings and murder.

Thomas felt so strongly about the inhumanity he had experienced and witnessed that he paid fifteen guineas for his passage from Barbados and another guinea to London from Portsmouth. It was an act of self-sacrifice and solidarity with those still suffering.

He was not the only person who fled to London in search of justice from the Lane family. Elizabeth Newton[52] also spoke with him, detailing the murder of field labourers by overseer Yard. He had 'threatened to put her in irons and kill her'. He is 'more cruel to slaves than ever, beats them unmercifully and puts them in iron for days together'. Like Thomas, Newton ran away to save her life. She pleaded – 'with her little girl in her arms' – with the absentee planter to grant her freedom. Desperate to return to Barbados to see her other children, she was also

---

49 Ibid., /290 pp.97-8.
50 Karl Watson, *The Civilised Island of Barbados. A Social History 1715-1816*, (Barbados, 1979), p.81.
51 Edmund C. Haynes et al (1910).
52 Elizabeth Newton was also the name of Thomas Lane's cousin. His brother and co-owner of Newton's – one of the oldest plantations – was John Lane. Is it also a coincidence that their ex-slave is named John Thomas?

fearful Yard would kill her if she did.[53]

These accounts of the pleadings of Elizabeth Newton and Thomas Lane provide an insight into life on plantations owned and managed by Haynes, such as Clifton Hall where he had absolute control over William Criss between 1808-1816.

BONDED LABOUR

The implementation of the Emancipation legislation on 1 August 1834 abolished the relationship between master and slave as one of property ownership, replacing it with an 'apprenticeship' system which committed the formerly enslaved to years of unpaid bonded labour. A small but huge cultural consequence of the act was the ability of the emancipated to legally define their names. William, like many, jettisoned his enslaved surname. At the Moravian United Brethren Church at Sharon, St. Thomas,19 June,1836, Brother John Taylor baptised him William Tull. He was admitted to Holy Communion three years later.[54] This was more than just an acknowledgement of his Christian faith. It was a right of passage, a real and symbolic act. For centuries people of colour were denied by law entry into the religion and the right to name themselves.

Criss was not a common surname at Clifton Hall where, according to the 1817 Slave Register there was just one other, John, aged fourteen. Was John William's brother? On the nearby four hundred acre Guinea plantation, also owned by Robert Haynes junior, the 1834 census indicates that there were another eight Criss's, including another William, aged forty.[55] It is reasonable to assume that this points to the development of family and kinship networks amongst the enslaved population across plantations. While we can speculate on interweaving of family and kinship ties, no definite answers can be provided. Corroborating evidence such as birth, baptism, marriage and other records are not available or have

53 Newton Papers, University of London Senate House Library, MS 523/973. Overseers, managers of the enslaved in the field, both White and Black, were notorious for their cruelty and acted with immunity.

54 Baptism Book 557, Barbados Department of Archives, Black Rock. Many thanks to Stephen Hopkins, a direct descendent of William, for this information. Taylor suggests a thriving congregation with 185 adults baptised and 81 admitted to Holy Communion in the year Easter 1835-36. *Periodical Accounts XIV* p.33 Moravian Archives, Muswell Hill, London.

55 1817 Slave Register T71/521; 1834 T71/558, N.A., London.

not been found.

However, before we conclude suggesting possible genealogical connections there is one more speculative consideration. William married Anna at Clifton Hill, St. Thomas, 8 December, 1838. The ceremony was presided over by Moravian minister, JG Klose and witnessed by William Skeet and CL(?) Savory. I have been unable to confirm the ancestry of William's wife, Edward's grandmother. However, on the 1817 Slave Register for Clifton Hall plantation there is a Nanny (Nancy?) Frances aged 1. Her birth date of around 1815-16 would fit the age of Anna as recorded when she died, 17 March 1896, aged eighty-one. The 1834 Register, for the same plantation lists a Nanny (or Nancy or Mary?) Frances, aged eighteen.[56] It is possible that, Nanny Frances, as part of the post-1834 cultural reconfiguration process chose to refashion her chattel name into the more formalised Anna Frances.

There is a preponderance of Frances/Francis on nearby Haynes Field plantation owned by Edmund Haynes, the brother of Robert, where seven – one adult and six children – are recorded. Three girls named with Frances as their surname are also found on the Clifton Plantation, owned by Henry Trotman. There is also an Anna, aged eighteen. Both Trotman and Edmund Haynes were friendly towards the Moravian church, providing physical resources and facilitating its presence on their land and plantations.

This still leaves unanswered the question of the genealogical origin of Anna's maiden name, Lashly.[57] There were three slave-owning Lashleys in Christ Church, Ralph, Edmund and John. Between them the 1826 Register lists a total of one hundred and seventeen enslaved in their possession. The 1829 Slave Register records Armel Culpepper owning twenty-two year old John Beauman Lashley.

The implementation of the 'apprenticeship' system forced the formerly enslaved to work, unwaged, forty-five hours per week. Refusal would mean absolute destitution: they would be thrown out of their shack and off the plantation. Initially, apprenticeships were proposed for twelve years, then reduced to six and finally abolished on most islands in 1838. Only Bermuda and Antigua chose to free all enslaved in 1834.

Unlocking the chains of nearly eight hundred thousand was a

---

56 1834 Slave Register T71/561, N.A., London. The handwriting of the ledger does not clearly define the name.

57 Included in the search is the spelling Lashley.

profoundly liberating moment, yet it did not radically transform existing power relations between people of colour and the White elite. Planters still owned virtually all the island's land. While they did not legally and physically possess their labourers anymore, they still held access to their means to live. No land was made available for sale or sustenance and the fabulously generous compensation paid to planters meant they were under no financial pressure to sell. They remained in control of the means of production: land, labour, tools and machinery. Historian Nick Draper argues the apprenticeship period of free labour needs to be reckoned into compensation payments.[58] The enslaved paid for their 'freedom' with forced labour. If this was calculated alongside the cash disbursements, enslavers received some ninety-percent of the pre-1834 enslaved value of each person. Emancipation so designed produced a scenario where the enslavers accumulated twice over.

In this fossilised pigmentocracy, people of colour, denied the ability to collectively advance, looked to individual solutions to signify their liberated status. Naming was one of these. It was a cultural tradition developed from the very beginnings of enslavement where individuals sought to retain their social identities and existence through retention of their original names or adoption of a self-chosen one. One of William and Anna's sons was baptised Samuel James. Three of Samuel's sons were given the middle names St Clair, Nathaniel and Irving. Liberated people of colour utilised their ability to name themselves which, by the action itself, said something about who they were and who they were not. It became, by context and circumstance, a political act.

FREE PEOPLE OF COLOUR

Freedmen – the generic term for manumitted people of colour – commonly renamed or retained their African denomination. Through growing crops, bartering and saving some managed to buy themselves out of their state of absolute oppression. By the seventeen seventies around five hundred 'freedmen' – this term included women – had managed to throw off their chains. By 1834 another six thousand had forced off their shackles, though it was still no more than five per cent of the population.

Under imperial law – passed by Parliament in London – as 'free'

58 T.M. Devine (ed.), *Recovering Scotland's Slavery Past. The Caribbean Connection*, (Edinburgh, 2015), pp.167-8.

people they had the same liberties as other British subjects. Yet, the consistent attitude by the planter elite toward this small but expanding social group was to pass laws confirming and embedding their inferiority. Prior to 1721 there was no legal recognition of the freed 'coloured' population. In July of that year this was attended to through a law which decreed that men holding civic power - in the Assembly, Vestry and courts - had to be White Christians. Eighteen years later, in an attempt to slow manumission it demanded the slave owner - the manumitter - pay a fee of £50 (£11,258) to the church warden and provide £4 (£900) per year to the freed person. Until the eighteen thirties free people of colour could not: testify against Whites in court, vote, serve on juries, attend parish schools or become Anglican ministers.

The plantocracy were anxious that the enlarging freed population would impact negatively on their own social and economic power, believing in times of social unrest they would naturally ally with their enslaved kith and kin. In 1802 Robert Haynes introduced a bill into the Barbados legislature proposing further limits on the amount of property free people of colour could own. Another prominent Assemblyman, John Beckles, spoke against it. He argued that Whites needed to encourage freed people of colour to see their class interests as best served by allying with fellow property owners. Restricting access to property acquisition would prevent this while relaxing obstacles to ownership would help drive a wedge between the freed and enslaved. His argument won and the bill fell.

Free people of colour were in the ambiguous terrain between exploited and exploiter. Governor Seaforth, a friend of Haynes, observed 'though not the property of other individuals, they do not enjoy the shadow of any civil right', applying the term 'unappropriated people': a state of limbo between people and property. Indeed, it was not uncommon for them to have to petition the governor to restore their manumitted status after being kidnapped as runaways by rapacious settlers seeking reward. Tragically, not all petitions were successful.

Panic at the growing population of free 'coloureds' was at its most intense at the turn of the nineteenth century when, in 1801, the manumission fee was raised to £300 (£22,635) for females and £200 (£15,090) for men plus an annuity of £18 (£1,358) and £12 (£905) respectively. The much higher fee placed upon females was a reflection of their number as the majority of the freed population: between 1801-10 female manumissions were fifty-seven per cent of the total. By 1829 this had grown to sixty-one per cent.

That women were better able to force their way into a state of limited freedom was itself often a reflection of their sexual oppression by planters who would choose the nubile and attractive for domestic work. The risk of rape was ever-present. It was not uncommon for women to be manumitted and left property on the death of their White master. The position of children was less clear: some were freed in their fathers Will; others remained enslaved; some were subsequently bought out of slavery by their mothers.

For enslaved men the most common route was saving whatever one could from selling produce grown on patches of land. They would then have to find a White sponsor to support their application. Mariners were sometimes sympathetic: forty-seven ship's captains and seamen were involved in the manumission of four hundred between 1795-1830. One procedure involved 'buying' the enslaved and pursuing the manumission through courts in the UK or other parts of the Caribbean. Between 1788-1834 an average of four hundred and eighty ships arrived in Bridgetown, providing a plentiful supply of potential helpers.

The other exit routes from enslavement were rebellion, suicide and running away. This latter option of deliverance invariably meant stowing away on a ship to escape the island. After the Somerset judgement in 1772 by Lord Chief Justice Mansfield - great-uncle of Dido Belle[59] - in which he effectively ruled a slave, from wherever they came, could not be returned to their owner England as an escape destination became more attractive. As discussed above, two escaped slaves from the Newton plantation appealed to their owner in London. In comparison,

---

59 Dido Elizabeth Belle (1761–1804) was born into slavery as the natural daughter of Maria Belle, an enslaved African woman in the British West Indies and Sir John Lindsay, a British career naval officer who was stationed there. He was later knighted and promoted to admiral. Lindsay took Belle with him when he returned to England in 1765, entrusting her raising to his uncle William Murray, 1st Earl of Mansfield and his wife Elizabeth Murray, Countess of Mansfield. The Murrays educated Belle, bringing her up as a free gentlewoman at Kenwood House, Hampstead, Middlesex together with another great-niece, Lady Elizabeth Murray, whose mother had died. Lady Elizabeth and Belle were second cousins. Belle lived there for 30 years. In his will of 1793, Lord Mansfield confirmed her freedom and provided an outright sum and annuity, making her an heiress. Source: https://en.wikipedia.org/wiki/Dido_Elizabeth_Belle accessed 15/11/2018.

hiding away as a fugitive in Barbados was difficult. Its lack of bush and forestation and high density of cultivation meant there were not many areas secretive and untouched. Most free 'coloureds' lived in eastern Bridgetown, around Roebuck Street and Marlborough Hill. Whilst males could be found in most skilled trades and women in selling products of domestic labour such as jam and pickles, some owners of the lodging houses, hotels, pubs and brothels - the last two known as 'tipling' or 'crimping' houses - were free women of colour. Sailors were valued customers and many sorts of business conducted leading to some women accumulating wealth and acquiring slaves. Nancy Clarke did so well with her hotel - left to her by fellow 'madam' Rachel Pringle Polgreen - she emigrated to London, living amidst aristocrats and gentry in Duke Street, St. James.

Maybe Polgreen also gave contact details to Clarke of an influential former customer at her Royal Naval Hotel brothel. Prince William Henry, Duke of Clarence, used the services available on a visit to Barbados in the seventeen-nineties. Along with members of his 49th Regiment, emboldened by unlimited rum, he concluded his visit by trashing the hotel. Having reached her comparatively privileged status by not being a passive recipient of injustice, Polgreen demanded the cost of refurbishment. In an act of unusual contrition, the future king William IV paid up. On her premature death aged thirty-nine she owned land, houses and at least nineteen enslaved. Her Will instructed six to be manumitted with the others left to them.[60]

As a great many of the largest plantation owners were absentee landlords, the inspiration and resources to create social and cultural institutions – public hospitals, theatres, higher education colleges, libraries, sports clubs and the like – signalling the intention of long-term settlement were largely non-existent. The architecture of civic life spoke to temporary White settlement where even third and fourth generation Europeans would often identify as expatriates rather than Bajan.

Given the legal limitations on their space for activity in civic life, free people of colour were compelled to work at anything and everything. And did. On their visit to Barbados in the eighteen thirties, during the apprenticeship period, two abolitionists from the USA, James Thome and J. Horace Kimball, found:

---

60 https://www.blackpast.org/global-african-history/polgreen-rachel-pring-le-1753-1791/ Accessed 22 May 2020. Rachel Polgreen's 1796 portrait by Thomas Rowlandson is owned by Queen Elizabeth's Royal Trust Collection.

One of the wealthiest merchants in Bridgetown is a coloured gentleman. He has his mercantile agents in England, English clerks in his employ, a branch in the city [of London], and superintends the concerns of an extensive and complicated business with distinguished ability and success. A large portion... of the merchants of Bridgetown are coloured. Some of the most popular instructors are coloured men and ladies, and one of these ranks high as a teacher of modern languages. The most efficient and enterprising mechanics of the city are coloured and black men. There is scarcely any line of business which is not either shared or engrossed by coloured persons, if we accept that of barber. The only barber in Bridgetown is a white man.[61]

The limited ability to own property and form relationships did allow for family relationships to develop whereby freed adults could buy their enslaved children and, if affordable, pay for their freedom without having to rely on inherited property or kind benevolence at death. Yet, the gulf between their individual and collective aspirations and the consistent absence of recognition by the rigid plantocracy increased tensions.

The political confidence of free people of colour grew during the final decade of the eighteenth century. The enslaved-led revolution in San Domingue (Haiti), the anti-colonial and egalitarian ideals of the American and French revolutions and the annual petitions to Parliament to ban the slave trade by the abolitionists in Britain, inspired greater assertiveness. In 1799 fifty-eight petitioned the governor and Council of Barbados with their *Humble Memorial and Remonstrance* requesting legal and civil rights. Their concerns were dismissed. An 1811 petition by free people of colour requesting they be allowed to testify in court was also rejected confirming that in law their existence had the same absolute lack of protection as the enslaved.

In addition to influential political events in the Caribbean two laws passed in Europe, both in 1792, may also have galvanised the determination of those prepared to come out as political activists: France decreed rights of citizenship for free Black people and those of mixed-heritage; and the union of Denmark-Norway banned the slave trade (though this law would not be effective until 1803). Amongst the enslaved, also, there was a sense that their status, with all they had consistently done to resist its continuance, was now being questioned by

61 Quoted in Claude Levy *Emancipation, Sugar, and Federalism. Barbados and the West Indies, 1833-1876* (Gainesville, Florida 1980), p.30.

these progressive forces in the wider world.

The dogged persistence of the revolutionary tremors in Haiti, the prize possession of France's Caribbean colonies, led by Toussaint L'Ouverture was a late-eighteenth, early nineteenth century manifestation of what seventeenth century enslaved revolutionaries believed: their condition could be overturned by collective action with a unity of purpose. Half a million Black people lived in Haiti, outnumbering Whites by about ten to one. This power of numbers organised behind an over-arching objective was crucial to their success. Those who rose up against the colonial administration comprised the enslaved, mixed-heritage free, runaway maroons and less-privileged and poor Whites. All these groups had nuanced social, political and economic agendas but nothing could be achieved for any without sweeping away the old regime. The French military was defeated by 1793 and slavery abolished. The British ruling class then sent their forces and within five years they too were defeated. L'Ouverture's revolutionaries then turned their attention to the adjoining Spanish slave colony of Santo Domingo and were once again triumphant.

The whole island was now liberated and renamed Hispaniola. Despite further French attempts to reinstall a colonial regime of enslavement and the death of L'Ouverture in a French prison, Haiti declared itself a republic in 1804. It was the first country in the world where the formerly enslaved had defeated their enslavers and created an independent state.[62] The profound importance and symbolism of this military and political triumph inspired Simon Bolivar to launch his campaign to end slavery throughout the Spanish colonies from Haiti in 1817. Wanting to create a federation of liberated states by his death thirteen years later, Bolivar succeeded in what is now Colombia, Venezuela, Ecuador and Peru where subsequent anti-slavery laws became the most advanced in the world. C.L.R. James argued the Haiti revolution as politically and socially profound and influential as the American and French.[63]

The Planters in Barbados were coming under increasing moral pressure from the Abolitionist movement and the revolutionary upsurges in the Americas. More significantly, the profitability of the sugar industry was decreasing dramatically as a result of foreign competition which led to oversupply and a concomitant fall in the price of sugar. The Planters

62 France never forgave Haiti for its insolence. In 1825 it forced the island to pay compensation, the debt of which resigned it permanently to poverty.
63 James, C.L.R., *The Black Jacobins. Toussaint Louverture and the San Domingo Revolution* (London, 1938).

responded with increased brutality, determined to hold on to what they had. Every last drop of profit would be squeezed out of their 'assets'. Levels of repression and terror were increased on the plantations as well as legislatively through such measures as raising the manumission fee.

Robert Haynes's diary reveals an incident that is instinctively repulsive, tragic but probably not unusual. A group of enslaved were walking back to their shacks after a long day in the fields when they heard a shout from a militiaman named Halls that he would kill them. Thinking it no more than a threat uttered to gratify his ego, they did not run but made way to let him pass. Reaching them, he bayonetted a mother of '5 or 6 children' who died on the spot. Most murders of this kind would go unreported and unnoticed because people of colour could not testify against Whites in court. Thankfully, two White witnesses referred it to magistrate Mr Justice Walton who, in court, said the law gave him no authority over the White militiaman. However, 'it was found that Halls had lain himself open to a penalty of £11.14s and he was ordered to be sent to prison until he paid'.[64]

Thome and Kimball found barbaric practices that may well have reminded them of their Southern slave states back home.

> White men made regular sport of shooting Negroes… one… young man had sworn that he would kill ten Negroes before a certain time. When he had shot nine he went to take breakfast with a neighbour, and carried his gun along. The first slave he met on the estate, he accused of being concerned in the rebellion. The Negro protested that he was innocent, and begged mercy. The man told him to be gone, and as he turned to go away, he shot him dead.[65]

Witnessing such carnage and having the psychological trauma burned in one's memory was, arguably, the common experience of most enslaved people. Such subconscious mental architecture was the psychological landscape of the inner plantation.

The ending of enslaved people trafficking in much of the British Empire in 1807 raised hopes in Barbados once more. Some interpreted the legislation as an end to their captivity rather than just their transatlantic transportation. It also reinvigorated the Abolition movement in Britain

---

64 Cracknell, (ed.), (1934), pp. 59-60.
65 Quoted in Hilary M. Beckles *Great House Rules: Landless Emancipation and Workers Protest in Barbados 1838-1938* (Oxford 2004) p.66

which had been instrumental in the achievement. Yet, the lack of any consequential material improvement to plantation life soon re-intensified the disillusionment, anger and frustration. The heady days of Barbados sugar dominating colonial trade was over. The American and Napoleonic wars restricted commercial shipping to and from the island and the tremendous 1812 volcanic eruption in St. Vincent, further depressed living standards. The people who paid most dearly were the enslaved, dependent as they were upon plantation owners for sustenance.

> The Negroes on many estates are in a perishing condition for want of necessary's of life... There is present much sickness prevailing all over the island, particularly of the lower class of the white people and Negroes.[66]

BUSSA UPRISING

This 1816 rebellion commenced on Easter Sunday, 14 April, spreading quickly across most of the southern half of the island. The population of around one hundred thousand comprised approximately ninety per cent enslaved. Of the remaining, approximately three thousand were free people of colour, a majority of the rest poor Whites. Planters formed a tiny proportion of this total. Thousands of people owned slaves: a few owning many and many owning a few. The latter included the manumitted who, unlike Whites, could not own plantations. The island's socio-economic demographic, therefore, represented an intersection of competing ethnic and class configurations.[67]

The conscious inculcation of fear and practical reign of terror by the plantocracy created an environment in which, for instance, poor Whites, unlike their predecessors in the seventeenth century, did not

---

66 Sharon, Barbados, 16 December 1812, letter from Brother J.N. Ganson to Christian Latrobe, London. Barbados Letters from 1768-1813 A Book p.141/2 Moravian Archives, Muswell Hill, London.
67 It was not until the nineteenth century that a freed man of colour, Jacob Belgrave, acquired a slave-populated plantation. See McNaught (2017) p.24. He is recorded as receiving £421.7s.11d (£48,449) compensation for 27 enslaved in 1836 https://www.ucl.ac.uk/lbs/claim/view/1961 Accessed 28 May 2020. In 1833 Whites still outnumbered free people of colour two to one.

see their collective improvement being achieved through alliance with impoverished and enslaved people of colour. Free people of colour did not automatically stand alongside the enslaved in times of revolt through fear – a manifestation of the 'inner plantation' – of losing what benefits they had managed to squeeze from a harsh and uncompromising system. Yet, the enslaved took inspiration from the mere existence of 'free' people of colour, even if their unshackled brothers and sisters were not always the most dependable fighting allies.

With the West India Committee fighting their cause in London the plantocracy defended their existence with confidence.[68] Their enslaved, they argued to anyone that would listen, were in better condition than Britain's industrial proletariat who lived stunted lives, worked longer hours and were more discontented. The British government had been instrumental in creating slave colonies and if they now tired of the project on moral grounds they, the planters, were happy to declare independence and continue as masters of their own affairs. Signalling their intentions, the Barbados Assembly rejected the imperial Parliament's 1815 Slave Registry Bill, designed to ensure there was not illegal trafficking after the 1807 Slave Trade Act.

Robert Haynes expressed his pleasure at the ending of the trade, saying he wished it had been twenty years earlier. (By the turn of the nineteenth century the plantocracy were supplying their labour power needs overwhelmingly by using the children of their enslaved.) He characterised the double-headed ambivalence of his class: in practice they could be cruel and unfeeling but publicly their concern for the well-being of their 'live' chattel investment could be misinterpreted as enlightened morality. Writing to Robert Long some months after the uprising he said he had trusted his work force and had no fear they would threaten his life or livelihood during the rebellion.

> The night of the insurrection I would and did sleep with my chamber door open, and if I had possessed ten thousand pounds in my house I should not have had any more precaution, so well convinced I was of their attachment.

---

68 The West India Committee was founded in 1735 as a political lobby on behalf of London slave trading merchants and Caribbean planters. By the nineteenth century the economic interests of the merchants and Barbados planters was diverging.

Three days before the rising, which some historians now argue was 'a collective political protest against slavery',[69] Haynes confirms his belief that 'the slaves of this island were never as happy since it was a colony'.[70]

However, a week after the suppression of the three day bloody rebellion, with the benefit of hindsight he observes:

What I have been for some months dreading has at length come to pass. On Easter night the 14th of April an insurrection of the slaves commenced in the parishes of St. Phillip and Christ Church, the slave population of which amount to about 19,000... most of the canes have been burnt, rum, sugar and provisions of various kinds have been plundered and destroyed to a considerable amount; and the neighbouring Parishes of St. John and St. George have partially suffered in a similar way. By a... movement of the regular troop and the militia... tranquility has been restored; only one white has been killed... I can calculate about 209 male slaves have been killed and executed and... 500 prisoners taken.[71]

A letter written by the Crown's representative in Barbados, governor James Leith, to his boss in London earl Bathurst, Secretary for the Colonies, comments on the deluded thinking of the planter elite who 'flattered themselves that the general good treatment of the Slaves would have prevented their resorting to violence'.[72]

At least fifty freedom fighters were killed in action – including Bussa – and around one hundred and forty-four executed. Over four hundred were arrested and held on ships in Carlisle Bay including, notes Lewis (1985), two Whites, a man and a woman. Many were transported, first to Honduras then Sierra Leone. McNaught observes that, to the planters 'the revolt... was not the heroic conflict it is painted as in modern Barbados, instead it was seen as the wilfully destructive action of a rebellious rabble'.[73]

---

69 Lilian McNaught, *The 1816 Barbados Slave Revolt*, University of Exeter MA Dissertation 2017.
70 Robert Haynes, 23 September, 1816, Newton Papers.
71 Ibid., 523/766
72 Letter from James Leith to Lord Bathurst, April 30th 1816, (CO 28/85) National Archives, London in McNaught (2017), p.42.
73 Ibid., p.12.

The leading figures were: 'General' Bussa who, Beckles suggests, was a West Africa-born member of the Bussa nation and chief ranger on Bayleys Plantation; freedman Joseph Washington Pitt Franklin who on victory was to become governor; Nanny Grigg, a literate domestic from the Simmons plantation; freedmen Cain Davis and John Sergeant; Johnny Cooper, a cooper, from Bayleys; King Wiltshire, carpenter, Bayleys; Dick Bailey, mason, Simmons; Jackey, driver, Simmons.[74] Contemporary evidence suggests Bussa was the military strategist, Franklin the political mastermind. Collectively, either freedmen or holding positions of responsibility and literate, they represented a social elite amongst people of colour. Paradoxically, this may have increased their frustration: the extreme contradictions of their daily experience juxtaposed, it may explain why they were so disciplined and committed in their preparation and planning. A more immediate spark, argues McNaught, was the rejection of the Slave Registry Bill which many enslaved interpreted as manumission legislation.

Two estates at the epicentre of the revolt, Bayleys and Wilshires, were notorious for vicious treatment of their enslaved and owned by absentee planter Reverend Alexander Scott of Parkside, Edinburgh.[75] However, Craton and McNaught argue against the assumption that this localised brutality was the primary reason for the revolt. Rather, it may explain preponderance of committed activists. Having two freedmen in the core group also suggests the cause was political rather than personal. Governor Leith even used their presence to blame free people of colour as a class, condemning the 'mischievous delusions of those who have availed themselves of every circumstance to influence the minds of the slave'.[76]

74 There is still debate amongst historians as to the character of the rebellion and the individual role of its leaders. McNaught and Robert Morris believe Bussa or 'Busso' was creole and in his fifties. Much of the surviving evidence is testimonies of the participants taken during court martial, under duress or torture and, according to McNaught, used to support a planter narrative of a few radical agitators stirring up trouble amongst a relatively content enslaved population.

75 Anonymous, *Remarks on the Insurrection in Barbados,* (London, 1816), in Lilian McNaught (2017) and Centre for the Study of Legacies of British Slavery, University College, London https://www.ucl.ac.uk/lbs/person/view/3202 Accessed 13 July 2021.

76 Proclamation enclosed to Earl Bathurst from James Leith, June 29th 1816,

The plantocracy crushed the rebels with characteristic ruthlessness. Their shacks and yards burnt to the ground, they were hunted remorselessly. There was a prolonged, ritualised theatre of terror staged across the island, executions by rope and axe symbolising a 'justice' of revenge. 'Even by the standards of an age whose penal system was characterised by blood-letting and public execution, the fate of the rebellious slaves was grotesque'.[77]

Governor Leith wasted no time in following up the ruling class's retaliatory massacre with a stern warning, issued a fortnight after the rebellion's end, that the enslaved would be crushed with even greater force should they try similar in future. Their condition, he emphasised, was permanent and unchangeable.

Since 1708 it had been illegal for enslavers to hire out their labour. The legislation also prohibited the enslaved selling for themselves their energy and muscle, known as huckstering. The mercantile instincts of planters and the economic necessity for more than a subsistence existence by the enslaved, however, overrode obedience to the law and it was widely ignored. In August 1818 a number of Whites in St. George made public their intent to enforce the prohibition.

Whereas many idle Negroes are allowed by their owners to traffic and huckster, to the great injury of the owners of property in general, the undersigned have therefore given this public Notice, as it is their intention tohave all such Negroes brought to Justice, should it be continued after this advertisement.

A year later the legislature passed a law re-confirming huckstering as illegal. Once more it was largely ignored. It symbolised the uneasy post-Bussa relationship characterised by violence, myopia and pragmatism on the part of the planters. They responded in a culturally consistent way through the continued use of force and terror while turning a blind eye to limited disobedience. Enslaved people fought back in the only way they knew how, through resistance by any means they felt able to offer. Beckles (2004) argues there was another attempt in 1816 to organise an

---

(CO 28/85) quoted in Lilian McNaught (2017), p.49.
77 James Walvin, *Black Ivory, A History of British Slavery* (London, 1982) p.236 quoted in Lillian McNaught, p.94.

uprising in Christ Church parish but the leaders were arrested and dealt with by court martial. Brandow (1983) notes planter Abraham Reece was murdered in July when he was mistaken for Mr Allamby, a character who attracted the hate of enslaved people in his parish of St. Thomas.[78] Yet, while the political representatives of the plantocracy were using uncompromising political language lingering after-thoughts include deliberation over its effect. Their intransigence and its impact upon the economic, social and political relationship between themselves and freed people of colour increasingly vexed their minds. Their 1817 decision to allow freed people of colour the ability to testify in court was, in this context, a pragmatic political decision that attempted to separate and extinguish any remaining feelings of unity between freed and enslaved. For the manumitted, it was a landmark legal progression that invigorated a bolder class confidence expressed through political lobbying.

For one Bajan freedman visiting his homeland, this judicial recognition was not worth the parchment on which it was written. St. Thomas-born Loveless Overton was a soldier in the King's Dragoon Guards, enlisting in Manchester in 1800 aged twenty. Witnessing a White beating an enslaved person, he stepped in. For this he was arrested, accused of being a Haitian revolutionary and deported back to England. However, while exercised at great personal cost his principled action has resulted in a favourable historical legacy, his image portrayed in oil-paint and his heroics the subject of research.[79]

Six years later, three hundred and seventy-three freedmen put their names to a radical statement demanding further rights and privileges known as the *Counter Address*. It was a reply to a public oath of loyalty to the Assembly by a group of twenty conservative free people of colour, led by plantation owner, enslaver and signatory to the 1811 petition, Jacob Belgrave, proclaiming their opposition to emancipation. The *Counter Address* supporters denied this group spoke for them as a class and were not content to limit their actions and aspirations to parameters set by the plantocracy. At least four freedmen named Tull – William M., John, John C., Thomas – were signatories which may shed some light on

---

78 James C. Brandow, *Genealogies of Barbados Families,* (Baltimore, 1983), p.488.
79 He is present in Henry Perlee Parker (1795-1873) *1st The King's Dragoon Guards, The Baggage Train* (1824) where he is referred to as an officer's servant. Allison Ramsey 'Fighting for Equal Rights/Rites: The Narrative of Loveless Overton' in *The Journal of the Barbados Museum and Historical Society Vol. 56* (2010):1-28.

why William Criss chose to change his name to Tull.[80]

Eventually, in 1825, the Consolidated Slave Law allowed Criss and his enslaved brothers and sisters to own property, testify in court cases and a reduction in their manumission fees. In return it gave planters immunity from prosecution for killing slaves in revolt, promised execution as the penalty for any person of colour who threatened the life of a White and confirmed that all Blacks were to be considered enslaved unless they had proof otherwise.

80 J.S. Handler, R. Hughes and E.M. Wiltshire, *Freedmen of Barbados. Names and Notes for Genealogical and Family History Research,* (Charlottesville, Virginia 1999) p.54. For list of signatories, *Barbadian,* 25 April 1824, see appendix 4.

Chapter Three
Enslaved Barbados

SUGAR

Barbados was for much of the seventeenth and eighteenth centuries the monarchy's most prosperous colony outside the British Isles. It was the second oldest in the Caribbean after St Kitts. While the narrative of acquisition that tends to dominate is written by the triumphant, the ownership of this small territory of twenty-one miles in length by fourteen in width in the south-eastern Caribbean was disputed from moment of claim. Some histories suggest that a ship commanded by Captain Simon Gordon and belonging to City of London merchant Sir William Courteen first 'discovered' the island in 1620. What is more certain is that the Anglo-Dutch Courteen Company occupied the island in 1625, claiming it for the British Crown. There was no reported resistance, the indigenous Arawak and Carib having been driven out by previous incursions. It is believed the first enslaved people and indentured servants were brought to the island by settler planters two years later.[81]

In a distorted version of 'finders keepers' where discovery, piracy and mercantilist capitalism merge, the patent for the island – permission from Charles I to personally exploit the resources and control administration through rent - was eventually granted to James Hay, first earl of Carlisle and a favourite of the monarch. He had loaned the king 'a very great sum of money' and possession of the island may have been to settle some or all this debt.[82] Hay immediately installed a replacement governor, Sir William Tufton, who used the prism of political patronage when overseeing the lease and sale of plots of land to planters and merchants. A 1673 list of the most 'eminent planters'[83] with holdings of between one hundred and one thousand acres includes many close to the Crown and affluent City of London merchants, such Robert Rich, earl of Warwick (three hundred and fifty acres) and Sir Peter Colleton (seven hundred acres)

81 Hilary Beckles, *A History of Barbados,* (Cambridge, 1990).
82 Roy Schreiber, 'First Carlisle: Sir James Hay, First Earl of Carlisle as Courtier Diplomat and Entrepreneur' in *Transactions of the American Philosophical Society* 74, 7, 1984, p.173.
83 https://www.geni.com/projects/Barbados-Eminent-Planters-1673/3290 accessed 10 May 2020.

A map published in the same year identifies 'tenn thousande Acres *of* Lande which Belongeth to the Merchants of London'.[84] Encouraged by Hay and Tufton – and subsequent governors and administrators – to use enslaved and bonded labour, early colonists grew wheat, tobacco, ginger, indigo and cotton. An over-supply from the Americas of the last two commodities collapsed their price in Europe in the sixteen forties forcing planters to diversify into other crops. Indigenous Arawaks from the Dutch colony of Essequibo, skilled in the cultivation of cassava, maize and other tropical foods were enticed to Barbados as advisors with the promise of payment and reward. Instead, planters enslaved them and the project collapsed. Consequentially, amongst the Arawaks of the region the reputation of English colonists was of untrustworthy cheats.

The transition to sugar-cane cultivation across the island was an economic decision that had its origins conflict between the Dutch and Portuguese over coveted sugar-producing territories in Brazil. They supplied eighty per cent of the European market and political tension between the two severely disrupted production. Barbados planters saw this as an opportunity to capture some of this lucrative trade. Settlers from Dutch Brazil, including many of Semitic origin, assisted with agricultural know-how and credit. One of these, David de Mercato, would be instrumental in revolutionising sugar production technology.

The Barbados soil and climate was ideal for this easily grown plant. The concentration of land-ownership meant that within a decade virtually the whole island was a sugar field.

The fact remains that the most spectacular and revolutionary commercial-industrial development of the Interregnum was the introduction of sugar planting to the West Indies.[85]

With the Restoration of the Stuart monarchy in 1660 the monopoly use in Barbados and the English Caribbean of an improved sugar-mill invented by de Mercato was granted by Charles II to governor Lord Willoughby and his business partner Lawrence Hyde, son of the Lord Chancellor. This allowed the governor greater use of political patronage

---

84 Richard Ligon, *A True and Exact History of the Island of Barbados*, (London, 1673), p.4.
85 Brenner (London, 2003) p.161.

as well as economic power as he could decide which planters would have access to this innovation.

The route from planting to processing involved an organised division of labour. Once the extremely repetitive and strenuous task of cane-holing had been done, the buds would be planted. Grown to full height, the cane would be harvested. The tall plants grew close together. In being harvested, the sharp edges of the leaves would cut labourers as they slashed away at their stems. The crop would then be carried to the sugar mill and fed through vertical rollers with the liquid channelled into the stifling boiling house where it would be crystallised by evaporation. Working inside in this extreme heat, intensified by the humidity outside, was as gruelling as field work. Finally, the sugar crystals would be transferred to coolers and potted into hogsheads. Lucrative and widespread, hogsheads of sugar soon became the island's currency of exchange. Estate windmills became so ubiquitous that the island was dotted throughout with revolving propellors. Williams (1964) argues that this precise division of labour provided the template for the factory system in the UK that was the organisational foundation of the industrial revolution.

Writing his analysis of Capitalism in the mid-nineteenth century, Karl Marx recognised similarities in the exploitation of factory workers, whether as wage labourers in the mills of Lancashire or enslaved labourers in the sugar plantations of Barbados. In both environments life was cheap, the owner wanting only biological muscle, a 'hand' or a 'slave'. Existence as a social being is unimportant and irrelevant.

The capitalistic mode of production (essentially the production of surplus value, the absorption of surplus value), produces thus with the extension of the working day, not only the deterioration of human labour power by robbing it of its normal, moral and physical, conditions of development and function. It also produces the premature exhaustion and death of this labour power itself. It extends the labourer's time of production during a given period by shortening his actual life-time ... The slave-owner buys his labourer as he buys his horse. If he loses his slave, he loses capital that can only be restored by new outlay in the slave-mart ... Considerations of economy, moreover, which, under a natural system, afford some security for humane treatment by identifying the master's interest with the slave's preservation, when once trading in slaves is practised, become reasons for racking to the uttermost the toil of the slave, for, when his place can at once be supplied from foreign preserves, the duration of his life becomes a matter of less moment than its productiveness while it lasts. It is accordingly a maxim of slave management, in slave importing countries, that the most effective economy is that which takes out of the human chattel in the shortest space of time the utmost amount of exertion it is capable of putting forth. It is in the tropical culture, where annual profits often equal the whole capital of plantations, that negro life is most recklessly sacrificed. It is the agriculture of the West Indies, which has been for centuries prolific of fabulous wealth, that has engulfed millions of the African race.[86]

Toil in the unforgiving sweat factory of the mill was on a par with the harsh, wearying, burden of field work.

Perpetual Noise and Hurry, and the only way to render a person Angry and Tyrannical, too; since the Climate is so hot and the labor so constant, that the Servants (we would say slaves) night and day stand in great Boyling Houses, where there are six or seven large Coppers or Furnaces kept perpetually boyling; and from which with heavy Ladles and Skimmers they Skim off the excrementitious parts of the Canes, till it comes to its perfection and cleans, while others as Stoakers, Broil as it were alive, in managing the Fires, and one part is constantly at the mill to supply it with canes, night and day, during the whole season of making sugar, which is about six months of the year.[87]

Seventeenth century anti-slavery campaigner and Barbados resident Thomas Tryon's unique description of a seventeenth century sugar mill graphically details their dangerous working environment with injury and death common, where 'hands and arms are crushed to pieces' and whole bodies could be ground to fragments. In the boiling house over-worked and over-heated operatives, over-powered by noxious 'sulphurous

---

86 Karl Marx, *Capital Volume One* (London, 1970), pp.265-6.
87 Seventeenth-century anti-slavery campaigner and Barbados resident Thomas Tryon *Friendly Advice to the Gentleman-Planters of the East and West Indies* (London,1684) quoted in Russell R. Menard *Sweet Negotiations. Sugar, slavery and plantation agriculture in early Barbados* (London, 2006) p.15.

fumes' would sometimes collapse into 'the fierce boiling syrups' where death may have compared favourably.[88]

Field-workers – 'praedials' – comprised three groups: First Gang – men, women and older children chosen for their physicality and strength; Second Gang – mothers, women, children and elderly – who did weeding, cleaning, tidying-up and other menial work; Third Gang, the most vulnerable and physically frail assigned child and medical care duties, such as looking after the new-born babies of mothers forced back into the field and looking after the sick whose death would represent a monetary loss to the enslaver. The working day was dawn to dusk. A roll-call would be taken in the field by 'a severe overseer'.[89] There would be half-hour breakfast mid-morning and a two-hour dinner break at midday. Work continued in the afternoon to sunset. The busiest period for this six day week was January-July where these working times would be extended.

It could be argued that domestic slaves were not so brutally exploited but this comparison would be a misleading. Working in the house of the master was seen as a privilege but like all 'benefits' they came with a cost. Female domestics were chosen primarily for their looks with the random terror of rape and sexual abuse a common experience. Men were picked for their perceived loyalty in the face of daily degradation.

European appetite for sugar spurred a labour-intensive agri-business that thrived on a cheap and durable workforce. Initially, planters used a mixture of bonded European, enslaved West African and indigenous Caribbean labour. Irish, Scots and English indentured servants – 'red-legs' – could be found working alongside the enslaved as field and domestic workers in the early decades of colonisation. They had usually arrived under coercion or force, as transported convicts, kidnapped or prisoners of war. After Cromwell's invasion of Ireland, 1649-53, alongside captured soldiers, thousands of beggars were also transported to the West Indies.[90]

When soldiers commanded by Henry Cromwell, Oliver's son, seized a thousand 'Irish wenches' to sell them to Barbados, Henry justified the

88 Thomas Tryon (London, 1684) quoted in (anonymous) *Thomas Tryon, Sheep, and the Politics of Eden* p.25 https://ueaeprints.uea.ac.uk/id/eprint/63014/1/Accepted_manuscript.pdf Accessed 9 May 2020.

89 Ligon, (London, 1673) p.44.

90 J.C. Beckett *The Making of Modern Ireland 1603-1923*, (London, 1966) p.110.

action by saying that 'although we must use force in taking them up', yet it was 'so much for their own good and likely to be of so great advantage to the public'. He also suggested 2,000 Irish boys could be seized for the same purpose: 'who knows but it might be a means to make them Englishmen'.[91]

By the middle decades of the seventeenth century Barbados was known to have a thriving slave market for all colours. Violence and contempt were integral features of the master-slave relationship. Richard Ligon, a Royalist exile who lived on the island in the late sixteen forties, found the brutality towards those of his colour particularly distasteful. For refusing instructions

> They are beaten by the overseer: if they resist, then their time is doubled. I have seen an overseer beat a servant with a cane about the head till the blood has followed for a fault that is not worth the speaking of and yet he must have patience or worse will follow. Truly, I have seen such cruelty there done to servants, as I did not think one Christian could have done to another.[92]

German Indentured servant, Heinrich von Uchteritz, was sold in Barbados in 1652 for eight hundred pounds of sugar. A political prisoner in London he had been transported along with thirteen hundred others. On his plantation were 'Christians, Negroes and Indian slaves'.[93]

Ligon noted the response this inhumanity provoked. The house and cane of planters James Holduppe and Constantine Silvester was burnt to the ground. On another occasion servants had planned to take over the island in revolution but were given away by a fellow servant. Eighteen plotters were subsequently executed. Barbados historian Jerome Handler (1982) suggests White indentured servants had, in the sixteen thirties, planned a revolt that was also terminated before fruition.

After completing their terms of servitude, usually between five and seven years, White captives would be allowed to sell their labour for

---

91 Liz Curtis et al, *Nothing But the Same Old Story: The Roots of Anti-Irish Racism*, (London, 1986), p.29.
92 Ligon (London, 1673) p.44.
93 A. Gunkel and J.S. Handler 'A German Indentured Servant in Barbados in 1652: The Account of Heinrich von Uchteritz' *Journal of the Barbados Museum and Historical Society* 33: 91-100 (1970).

a wage. For this reason, to planters, they did not represent a viable, long-term investment. A enslaved person could be bought for life – on average seventeen years – while a bonded labourer allowed a wage after seven years. By 1660 the enslaved population in Barbados was around twenty-seven thousand. Between 1662-67 the Stuart monarchy's *Royal Adventurers Trading into Africa* (RA) transported, each year, approximately six thousand West African captives to the island with private traders shipping a similar amount annually.

The estate owners and managers also encouraged biological reproduction so that the supply of new labour could be provided from within – Creoles – rather than continuously buying imported, 'unseasoned' captives who tended to be more rebellious. In contravention of their Christian moral codes many encouraged and facilitated polygamy to increase reproduction rates. The success of this bio-engineering and booming sugar exports changed the ethnic balance of the population. By the sixteen eighties people of colour comprised thirty-eight thousand compared to around twenty-three thousand Whites.

Conscious of their security being threatened from this rising Black population the Barbados Assembly, dominated by large-acreage planters, passed in 1676 a law forbidding the teaching of Christianity to enslaved people: spreading the word and teachings of the bible would inevitably inspire an interest in literacy, self-education and ideas of equality.

The Anglican church on the island acted in the support and defence of the class it represented. It reflected in its thinking and actions the (largely privileged) White people who worshipped within. Since 1661 Church of England (CoE) clergy in the West Indies were chosen by the Bishop of London to ensure all were on message.

SLAVE CODE

The Barbados Assembly enacted the foundational pillars of its slave code – *An Act for the Governing of Negroes* – in 1661. It was the first of its kind in the Caribbean and was adopted as a template for other societies built upon enslavement, such as the Carolinas in North America.

Whereas the Plantations and Estates of this Island cannot be fully managed, and brought into Use, without the Labour and Service of great Numbers of Negroes and other Slaves: And for as much as the said Negroes and other Slaves brought unto the People of this Island for that purpose, are of Barbarous, Wild, and Savage Natures, and such as renders them wholly unqualified to be governed by the Laws, Customs, and Practices of our Nations: It therefore becoming absolutely necessary, that such other Constitutions, Laws, and Orders should be in this Island framed and enacted for the good Regulating and Ordering of them, as may both restrain the Disorders, Rapines, and Inhumanities to which they are naturally prone and inclined, with such Encouragements and Allowances as are fit and needful to their Support, that from both, this Island, through the Blessing of God thereon, may be preserved, His Majesty's Subjects in their Lives and Fortunes secured...[94]

Conditions imposed upon the chattel slaves were imprisonment within plantation boundaries unless given specific permission to leave. Even then a signifying uniform – 'livery' – had to be worn and return time stipulated. No implements such as 'clubs or wooden swords' were to be carried. The owning, carrying and playing of musical instruments was prohibited. 'Negroes... found out of the plantation of his or their master or owner at any time' should be whipped. Slave shacks were to be searched every fourteen days. If any man of colour, enslaved or free, acts violently toward a White person, they will be whipped for the first offence, severely whipped, their nose slit and their face burned with a hot iron for the second. A third violation would entail whatever punishment 'the Governor and Council 'decide. However, it added the caveat that a slave could strike a Christian if it was in defence of another White person, such as their 'Masters, Mistresses, or Owners of their Families, or of their Goods'. The code also stipulated differing amounts of reward for the return of runaways.

It unconsciously acknowledged the enslaved's continuous resistance to their condition through 'many heinous and grievous Crimes, as Murders, Burglaries, Robbing in the High-ways, Rapes, Burning of Houses or Canes' attributing these to 'the Baseness of their Condition'. Yet, as property, they did not qualify for trial by jury. Rather, two Justices of the Peace could co-opt three householders and together they could administer 'justice'. If 'guilty', they were then obliged to force another

94 http://pryan2.kingsfaculty.ca/pryan/assets/File/Barbados%20Slave%20Code%201688%20(repealed%20the%201661%20code).pdf Accessed 12 May 2020.

enslaved person(s) to carry out the execution.

The three strikes and out rule was a feature of the code. Third violations of the same offence, if not carrying the mandatory sentence of death, allowed those in authority to apply their choice of punishment which could – and often did – include execution. If the 'crime' was rebellion, mutiny or insurrection martial law could be declared and four militiamen decide punishment by Council on the spot. This would certainly be execution for the main protagonists and severing of limbs for others. Death could be drawn out over a number of days by slow burning and the cutting out of entrails while still alive. For losing their human property, the slave-owners would be compensated damages out of public funds with up to £25 (£4,718) for each. If it could be proved that the Negroes acted rebelliously because of ill-treatment, their owners would not be compensated.

Killing or injuring an enslaved person by 'accident', in whatever circumstances, would not be deemed a crime or punishable in any way. However, if their property and killed by 'Wantonness… Bloody-mindedness or Cruel Intention' the culprit would pay a £15 (£2,831) fine. If the enslaved was another's property, the fine was £25 (£4,718) coupled with a promise of future good behaviour. Additionally, if a White settler thought *a Negro* out at night was intending to steal their property they could kill without having to 'be accountable for it'.[95]

The slave code used the term 'Negro' and 'slave' interchangeably as if one cannot exist without the other. Prior to its enactment, White indentured servants and West African enslaved had both been treated with brutal ferocity. However, plantation owners were well aware of the risks should these dispossessed ethnicities find common cause. The planters had been in receipt of many Scots, Irish and some English political prisoners who, with a dubious legal status – were they slaves or indentured servants? – had nothing to loose in plotting insurrection with their fellow brown-skinned captives. It was necessary to drive a wedge between them. As early as 1636, the Barbados Council had decreed that Africans and indigenous Caribbeans were slaves for life, White servants however were offered the prospect of 'freedom' once their period of indenture was completed. Yet, continued collaborations, most notably

---

95 Many former slave states in the USA have retained a similar law, which allows lethal force to be used on mere suspicion. Contemporary legislation reflecting the same rationale are called Stand Your Ground Laws. At least 27 states have enacted some form of this law (2020).

manifest in the brutal suppressions of 1655, were a likely major catalyst leading to the imposition of the Slave Code in 1661.

The legal status the code transposed upon the African was one of passive object: anything could done to them with virtual immunity while they had with no recourse to the law for protection as human beings. They were not recognised as sentient people, just animalistic brutes. It gave planters free hands to beat, whip, slash and kill. Africans and Creoles of African descent could not give testimony against Whites. White planters would not stand witness against another of their kind for ill-treatment or killing for reasons of self-protection: such inhumanity to their chattel was the norm.

The code introduced a dual legal system, hammering a wedge between enslaved and servants. It offered rewards to Whites for informing, capturing and killing rebellious people of colour. While it talked of two groups, 'Christians' and 'Negroes/Slaves' it only recognised the latter as property. As feeling, thinking, people they were non-existent, instead just animate chattel. Yet, here lies the profound contradiction at the heart of the code's inferred conceptualisation of the enslaved. While denying their status as human beings, they recognised that they were living beings with agency.

The plantocracy used the law and legal system as an instrument of terror. While simultaneously using the code to protect themselves, it was not a refuge the enslaved could use to protect themselves against injustice. There was no concept in the code of equality under the law as we would understand it today. The 'rights' of the Masters were the only rights that mattered. The juridical system was a device and tool to exploit the absolute extraction of their slaves' labour power; to hire them for cash or kind; to sell them for cash or kind; to maintain the ability to reproduce biologically, at minimal cost, the social structure of enslavement. The code's laws applied to Negroes, but law as part of society's infrastructure was not relevant to Negroes. Existing in a constant state of natural injustice, the enslaved were outlaws where just their biology was useful, as a repository of financial return.

The 1661 Barbados slave code could arguably be the first that legally enshrined a social, economic and political system that became known in the twentieth century known as apartheid. From this moment on, it may well have been the hope of the plantocracy that class collaboration between White bonded servants and Black enslaved, witnessed in 1655, would be viewed by the former as unviable.

Without the code Barbados, as the Stuart's jewell in their colonial crown, could not have prospered as it did. Charles II, the Duke of York, Prince Rupert and other members of the royal household who were the majority shareholders of the RA, were determined to protect and enhance the island's ever-increasing revenue flow to the royal exchequer. The Crown's consultative committee on colonial affairs, the Council of Foreign Plantations, also had a number of commissioners with financial and land interests in Barbados including Willoughby, James Drax, Thomas Povey, Henry Walrond, John Morrice and Thomas Crispe. The creation and enactment of the code, if not inspired by Crown and Merchant self-interest, would undoubtedly have had its unqualified support. Otherwise it would not have been sanctioned by the Court and Parliament in London who had the power of veto on colony-enacted legislation.

While the code galvanised the planters' regime of terror, it did not immediately extinguish the enslaved's spirit of collective rebellion. The plantocracy's characteristic response was a revision and strengthening of its laws.

Chapter Four
Resistance

The enslaved constantly and consistently resisted and rebelled. It was the undeniable reality in the ultimate objective of seizing control of their lives. Beckles argues they were politically conscious, as individuals and as a class, acting against personal injustice and in furtherance of their collective emancipation. They 'rebelled when they could, and accommodated when they had to'. As such they created a distinctly radical tradition revolving around the core themes of freedom and 'the right to create a life of their own'.[96]

Resistance could take many forms. Covert modes included not obeying instructions to the letter; not hearing a demand correctly; sabotaging a task; contriving an accident; refusing to show emotion, such as pain; and keeping African names and cultural practices. These forms could be daily occurrences, part of an individual's ingrained behaviour and way of being, their modus operandi.

Overt modes tended to be more physically explosive and expressive, such as practising Obeah,[97] running away, self-mutilation and suicide; if collective, take the form of group escape, rebellion, revolt and uprising.

Alongside were incremental methods that combined both modes, such as growing surplus crops on patches of ground to sell for cash that in time could be used to buy freedom; or manipulating the emotion of an owner in the hope of future manumission.

This culture of resistance to enslavement and servitude began from the moment people were deprived of their status as a social beings. It developed further during the Middle Passage and consolidated while living through prolonged hell on alien soil. The way planters lived betrayed an awareness of this. Ligon described how their residences in the mid-seventeenth century were architecturally designed for defence against revolt.:

96 Hilary Beckles *Black Rebellion in Barbados. The Struggle Against Slavery 1627-1838,*(Bridgetown, 1984), pp. 2,4.
97 Obeah was the belief in, and practice of, West African cultural traditions that drew upon magic and the supernatural. See http://www.people.vcu. edu/~wchan/poco/624/harris_south/Obeah%20and%20Myal.htm Accessed 11 May 2020.

Their houses, many of which are built in manner of fortifications and have lines, bulwarks, and bastions to defend themselves in case there should be any uproar or commotion… either by the Christian servants, or Negro slaves. [Rain water collected and stored internally could be used] whilst they are besieged; as also, to throw down upon the naked bodies of the Negroes, scalding hot; which is as good a defence against their underminings as any other weapon.[98]

He records the burning of a boiling house by enslaved – under the pretence of an accident – that occurred before his arrival on the island. During his first year of residence a planned rebellion by servants was foiled and punished with eighteen executions. Enslaved Blacks and indentured Whites were rising up forging a class unity which overrode ethnic difference. The Barbados Council, a governing body appointed by the Crown on nomination from the governor, was informed in 1655 that Africans and Irish had joined together in rebellion. Governor Daniel Searle immediately banned all Irish servants from possessing weapons.

Communities of runaway Africans – Maroons – hid in woods and caves. One of the earliest maps of Barbados, published in Ligon's book, has an illustration of a pursuing enslaver on horseback firing a gun at fleeing captives, suggesting it was a common feature of island life. Planters feared Maroons would foment this condition into their enslaved brothers and sisters through some kind of osmosis. One of the laws of the slave code was directed specifically at this phenomenon. Armed planters could hunt down and recapture Negroes dead or alive. If the runaway had been 'free' for six months or more a reward of five hundred pounds of sugar could be claimed. This would be doubled if the person had escaped a year or more. After the forests were cleared to create more sugar fields, while Maroon communities disappeared their legend and legacy spread to other enslaved peoples in the Caribbean, such as Jamaica, where they became an unconquerable feature of plantation society.[99]

---

98 Richard Ligon (London, 1673) p.29.
99 J. Handler 'Slave revolts and conspiracies in seventeenth century Barbados' in *New West Indian Guide/Nieuwe West-Indische Gids* 56 (1982), no: 1/2, Lieden, 5-42, p.9. http://jeromehandler.org/wp-content/uploads/2009/07/Revolts-82.pdf Accessed 13 May 2020. In the US during the mid-nineteenth century Samuel Cartwright diagnosed runaway slaves as suffering from a mental illness he 'diagnosed' as Drapetomania. His concept became part of

The overwhelming majority of the enslaved population in the seventeenth century was Africa-born 'saltwater slaves'. They believed that suicide would return their embodied souls home where they would live eternally with ancestral spirits. Humphrey Walrond, determined to eradicate self-expiration on his estate, forced some fellow believers to raise up on a tall wooden spike the head of a recent suicide as proof that without the head the body cannot transfer to one's treasured place of birth.

Despite the code Negroes continued to meet collectively to sing, dance, discuss and plot recovery of their unchained lives. It did not nullify their resistance or calm the anxieties of the exploiters.

An uprising by mainly Akan-speakers in May 1675 was said to have been inspired by a runaway. Involving hundreds and in gestation for at least three years, the freedom fighters envisioned an island devoid of White enslavers and run much like their lamented Gold Coast kingdoms. An imagined re-creation of home. Unfortunately, the design was discovered with the majority of the leaders ritually destroyed: seventeen were executed, six burned alive and eleven beheaded – their bodies pulled along the streets of Speightstown before being burned like the others – while five more killed themselves to escape such fate.

In May, 1683, governor Sir Richard Dutton instructed military on horseback to ride out on Saturdays and Sundays looking for 'disorderly meetings of Negroes who assemble in several places in great numbers at those times, to the terror of the inhabitants'.[100] His order was symptomatic of a more or less permanent state of anxiety characterising planters. No concrete evidence of an uprising was found but nevertheless, on the principle of no smoke without fire,

> four of five for examples sake were well whipped for terror to others, and one old Negro man… was… burned alive for uttering some insolent words upon the Christians beating some Negroes, which struck terror into his mistress.[101]

---

a body of knowledge labelled in the twentieth century as Scientific Racism, that attempted to de-legitimise individual and social responses to structural racism.

100 Richard Dutton to John Witham May 1,1683. CO/1/51, N.A. quoted in J. Handler (1982), p.19.

101 Ibid., p.20.

Within just a few years, the nightmare scenario for men like Dutton of inter-ethnic class unity again raised its head, a collaboration that many of the settlers fervently hoped had been extinguished with the slave code. The scare of 1685-6 held that Negroes and Irish servants were planning an uprising to eradicate their mutual exploiters. Acting governor and member of the Royal Africa Company (RAC), Edwin Stede, ordered twice daily searches of slave shacks, morning and evening. Nothing was found yet, as in 1655, a signal of terror needed to be transmitted: a number of Irish were imprisoned and Africans executed. What began as a phantom in the minds of anxious Whites culminated in the reality of killing and forced confinement.

This episode focussed minds within the governing bodies of the island. A rewriting of the code to restrict further the enslaved population was enacted in 1688. It went into greater detail on the control of behaviour and the sanctions used to enforce compliance. A revived law from 1682, outside the code but related, addressed the issue of a declining White population and its effect upon their ability to impose internal security. The exodus of poor Whites once they had finished their terms of servitude, often to other islands where land was obtainable, had severely depleted manpower available to the militia. It was a preoccupation that became heightened with the next rebellion several years later.

Like the planned uprising of 1655, the 1692 design was also years in preparation, involved inter-ethnic class unity and envisaged taking complete control of the island. While the leading protagonists and architects were people of colour – enslaved and 'free' – there was collaboration with Irish servants. The latter's role was to infiltrate Bridgetown armoury, get the guards drunk, take their keys and open the doors to the arms store. The wider detail of the elaborate plan involved a mature military strategy that was remarked upon by governor Kendall, *those villains are but too sensible.*[102] An example was the flexible adaptation of the leaders – Hammon, Ben, Samson and Sambo – who postponed a couple of times the trigger date for commencement: the war with France had seen large English naval forces anchoring in Carlisle Bay, with each suspension involving a recalculation of dates and timings.

Participants swore an oath to secrecy. Most were Barbados-born Creoles rather than saltwater Africans. For the plantocracy, this was a new and frightening characteristic with the leading activists from skilled

102 James Kendall, Letter to Lords of Trade, November 3, 1692. CO 28/1, N.A. in J. Handler (1982), p.27.

trades and positions of responsibility. The authorities foiled it before implementation. On being alerted, the governor invoked martial law and thirty revolutionaries from twenty-one plantations were immediately punished. To strike terror into their brothers and sisters Samson, Ben and Sambo were sentenced to be hung in gibbets and left to starve to death, whereupon their heads would be severed from their bodies and placed on pole. Their torsos and limbs to be quartered and burned. Only naming the others could save them. After four days in the gibbets and the expected rescue by fellow insurrectionists not occurring, Ben and Sambo agreed to confess while Samson remained true to his oath. Sambo died on release, while Ben named names. Consequently, hundreds of slaves were arrested with many hanged and burned, some by the same method of execution suffered by Samson. As well, Alice Mills was paid ten guineas for castrating forty-two rebels. Thankfully, some of the named managed to escape apprehension.

The ruling class responded with further legislation that encouraged informers with manumission and passage to a destination of choice; or a cash payment while remaining enslaved. Five other pieces of legislation were passed before the year's end with a similar purpose and objective: to make rebellion and insurrection more difficult; and when it did manifest to suppress ruthlessly. By the end of the seventeenth century Barbados had legalised terror as the acceptable method of control of its enslaved population.

There were more rumours, scares and alarms about uprisings in the early years of the new century. A few dwellings were fired in Bridgetown in late 1701 resulting in the execution of an unconfirmed number of slaves but no rebellion followed. Indeed, the formal legalisation of the reign of terror instituted by the slave code and its subsequent additions and amendments, appears to have led in turn to the greater use of increasingly covert and nuanced modes of resistance. A Moravian minister of colour recalled how a carpenter that had been torn from his wife and child through auction, only to rebuild a family once more in his new location was so desperate on being sold a third time that when the auctioneer instructed him

to expose his limbs and wield his tools... he bent on his knee and spread out his right hand on a log timber near by, and resting the adze on his knee, and lifting the sharp tool with his left hand, with a couple of rapid strokes he cut off his right hand, and said 'there, now – who will buy me'.[103]

THE MIDDLE PASSAGE AND RESISTANCE

For West Africans, victims of the largest forced migration in history, if having your status as a social being stripped from you was not enough, the unimaginable horror of the Middle Passage was an additional, hellish torment.[104] Men, women and children chained at the hands and ankles were packed horizontally as tight as possible on the floors below deck. Awash in their collective excrement, urine, sweat and vomit the journey south west could take weeks, often months. Each day they would be brought in groups onto the deck to 'dance' in the light and given – if they were lucky – water and one meagre portion of either beans, corn, yams, rice or palm oil. The noxious, over-powering stench marked out slave ships long before they were seen.

John Hart, captured with his mother and sister, described their experience of being enslaved and transported from their home of Sierra Leone. Tellingly, he writes of his kin and former self in the third person.

The Spaniards immediately seized all three, and conveyed them to a boat, which was lying in a creek of bushes. They were then, with many more conveyed to a ship which was lying at the mouth of a river, where they were then put on board, they were then taken below in the ships hold were [sic] there where [sic] a great many more. Not being used to close confinement they were nearly all suffocated and only being allowed two hours upon deck to see daylight with a strong guard of Spaniards over them, and their diet being only one quart of

103 Reverend H. Moore and Mr G.R. Potter, *1838-1878 Emancipation Jubilee. Address Delivered in the Moravian Chapel in Demerara*, (1888), pp.10-11.
104 This was the middle leg of the triangular trade, from West Africa to the Americas – the Caribbean, North, Central and South America. Called the triangular trade because ships would leave European ports with manufactured goods such as ironware and weaponry, exchange some of these in West Africa for gold, captured people, spices, ivory and cloth before selling the enslaved and other manufactured commodities in the Americas in exchange for tobacco, sugar and spices. Thus, on each leg of the journey the ships would be laden with saleable commodities.

rice a day, from the time they were stolen until the time they arrived in Charleston.[105]

Many did not survive, between fifteen and twenty-five per cent dying from mental anguish and suicide, disease, brutal treatment, malnutrition or murder. Sometimes it was much higher. The captain of slave ship *Hannibal*, Thomas Phillips, noted that of the seven hundred transported from West Africa, only three hundred and seventy-two were still breathing on reaching Barbados.[106] Discarded as unwanted waste, without ceremony or any acknowledgement they were human beings mothers would see their children thrown overboard, women their sisters, men their wives.

DNA test results for Edward's elder brother William's great grandson, Graham Humphrey, suggested a four per cent West African – Nigeria, Ghana, Benin and Togo – antecedence.[107] Researching Tulls in the Barbados and UK Archives revealed Quamin Tull, a free man of colour resident in St. Michael owning one enslaved person.[108] It is not known if he is related. His significance in this part of our story lies in his insistence on proudly retaining and proclaiming his West African heritage through his name, a weapon of resistance. Quamin is male-gendered Akan for Saturday (Quamino, female). Quamin's and Edward's direct ancestors survived the Middle Passage. They may well have had brothers, sisters, aunts, uncles, mothers, fathers, cousins and friends who did not. Amidst the warm sun, fertile soil and lush vegetation they left beloved people and cherished memories. By situating a Tull with a West African name aboard a Barbados-bound ship we can re-humanise, reclaim them from just a number on the cargo ledger sheet. It is a profound moment of empathy with obliterated identities; bodies deformed, abused and crushed. On reconfiguration over four thousand miles across the Atlantic, Quamin and Edward's forebears would have an objectified shape forced upon them that had no relevance to their

105 John Hart *A Narrative of the Life and Sufferings of John Hart, a native of Sierra Leone, Africa, from which place he was stolen away by a company of Spaniards, and brought to the town of Charlestown*, (London,1842), p.2.
106 Thomas Phillips, 'A Journal of the Voyages made in the Hannibal', in A. Churchill (ed.), *A Collection of Voyages and Travels Volume 6*, (London, 1746).
107 Email correspondence between author and Graham Humphrey, 20 January, 2020.
108 1832 Slave Registry, T71/552, St. Michael, 221, 2nd, N.A., London.

previous lives. The past was washed away with blood. A hellish journey to a hellish existence.

While a factor for the RAC in Barbados, Edward Stede detailed the number of enslaved forced aboard company ships at *Arda* port (Ardra, southern Benin) and landed at Barbados for the month of December, 1678: *Arthur*, four hundred and seventeen on embarkation, three hundred and twenty-nine at disembarkation; *Martha* four hundred and forty-seven reduced to three hundred and eighty-five; *Coaster* one hundred and fifty to one hundred and thirteen. In total, from one thousand and fourteen, one hundred and eighty-seven did not survive the Middle Passage.[109] Davies notes that the RAC ship *Francis,* sailing from Calabar to Nevis, lost one hundred and ninety-nine of its two hundred and sixty-seven enslaved. The Committee of the Privy Council, investigating the trade in 1789, found the previous eight years RAC ships lost an average of twenty three and a half per cent.[110] Maddison estimates that between 1500-1820 out of eleven million suffering the Middle Passage, one and a half million did not survive.[111]

To this incalculable suffering there was continuous resistance – described by Equiano as the 'cry of the human soul within' – in West African coastal communities and aboard slave ships, taking myriad forms.[112]

Slave ship surgeon Alexander Falconbridge had first hand knowledge.

As very few of the negroes can so far brook the loss of their liberty, and the hardships they endure, as to bear them with any degree of patience, they are ever upon the watch to take advantage of the least negligence in their oppressors. Insurrections are frequently the consequence; which are seldom suppressed without much bloodshed. Sometimes these are successful, and the whole ship's company is cut

---

109 Elizabeth Donnan (ed.) *Documents Illustrative of the Slave Trade, Volume 1 1441-1700*, (Washington, 1930) p.240. So strategically important was Arda that the Duke of York attempted to visit the King and sign articles of trade in 1664. Calamitously, he was captured by Dutch naval commander De Ruyter and taken to Holland as prize.
110 Davies, (1999), p.292.
111 Angus Maddison *Contours of the World Economy, 1-203 A.D.. Essays in Macro-Economic History* (Oxford, 2005) p.224.
112 Vincent Carreta, *Equiano The African. Biography of a Self-Made Man,* (Georgia, 2005) p.105.

off. They are likewise always ready to seize every opportunity for committing some act of desperation to free themselves from their miserable state; and notwithstanding the restraints under which they are laid, they often succeed.[113]

A contemporary, Charles Davenant, describes a kidnap method called 'boating'. This involved enslavers setting out from their ship on a small craft with goods to trade upriver and returning with captives from wherever they could be had and by whatever means.

Very gross and barbarous acts of inhumanity, seizing and taking away with them all the Negroes they could surprise along the coast, robbing canoes on the water, forcing women, boys and girls along with them from the shore, shooting at boats, and killing such Negroes as refused to answer their call.[114]

Falconbridge witnessed one hundred and twenty brought back through 'boating' and felt it was a common mode of people stealing. It became more widely known as 'panyarring'. Andrea Stuart poignantly describes its brutal reality.

Spirited away from their communities, many as a result of inter-ethnic conflict... The men were bound together into coffles, linked by wood and rope and chain, with the women and children straggling alongside, free of shackles but ever vulnerable to violence and opportunistic sexual abuse.[115]

---

113 Alexander Falconbridge, *An Account of the Slave Trade on the Coast of Africa,* (London, 1788) quoted in Melville J. Herskovits *The Myth of the Negro Past* (New York, 1941) p.88. He later became an active abolitionist.
114 Charles Davenant 'Reflections upon the Constitution and Management of the Africa Trade etc' in Charles Whitworth (ed.) *The Political and Commercial Works of that Celebrated Writer Charles Davenant L.L.D.V.* (London, 1771) quoted in William A. Pettigrew, *Freedom's Debt: The Royal Africa Company and the Politics of the Atlantic Slave Trade, 1672-1752,* (Virginia, 2013), p.188.
115 Stuart, (2012), p.89. The creation of war between West African ethnic groups was an instrument of trade used by European people traffickers. Through the cultivation of historic animosities between rival chiefs and the supply of devastating weapons to their favoured ally, the traders would reap

A major uprising occurred on Dog Island in the Gambia River in the summer of 1667. It was the site of an RA fort where captured Africans were held. They rose up and took repossession. Thirty of their English captors were slain. The crew of the company's enslaver *John,* anchored in the river, recaptured the soil but not the people: around forty were killed, the rest escaping. A member of Charles II extensive spy network, Cowes-based John Lysle, reported the rebellion to under-secretary Sir Joseph Williamson, head of Intelligence and member of the RA explaining the delay in the ship's return. In mitigation, he emphasised it had still brought back valuable commodities: reed, wood, logwood, wax and elephants teeth.

Coastal communities would try to liberate the captured while the ships in which they were entombed lay at anchor. These vessels would sometimes be dormant for months while company traders and militia went about their business, such as 'boating'. RAC factor in Gambia, David Francis, reported in January 1715 that the king of Barra and his men had attacked the company's vessels, successfully seizing the *Snow*.[116] Similarly, the coastal community of New Calabar assisted the uprising of the enslaved aboard the *Nancy*. Hearing guns being fired they rowed out en-masse to the vessel, took control, removed the commodities and returned to shore with the freed rebels after setting loose the ship.

At Cong Point, the Blacks of Saboe and Mauree attacked RAC soldiers, several losing their lives in the battle.[117] In the case of Mauree (Moree), four miles to the east of Cape Coast Castle, this culture of fierce resistance to outsiders with hostile intent carried through generations. The journal *Transactions of the Aborigines Protection Society* records that two thousand inhabitants of this 'deadly and utterly uncared for' ghetto, rebelled against the colonial authorities in February, 1899. They demanded their taxes be used, at least in part, on civic improvement of their destitute

the reward of prisoners of war that could then be enslaved and sold in the Caribbean.

116 Ruth A. Fisher (ed) *Extracts from the Records of the African Companies* (London,1929) p.51. *Snow* was a generic term for a particular kind of ship that was rigged in a certain way. The Slave Voyages database, while not finding a ship with that name does provide details of the Dolphin Snow which acquired people in Gambia to enslave and was 'destroyed, lost or sold as a result of slave rebellion' in 1734. https://slavevoyages.org/voyage/database Accessed 15 April, 2020.

117 Fisher, (ed), (1929), p.33.

lives. In response the British colonial militia killed over forty were and injured many more in a show of brutal and barbaric force.[118]

At Sierra Leone mothers and women of enslaved loved ones imprisoned aboard an RAC ship in 1728, gathered angry and emotional on the shoreline, crying out for their release. The master of the enslaver warned through a 'speaking trumpet' that if they did not calm down he would hang the captives.[119]

Some sixty or so years after the first attempt by the Guinea Company (GC) to mine for gold the RAC, under the Duke of Chandos, tried to revive the idea by using Cornish miners. Attacks by local people doomed the venture as the men from the West Country were reluctant to leave the company fort. In their earlier quest rather than pay for local African labour they used Scots prisoners captured in the Civil War. Fifteen hundred were shipped as slaves. According to a contemporary account, on departure they violently resisted with two Scots drowning in a series of skirmishes.[120] Unfortunately, their fate is not known nor that of the mining venture itself.

A fight-back by captured Africans held aboard the RAC's *London Galley* anchored just off Cape Coast Castle, Gold Coast (Ghana) in 1704 resulted in a massacre of thirty of their number with three Whites also slain. A rising by captives imprisoned on the *Mary* four years later at the same place saw three Africans dying of their wounds with thirty-three drowned.[121] The writer does not say how.

At times the enslaved were successful in restoring their status as social beings: a rising on the River Gambia in September 1731, resulted in seventeen Africans restored.

Writing from Cape Coast Castle in 1752 an RAC factor observes

The Negroes will suffer us to amuse ourselves with what words please us best, but when we come to explain these words by Actions, and attempt to carry matters with a high hand, I find they ever have opposed us, and I may venture to assure you they ever will.[122]

118 *Transactions of the Aborigenes Protection Society 1890-96*, 4, 1, p.79.
119 Fisher, (ed), (1929), p.36.
120 Bulstrode Whitelocke, *Memorials of the English Affairs from the Beginning of the Reign of Charles the First to the Happy Restoration of King Charles the Second,* (1853), III, 1682:353–54 in Svalastog (2018) p.134.
121 Ibid. pp.31, 37.
122 Ibid. p.79.

Physical opposition to Middle Passage enslavement was so common and presented such a risk to profits that it warranted the creation of a special type of marine insurance against mutiny, rebellion, suicide and other unnatural causes of death. This, in turn led, to the development of another barbaric practice: masters of slave ships having sick Africans – a condition not covered by any insurance – thrown overboard to drown and then fraudulently claim for loss of cargo. The most infamous case was that of the *Zong,* sailing from Accra to Jamaica, where Captain Luke Collingwood ordered overboard one hundred and thirty-three over three days after sixty – and seven White crew – had died of illness. On the third day the final thirty-six rebelled and fought back. Eventually subdued, they were shackled in irons and thrown into the ocean. Rather than wait to be murdered, ten preferred suicide, jumping into the sea and drowning. In total one hundred and thirty-two captives perished after one climbed back on board undetected. The Liverpool-based owners of the Zong, a banking and slaving firm dominated by the Gregson family, filed for insurance compensation for loss of their 'commodities'. The underwriters refused to pay which led to an insurance trial at the Guildhall, London. The jury affirmed the right of the firm and Collingwood to murder the Africans.

The court case brought by the insurers was highly unusual in seventeen eighties London in highlighting the horrors of the Middle Passage. It also boosted the Abolitionist cause after the prosecution was brought to the attention of a leading member, Grenville Sharp, by formerly enslaved Olaudah Equiano. A subsequent campaign by Equianao, Sharp and fellow Abolitionists for a trial of mass murder was unsuccessful. The celebrated artist J.M.W. Turner was so appalled and moved by the affair that he commemorated the dead in a painting entitled *Throwing Overboard the Dead and Dying, Typhoon Coming On.*[123]

Tragically, this massacre at sea was not the only one of its kind. A decade later another Liverpool slave trader claimed compensation for one hundred and twenty-eight captive Africans who had been starved to death during the Middle Passage. This time, however, the merchant of death lost. This may have been a consequence of the Dolben Act of 1788 which restricted insurance of the enslaved.[124]

123 David Dabydeen, John Gilmore and Cecily Jones (eds.) *The Oxford Companion to Black British History* (Oxford, 2007) p. 534-535.
124 The *Zong* case, surrounding publicity and Abolitionist campaign led to the Dolben Act 1788 which regulated transportation conditions during the

Lloyds List, the house journal of the (English) insurance industry, grew exponentially in great part because of the seventeenth century Navigation Acts and explosion in human trafficking. A curious feature is that it provides numerical information on uprisings aboard slave ships. Between 1689-1807, of one thousand and fifty-three vessels lost by owners some eighteen per cent – around one hundred and eighty eight – were due to insurrections or conflict with coastal communities.[125]

One of these successful rebellions was aboard the London slaver *Industry.* Four days into their journey from Gambia to Carolina, North America African captives rose-up and killed virtually all the crew (save two). Sailing to Sierra Leone, they recaptured their freedom.

Evidence… does lend itself to the speculation that the ordinary folks in the coastal societies – people who were not in government, were not soldiers or traders, and held no slaves – were appalled by the trade in fellow human beings conducted daily on a vast scale before their very eyes. Some of these may have assisted the export slaves in their insurrections on the African coast. They may also have expressed their disapproval by attacking the European traders whenever this could be done with very little risk to themselves. All this would help to explain why far more insurrections by the export slaves occurred on the African shores than in the Atlantic crossing.[126]

Another Middle Passage (planned) uprising was not so successful. During a May 1751 voyage Captain John Newton writes of a plot being discovered just hours before it was due to commence. A captured African, who had been unchained because of a large ulcer, was seen handing a large marline spike through the deck gratings to his brothers and sisters below. In under an hour, twenty had broken free of their irons and were ready to seize the ship. The following day six of the freedom fighters were tortured as punishment. Newton records other

---

Middle Passage for West African enslaved. It also prohibited their insurance against loss unless it was cover for piracy, natural disaster, insurrection, barratry and fire.

125 Joseph Inikori, 'Measuring the unmeasured hazards of the Atlantic slave trade: documents relating to the British trade', *Revue française d'histoire d'outre-mer,* 83, 312, 3, (1996), pp.53-92. http://www.persee.fr/doc/outre_0300-9513_1996_num_83_312_3457 accessed 19 April 2020.
126 Ibid, pp. 89-90.

similar incidents on his ships in 1750, '51 and '52 suggesting these events were frequent and/or his management was particularly brutal.

ENSLAVEMENT AND RESISTANCE IN SCOTLAND

The celebrated ruling in the Joseph Knight v John Wedderburn case of 1778 that enslavement was illegal was not the first instance in Scotland of litigation as an instrument of resistance. Twenty-two years earlier the Ayrshire enslaver of James Montgomery tried to forcibly send him to Virginia. Escaping to Edinburgh he was caught after newspaper advertisements publicised his unauthorised liberation. Imprisoned in the Tolbooth, Montgomery began litigation claiming his baptism as a Christian while in Scotland effected his freedom. He died before the case could be heard.

In 1769 David Spens, enslaved by absentee Caribbean planter Dr David Dalrymple of Methil, Fife, also resisted by running away and then litigation, offering the same evidence as Montgomery. Dalrymple accused Spens of pia fraus (pious fraud), in that he had sought baptism not because of a desire to embrace Christianity but as a route to emancipation. In his testimony to the court Spens addressed this claim.

I am now by the Christian Religion Liberate and set at freedom from my old yoke bondage & slavery and by the Laws of this Christian land there is no Slavery nor vestige of Slavery allowed nevertheless you take it upon you to exercise your old Tyrannical Power over me and would dispose of me arbitrarily at your despotic will & Pleasure and for that end you threaten to send me abroad out of this Country to the West Indies and there dispose of me for money.[127]

Spens received support from the community: he had taken the surname name of the minister that baptised him; offered sanctuary as a fugitive in the house of a Wemyss farmer; had his courts costs paid for by local miners, salters and farmworkers. Winning his freedom through the untimely death of Dalrymple, he returned to Wemyss and worked

127 Dalrymple v Spens and Henderson (1769-70), National Records of Scotland, https://www.nrscotland.gov.uk/research/learning/slavery/dalrymple-v-spens-and-henderson-1769-70 Accessed 5 February, 2021. Records of the Knight v Wedderburn and Montgomery v Sheddan cases can be found via this page.

for the farmer who selflessly provided refuge, becoming a respected and popular resident.[128]

It would be morally understandable and intellectually rational for every enslaved person in Scotland, whether believers or not, to have sought baptism as a means of resisting enslavement. There are instances of people of colour undergoing the ritual from at least the sixteenth century when ultra-religious James IV oversaw the baptism of two African women, Margaret and Helen. At Edinburgh's Abbey Church, Canongate in September, 1686, John Drumlanrig, the Duke of Queensbury's ten year old slave 'made public profession of the Christian Faith and solemnly engaged to live according to it'.[129] Chief minister to the king, John was part of an influential household and it would be interesting to know how his status was legally affected by this inferential disavowal of heathenism. As a Christian he was now able to enslave others who were not of the faith.

Evidence of eighteenth-century resistance through absconding by enslaved is revealed by adverts in newspapers. Numerous owners provide details of their runaways and offering rewards for capture and return: Gustavus Brown of Glasgow and Dalkeith requested readers keep a look out for eighteen year old Ann with a two guinea reward offered; capturing London, the property of Captain Oliphant from Muirtown, Perthshire brought a lesser bounty of twenty shillings; the substantial sum of four guineas was to be had for the return of Samuel Ramsay belonging to David Frazer of Arbroath.

Runaways were mostly males in their late teens or young adults in their twenties. Of the runaways described in the Edinburgh and Glasgow press [of the mid-eighteenth century] 9 were teenagers (two were young as 14 and 15 respectively), 3 were in their twenties,1 was in his thirties and 3 had no ages given. Only one slave was 30 years old which might indicate that older slaves were less likely to abscond possibly because of maturity, infirmity, reluctance to abandon long-standing friendships or family ties, or resignation to… [their] situation.[130]

---

128 Fryer, (1991), p.206 and fn13 p.541 and June Evans, *African/Caribbean in Scotland. A Socio-Geographical Study*, Ph.D dissertation (1995), University of Edinburgh, p.71. Miners and salters existed within a form of serfdom in eighteenth century Scotland which may explain their empathy for Spens.
129 Evans, (1995), p.68.
130 Ibid., pp.73-4.

Pleas for their return appealed to vigilantes. The sight of a 'strolling Negro' inspired Glasgow merchant Mr Andrew Ramsay to apprehend the felonious walker.

Whoever owns him, and gives sufficient marks of his being theirs… may have him again upon Payment of Expenses laid out on him, otherwise the present possessor will dispose of him at his Pleasure.[131]

The enslaved were cheaper, more reliable labour for aristocrats and merchants than hiring waged servants. With Glasgow an integral port in the triangular trade supply was not difficult. It would not have been uncommon to see enslaved people in Scotland shackled with iron collars or other impediments as a mark of their chattel status. If the 'strolling Negro' was free of such things the cultural imperative was to assume they were absconding. This was the cruelest of inescapable contradictions entwining people of colour: walk as if free and you are an absconder; walk in metal and you are free to go about your business.

Oronoce, servant of Dugald Stewart, the Laird of Appin – the locale of Edward's daughter Jean and husband Duncan in the nineteen nineties – was arrested and thrown into gaol in the summer of 1750 for wearing tartan after it was banned. As Evans (1995) notes, the satire here is that Scottish mills supplied the Caribbean plantations with cheap plaids that the enslaved were forced to wear.

Born during the Middle Passage abolition activist, author and composer Ignatious Sancho (c.1729-80) was enslaved by three sisters in Greenwich, London. Befriended by John, second Duke of Montagu, a relatively enlightened man he encouraged the adolescent to read and write. Eventually becoming butler to the duchess of Montagu, Sancho visited the north of Scotland *in* 1770 (while the clearances were underway). Writing later from Dalkeith, Sancho reassures his friend: 'We came home from our Highland excursion last Monday night, safe and well – after escaping manifold dangers'. Despite the alarms the African was captivated by its nature.

Inverary is a charming place – the beauties various – and the whole plan majestic; there are some worthy fouls on the spot, which I admire more than the buildings and prospects. We had herrings in perfection – and would have had mackarel; but the scoundrels were too sharp

131 *Edinburgh Evening Courant*, Thursday 20 April 1720 in Evans,(1995), p.52.

for us and would not be caught. The Loch-Loman – Ben-Loman – Domiquith – and Arsenhoe – with Hamilton and Douglas houses – are by much too long for description by letter.[132]

A year or two before this adventure Sancho was painted by the renowned artist Thomas Gainsborough around the same time that he created a portrait of the Duchess of Montagu. He gained his liberty and not a little wealth on her death in 1751 where he was bequeathed seventy pounds (£16,190) and an annuity of thirty pounds (£6,938). With this economic security plus income from his books and composition, the property he then acquired made him eligible to vote. Doing so in 1774 and again in 1780 suggests he was the one of the first Black Britons to participate in a General Election.

The Montagus were not the only aristocrats with the mystifying predilection for extracting the labour of brown-skinned captives for use in their homes and estates then sponsoring immortalisation of this exploitation in oils. Anne, duchess of Monmouth and Buccleuch and the second Duke of Perth are also captured on canvas with enslaved children.[133]

Domestic trafficking of enslaved people of African heritage in Britain was through private agreement or, according to the June 1772 edition of the *The Scots Magazine,* at auction. Two adverts offering for sale eleven year old *Negro Boy*[s] appear in the *Edinburgh Courant,* 27 September and 6 December, 1766 though Evans could find no corroborating evidence to support the existence of slave auctions.[134] After the Somerset and Knight judgements public sale notices and advertisements declined rapidly.

---

132 Ignatious Sancho to Mr K, Dalkeith, 16 July, 1770 in *Letters of the Late Ignatious Sancho, An African,* Vol.1, (London, 1782), pp.27-8.
133 Evans, (1995), pp.49-50.
134 Ibid., p.63.

Chapter Five
The Monarchy, City of London and the Trade of Enslavement

THE TUDORS

From the late fourteen hundreds, Portuguese and Spanish traders, including state sponsored and independent pirate 'adventurers', were active in the Caribbean and the Americas settling and colonising. Until the mid-seventeenth century Iberian commercial shipping and naval forces dominated the Atlantic, a reflection of these kingdom's political power, deriving in large part from their relationship with the papacy. It is more than possible Barbados had been considered by these for colonial settlement but the island was never claimed.

The acquisition of gold, spice, cloth, ivory and enslaved people from West Africa was characterised by tense and often bloody competition, accelerating during the sixteenth century as British, Dutch, French and Danish adventurers joined the treasure hunt. This hostile seafaring environment meant the protection from respective Crowns was crucial: calling upon the navy to convoy precious cargo in times of war; or requesting diplomatic assistance when ships and treasure had been seized as 'prizes'.

Tudor monarchs supported this sea-based commercial expansion. During the fifteen twenties and thirties Plymouth merchant and mariner William Hawkins, a favourite of Henry VIII, made at least three pioneering voyages to the coasts of West Africa and Brazil in search of gold, ivory and pepper and other prizes. On his second voyage to Brazil around 1530 he returned with a 'savage king' for whom Hawkins left sailor Martin Cockeram of Plymouth as surety. A meeting with Henry took place at his palace in Whitehall. After a year the indigenous king returned to Brazil with Hawkins. The nature of the relationship is not known, though it is implied in records of the voyage that the Brazilian king came consensually.[135] Hawkins sought royal backing in 1536 when he asked Henry's chief minister, Thomas Cromwell, for

---

135 Sir Clements Roger Markham 'The Hawkins' Voyages during the reign of Henry VIII, Queen Elizabeth and James I' in *Works Issued by the Hakluyt Society* No. LVII (London, 1878).

£2,000 (£1,663,954) four brass guns and a last of powder (stock of gunpowder).[136]

Iberian dominance in the Atlantic resulted in Portuguese claims to the Guinea coast of West Africa dating from 1471. However, the acquisitive mercantilist culture of the City of London inspired the Duke of Medina Sidonia, Spain, a decade later to contract two merchants, John Tintam and William Fabian, to plan a voyage to Cape Verdes, West Africa. The objective was to establish a fortified camp for future enslavement missions.[137] The enterprise never materialised due to the intervention of Edward IV, who prohibited all trade to the Guinea coast by English traders in deference to the Portuguese monarch, John II. This did not stop a number of other Spain-based English merchants – Nicholas Arnold, William de la Founte and brothers Thomas and John Bridges – from participating in these early moments of the Atlantic triangular trade. While Thomas, who had lived and traded in Seville from 1491, did not return to England, John pursued a trading and political career in the City of London, becoming sheriff in 1513-14 and Lord Mayor six years later.[138]

English commercial interest in West Africa and the south and eastern Atlantic revived with William Hawkins voyages but lay dormant for a decade or so after until Royal Navy vice-admiral Thomas Wyndham's ventures in the fifteen fifties. A volatile merchant-mariner, during the Anglo-Scottish war of the fifteen forties he had built a reputation as a ruthless invader, burning to the ground Balmerino Abbey, Elcho nunnery and the town of Dalkeith. While his war ships patrolled the Firth of Forth estuary, the Norfolk-born commander made a habit of seizing foreign trading vessels and their cargoes.[139] It may have been his rampaging and looting in Scotland that gave Wyndham a taste for

---

136 Kenneth R. Andrews *Trade, Plunder and Settlement: Maritime Enterprise and the Genesis of the British Empire 1480-1630* (Cambridge, 1984) p.59. The Guinea coast is taken to mean the southern coast of West Africa, from Volta River in the west to the Niger Delta in the east.

137 Andrews, (1984), p.58.

138 Heather Dalton *Merchants and Explorers: Roger Barlow, Sebastian Cabot and Networks of Atlantic Exchange 1500-1560* (Oxford: 2016) p.28.

139 He gave one captured vessel to his warrior nephew, Sir John Luttrell, a feudal baron of Dunster Castle, Somerset, whose Norman ancestors were given land and labour in the county by William the Conquerer. https://en.wikipedia.org/wiki/Feudal_barony_of_Dunster accessed 30 March 2020.

acquiring forcibly the goods of others under royal sanction.

He is documented as having captured 'two Moors' during his voyage to Morocco in 1551.[140] Along the way they fought with the inhabitants of Lanzarote where eighteen Spaniards and six crew were killed.

Two years later Wyndham made a second voyage to Africa, backed by Sir George Barne, Sir John Yorke, Nicholas Lambert and other City of London merchants along with experienced Portuguese mariner, Captain Antonio Pinteado, who knew well the West African coastline. In preparation the enterprise received backing from Edward VI (though he died a few weeks before embarkation). Three ships, the royal vessels *Primrose, Moon* and *Lion,* sailed to the Guinea coast. Aboard were some of merchant backers, such as Nicholas Lambert, who may have been the son of Nicholas Lambert, former Alderman, sheriff and Lord Mayor of London.[141] The expedition was again characterised by the hallmark's of Wyndham's naval career.

Wyndham's voyage is remarkable in several respects, but most of all for his aggressive, predatory and brutal conduct of it.[142]

Coastal settlements en route were raided and burned. The tyrannical master fell out with Pinteado, forcing him to navigate to Benin, where many of the crew fell sick and died, including Wyndham. The *Lion* was abandoned and left behind for want of men to sail her. Pinteado also died, imprisoned on the return voyage by disillusioned crew members enraged by Wyndham's brutality and the extraordinarily high mortality rate after Pintaedo had charted their course to the pestilential coast.

A 1554-55 expedition to the Guinea coast in the ships *Trinity, Bartholomew* and *John Evangelist* by mariners Robert Gainsh and John Lok – son of a City of London alderman – included merchant John Berin. An essay of their trip, possibly written by Gainsh, allows an insight.

The elephant… is the gentlest and most tractable of all beasts, and understands and is taught many things, so that it is even taught to

---

140 *Hakluyt's Collection of the Early Voyages, Travels, and Discoveries of the English Nation* (London, 1810).

141 http://www.e-reading.life/chapter.php/80243/52/a-general-history-and-collection-of-voyages-and-travels-vol-vii.html#footnote201 accessed 23 March 2020.

142 Andrews, (1984), p.106.

do reverence to kings, being of acute sense and great judgment... Negroes; a beastly living people, without God, law, religion, or government... In dealing with them, it is necessary to behave with civility and gentleness, as they will not trade with any who use them ill.[143]

Despite the observation about the need to respect their hosts' customs, the Englishmen captured five adult men from the coastal town of Shama (Ghana). Three were named: Anthony, Binny and George. The plan was for all to learn English and return as facilitators of trade between their chiefs and the mariner-merchants.

The following year, an influential City merchant and navigator, Cumbria-born William Towerson of the Worshipful Company of Skinners, attempted to trade on the same coastline. A major obstacle was convincing the West Africans that he had no desire to enslave. This was difficult. He was pleading with those who had encountered Wyndham, Gainsh, Lok.

None of them would come near us; being as we judged afraid of us; because that four [actually five] men were taken perforce the last year from this place.[144]

Towerson's observation confirms Gainsh's: to trade, respect for the indigenous people and their customs was essential. He was an organiser and leader of three expeditions to West Africa returning with exotic curiosities such as elephant tusks and chillies but even more alluringly, hundreds of pounds weight of gold. It is estimated that in this early trade for the precious metal – exchanged for brass, copper and tin – merchants could anticipate returns ten times their investment.[145] However, by the time of his third and final voyage in 1577, whatever the profits, respect for the economic and social customs of his hosts had disappeared. Angered

143 Section 111. Voyage to Guinea, in 1554, by Captain Jon Lok in Hakluyt's Principal Navigations (edition of 1598–1600), vol. ii. pt. ii. pp. 23–52 from https://en.wikisource.org/wiki/Towerson,_William_(DNB00) accessed 30 March 2020.
144 William Towerson quoted in Miranda Kaufmann, *Black Tudors. The Untold Story* (London, 2019) p.183.
145 William Robert Scott, *The Constitution and Finance of English, Scottish and Irish Joint-Stock Companies to 1720*, vol. 2 (Cambridge, 1912), pp.4-5.

by this response of the people of the Mina Coast, with his flotilla of four ships, Towerson ordered the destruction of two coastal towns.[146]

During the early fifteen sixties, John Hawkins was making it known amongst interested London merchants that he would like to do as his father William had done and trade on the West African coast. The latter's success in turning a profit – and his reputation as a man who could be ruthless, having killed a man in a tavern fight before he was twenty – opened doors. A syndicate of City of London merchants and politicians, including two Lord Mayors and organised by Hawkins' father-in-law and treasurer of the navy, Benjamin Gonson, provided finance of £5,000 (£2,354,925) for commodities that could be traded, such as copper pots, tools and weapons.[147]

There was one crucial difference between this first, speculative 1562 voyage and those of his father William: it intended to capture and enslave. The Queen, Court and City of London – the state – backed this pirate venture, if not personally then politically. All had become envious of the lucrative Portuguese and Spanish dominance of the triangular trade and de facto colonisation of much of the West African coast, Caribbean and Americas.

The commencement of the English slave-trade was no afterthought but the original foundation for the venture [as] Hawkins [thought of Negroes as being] 'very good merchandise in Hispaniola'.[148]

John Hawkins, with his cousin Francis Drake and ships, *Saloman, Jonas* and *Swallow* soon made their presence known along the coastline of what is now Sierra Leone, capturing a number of Portuguese vessels carrying tradable cargo and between three and five hundred enslaved West Africans. The highest (Iberian) estimate calculates five hundred and twelve ships.

---

146 Hakluyt's *Principal Navigations* (edition of 1598–1600), vol. ii. pt. ii. pp. 23–52 from https://en.wikisource.org/wiki/Towerson,_William_(DNB00) accessed 30 March 2020.

147 The merchant backers included Sir Lionel Duckett and Sir Thomas Lodge. Four times Master of the Mercers' Company, Duckett served as Lord Mayor London, 1572; Lodge, of the Worshipful Company of Grocers, was Lord Mayor as the voyage took place in 1562. For further information on the political and economic relationship between the early English slave traders and Queen Elizabeth I see Harry Kelsey, *Sir John Hawkins. Queen Elizabeth's Slave Trader* (London, 2003) pp.4-14.

148 Scott, (1912), p.8.

Whatever the true figure, Hawkins is said to have sent Drake back to England with a ship-load of coins, jewels and West African artefacts – 'dead' goods – while he traded his 'live' enslaved in the Spanish Caribbean.

Before returning to England in September 1563, however, much of his treasure had been recaptured by the Spanish. Despite Elizabeth's intervention the Spanish Crown refused to hand-back the captured cargo. Yet, even with these losses, the expedition is said to have made a profit of between forty and sixty per cent.[149]

The Spanish monarch, Philip II, subsequently banned all English ships from trading in Spanish ports and their Caribbean colonies. It would not allow any foreign incursions into the Iberian monopoly of the slave trade. This was a huge economic and political setback. Hawkins' irritating excursion into their territory had produced a powerful response. However, the lure of potential riches was so great that, instead of restraint in the face of more powerful rivals, the English state effectively decided to up the ante and support further piratical ventures.

Hawkins's second treasure hunt the following year attracted even more interest, especially from the Court. As well as the queen, the earls of Leicester and Pembroke and Lord Clinton reached into their purses. City of London merchants provided the additional finance. Four ships would sail, with Elizabeth supplying the 700 ton *Jesus of Lubeck,* five times larger than any ship on the previous expedition. She would also spend £250 (£109,182) per ship for fitting out and be responsible for crewing. For so doing, she forbade any private trading on the expedition. The syndicate of merchants – including again Lord Mayor, Sir Thomas Lodge and father-in-law Gonson – as before would stock the ships with tradable goods. If the venture made a loss, they would be liable.

Elizabeth, her closest advisor and secretary of state William Cecil, Lodge and the other members of the syndicate at home in London may have worried about their investment. They would not see the ships again for a year. If extra grey hairs did appear under their wigs it was unnecessarily so: Hawkins had to procure two additional vessels to carry the booty home. This was after they had imprisoned aboard some three hundred indigenous people from the Guinea coast, enslaved them and sold them – through the use of naked force – in the Spanish Caribbean colonies for ginger, sugar, pearls and animal hides worth £10,000

---

149 State Papers, Dom., Eliz. xxvi. 44, Cal 1547-80 in Scott, (Cambridge, 1912), p.5.

(£4,367,295).

Hawkins and others like Raleigh, Drake and Frobisher became mythologised in popular culture as daring 'sea-dogs' tweaking the King of Spain's beard. The ruthless, murderous nature of their voyages was less often commented on.

The blowback to sea-dog Hawkins's latest skirmish with Spanish and Portuguese ships resulted in English vessels in the Atlantic and Caribbean being treated with even more hostile suspicion. Increasingly, the Spanish and Portuguese navies, along with private Iberian ships and pirates made trade difficult with raids and seizures.

The Spanish ambassador, hearing rumours of a third slave venture, persuaded the Crown to stop it. Hawkins simply arranged for Captain John Lovell to command the pirate ships in his place, with relation Francis Drake as a senior member of the crew. Hawkins-less, they sailed from Plymouth in the Autumn of 1566.[150]

Capturing enslaved people from Portuguese ships and forts along the Guinea coast and selling to the Spanish, the first stage of Lovell's voyage went to plan. From then on, it did not. Local antagonism meant they could not trade peaceably. Unable to sell most of their enslaved humans they were forced to abandon ninety-two West Africans to their fate at Rio de la Hocha on the South American mainland. Andrews argues that this was because Lovell, unlike his employer, did not have enough firepower to negotiate a deal the local Spanish could not refuse. A less-detailed but more emphatic perspective suggests Lovell returned with around fifty enslaved people on board the *Swallow* with the venture still making a profit.[151] The writer fails to say what happened in England to the human cargo.

Hawkins immediately proposed a fourth voyage even though the Iberian diplomatic and military furore was escalating. Despite the risk and the relative failure of Lovell to conjure the anticipated returns on investment, the merchant backers that had previously provided were joined by others with Court and government attitudes encouragingly warm. William Cecil recognised that if Elizabeth's international power and influence was to rival Spain and Portugal, competitive engagement with their shipping and seagoing commerce was essential. To succeed,

---

150 Andrews (1984) p.125.

151 Hugh Bicheno, *Elizabeth's Sea Dogs. How England's Mariners Became the Scourge of the Seas* (London, 2013) p.89.

state support would have to be at the heart of the enterprise.[152]

Compared to his other expeditions, the tonnage and number of ships planned for this venture was greater: one thousand three hundred and thirty-three and six respectively. Of these, the *Jesus* and the *Minion* were navy ships. Another, the *Judith,* was commanded by Francis Drake. This considerable flotilla emboldened Hawkins. Before sailing from Plymouth in 1567, he signalled his hostile intent toward Spanish shipping by firing canon warning shots at a squadron of their warships anchored in the Devon seaport. This gesture of martial strength was combustible and risky. Not least because Hawkins' primary intention was to sell his captured, enslaved West Africans in Spanish America.

The fleet moved on to the African coast in search of human cargo... In addition to robbing the Portuguese of a number of slaves, the English intervened in a tribal war, accepting prisoners-of-war as payment for services rendered. By the time he set out for the Caribbean, Hawkins had acquired nearly five hundred slaves and three more vessels for his fleet.[153]

Bicheno enthusiastically describes how Hawkins deployed his tried and trusted method of using barbaric force to encourage locals to trade: the village of Cacheo on the River Gambia was razed and looted, citizens captured and enslaved; the flotilla's passage along the Guinea coast characterised by killing and looting.

Arriving in the Spanish West Indies with between four and five hundred enslaved chained to the timbers below deck, Hawkins coerced locals into buying some two hundred. His actions were vengefully reciprocated. Attacked by Spanish vessels and pirates, the English slave trader lost the use of two ships.

---

152 While willing to sanction the capture and enslavement of West Africans if they could be sold at a profit, Elizabeth did not want to see them living freely in England. She issued three proclamations between 1596-1601 instructing Africans be banished and/or sold to Spain and Portugal in return for British prisoners. Peter Fryer, *Staying Power. The History of Black People in Britain* (1991) pp11-12; Weissbourd, Emily. "Those in Their Possession': Race, Slavery, and Queen Elizabeth's 'Edicts of Expulsion." *Huntington Library Quarterly*, vol. 78, no. 1, 2015, pp. 1–19. www.jstor.org/stable/10.1525/hlq.2015.78.1.1. Accessed 10 Feb. 2021.
153 Andrews (1984) p.126.

Sailing home – with seventy unsold people – they encountered storms and sought shelter. The flotilla anchored at the island of San Juan de Ulua, off the coast of Mexico, the most prized of Spain's seizures in the Americas. In the harbour were twelve ships laden with gold and silver, awaiting collection by the Spanish fleet. Coveting the treasure, Hawkins launched a ferocious attack.

In this mother of all battles, he was accused of abandoning the *Jesus* and her crew. When his ship, the *Minion,* eventually docked at Plymouth, of his two hundred or so crew who left San Juan de Ulua, only fifteen made it home. Amazingly, some of his enslaved survived.

The 1567-68 expedition damaged him. It failed to make substantial profits or force the Iberian powers to open their trade to English ships. He called it his 'sorrowful voyage'. Yet, proud of his reputation as a sea-dog, he incorporated an image of an enslaved, shackled African into his coat of arms.

While the Crown and City of London recognising his pioneering efforts at encroaching upon the Iberian-dominated slave trade, the San Juan de Ulua episode distanced for a while some courtiers and merchants who had been friends and business partners. Elizabeth, though, stood by him. When he was stabbed in 1571 she sent her personal physician to attend. Always a controversial figure, Hawkins remained very much in public life becoming MP for Plymouth in 1571. In 1578 he was appointed Treasurer and Comptroller of the Royal Navy after the death of his father-in-law Benjamin Gonson, who had been instrumental in arranging financial backing for his slaving expeditions. Ten years later he was knighted.

It would be twenty-five years before he again visited Spanish America with his now famous cousin, Sir Francis Drake. It was their last piratical venture together, both losing their lives on the expedition.

Voyages to West Africa and the Caribbean by other merchant-mariners including Drake and Hawkins' brother, William, continued in the fifteen seventies. Crown interest and involvement in these ventures was determined, now, more by economic considerations rather than adherence to a strategic political design. Scott asserts that Elizabeth received between £250,000–300,000 (£110,324,958–£132,389,949) from Drake's piracy alone.[154]

The formation of the Senegal Adventurers (SA) in 1588 saw the

---

154 Scott, (1912), p.500.

merging of official state and commercial objectives in the trade to West Africa. The joint-stock syndicate of eight merchants from London and Devon that comprised the SA concentrated their trading activities between the Senegal and Gambia rivers, their royal patent guaranteeing monopoly rights for ten years. (Previously, similar monopoly trading rights given by the Crown dissolved after each voyage.) It was a business model that would come to characterise the Stuarts' royal slave trading companies.

Meanwhile, in 1592 other English merchants were granted a royal patent to trade along other parts of the West African coast. The granting of monopoly rights both to the SA and the other merchants had the practical effect of providing royal protection. It marked in the Crown a formal commitment to make available the powers of the state for economic ventures that would rival Iberian power in the West Africa and Caribbean theatres of trade. While detail about these traders and their activities is scarce, it is reported that on a trip to Sierra Leone in 1607 sailors performed Shakespeare's Hamlet.[155]

THE STUARTS

A peace treaty signed by James I & VI with Spain in 1604, one year after the death of Elizabeth, accepted that the Caribbean was a Spanish domain. This momentarily dampened enthusiasm in the City of London for financing Atlantic ventures that now would not have the unreserved protection of the Crown.

It would not be until 1618 that another Africa company was formed, 'The Governor and Company of Adventurers of London trading into the parts of Africa', known as the Guinea Company (GC). Its affluent and powerful stockholders had secured from James monopoly rights for all English commerce, including trafficking enslaved people along the West Africa coast. Members close to the Court and Parliament included Robert Rich, soon to become the second earl of Warwick. Others were prominent merchants in the City of London like Sir William St John. Some had, or would acquire, controversial backgrounds. The son of Sir John Hawkins, Sir William, was imprisoned for eight years by the Spanish in South America for raiding slave ships. Sir Giles Mompesson MP eventually had to flee England only three years later over allegations

---

155 R. J. Blakemore 'West Africa in the British Atlantic: trade, violence, and empire in the 1640s'. *Itinerario*, 39 (2) (2015) pp. 299-327: http://centaur. reading.ac.uk/71911/ Accessed 10 April 2020.

of corruption discussed in Parliament. One of the most detested personalities of his age, his name became synonymous with cheating, fraud and embezzlement, so much so that a play was written about him.[156] There was no shortage of material to draw upon. He once threatened wire-workers in the gold thread industry with death in prison if they did not submit to his authority.[157] Sir Robert Mansell MP, while treasurer of the navy, had had his malfeasance exposed in a 1609 investigation. He was gaoled in Marshalsea Prison four years later for further corruption and theft. This did not stop him getting a £16,000 (£4,097,934) wedding gift from James in 1616 and being appointed by the latter as Vice-Admiral of England in the same year the GC was formed.[158] The two merchants who came quickly to dominate the company were John Davies and Humphrey Slaney whose relationship was often turbulent and litigious.

The main problems of the early Guinea Company stemmed, not from its inexperienced courtiers… but instead from its experienced merchants. Their loyalty had never been to the company but to their own personal affairs.[159]

The king would have a share of the company's profits for the granting of the monopoly whose main trade, initially, was in 'dead' commodities such as gold, timber and cloth rather than people.[160] He also received a loan of £50,000 (£12,576,250) from the merchant adventurers in the year the company was formed.[161] Ekelund and Tollison suggest the

156 *A New Way to Pay Old Debts* by Phillip Massinger.
157 Scott, (1912), p.177.
158 See Appendix 1 for the list of members, courtesy of J. M. Svalastog, *Mastering the worst of trades : England's early Africa companies and their traders, 1618-1672* PhD dissertation (2018) University of Leiden (1988), pp. 222-3.
159 Svalastog, (2018), p.86.
160 The Stuarts increasingly used their power of the Royal Prerogative to grant monopoly patents to traders to create an income source that was independent of Parliament. The latter responded by passing the Statute of Monopolies Act 1624 stripping the Crown of this power. However, Charles 1 found a loophole in which the law did not apply to 'corporations for the benefit of trade' and 'companies of merchants'. See Robert B Ekelund Jnr and Robert D Tollison, *Politicized Economies: Monarchy, Monopoly and Mercantilism*, (Texas, 1997), p.79.
161 Frederick C. Dietz 'The Receipts and Issues of the Exchequer During

rising mercantilist class of the City of London bought their monopoly privileges through such 'loans'.[162]

James and the royal household were notorious for paying late or failing to settle bills. Despite enormous sums going in and out of the royal exchequer smaller creditors, including workmen and suppliers, often had to repeatedly plead for their money.[163]

A trader in West Africa on behalf of the GC, Richard Jobson, travelled in 1621 to the River Gambia. He wrote that he found the Mandingo people initially wary of traders they had not encountered before in case they were enslavers. He describes them as friendly and trustworthy and was angered by the unfair stereotypes that he had hitherto drawn upon.

We finde the natives to embrace us withall, not onely clearing our own doubts, which before knowledge must of necessity be, but likewise disapproving, and altogether confounding the reports and speeches of all those, who, to serve their own ends, gave, the people above to be a bloody and dangerous nation.

Jobson's enlightened views were unusual. The common refrain among European enslavers was Africans were heathen and barbarous. He was firmly against buying 'any that had our own shapes'.[164] This respect travelled both ways. He was able to build a trusted relationship with the representative – cabashier – of local traders, Buckor Sano, who facilitated meetings and exchanges.

The reflections of Thomas Bowdich of the Company of Merchants trading to Africa on his colonising expedition to the Ashante kingdom, Gold Coast in 1817, also contradicted contemporary stereotypes. He was struck by the opulence of the social elite of its main town, Kumase and the scale and eloquence of much of its architecture. He estimated the market place to be a mile in circumference. One of the main thoroughfares was one hundred yards wide. Streets were swept daily,

the Reign of James I and Charles I' (vol.XIII, 4) in Sidney Brayshaw Fay and Harold Underwoood Faulkner (eds) *Smith College Studies in History Volumes 12-14 1926-29* (Northampton Mass., 1929).

162 Ekelund Jnr and Tollison, (1997), p.172.

163 Scott, (1912), pp.171-2.

164 Richard Jobson *The Golden Trade or A Discovery of the River Gambra, and the golden Trade of the Aethiopians*. First published London 1623. This edition (London, 1968) p.197 & p.112.

waste collected. The wealthy had indoor toilets. Personal hygiene such as bathing regularly, cleaning teeth, shaving bodily hair and wearing clean clothes was a cultural sign of affluence and power.[165]

Scottish king James VI on assuming the English throne in 1603 as James I moved to alter the political climate surrounding the activities of the Atlantic trade. In 1604 he concluded a peace treaty with Spain and ceased the practice of providing Letters of Marque to English privateers. These letters had made their freebooting activities legal under English law. In order to open up wider sea going commerce, enthusiasm for slave trading and willingness to antagonise the Spanish and Portuguese who dominated the Atlantic trade routes would have to be curtailed.

A more peaceful commodity trade was the preferred practice, considering the potential it held for trade in gold. In addition to the perspective of the African states on the coast, any official sanctioning of English slave trade with the Spanish territories would be perceived as an affront to the Spanish authorities attempting to enforce protectionist policies within its territories. As a result, there was a gradual increase in the granting of more detailed and restrictive patents causing a de-facto, if not openly intentional, separation between the English official trade in commodities, including gold, and the taking of slaves to trade for profit... The best way to achieve necessary stability and security around the trade was a discontinuation of abductions along the coast in combination with the establishment of trading centers on plots granted by interested African states along the coast.[166]

However, peace with Spain did not stop English pirates from trading in enslaved people. A year after the parchment was signed the captain-general of the Spanish Atlantic squadrons impounded an English pirate ship that was sailing to the North African coast to sell as enslaved people it had seized from a Spanish vessel.[167]

165 Thomas Bowdich *Mission from Cape Coast Castle to Ashantee, &c.* (London, 1819). Though it needs to be emphasised this public grandeur and civility reflected the lives of a small privileged elite, whose elevated status rested to a large extent upon the exploitation of enslaved labour.
166 Svalastog, (2018), p.46.
167 Clive Malcom Senior *An Investigation of the Activities and Importance of English Pirates 1603-40* , Ph.D dissertation, University of Bristol, (1972) p.129.

Two years before Jobson's visit to West Africa, English pirates sailing the *White Lion* owned by the second earl of Warwick, seized enslaved Angolans from a Portuguese ship and traded them at Providence Island, the first group of captured Africans recorded as sold in North America. Earlier, in 1614, a flotilla of thirteen English pirates ships sent into the port of Tuscany two of their number with twenty enslaved captives under the decks as a present for the grand duke in return for the safe conduct of their treasure-laden vessels.[168] The slave voyages database records captain John Powell in the England-registered ship, *Hopewell*, selling enslaved Africans seized from a Portuguese ship as 'prize' in 1617.[169]

While pirates continued to act as they always had done, independently of the state – even when they were sponsored by powerful members of the ruling class such as Warwick – GC merchants worked to build contacts, relationships and trading posts in West Africa, particularly the Gold Coast.[170] Representatives – factors – were stationed in fortified settlements at Anamaboe, Kommenda, Kormantin and Winneba.

In London, continuous jostling for supremacy by the two merchants dominant in the GC, John Davies and Humphrey Slaney, was creating a fractious operating environment culminating in Privy Council adjudication. The company struggled to make a profit. This was exacerbated by the governor, William St John, disappearing with investors money in 1624.

There was a resurgence of hope engendered by Charles I taking the Crown the following year. He invested, lent a naval vessel as protection and granted new concessions to the West African coast with a new patent in 1631. The king is also believed to have had shares in the company.[171] In return the GC, with London merchant Nicholas Crispe now the largest stakeholder, promised gold.

The growing interest in trade to West Africa and the Americas soon spread to Scotland. In 1634 Charles I granted a charter to the Scottish Guinea Company created by four members of his Court there. However, a disastrous voyage to Kormantin a couple of years later quashed enthusiasm for further ventures. More than half a century later a second slave trading initiative, the Company of Scotland trading to Africa and

168 Ibid. p.163.
169 https://slavevoyages.org/american/database accessed 8 April 2020.
170 Now Ghana.
171 Scott, (1912), p.13.

the Indies, sought to capture Africans, colonise land and compete with the English mercantilists. Created in the 1690s by William Paterson, a key figure in the establishment of the Bank of England, its birth gained momentum in the wake of legislation passed by the Scottish Parliament in 1693, *An Act for Incourageing Forraign Trade*. The company was met with organised hostility from the established slave trading network south of the border who campaigned against its legitimacy to trade at Court and in the colonies. Its attempt at establishing a colony at Darien, New Caledonia (Panama) built upon enslaved labour failed disastrously. One of those buried there was Lord Mungo Murray. He took with him much of father's wealth. John Murray, Marquess of Atholl had invested £500 (£88,144). Numerous members of Scotland's ruling class had their riches dissipated by the collapse. It hastened a controversial political development to which some had hitherto been staunch opponents, the 1707 Act of Union. A seductive condition of Scottish parliamentarians agreeing to the union was full compensation for Darien losses, with an additional bonus. Robert Burns derided those willing to sell the political independence of their country for 'English gold' in his poem/song 'Such a Parcel of Rogues in a Nation'. The integration opened the English slave trade to Scotland-based aristocrats, merchants and their companies.

City of London merchants not members of the GC but wanting to profit from participation in the trade – known as 'interlopers' –organised private ventures. Maurice Thompson, William Pennoyer and Samuel Vassall were particularly active. Thompson specialised in exploiting opportunities overseas and was one of the most politically powerful merchants of his age. He eventually joined the GC in 1647 and became a prominent planter in Barbados. He planned his first expedition over twenty years earlier with partner Thomas Combes. The pair sailed three ships to West Africa, enslaved sixty, transporting them to England's first Caribbean colony, St Kitts. They returned with twenty-thousand pounds weight of tobacco.

After a spell in prison, Thompson planned another voyage with John Crispe, who may well have been a relative of Nicholas Crispe, the controlling force of the GC. Their design was 'to trade 'niggers' and carry them to foreign parts'.[172] However, the GC found out and by order of the Privy Council stopped the slavers' ships from leaving port.

Another dispute involving leading members of the company, John Wood and Rowland Wilson, led to them petitioning Parliament's

---

172 Svalastog, (2018), p.110.

Committee for Foreign Plantations in 1646.[173] They accused shipmasters Robert Shapton, Miles Cawson and James Smith – living in Barbados with his family – of being interlopers on the West African coast at Cape Verde having

> By force & violence tooke the Native people being Blackes from the shoare, putt them aboard their ships, and carried them for the Barbados where they sould them to planters [which] tendeth much to the destruction of that Trade and Commerce, which your petitioners have in those parts, & to the dishonour of our nation.[174]

Witnesses said the trio were working for veteran enslaver and colonialist the earl of Warwick, now a member of the Committee for Foreign Plantations, who would be paid 'the 5th Negroe of all they should take'.[175] They added that they had planned to attack the town of Portudal from where they intended to steal people for enslavement. The outcome of the petition is unknown but, as Blakemore argues, it would not be surprising if the earl of Warwick had not protected his contractors. The question left begging is that of Warwick's three-way conflict of interest: as a member of the GC; a private enslaver; and member of the state body overseeing and regulating colonial trade and settlement.

RESTORATION

The effect of the Civil War and the Republic, 1642-60, upon Barbados, the triangular trade and the narrative of justification is discussed in more detail in chapter five.

While the Restoration of the Stuart monarchy with Charles II in 1660 'opened with harmony between traders and the Crown',[176] within a few years this dynamic had fundamentally changed. Via the Royal Prerogative

---

173 Inikori (2002) writes that there had been a private trading firm, Wood and Company, doing business at Sherbro, Guinea Coast since the early 1620s. It is very likely that John Wood was either the owner or played a prominent role.

174 TNA HCA 30/849/636 (National Archives) in Blakemore (2015).

175 Ibid.

176 Christopher Hill, *The Century of Revolution 1603-1714*, (London, 1974), p.189.

the king was determined to become as financially independent of Parliament as possible. He recognised the importance of the trades in gold and enslaved people to this. 'A new form of 'gold fever' seemed to grip the palace of Whitehall'.[177] One of the first patents granted through the Prerogative was, in December, to his newly established family firm, the Royal Adventurers Trading into Africa (RA) allowing a monopoly of English trade in West Africa. For this Charles would receive two-thirds of all gold found which, once on English soil, would be minted into Guinea coins with, symbolically, an elephant's head on one side.[178]

The king's accounts show a number of payments to RA treasurer, Thomas Holder, 'for His Majesty's adventure in the business of Guinea'.[179] More than half of those listed in the patent were royals and aristocrats. They included his brother the Duke of York, his cousin Prince Rupert, his sisters Mary, the Princess Royal and Princess Henrietta. Each of the thirty persons named in the charter invested £250 (£50,646). It signalled the importance the Stuarts put upon the colonial enterprise and in particular the triangular trade.[180] It also effectively ended the East India Company's (EIC) involvement in the West Africa trade though they did suggest to the Duke of York that a division of labour be agreed, his company controlling enslavement, they gold and ivory but without success.

To ensure close supervision and unified policy and action, a Council of Foreign Plantations was created with Noell and Povey as members. Both had managed, with apparent ease, to make the social and political transition from influential actors in the republic to equally powerful personalities in the restored monarchy.

One of Charles II's earliest acts was to establish a committee of the Privy Council to collect information and offer advice about the colonies… Noell, Povey, and Drax, experts in high favour with Cromwell, were influential after 1660.[181]

177 John Callow, *The Making of King James II. The Formative Years of a Fallen King*, (Stroud, 2000), p.240.

178 Ibid. p.241.

179 *Calender of State Papers Treasury Books Vol 1 1660-1667*, (London 1904), pp.312, 314, 383.

180 See Appendix 2 for list of members, courtesy of Svalastog, (2018), p.224.

181 Hill, (London, 1974), p.184.

Noell was soon knighted with Povey becoming the Duke of York's treasurer. Samuel Pepys, working as a senior bureaucrat in the navy, was not impressed. His diary entry, 16 April 1664, notes 'the simple Povey, of all the most ridiculous fools I ever knew to do business'.[182]

The RA was a collaboration between the Stuarts and the City of London. Both institutions were dependent upon each other, a relationship mutually beneficial and expedient, economically and politically. The City merchants had the money and the Crown political power – mitigated by Parliament – both parties wanting some of what the other had.

The Duke of York and cousin Prince Rupert were the most influential voices in defining policy and objectives. Meetings of the ruling body, the Court of Assistants, were held in York's rooms in Whitehall Palace. Rupert's ability to lobby the king and influence his advisors was instrumental in the creation of the company. It facilitated the realisation of his obsession to return to the Guinea coast and find the source of its, hitherto, most sought after and precious commodity, gold. The many Civil War years at sea attacking the new republic's ships, such as his plunder of GC vessels in 1651, instigated this irrepressible desire. With York as Lord High Admiral of the navy, the duo had opportunity to use the country's ships to accumulate wealth for the family, patriarch Charles having given permission for them to sequester vessels. Crown and company interest merged and became indivisible.

A revised Navigation Act 1660 sought to restrict further the ability of foreign ships and sailors from competing with English trade in its ports and colonies. Many City of London merchants who were overseas traders welcomed the law.

At the Restoration, many merchants viewed Crown interest in the imperial project with acquiescence: they welcomed cooperation between Crown and Parliament in passing the Navigation Acts to combat foreign competition and believed that the Crown's prerogative rights might be employed to mutual advantage.[183]

Not all did, however. Especially those who wanted the freedom to go about their business unrestricted, a bourgeoise liberty that had been a

182 Svalastog, (2018), p.1.
183 Nuala Zahedieh *The Capital and the Colonies: London and the Atlantic Economy, 1660-1700*, (Cambridge, 2010) p.116. There were three further Navigation acts, with similar purpose.

fundamental principle fought for in the Civil War.

Parliament in the same year voted the king lifetime control of customs for personal use. The revenue would be less difficult to administer and collect if all goods were transported in England-registered ships. The act also enhanced the power of York as controller of the state's fleet. The two brothers ensured that expenditure on the navy increased dramatically during these early years of the Restoration, rising from £168,919 (£31,881,167) in 1661-2 to £516,383 (£106,767,939) two years later.[184]

In 1662 three ships sailed to the Gambia, each costing £5,000 (£922,531) for crew and provisions. A further £17,500 (£3,228,859) was invested in tradable commodities that could be exchanged for gold and people to enslave. To cover these costs York raised his stockholding to £3,600 (£664,222), against £800 (£147,605) each from the king, Prince Rupert and the Duke of Buckingham and £400 (£73,802) each from the Queen Mother and the duchess of Orleans. Forty RA ships made the voyage south east to West Africa in the first three years.[185]

THE STUART SLAVE TRADING COMPANY

In 1663 a renewed charter from Charles decreed the RA sole rights to the English trade in people trafficking in West Africa for a thousand years. A revised subscribers list contained the king, queen, the queen mother, a prince, three dukes, seven earls, a countess, six lords and twenty-five knights, who held around twenty-five per cent of the stock. The majority of the rest was held by City of London merchants and gentry.[186] Negotiations prior to the renewal had concentrated upon refocussing the main activity of the company: 'to furnish his Majesties American plantations with Negroes at certain and moderate rates'.[187] Rupert's obsession with gold had been subsumed. Enslavement was now considered by the Crown as more viable and necessary corollary to the enlargement of its possessions in the Caribbean.

---

184 *Calender of State Papers Treasury Books Vol 1 1660-1667*, (London 1904), p.xxxii.

185 W. Noel Sainsbury (ed.) *Calender of State Papers, Colonial Series, America and West Indies 1661-1668* HMSO (London, 1880) number 618 p.175.

186 Fryer, (1984), p.21.

187 *The Several Declarations of the Company of Royal Adventurers of England trading into Africa.*

Thereafter, the Duke [of York's] personal fortune became increasingly tied to the success or failure of the slave trade, and he did everything in his power to foster its growth... There is solid reason to credit him with the formal establishment of the British slave trade.[188]

This reconstituted RA was characterised by a more aggressive policy of colonial expansion through monopoly trade and settlement that had strategic alignment with the Stuart goal of enlarging its international power and prestige. The desire was to build a permanent imperial authority in West Africa and dominate the Caribbean through settlement and plantation. The company would, effectively, be able to make laws, execute martial law, appoint governors and raise a military force. These extensions of legal authority were designed to have a number of beneficial political, economic and military consequences for the Stuarts, home and abroad. Developing was an imperial infrastructure with the Crown, the Court and the City of London at its heart.

One department of this infrastructure – to ensure accumulated capital found its way into the royal exchequer as smoothly as possible – was the Receiver General of the Revenues payable from his Dominions, Colonies and Plantations in Africa and America.

A greater number of the most influential merchants in London including veterans of the GC and EIC such as Sir Nicholas Crispe, Sir Martin Noell (and two of his brothers) and Thomas Povey bought stock.[189] The trio, as members of the Council of Foreign Plantations – for which they received £300 (£62,028) a year – would also be able to do all in their power to ensure their private investments were publicly protected. The following year the Council issued a 'proposition' detailing the policy of supplying forced labour in the colonies:

Blacks [should be] bought by way of trade, and sold about 20l. [£20 (£4,197)] a head, the most useful appurtenances of a plantation and perpetual servants. The whites divers ways gathered up in England, a few from Ireland or Scotland, transported at the rate of about 6l. [£6 (£1,259)] per head... Ways of obtaining these servants from felons condemned to death, sturdy beggars, gipsies, and other incorrigible

188 Callow, (2000), p.242.
189 See Appendix 3 for list of members, courtesy of J.M. Svalastog (2018) p.224.

rogues, poor and idle debauched persons.[190]

The supply of enslaved Black people 'by way of trade' could, of course, only be done by the RA. The practice of forcibly transporting peasants and artisans from the British Isles to colonies began in this century. They were usually convicted people – there were over three hundred capital offences in England – people living outside mainstream society or Gaelic prisoners of war. It had the dual effect of exiling people the state did not want and furnishing colonial merchants and planters with servile labour they desperately needed. On the slave ship *Hopewell* which sailed for the Americas in February, 1634 was one such persona non grata, Thomas Browne, aged 11.[191]

In his seminal history of the umbilical link between the triangular trade and the development of industrial capitalism, Eric Williams claimed Bristol magistrates with land in the Caribbean were using harsh sentences of transportation for trivial offences in order to supply labour for their plantations. He cites the notorious Judge Jeffreys who imposed sentences of transportation upon many of the followers of the Duke of Monmouth after their failed rebellion of 1685. His fondness for trying the accused at the rate of five hundred a day and handing out maximum sentences created such anger amongst the populace of the West Country that his court was named the Bloody Assizes.[192] Hill (1974) asserts that Queen Mary, wife of James II, made a profit from the transportation of the rebels.[193] Transportation after being captured in war or convicted in court became an integral part of the formal criminal justice system during the seventeenth century.

As early as 1643 articles appeared in the London press advocating transportation for Loyalist sympathisers. The largest deportation

---

190 Number 791 'Report of Committee of Council of Foreign Plantations', Col. Entry Bk, XCII, pp.275-283 in W. Noel Sainsbury (ed.) *Calender of State Papers, Colonial Series, America and West Indies 1661-1668* HMSO (London, 1880) p.229.

191 John Camden Hotten (ed.) *The Original Lists of Persons of Quality; Emigrants; Religious Exiles; Political Rebels; Serving Men Sold for a Term of years; Apprentices; Children Stolen; Maidens Pressed; And Others who went from Great Britain to the American Plantations 1600-1700* (London, 1873) p.128.

192 Williams, (1964), p.15.

193 Hill, (London, 1974) p.206.

from England occurred after the battle of Preston in 1648 when an unknown number of the 9,000 Scottish prisoners who had been captured were transported. Other prisoners of war also ended up in the New World after the battles of Dunbar and Worcester. In 1654 the Parliamentary commander in Highland Scotland was empowered to transport all those he encountered under arms to the plantations. Thereafter further transportations occurred in the wake of the Argyle and Monmouth rebellions of 1685 and the 1715 and 1745 Jacobite rebellions... Many others were transported out of Ireland in the aftermath of the Cromwellian invasion of 1649–1653. Contemporary accounts put the number of felons, vagrants and prisoners of war conveyed to Barbados in the 1640s and 1650s at 12,000... Beckles estimates that between 1645 and 1650 at least 8,000 indentured servants arrived in Barbados, many of whom were transported... By 1652 justices of the peace were empowered to apprehend beggars and vagrants and send them to ports for trans-shipment to the New World. Four years later judges were ordered to send lists of criminals convicted in assizes to London in order to identify suitable recruits. In the same year 1,000 London poor were sent to Barbados.[194]

The incestuous nature of Stuart control of West Africa and Caribbean trade is illustrated graphically by the five year licence for transportation issued by the king in November,1664.

To Sir James Modyford to take all felons convicted in their circuits and at the Old Bailey [for] transportation to Foreign plantations and transmit them to Sir Thomas Modyford, Governor of Jamaica.[195]

Sir James, a member of the RA, had been governor of the newly seized Jamaica before his older brother, Sir Thomas, took over. Both had landholdings and plantations on the island. James had over one thousand acres but was now employed by his brother as London-based agent for the colony. Thomas had originally emigrated from England to Barbados two decades earlier. He bought land, established a plantation

194 Hamish Maxwell-Stuart 'Transportation from Britain and Ireland, 1615–1875.' *A Global History of Convicts and Penal Colonies*. Ed. Clare Anderson. (London, 2018). pp.189–90. http://dx.doi.org/10.5040/9781350000704.ch-007 Accessed 16 June 2020.
195 Sainsbury, (ed.), (London, 1880), number 866, p.257.

while also becoming a factor for the GC. For a short time he was governor. In Jamaica he is said to have used 28 servants from England.[196]

Scotland was also transporting convicted people to the Caribbean.

Four young men scourged by the hangman through Edinburgh, burnt behind the ear, and delivered up to be sent to Barbados, for abusing James Scott, minister at Ancram, in time of sermon.[197]

The Modyford brothers were cousins to the powerful and influential George Monck, the first Duke of Albemarle, who was close to the king and one of the founder members of the RA. Monck's support for the parliamentary cause during much of the Civil War and his success as a leading commander in the New Model Army did not weigh against him after the Restoration. Indeed, he is credited for using his military reputation and strategic know-how to create the relatively secure conditions for the settlement and return of the monarchy. His military, business and political career exemplifies the fluidity of alliances that was a familiar characteristic within the ruling class. Networks of affiliations were largely built on the dual principles of (long-term) strategy and (short-term) expediency. This arrangement of his cousins suited all parties whatever their previous allegiances.

The trawl of society's poor and unfortunate to provide free and inexpensive labour on the slave ships and in the colonies became an industry. Eric Williams writes that kidnapping became a notorious practice in the ports of London and Bristol. The practitioners became known as 'spirits' and were despised in the communities they preyed upon. 'It was enough to point a finger at a woman in the streets of London and call her a 'spirit' to start a riot'.[198] Proposal for laws that would have interfered were rejected, such as a bill against stealing children. Many people had a lot to lose.

In the transport of felons, a whole hierarchy, from courtly secretaries and grave judges down to gaolers and turnkeys, insisted on having a

196 Hilary McD. Beckles, 'Plantation Production and White 'Proto-Slavery': White Indentured Servants and the Colonization of the English West Indies, 1624-1645' *The Americas* 41.3 (January 1985), pp. 21-45.
197 Sainsbury, (ed.), (London, 1880), number 1113, p.351.
198 Eric Williams, *Capitalism and Slavery*, (London, 1964), p.14.

share in the spoils.[199]

However, as a compromise colonial merchants, ship masters and planters who had to deal with the resultant anger and indiscipline of unwilling and far from home sailors, petitioned the king create a register of those travelling to the plantations. Voyages to West Africa were dangerous and lasting months, had a high mortality rate. A rebellious crew just made things worse. Thirty-eight of the crew of the *Amity* died during their 1661 expedition.[200] Understandably, these employments were, at the best of times, not popular amongst sailors even though pay rates tended to be a little less parsimonious. To get around crew shortfalls, slave ship masters organised press gangs in port towns to kidnap drunken sailors. If there were not enough inebriated stumbling the streets, they would raid taverns and kidnap.

On occasion, sailors would refuse to keep aboard people against their will. Eight crew of the Mary obstinately opposed transporting to the Caribbean 'innocent' Quakers whose only crime had been to 'walk in fear of the Lord'.[201]

For the Crown, the planters and the Modyfords this supply of forced unpaid labour was a necessary ingredient in developing the island's economy, their wealth and the state's imperial power. Sugar production in the English Caribbean was booming. Barbados as the largest exporter, required ever more labour. However, colonial merchant-planters settling other islands, like Renatus Enys in Suriname, pointed out the downside of monopoly enterprise.

The country begins to be populous, partly with supplies [of slaves] which arrive weekly (within the last two months nine ships have been consigned here), and partly with a succeeding generation, for the women are very prolifical and have lusty children... Were the planters supplied with negroes, the strength and sinews of this western world, they would advance their fortunes and his Majesty's customs. The sworn enemies of the colony are the Dons of Barbadoes, whose interest is to keep the planters in that island to balance the power of their negroes; therefore they use their utmost means to disparage the

199 Ibid.
200 George Frederick Zook, *The Company of Royal Adventurers Trading into Africa*, Ph.D dissertation (1919), Cornell University.
201 Sainsbury, (ed), (London, 1880), number 909, January 7th, 1665, p.266.

country, but their hyprocrisies are discovered, and several families are transporting thither. It is reported that some of the Royal Company, who are eminent Barbadians, endeavour the diversion of all supplies of negroes from this place, which will prove a detriment to his Majesty, there being no colony more hopeful than this, especially for any design against the Spaniard.[202]

Enys's observations are astoundingly revealing: he acknowledges both the source of settler wealth in the plantation colonies, 'negroes, the strength and sinews of this western world' and the power and preeminence of those powerful Barbados merchants and planters – 'the Dons', of whom Martin Noell was one of the most prominent – and their umbilical link with the RA which had bought 250 acres on the island.

Voyages to West Africa became more numerous and fleets larger. Royal navy ships *Welcome*, *Sophia* and *Rosebush* were requisitioned for use. In the summer of 1664 eight ships were readied with £50,000 (£10,382,737) worth of goods and supplies for the company's permanent factories and garrisons. They requested naval protection in case of attack.

Charles II, meanwhile, was making clear his determination to advance the imperial project. He instructed the governor of Barbados, Francis Lord Willoughby

to use all prudential means to advance the wealth of the King's dominions in these parts… to take special care of revenue… [and to] treat with the natives… or if injurious or contumacious, to persecute with fire and sword.[203]

---

202 Written in 1663 from the newly acquired plantation colony of Suriname by City of London trader Renatus Enys to Sir Henry Bennett a senior member of the government. Charles II formally granted Francis Lord Willoughby, the governor of Barbados, and Laurence Hyde (later 1st earl of Rochester), the proprietorship of Suriname in return for 30,000 acres, 2,000 Ibs of tobacco and one-fifth of all gold and silver. He allowed it to be called Willoughbyland https://www.british-history.ac.uk/cal-state-papers/colonial/america-west-indies/vol5/pp166-171 November 1663 accessed 11 April 2020 and Sainsbury, (London, 1880), p.131.
203 Sainsbury, (ed.), (London, 1880), number 489, p.142.

The instruction became the modus operandi of RA. York and Prince Rupert implemented their family patriarch's wishes with brutal savagery. The company was, by 1665, employing over one hundred ships while expecting a return of between £200-300,000 (£44-66,000,000).[204] On one voyage, the council of war on the *Jersey* decided to destroy *Anta Castle* on the coast of West Africa and loot all they could.[205] The willingness to resort to 'fire and sword' meant confrontation would inevitably intensify. This aggressive Atlantic policy hardened Dutch anger, with the hostility breaking out into the second Anglo-Dutch war of 1665.[206]

Much of this conflict was fought in the Caribbean, with the French assisting the Dutch in the hope of colonising islands held by the Stuarts. Indeed, islands were lost and won back in a series of tit-for-tat attacks and counter attacks. After two years of blood-letting, peace was resumed through the Treaty of Breda with settlement of territorial possessions and trading rights in West Africa, North America and the Caribbean. This would, however, not end the brutal trading rivalry in these regions.

The war had commenced just after the RA had signed a contract to supply the Spanish plantations in the Americas with enslaved Africans. This trade was known as the Asiento. The licence was held by Genoese partners, Grillo and Lomellino, who subcontracted the RA to supply three thousand five hundred per year. The captives would be shipped to Barbados and Jamaica from where they would be distributed to Spanish colonial territories. It was potentially very lucrative and opened up the company to trading in this larger and more affluent market.

The conflict with the Dutch prevented the Stuart's firm from fulfilling its supply promise and their contract was not renewed. The failed Asiento deal particularly upset the Barbados planters who, with their booming sugar plantations, were ever more reliant on the RA for their labour needs.

On Restoration, the king's closest and most trusted advisors, the Privy Council, assumed direct management of the colonies. They were later assisted by a series of consultative committees and boards, such as the Council of Foreign Plantations. This centralisation of power in the

---

204 Zook, (1919), Cornell University.
205 Sainsbury, (ed.), (London, 1880), number 699, p.197.
206 In that year the plague claimed 100,000 victims in London – including Martin Noell – a quarter of the population. Charles fled to the relative safety of Oxford. The following year was the Great Fire which left between 70-80,000 without home and shelter.

implementation of imperial policy reflected the importance of the slave trade in facilitating colonial expansion in the Americas. Imports from and exports to the region were increasing annually. Between 1607-89 London merchants created at least fifteen companies to pursue Atlantic trade and colonisation.

The trade industrialised during the second half the seventeenth century. Africans were packed tighter into ships' holds, more slaving vessels sailed the triangular route carrying more manufactured goods and transporting back to England ever-increasing African and Caribbean commodities, especially sugar. The colonial population grew from an estimated one hundred and forty-thousand in 1660 to four hundred thousand by the beginning of the new century.

This rapid increase in trade and traffic necessitated an enlargement in naval capacity. We have noted already how the Charles supported a near trebling of expenditure on the English navy, under the command of his brother the Duke of York.[207] This expansion of size and activity was most noticeable in its Atlantic fleet. By the mid-sixteen eighties it employed approximately six thousand three hundred sailors compared to around three thousand two hundred and forty twenty years earlier. Ekelund and Tollison describes the role of the navy in protecting the triangular trade as state-funded 'cartel enforcement services'.[208]

Even with the Stuart's enthusiasm for making available state resources to the RA, the expected cash bonanza was not materialising. The second Anglo Dutch war and the failure of the Asiento deal disrupted many plans. As a consequence it decided in 1667 to issue licences to private traders. In return, it stipulated all licensed ships carry one-tenth of their cargo for the company. Prince Rupert, never slow to seize a business opportunity, acquired a licence. By the sixteen eighties this private dimension to the trade was worth half of the company's.[209]

Opening up the trade to privateers may have diluted company profits but for the Crown, with complete control of customs' duties, it had the opposite effect. An agreement with the planters in Barbados in 1663 resulted in the king receiving an additional customs duty of four and a

---

207 The Duke of York consistently agitated for more funds for the navy. In 1669 he wanted *£220,000 (£48,308,965) more than the £200,000 (£43,917,241) appointed for the Navy this year, Calender of Treasury Books Vol.3 1669-72 Pts 1&2,* Number 56, Wednesday 21 April ,1669.
208 Ekelund Jnr and Tollison, (1997), p.181.
209 Zahedieh, (2010), p.105.

half per cent upon all 'dead' commodities exported from the island of which the greatest by far was sugar. It was then reckoned to be worth annually around £8,000 (£1,678,916). Personally, Charles II also received from the RA an annual dividend of £322 and ten shillings (£67,264). Governor Lynch of Jamaica estimated that every enslaved person was worth £20 (£4,165) per year to the king.

The RAC, created in 1672 after the legal dissolution of the RA, included the dukes of York – as governor – and Buckingham, Prince Rupert and the earls of Shaftesbury (as sub-governor),[210] Arlington, Craven and Bath amongst others. Four out of five of Charles II's 'Cabal' – his closest advisers – were subscribers. Of the more numerous City of London merchants we find many names long associated with the trade: Sir Nicholas, John and Thomas Crispe, Sir Peter Colleton, Sir Richard Ford, Ferdinando Gorges, Charles Modyford, Humphrey and John Morrice, Thomas Povey, Sir Robert Vyner, Edward Colston and four members of the Dashwood family. Lord mayors, MPs and aldermen they were some of the richest and most powerful people in Britain. The company's call for subscribers raised £111,000 (£25,588,199). Over the next few years a concentration of power saw just fourteen shareholders (out of two hundred) with more than £1,000 (£232,620) stock, York having £3,000 (£697,860) and Shaftesbury £2,000 (£465,240). Callow estimates that York was receiving twelve per cent (£83,743) per year on his investment.

There can be little room for doubt that private profit, as opposed to the national good, remained the primary motivation behind all of his trading schemes.[211]

On inception, the RAC became the largest joint-stock company in England after the EIC. The enthusiasm of the aristocracy and the mercantilist class for this new incarnation of yet another Africa company reflected the positive influence the triangular trade was having upon their political economy. The colonial empire and associated domestic trades and businesses were developing, expanding and booming: shipbuilding, the manufacture of iron and cotton goods, production of commodities based upon sugar and tobacco, insurance and finance. By

---

210 The post of sub-governor was established because governorship of the RAC was reserved for the royal family. See Jose Rowell Tapac Corpuz (2019).
211 John Callow, (2000), p.263.

the mid sixteen eighties plantation shipping would account for forty per cent of London's total overseas trade. Of the fifty nine biggest colonial merchants in England, nine owned plantations and thirty-two had kin in the colonies with Barbados the centre of settlement and trade.[212]

From the £111,000, £34,000 (£7,909,080) was allowed for the three RAC forts at Cape Coast, Sierra Leone and the Gambia, a commitment that signalled the permanence and importance of their function. Another eight forts were built using the labour of hundreds of enslaved (child labourers in parenthesis): at Cape Coast Castle, three hundred and sixty seven (seventy six); Commendah, twenty two (five); Secondee, ten (three); Dick's Cove, forty eight; Tantumquerry, ten; Winnebah, thirteen; Accra, thirty one (four); Whydah, one hundred and eighteen (twenty seven).[213]

These forts were used as holding depots before transportation to the Americas. The enslaved were branded upon the right breast by a burning iron with the letters DY to denote they were the Duke of York's property, an inerasable marker should they try to escape. Later, after his proprietorial dominance of the company had declined the enslaved, if they were held captive at Bance Island Castle had burned into their breast RACE – Royal Africa Company of England – and S for Sierra Leone.

The nature of this Atlantic trade with individuals having fingers in many pies engendered a complex relationship dynamic between the Court and merchants that was often tense, suspicious, competitive and conflictual. Larger colonial merchants were becoming increasingly frustrated at the Stuart's absolutist tendencies and liking for the Royal Prerogative, both at home and in the colonies. As the seventies transitioned to the eighties they looked to restore the power of Parliament and the City of London.

It was Charles, however, who went on the offensive: proroguing Parliament in the last year of the decade; withdrawing the royal charter from the City; and imposing royal governance. It was as if nothing had been learned from the Civil War when his father had upped the ante in the conflict between Crown and Parliament by storming the Commons and attempting to arrest members.

This mirrored a similarly aggressive policy towards the colonies that

212 Nuala Zahedieh (2010) pp. 83, 286, 287.
213 J.J. Crooks *Records Relating to the Gold Coast Settlements from 1750-1874* (London, 1973) pp.3-7. Thanks to the late Frank Cass for bringing this book to my attention.

had been in operation since the mid-seventies. Governors of Caribbean islands were appointed with a brief to subdue increasingly recalcitrant local legislative councils and assemblies, and increase revenue to the Crown. Some governors took this as a green-light to fill their purses. Dutton of Barbados in five years accrued £18,000 (£4,019,550) in salaries, perks, bribes and 'presents' from the Assembly. Meanwhile, the RAC's resident planter-enslaver Sir Peter Colleton, as president of the governor-appointed Barbados Council, was looking after company business.

The Absentee planter-enslavers and Barbados merchants responded to what they felt was an unfair wielding of arbitrary power by meeting weekly at the Cardinal's Cap tavern, Cornhill, London to organise representations to the Lords of Trade and Plantations and its successor, Lords Committee of Trade.

The death of Charles and the crowning of his brother York as James II in 1685 enthroned England's preeminent aristocratic enslaver, a reputation unrivalled since the death of his cousin Prince Rupert three years previous. The Stuart mercantilist ethos, expressed in their family motto *regio floret patricino commercium, commercioque regnum* – the kingdom and king flourish alike through the encouragement of trade – was embodied in James. Continuing as governor of the RAC he used his status to ensure the company's profitability. He was also its biggest shareholder until 1688 when he passed his holding to courtier James Grahme MP, secretary of the company.[214]

James' overlapping and mutually beneficial roles as king and RAC governor and his ability to use the Royal Prerogative to achieve his ends, was good for company business. The RAC became the biggest slave trading company in the world. In recognition, the company gifted five hundred guineas (£124,663) in 1677 for his 'extraordinary services.' This was over and above his investment income. Davies asserts 1672-91 was their most profitable period.

All the original subscribers to the African company who sold their

214 A trusted member of the royal household the shares were part-surety for a loan of 6,000 ducats (c.£685k 2020) to the king, https://www.historyofparliamentonline.org/volume/1660-1690/member/grahme-%28graham%29-james-1650-1730 Accessed 31 July 2020. Graham was also keeper of the privy purse and master of the buckhounds. See Jose Rowell Tapac Corpuz (2019) p.53.

holdings before 1691 must have made satisfactory if not spectacular profits as a result of capital appreciation. James II, for example, held fully paid up stock of £3,000; he received in dividends £3,480 and sold for about £5,730. Thus his total profit was around £6,210 spread over seventeen years, the equivalent of an annual return of twelve per cent. There were others in the same happy position.[215]

The pursuit of undisguised self-interest by James that had characterised his career as duke inevitably brought social, economic and political tensions between the Crown and wider Mercantilist class to a head. One of the primary reasons he felt able to assert his will over Parliament and the free trade mercantilists in the City of London was the increasing revenues pouring into the royal exchequer from the triangular trade. In 1668-89, for example, sugar from the West Indies paid customs of £18,000 (£4,610,552). During 1686-7 over £168,380 (£40,742,238) in *impositions* – duties – from tobacco and sugar, produced with enslaved labour supplied by the RAC or traders licensed by the company, was paid into the same exchequer.[216]

Barbados exported more sugar to Britain than anywhere else and was the English Caribbean's foremost market for the auction of enslaved West Africans. Customs duties were rising because of the growth in imports and exports. In the first year full year of his reign his unique four and half per cent customs duty on exports from Barbados yielded £17,658 (£4,186,424). Between 1670-1688 it returned £81,000 (£16,794,621).[217] This income ensured James II was not solely reliant on Parliament for his money supply.

This internecine conflict within factions of the ruling class fed into the discontent of the general population in London, devastated by the recent plague and fire. In a period of wealth concentration and mass poverty – the top income group had an income thirty-five times bigger than the lowest where life expectancy was thirty-six years[218] – the more frequent occurrence of rioting in London worried the wealthy.

Parliament, representing the power of merchants operating outside

215 K.G. Davies (1999) pp. 156, 74. £6210 = £1,564,399 (2019).
216 Statement N. *The Receipts of the Exchequer 1686-94*, Add. MS., 17,756, ff. 16b., British Library, London.
217 Ibid. p.216.
218 Angus Maddison (Oxford, 2005) p.275. John Gaunt's study of London published in 1662 showed just 3% of people survived beyond 66 years of age.

the magic circle that had monopoly powers granted by the Crown and aristocrats hostile to the new king for religious reasons, acted to avert a second bloody revolution they feared would this time be led by the masses. James was kicked off the throne in the Glorious Revolution of 1688 which asserted the the constitutional supremacy of Parliament over the Crown.

The political ramifications of the overthrow of James by William of Orange led to greater coordination between the Crown, Parliament and the City over the imperial project. In particular, revenue from the colonies was now filtered through Parliament, which prevented the monarchy from using the income as a cash cow to fund its exertion of arbitrary power.

While William III may not have overtly expressed the same obsessive enthusiasm for the trade in enslavement he had no moral or religious objections to maintaining a personal involvement. He picked up where James had left off and took on the governorship of the RAC and accepted a substantial stockholding of £1,000 (£256,142). He also recognised the political and military value of the company in providing a settled defence force in Africa and the Caribbean against France and other nations with competing imperial designs.

A series of Parliamentary enquiries into monopoly patents in the sixteen nineties resulted in the triangular trade being opened up. In this new environment, even without the sheltering protection of the Crown, Parliament agreed the RAC's costs relating to the upkeep of its factors and forts in West Africa would be subsidised with a ten per cent tax on goods exported to Africa. In the seventeen-thirties Parliament granted £10,000 (£2,164,924) per year for the purpose. Not all were happy with the company's accounting methods. A report laid before the House of Commons in 1708-09 accused it of inflating its costs by ten times in order the ten per cent would pay the full outlay.[219]

Though it had not engaged in the business of direct enslavement for two decades, the dissolution of the company in 1752 ended an eighty year existence in which it had been instrumental in establishing the role of key institutions of the British state as the world's biggest traders in enslaved human beings. During its existence the number of slaves

---

219 *An Extract Out of the Report of the Lords Commissioners of Trade, Laid before the House of Commons in 1708-08 setting forth the Fictitious and Real Accounts of the African Company for the 10 per Cent Duty* held in British Library Rare Documents Department.

carried by British ships increased six fold and soon accounted for fifty per cent of the total trade. Between 1673-1711 the RAC forced onto the soil of the Caribbean colonies over ninety thousand chained West African human beings. From the captives' shores they embarked with many more.

The Company of Merchants trading into Africa (CMA), a syndicate of enslavers from London, Liverpool and Bristol formed in 1750, filled the space vacated by the RAC. Within ten years, one hundred and forty-six of its ships with a capacity to carry thirty six thousand sailed to West Africa from British ports. Twenty years later their vessels' capacity had risen to forty seven thousand. By the end of the century, Liverpool has overtaken London as the world's biggest slave trading port. Profits on each triangular voyage out of the northern city averaged between sixteen and thirty eight per cent.

The royal family continued to support and defend slavery: William and Mary's successor George III opposed ending the trade; the Duke of Clarence, later William IV, attacked abolitionist Wilberforce as a hypocrite and fanatic; royal family members in the Lords consistently voted against bills to ameliorate enslavement. The CMA had its permanent African militias for defence of its possessions subsidised by the state until the eighteen twenties. From its creation to 1815 it received £963,000 (£163,753,119) in grants from the Treasury confirming Williams' assertion that 'the British government was uniformly consistent in its encouragement of the slave trade'.[220]

The economies of the UK and its imperial possessions were transformed as were the bank accounts of many investors. The exponential growth of the populations of the cities most involved in the trade reflected this: Liverpool exploded from around four thousand in 1680 to eighty three thousand in 1801; Bristol from twenty thousand in 1700 to three times that just over hundred years later with London nearly doubling in the same period. Williams argues the economic growth and development caused by the triangular trade was a major factor in the first capitalist revolution occurring in Britain. He cites the industrial organisation of the Africa companies and the colonial territories with factors, factories and sugar plantations characterised by a strict division of labour. The sugar-mills in the Caribbean were possibly

---

220 Figures for CMA grants from Africa Company records 1601 in Hilary Jenkinson 'The Records of the English African Companies', *Transactions of the Royal Historical Society*, 3, 6, (1912), p.213. Eric Williams (1964) p.40.

'the most advanced technical installations of the time' and created the organisational template for the eighteenth-century cotton mill, the key industry characterising Britain's industrial revolution.

The new colonial markets... encouraged the development of new industries and changes in organisation and techniques which underpinned a broadening, as well as a deepening, of England's industrial base.[221]

The trade enlarged the size, power and wealth of the City of London. The Bank of England was created by City merchants in 1694 in large part to provide a more efficient, centralised and ready supply of credit for the imperial project and associated domestic expansion. Some of the biggest private banks were created by slave traders, such as Heywoods in Liverpool and Barclays Bank which still operates. The Phoenix Insurance company was established to protect colonial merchants against loss, including cover of their human cargo.

Enslavement as a means of supplying colonial labour for the extraction of absolute surplus value was the primary ingredient in the creation of an imperial state in which British monarch's ruled over people they had never seen. Queen Victoria gloried in her role as Empress of India. A fixed, permanent sign along the seashore boardwalk in Carlisle Bay, Bridgetown, Barbados in 2020 denies the Crown's responsibility for accidents while walking.

---

221 Zahedieh, (2010), p.257.

Chapter Six
Civil War, the Republic of England
and the Moral Economy of Enslavement

CIVIL WAR 1642-51

The predilection of Charles I for the use of the Royal Prerogative and sidelining Parliament antagonised members of the House of Commons and powerful, often overlapping, bourgeoise factions in the country and City of London. Colonial merchants and planters not patronised by the Crown, not gilded with a patent, instead took to interloping and privateering. In so doing they allied politically with social forces, such as rural sections of the land-owning gentry, that sought regime change as a solution to their perceived grievances. Yet, the wars fought in England, Wales Ireland and Scotland were characterised by a fluidity of alliances that saw influential and powerful individuals – such as Sir Richard Grenville, Lord Maudant and George Monck, the Duke of Albemarle – change sides and beliefs.[222]

In the early years of the revolution, 1640-42, there was sporadic, popular uprisings of peasants, artisans and small producers: rent strikes, the looting of country houses and demands for bread and justice. Arising out of this social, political and economic turbulence were the profoundly progressive grassroots movements of Levellers, Diggers and Ranters. The Ranters we might describe as Bohemian anarchists. They rejected the restraints of Puritanism on sex, food and alcohol and were the 'free spirits' of the revolution. Less numerous than the Levellers and Diggers their nomadic, unpredictable indulgences frightened the life out of all sections of the (competing and factionalised) ruling class of the sixteen fifties.[223]

With the trial of Charles I in early 1649 for being a 'tyrant and murderer; and a public and an implacable enemy to the Commonwealth

---

222 Andrew Hopper *Turncoats and Renegades: Changing Sides During the English Civil Wars* (Oxford, 2012) p.95.
223 Norah Carlin *Marxism and the English Civil War* (Autumn, 1980) https://www.marxists.org/history/etol/writers/carlin/1980/xx/civilwar.html accessed 26 April 2020. It could be argued that these the progressive, proto-socialist factions were economic, social and political descendants of the 1381 Peasant's Revolt which demanded abolition of the poll tax, forced labour and serfdom.

of England' and the statement by Parliament that 'the office of the King in this state is unnecessary, burdensome and dangerous to the liberty, society and public interest of the people'[224] on his execution it looked as if the political mood of the new republic was aligning with the radical sentiment of the Levellers and Diggers. However, over the next decade the prevailing socio-political alliance that triumphed was dominated by historically powerful people and organisations. Indeed, it was City of London merchant and Lord Mayor, Sir Christopher Packe, who, in 1657 ,offered the Crown to Cromwell.

The political and social upheaval caused by the Civil War in the British Isles exacerbated to serious political and social division within the planter class in Barbados. Additional to the republican cause, the egalitarian ideas of the Levellers and Diggers in England led to bags under the eyes for many of the staunch monarchist majority. The danger of revolutionary ideas blowing across the Atlantic and inspiring oppressed people to think and act for themselves was a seminal issue for all planters, whether republican or royalist. Keeping their captive populations in ignorance of any emancipatory ideas traditionally lay at the heart of their refusal to allow the enslaved literacy. It was reflected, for example, in their hostile attitude to Quakers, such as Thomas Tryon, who did try to proselytise amongst plantation labourers.

The class conflict between the Crown and Parliament exposed and accelerated already existing political tensions developing within the Barbados plantocracy. The sixteen forties sugar boom spurred a monopolisation of land with its resultant expression in the island's internal power relations. Before the transition to sugar, Ligon estimated Major Hilliard's estate of five hundred acres could have been bought for £500 (£125,032). In 1647 half was sold to Modyford for £7,000 (£1,327,910). A small group of Crown appointees and merchant planters, including Francis Lord Willoughby, Thomas Modyford, Daniel Searle, Henry Walrond, Sir Peter Colleton and the Noell and Drax families, acted to create the economic and political foundations to enable them to accumulate vast land holdings and dominate political life. However the Civil War revealed fault lines within this dominant class of merchant-planters. These were widened to breaking point in 1651 when Willoughby as governor declared the island would remain

224 Both quotes in Andrea Stuart *Sugar in the Blood. A Family's Story of Slavery and Empire*, (London, 2012) p.74.

loyal to the Crown despite England having declared itself a republic. It became known as the Horrid Rebellion. Even though royalists had been arriving on island both as political exiles and speculators in the sugar boom, there was no unanimous political consensus: Walrond, for instance, rallied alongside Willoughby and the Stuarts, while Drax and Modyford stood with the Parliamentarians. In the House of Assembly the Royalist majority passed *An Act for the Unity of the Inhabitants of the Island*. It required the primary allegiance of all non-enslaved inhabitants to the island's government. Those unwilling to swear loyalty were disarmed. Influential and vocal supporters of the Parliamentary cause had to pay a bond or face expulsion. Some did leave and lobbied Cromwell and the Roundheads in London to take action.

A major fissure also was the recently passed Navigation Act which severely curtailed trade with non-English ships. It was particularly aimed at the Dutch who had come to dominate the Atlantic trade. But the Hollanders also supplied the island with enslaved West Africans, the lifeblood of plantation production. It was a complicated dilemma for many planters. Monopoly trade was an instrument of the Royal Prerogative and used to enhance crown income and power. Many planters preferred open trading, irrespective of flag and nationality, because they believed it would better suit their economic needs. Parliament's policy reflected the competing political ideologies jostling for preeminence. Many of the City of London merchant-planters who had been attracted by the sugar boom and had bought large plots were supporters of restricted trade because it protected them from foreign competition. As mercantilists they would have numerous trading arms, such as being members of the GC with the supposition that the net result would be positive for their balance sheets. For many smaller planters, however, the Navigation Act merely raised the cost of the commodities they had to buy.

The political deadlock was eventually resolved by force with Cromwell ordering a fleet of seven ships and over eight hundred mariners to restore metropolitan authority. Imposing a blockade and then invading with hundreds of soldiers, Bridgetown was captured costing the lives of a reported thirty resistors. Eight were captured and two hanged. Very soon the Charter of Barbados was agreed with partisan behaviour and speeches from the past being erased from official memory as a condition of the peace.

The sixteen forties and fifties saw increased English activity in the slave trade by the GC, interlopers and pirates. The Transatlantic Slave Trade Database records at least seventy-seven voyages by English ships. English merchants and planters were now colonising islands in the Caribbean and entrenching themselves in West Africa, often through the auspices of the company.

Barbados was now established as the first port of call because of its geographical position and, as a consequence, the premier market in enslaved people in the English Americas. At the beginning of the forties it had a few hundred enslaved Africans; by 1660, twenty-seven thousand. The company was the major provider, especially after the passing of the first Navigation Act in 1651. It also bought two hundred and twenty-five acres of land for plantation production using enslaved labour. It stationed a factor, John Ballow, on the island to look after its growing investment.

When the GC's patent came up for renewal that year, the monopoly was restricted to a narrower stretch of the coastline, the greater part in what is now Ghana. This triangular trade was becoming increasingly competitive with English interlopers, pirates and Spanish, Portuguese, Dutch, French and Danish merchant ships rivalling to capture and enslave. One voyage to the River Gambia during the autumn of that year planned to 'buy as many lusty negroes as possible'[225] and sell them in Barbados. It did not go well. Apart from accidentally blowing up with gunpowder their purchases and the village in which they were stored, a rampaging Prince Rupert, nephew of Charles I arrived in the river. His Cavalier fleet had recently been decimated by the Parliamentary navy and he was in a vengeful mood, looking to attack vulnerable English ships en route to the Caribbean. Plundering what he could from company vessels, Rupert heard rumours of gold mines further up river. He did not have time to fully investigate because of the changing seasons and his fleets' consequent need to embark. Yet, the allure never left him. On hearing the news in London, GC grandees may well have felt doubly aggrieved: a few years earlier it had lent the exiled Prince Charles £500 (£88,425) and two ships.[226]

---

225 Quoted in Svalastog, (2018), p.132.
226 Guinea Company ships had also been attacked in 1648 by Lord Willoughby of Parham, while a vice-admiral of the Royalist naval forces.

England was also at war with the Dutch, 1652-4. The most powerful seafaring nation in the Northern Atlantic it further hindered the GC's ability to trade. One of the contributing factors in causing the conflict was the Navigation Act, passed a year before the outbreak by the Rump Parliament of the new republic. The law prohibited foreign ships from transporting goods from Asia, Africa or the Americas to England or its colonies. It was designed to help companies like the GC by handicapping foreign competition, particularly the Dutch and to a lesser extent the Portuguese.

Planters in Barbados, led by governor Lord Willoughby of Parham, were overwhelmingly opposed to the law and refused acceptance. They feared it would raise the purchase price of enslaved people if the GC and English merchants were their only suppliers. Dutch and other foreign ships continued to anchor in Carlisle Bay and trade in Bridgetown. In response, Cromwell sent a Commonwealth naval fleet to remove Willoughby and force the planters compliance. The republic's government, the Council of State, resolved to exercise much closer scrutiny and control of affairs in Barbados and the colonies generally.

For merchant planters who were also members of the company such as Martin Noell, Thomas Povey, John Wood and Maurice Thompson these legal and economic developments were welcome. Noell's two brothers, Steven and Thomas, lived on the island overseeing their plantation and investments. The family were close to governor Daniel Searle who had replaced Willoughby. Martin Noell was also brother-in-law to Sir John Thurloe, secretary to the Council of State and moved in influential circles in London. Svalastog argues Noell and Thomas Povey were instrumental in shaping these new state arrangements for the colonies.[227]

The EIC had the monopoly of English trade for the Indian subcontinent. A more profitable company, it courted royal favour with annual grants of money to the king, which by the early 1680s were £10,750 (£2,400,789).[228] Some EIC members were also GC members, such as Maurice Thompson, who was governor and John Wood. By Christmas 1657 it was decided that the GC would sell its charter to the EIC for £1300 (£288,627) per year. For their large East Indiamen ships sailing east stopping off at GC forts in West Africa for provisions made

---

Soon after he was appointed governor of Barbados.
227 Svalastog, (2018), p.151.
228 Scott, (1912), p.535.

logistical sense. Also, the gold traded there was a valuable commodity in Asia. There is no definitive answer as to why the EIC was reluctant to exploit the slave trade but it is telling that influential individuals within the company were private slave traders and may well have not wanted the EIC to muscle in on their lucrative business.

THE MORAL ECONOMY

It has been argued by some contemporary historians that the trade in enslaved people, though industrialised by the Crown and City of London, was not a practice created by the British ruling class. Their argument is characterised by a moral equivalence: African societies enslaved people and had bartered with traders from the north of the continent for generations, therefore it would be wrong to judge past behaviour with contemporary values. Simply put, if Africans were selling each other we cannot condemn non-Africans for wanting a piece of the action. Hugh Bicheno's vociferous ejaculation encapsulates this stance. He directs his anger at another historian for daring to entitle his 'prissy' book about John Hawkins, *Queen Elizabeth's Slave Trader*. If he had not engaged in people trafficking on 'moral grounds' Hawkins's existence would probably merit no more than a footnote, he argues. It was his buccaneering slave-trading, his sea-dog status, that has invested his existence with posterity. We cannot condemn him for that because

It should be borne in mind that the administration and the army of the Ottoman Empire was entirely manned by slaves, that all galley fleets including those of His Most Catholic Majesty the King of Spain, His Most Christian Majesty the King of France, and even those of His Holiness the Pope were rowed by slaves... The Muslim trade in African slaves began much earlier, ended much later, and involved far greater numbers than the transatlantic trade, which began (slowly) in 1502. Throughout the 16th and well into the seventeenth century Portuguese slave traders had a virtually unchallenged monopoly in the Atlantic.[229]

This stance of 'they are doing it, so I/we can' suggests no actions can be morally evaluated in binary terms, right or wrong. It also denies the socio-religious contract which underpinned most Christian societies:

229 Hugh Bicheno, (London, 2013), p.72.

the rule of law as guided by biblical precepts. Piracy was illegal, to steal another's property – as slaves were defined – is thus a crime and violates the tenth commandment, thou shalt not covet thy neighbour's goods.[230] On the Memorial to John Hawkins at St Dunstan in the East Church, City of London the inscription reads: 'One fearing God...'

Paradoxically, to get around the illegality and moral depravity of people stealing, traffickers evoked the Christian worth of their enterprise: we are taking people out of barbarism into a civilised God-fearing society. Yet, there is an absence of statements in the public domain where an enslaved or formerly enslaved person has celebrated their de-humanised condition as an improvement on their previous existence. Mary Prince in her autobiography argued

> I have been a slave myself – I know what slaves feel... The man that says slaves feel quite happy in slavery – that they don't want to be free – that man is either ignorant or a lying person. I have never heard a slave say so.[231]

This voice of this formerly enslaved woman was published in the nineteenth century. People of African heritage had shouted in condemnation for the previous three hundred years but their cries were muted – often forcibly – save a few, rare, heroic exceptions.

Their confidence in speaking out was boosted exponentially by the Somerset judgement of 1772 when Lord Chief Justice Mansfield ruled that sending enslaved out of England against their will was illegal. London's Black community, estimated by the *Gentleman's Magazine* in 1764 to be twenty-thousand, celebrated their joy. A few days after the court case, around a couple of hundred people, the majority of distinct African heritage, got together at a Westminster tavern and danced the night away. The joy was reignited six years later by judgement in the Knight v Wedderburn case in Edinburgh that slavery was not recognised in Scottish law. Tragically, the enslaved initiator of the hearing, Joseph Knight, died during the process so was not able to celebrate and benefit from his emancipation. Yet, a form of internecine justice did occur.

---

230 The bible is equivocal about slavery, as is Christianity itself. There is both condemnation and acceptance.

231 Mary Prince, *The History of Mary Prince, a West Indian Slave, as Related by Herself* (ed. Moira Ferguson) quoted in Dabydeen, Gilmore and Jones (2007) p.379.

Robert Wedderburn, the mixed-heritage son of the other party in the case – a Scottish doctor and absentee Jamaica plantation owner – became a renowned activist in the abolition movement. Robert's mother, Africaborn Rosanna, was enslaved; he, the progeny of his father's rape. His brother, James, was also conceived through violence. Robert devoted his adult life to abolition as a radical Methodist preacher and publisher. He was also an active member of the London-based Society of Spencean Philanthropists. His periodicals, *Forlorn Hope* and *Axe Laid to the Root* were megaphones of opposition to enslavement. He is discussed further below.

During the seventeenth century (and before), there were individuals and communities who rejected slavery outright. In England, more than a decade before the creation of the RA the Levellers and Diggers, protosocialist groups in the Civil War era, were having debates and issuing pamphlets proclaiming the equality of all humanity. An anonymous Leveller pamphlet of 1648 argued

for all men being a like priviledged by birth, so all men were to enjoy the creatures a like without proprietie one more than the other, all men by the grant of God are a like free, and every man individuall, that is to say, no man was to Lord or command over his own kinde: neither to enclose the creatures to his own use, to the impoverishing of his neighbours...[232]

The title page of this anonymous pamphlet reads *Light Shining in Buckinghamshire, or A Discovery of the main ground, original Cause of all the Slavery in the world, but cheifly in England: presented by way of a Declaration of many of the welaffected in that County, to all their poore oppessed Country men of England, &c.*[233] It states 'their principles to free all alike out of slavery'. It points the finger at kings and the institution of the monarchy for the cause of 'all the slavery in the world. Kings are the root of tyranny [and] slavery' yet, despite their claim to be divinely chosen by God, are they not mere mortals like the rest of us? In England did not William the Conquerer become king through murder? Drawing upon biblical imagery and precepts it asserts kings do the work of the Devil. Through their greed they take far more than they need from the societies in which

232 Quoted in George Sabine, ed., *The Works of Gerrard Winstanley* (New York,1965).
233 Ibid.

they live. They continuously propagate war to further increase their power and wealth. As such it is the duty of all to resist and 'to free all out of slavery [by] the removal of the Kingly power'.

A powerful and prescient revolutionary tract it demands freedom and the abolition of those people and institutions that stand in the way. 'For the People will no longer be enslaved by you, for the knowledge of the Lord shall enlighten them'. Here we find an unconscious but loud rebuttal of the practice of English planters in the Caribbean who refused to allow their enslaved labourers to learn to read and write in the fear that it would then lead them to know the bible and in so doing understand the hypocrisy of their masters. It is also a wonderfully humorous work that irreverently dissects the sycophantic hierarchy rulers depend upon.

What, will they creep in one anothers arses for honour? Why, oh, his Majesties breath of Honour it may be blows out There, and therefore he holds up his gown that it might blow him that holds it up, and makes him be called Sir.

Referencing the use of war to further kingly power and wealth, the manifesto exposes a common method of accumulating enslaved Africans whereby English traders would foment hostility between different tribal communities in order to buy captured prisoners. So prevalent was this practice that RAC records show an average of one hundred and fifty thousand firearms exchanged annually for humans.[234]

It recognises also the use of patents and monopoly power and the elevation of merchants and corporations as an instrument to galvanise the power of kings and divide people against each other.

All Charters, Pattents, and Corporations was devised onely to up-hold the Kings Tyranny, Greatnesse, and Interest; and because the people did rise in many parts for their Priviledges and Right; and he being in straights and knowing not how to uphold his tyranny, devised a way to set the people one against another, by making some Free,

234 Steven Napier 'The Royal African Company' in Leslie M. Alexander and Walter C Rucker (ed.) *Encyclopaedia of African-American History, Volume 1* (California, 2010) p.96. During the period 1681-1699 the RAC was involved in numerous conflicts both with resistant tribes and assisting one side against another. See Jose Rowell Tapac Corpuz *Essays on the Royal Africa Company and the Slave Trade*, Ph.D (2019), University of Warwick, p.116.

some Forreigners, &c. and so deviseth these Patents and Charters in all populous Cities and Towns throughout the Realm to uphold his Interest.

Political brothers of the Levellers, the Diggers led by Gerard Winstanley, William Everard and others argued land belonged to no-one and everyone. It should be held in common for the benefit of all. Wigan-born Winstanley, a former cloth merchant in the City of London, became disillusioned by his trade.

> For matter of buying and selling, the earth stinks with such unrighteousness, that for my part, though I as bred a tradesman, yet it is so hard a thing to pick out a poor living, that a man shall sooner be cheated of his bread, then get bread by trading among men, if by plain dealing he put trust in any.[235]

He instead advocated an early form of communism, taking a more radical position on religion than the Levellers. Diggers cultivated common land in Surrey, Northamptonshire, Kent and Buckinghamshire demanding the right to self-sustenance. Their simple but profound principle was that if you, as an able-bodied person, needed the forced labour of others to dig and plant the land you were cultivating, you had too much.

> And the truth is, experience shows us, that in this work of Community in the earth, and in the fruits of the earth, is seen plainly a pitched battle between the Lamb and the Dragon, between the Spirit of love, humility and righteousness... and the power of envy, pride, and unrighteousness... the latter power striving to hold the Creation under slavery, and to lock and hide the glory thereof from man: the former power labouring to deliver Creation from slavery, to unfold the secrets of it to the sons of man, and so to manifest himself to be the great restorer of all things.[236]

235 Gerard Winstanley *The Law of Righteousness* (1649) quoted in John Simkin, *Gerard Winstanley* (1997) https://spartacus-educational.com/STUwinstanley. htm Accessed 22 April 2020.
236 Gerard Winstanley letter to General Thomas Fairfax (June,1649) quoted in John Simkin (1997) https://spartacus-educational.com/STUwinstanley. htm accessed 22 April 2020.

The Levellers and the Diggers with their pleas for equality, internationalism and collective ownership, were brutally crushed by landlords, country gentry and merchant factions of the Parliamentary cause. Cromwell's New Model Army, under the command of Fairfax defeated, in May 1649, the Leveller soldiers who mutinied at Salisbury some days earlier.

By close of the following year, for daring to confront slavery and hierarchy both movements had been physically extinguished: killed, beaten, burned out and imprisoned.

Winstanley's vision of society had no place for hierarchy and exploitation.

> [He] hoped that the revolution in England would mark the beginning of a better state of affairs, in which true freedom would be made possible by the abolition of private property and wage labour and the establishment of an egalitarian communist society... He envisaged a reorganisation of society that would enable the poor to assert themselves as part of the nation. He... really tried to grapple with the problem of fitting the whole people to run a democracy... And by people he really did mean all the people.[237]

The democratic imagination of the Diggers and Levellers still inspires. Every summer – pandemics permitting – the Wigan Diggers Festival commemorates its famous son through song, poetry and art themed around Winstanley's socialist values; while the Putney debates and principled mutiny of the Levellers, consistently and universally foment discussion, debate, deliberation and action.[238]

Preacher Thomas Fuller, in his 1642 book *The Holy State*, complained of the brutality of throwing Negroes overboard when captured as prizes, asserting they too were God's children. Clerics Francis Brokesby and Morgan Godwyn protested the degradation of enslavement loudly in their writing and speeches as did Quakers George Fox and Thomas Tryon

---

237 Christopher Hill, 'The Poor and the People in Seventeenth Century England', in F. Krantz (ed.), *History from Below: Studies in Popular Protest and Popular Ideology*, (Oxford, 1988), pp.49-50 in Brian Manning, 'God, Hill and Marx', *International Socialism*, 59, Summer, 1993, p.93.

238 *The Last Stand of the Levellers* https://www.marxist.com/last-stand-of-the-levellers.htm Accessed 20 May 2020.

and Presbyterian Richard Baxter.[239] Spanish Capuchin friar Francisco Jose de Jaca, wrote about witnessing the suffering of Africans enslaved by his compatriots and transported to South America. As punishment for their crimes he advocated excommunication for the enslavers and freedom for the victims. He was supported by Frenchman, Epifano de Moirans, whom he met in Havana, who also penned a condemnation. Both, as a consequence, were imprisoned and had their freedoms curtailed.[240]

These brave seventeenth-century voices, angry at enslavement in all its forms and willing to put their life and liberty at risk in opposing, have echoed through the centuries. They call out the lazy and mistaken notion that such barbaric practice was morally acceptable or politically tolerable.

ABOLITION NARRATIVE

The conventional slave trade narrative has centre stage the abolition story peopled by heroic figures from Britain's aristocracy, gentry and artistic community: Wilberforce, Clarkson, Granville, Buxton, Cowper, Blake, Southey, Turner and others with a supporting cast of ex-slave activists and writers such as Mary Prince, Olaidah Equiano, Quobna Ottobah Cuguano, Ignatious Sancho and Albert Ukawsaw Gronniosaw. However, as Williams (1964) and Pettigrew (2013) argue, the overwhelming feeling and sentiment amongst the ruling class was persistently, doggedly and unreservedly in favour of the trade. Lord Nelson, the hero of Trafalgar whose towering statue in the central London square carrying his name keeps imperious watch upon Whitehall and Parliament, was vocally opposed to ending the trafficking of enslaved people.[241] The church bells of triangular trade

239 Peter Fryer (London, 1984), pp 146-150. Quaker Thomas Tryon lived in Barbados during the 1660s writing *Friendly Advice to the Gentleman-Planters of the East and West Indies* (London,1684).
240 Francisco Jose de Jaca *Resolución sobre la libertad de los negros y sus originarios, en estado de paganos y después ya cristianos* (1681) (*Resolution on the Freedom of Blacks and Their Origins, in the State of Paganos and Después ya Cristianos*); Epifano de Moirans *Servi liberi seu naturalis mancipiorum libertatis iusta defensio* (1682)(*A Just Defence of the Natural Freedom of Slaves: All Slaves Should be Free*).
241 His wife, Frances Herbert, was born into the West Indian colonial elite and owned enslaved people.

port Bristol rang out in celebration of the failure of Wilberforce's first abolition bill in 1789. Each year he re-presented the bill and each year it was defeated by a majority of Parliamentarians until 1807 when finally it was passed at the eighteenth attempt.

Not until 1823 did the British government actively pursue a policy of ameliorative reform of slavery by limiting the working day to nine hours, allowing Saturday as a day off and protecting captives from arbitrary punishment. These changes were met with fierce opposition by colonial planters which in turn ratcheted-up the ever growing and widening sentiment of rebellion and revolt amongst those who created their wealth.

The primary cause of the legal abolition of enslavement in 1834 in most of the British Empire was not because of a moral awakening by the ruling class as to its horrors or an overwhelming preference amongst our legislators for 'free' trade that included an unrestricted labour market. Millions of people subject to colonial rule in India (including Pakistan and Bangladesh), Ceylon (Sri Lanka) and St Helena were not included. It ended, fundamentally, because of resistance, rebellion and revolt from the enslaved themselves across the Caribbean and Americas. Foremost in these uprisings was the Haitian revolution and the declaration of a republic by self-liberated ex-slaves who defeated successive French and British armed forces sent to bludgeon them back to captivity. This created seismic political waves that engendered fear, alarm and nervousness amongst the ruling classes of the Caribbean and metropolitan Europe in the first decade of the nineteenth century.

This perspective of emancipation as propelled primarily by the un-emancipated does recognise the value and impact of the abolition movement and the activism of its participants. Williams acknowledges their contribution:

> The British humanitarians were a brilliant band. Clarkson personifies the best in the humanitarianism of the age… Clarkson was one of those friends of whom the Negro race has had unfortunately only too few.[242]

However, it places front and centre those dynamic and powerful agents of progressive change, the enslaved, as spearheading their own liberation.

242 Eric Williams (1964), p.179.

Chapter Seven
Building and Breaking Up.

Edward's written and oral legacy provides no clue or explanation as to why his father chose to settle in Folkestone. Neither does Daniel's *Journal*. However, a *Folkestone Herald* obituary of his brother Walter, published 20 April, 1918, names one of the town's former coastguards, Richard Tiddy, as someone who assisted Daniel in settling and finding work. Born in Cornwall in 1810, Tiddy is reputed to have sailed as crew to Barbados after the 1833 Abolition Act to spread news of emancipation.

> I have heard several times the late Richard Tiddy tell with pride how he was one who accompanied the captain who carried the good news to the West Indian slaves, and with what joy they received the news that England had paid their ransom and that they were no longer slaves but free men. The scene said he was indescribable... Daniel, father of Lieutenant Tull, came to this country, being anxious to improve his position and came in touch with our old friend Richard, who, with another townsman, W.L. Martin, showed him great kindness. He worked for some years for the late John Holden, J.P., who took a keen interest in him, and for years was a member of the Grace Hill Church and Choir.[243]

Councillor Kingsmill uses the word 'ransom' when referring to the compensation paid to enslavers. Is it indicative of a perspective that recognises the perverted morality of planters and merchants demanding payment to free their captives?

It is clear from Kingsmill that Daniel soon found friends in Folkestone who helped him settle and find work. Surviving records of the Elham (Poor Law) Union and Grace Hill Methodist Chapel provide evidence of Holden's paternal influence. A prominent local politician, twice mayor of Folkestone, a worshipper at Grace Hill, he figures consistently in Daniel's orbit where participation in church and choir was the focal point of his social life; where friendships and relationships were made and developed. Edward's father benefitted from Holden's 'keen interest'.

---

243 Written by Councillor J. Kingsmill.

The latter and his family had been principal financial contributors to the building of the church during the eighteen sixties and were preeminent in the Methodist community and Folkestone civic institutions, such as Elham Union and local government.[244]

Tiddy died on the last day of January, 1896 and was commemorated with an obituary in the *Folkestone Herald*. The participation of one of the town's 'oldest and most respected inhabitants' in proclaiming emancipation featured as a core marker of his life.

Within the last few days death has robbed Folkestone of... Mr Richard Tiddy who... attained the ripe age of 85 years... His whole life has been full of incident. He had served under three monarchies, was connected with the navy in the time of the old mail packets, carried the Emancipation Bill to the West Indies, assisted in freeing five islands from slavery and made what was at the time the quickest voyage on record. He served two and a half years active service in the Crimean War and his bravery for saving life has been acknowledged on more than one occasion. The passing of this good old salt will be lamented by a large circle of relatives and friends by whom he was much loved and profoundly respected.[245]

Daniel may have been one of those friends saying their last goodbye at the graveside.

Not only did he manage to earn a living at his chosen trade, an achievement in itself for a Black migrant in late nineteenth century Britain, he also found love with Alice Elizabeth Palmer, a country lass from a family of Kent agricultural labourers. It is possible they met at Grace Hill. With no Moravian church in the town, the Methodists would have been an acceptable non-conformist alternative. They had been active in Barbados amongst people of colour with J.R.F. Tull becoming a Methodist pastor.

After four years in the thriving coastal resort and port, Daniel married

244 Elham Union Minute Book, G/EL/AM 22; Grace Hill Church Poor Stewards Cash Account Folkestone 1870, M13/6/2/8; quarterly membership ticket of John Holden for Wesleyan Methodist Church, Grace Hill, Folkestone, September 1897, M13/6/7/2. Kent History and Library Centre, Maidstone.
245 'Felix', 'About the Neighbourhood', *Folkestone Herald*, 8 February 1896. Many thanks to Lynne Ewart for providing this obituary.

Alice 25 February, 1880, at Grace Hill Chapel. He was living at 14 Darby Road. 'A tender plant',[246] his wife resided at 18 Ford Road. She was born at Elms Farm, Hougham, near Dover in 1853, the only daughter of Sarah-Ann (née Taylor) and farm labourer Stephen Palmer. It was a courageous act for both lovers.

MISCEGENATION

White women marrying men of colour was unusual but not unknown in Kent during the eighteen eighties. Indeed, another mixed heritage family of African Caribbean and White descent were living in Sheerness. Thomas Brown, a Guyana-born son of a freed slave and petty officer in the Royal Navy married Elizabeth Rump, a laundress. They had three children. In a remarkable parallel to Edward's fate, their two daughters and son were orphaned and in 1883 the latter, Donald, was placed alone in Greenwich Royal Hospital School. Refused entry into the Royal Navy he became a merchant seaman, eventually marrying suffragette Eliza Adelaide Knight and taking her name. An active trade unionist, working at Woolwich Arsenal he was awarded both the Edward Medal and the Carnegie Hero Fund Medal for a 'Deed of Sterling Bravery' in preventing a serious explosion and loss of life by single-handedly dragging out of the depot a batch of exploding ordnance.[247]

What would have been unknown is for these inter-ethnic couples to be able enjoy their togetherness in anonymous tranquility. The Reverend Duncan Finlayson, who married Edward's daughter Jean, recalled an incident on their honeymoon. Nearing the breakfast room on the first morning of their honeymoon at Bridge of Orchy hotel they heard an anonymous diner telling his companions in a loud, emphatic voice that, on hearing the news that a friend had married a 'nigger', promised there would be 'no tar in his family'. On entering the dining room Duncan, an ex-boxer, wanted to silence the him with his knuckles but was persuaded

---

246 Sarah-Ann Palmer to Daniel, Monday 26th [month unclear] 1880, Finlayson Family Archive. The 26th fell on a Monday in January, April and July in 1880.

247 Beverly Burford and Julian Watson, *Celebrating Black and Asian History in Greenwich*, (London's Museums, Archives and Libraries, undated), pp.9-12. Eliza was a founder member of the Communist Party in Britain. Her daughter Winifred Langton, 1909-2003, a lifelong member of the CP, wrote her family's biography *Courage*, published 2007.

otherwise by his resilient, thicker-skinned wife.

In Barbados a relationship of love between a female of European origin and an enslaved man of African descent would have been unseen in public. A male captive of colour could open himself to instant punishment, including death, merely touching, inadvertently, a White woman's skin. After emancipation apartheid, previously configured through the slave code, was refuelled through a doubling down of moral surveillance. One of the rules for apprentices and employees on the Drax Hall estate forbade inter-ethnic relationships: 'any white woman who cohabits with a color'd Man, now so common' would be exiled.[248] William Sewell, visiting in the eighteen fifties, remarked upon inter-ethnic relationships but with the assumption that what he was referring to was, without fail, a relationship of White, patriarchal power.

The amalgamation of the two races is nevertheless very general, and illicit intercourse is sanctioned, or at least winked at, by a society which utterly condemns and abhors a marriage between two people of different color. There are cases, it is true, where white people have intermarried with mulattoes, but they are rare, and I know of none where the white is a born Barbadian. A white man who marries a half-caste is nearly always an Englishman, who comes to the West Indies with little or no prejudice against the race, and is ignorant of the unanimous feeling that on this subject, secretly pervades the whole of Barbadian society.[249]

While tolerance illuminated the reception Daniel encountered from his working class mother-in-law and her family this was in contrast to the wider cultural environment which was increasingly prim, fearful and intolerant in attitudes towards sexuality and miscegenation.

Sex is at the very heart of racism. Racism is not simply caused by sexual apprehensions, and there are many other factors involved... but the

---

248 Melanie Newton, 'The Children of Africa in the Colonies': Free People of Colour in Barbados During the Emancipation Era, 1816-1854, Ph.D dissertation, University of Oxford, 2001, p.187.
249 William G. Sewell, The Ordeal of Free Labour in the British West Indies, (London, 1861), pp. 67-68 quoted in Melanie Newton, 'The Children of Africa in the Colonies': Free People of Colour in Barbados During the Emancipation Era, 1816-1854, p.189 footnote 28.

peculiarly emotional hostility towards black men which it has so often engendered requires a sexual explanation. From New Orleans to New Guinea, from Barbados to Bulowayo, from Kimberley to Kuala Lumpur, the quintessential taboo to be explained is the white man's formal objection to intimacy between black men and white women.[250]

This social mood, percolating downwards, was inextricably linked to the zenith of the British ruling class's imperial project. Through an ideology that proclaimed a hierarchy of 'races', the violent accumulation of territory and depravities of colonisation were justified with the moral defence of the civilising mission.

Daniel's colour, therefore, represented negative equity in an economic system constructed around the notion of racial difference. Yet, the cultural capital he had managed to acquire through his training as a carpenter, his literacy and his non-conformist belief, signified upward social mobility for Alice in the eyes of her proletarian family.

WORKING CLASS METHODISM AND TOLERANCE

His status would also have been enhanced in their eyes through his role of Visitor on behalf of Grace Hill Chapel's Wesleyan Benefit Society. Established in 1879 its function was to respond to pleas for financial help from members of the congregation suffering hardship. Applicants would be called upon at home by Visitors who had the authority to provide immediate relief of up to one shilling. Additional support would require the agreement of the superintendent of the society. The overseeing group, the Wesleyan Home Mission Committee, comprised three members of the Holden family, including Daniel's sometime employer, John. At a meeting of the committee and Visitors, 27 January, 1880 a number of candidates for help were discussed. 'Mr Dunscombe and Mr Tull spoke to these being deserving cases [and] have particulars of their visits to them'.[251]

Visitors were appointed by the committee. John Holden employed Daniel and knew him socially and spiritually as a member of the church.

250 Ronald Hyman, *Empire and Sexuality. The British Experience*, (Manchester, 1991) p.203.
251 Wesleyan Home Mission Committee and Wesleyan Benefit Society, Folkestone, Tuesday 27 January, 1880, M13/6/1/16, Kent History and Library Centre, Maidstone.

He, seemingly, had no qualms in entrusting the carpenter with a position of responsibility which involved disbursing church funds. From Daniel's perspective, visiting poor Whites and having the power to financially assist and improve their situations would have been a new experience and unique cultural phenomenon.

The Palmers loving acceptance of Alice and Daniel's relationship is evidenced with the words of Sarah-Ann Palmer to her prospective son-in-law after he asked to marry Alice. Writing an affectionate, thoughtful commentary on the meaning of marriage, throughout she refers to him as 'Dan; dearest child; my intended son'. It is a refreshingly open-minded welcome note from the Palmer family, with an absence of contemporary stereotypes and prejudices. It speaks of an alternative, egalitarian vision of the world where acceptance and rejection of people and persons is premised upon the quality of their behaviour.

> You have asked me for my only daughter… there are two things I must beg of you and the first is of the most importance that you will be kind to her for she is a tender plant… the other is that you will never take her out of England whilst I am alive. Do not think Dan in raising these two things that I doubt your love for her on that point I am perfectly satisfied your actions have shown that and your respect for the family… sharing in one another's joys and sorrows you will find the path at times very rough and uneven but you must bear with one another's weaknesses and try and help one another… kindest and best love to your dear self… dearest child.[252]

Over sixty years after it was written, its love, tolerance and humanity was recalled by Edward's sister, Cecilia, writing to the Reverend Duncan Finlayson.

> Some day Duncan I will let you read a letter from my mother's mother when my dad was asking for her in marriage. It is a beautiful letter from a mother to her future son-in-law and I wonder how many have been written like that. Grandma must have been a good woman and hereditary does count.[253]

---

252 Sarah-Ann Palmer to Daniel, Monday 26 January 1880, Finlayson Family Archive.
253 Cecilia Tull to Reverend Duncan Finlayson, 14 September 1942, Finlayson Family Archive.

Alice and Daniel's marital home in the 1881 Census was 8 Garden Street, Hythe, Folkestone. Bertha, their first child, born 9 February that year tragically survived only five weeks. Though devastating, her death was not an unusual occurrence in working-class communities. Infant mortality rates were much higher than present and parents harboured inherited fear, expectation even, of premature loss.[254] The birth of William Stephen Palmer, 7 April 1882 – named after each grandparent – was, therefore, celebrated with great joy by the Tulls, including those in Barbados. In her letter of 25 March 1883, Anna writes: 'We are very glad to hear that your wife has had a safe delivery with a son you must give him a dozen kisses from us'.

Surviving letters written to Daniel by his mother and future mother-in-law suggest he was surrounded by loving families. Neither the Kent Palmers nor Bajan Tulls were prosperous. The wages of Alice's brothers, agricultural labourers William and Robert, is recorded in 1898 as fourteen shillings per week, one shilling and a halfpenny under the UK average.[255] Yet what they lacked in material resources, the Palmers more than made up in love and support.

His mother's letters suggest Daniel was also aware of his responsibility as an economic migrant to his family in Barbados. In 1878 she replies to her son: 'Most humble thanks for your gift... it was very acceptable I do assure you. . . our little hut wanted great repairs, so it came in grand.' She also thanks him for a photo portrait of himself he included while also explaining that four shillings of the pound (of twenty shillings, £120) he sent had to pay for the excess weight of his letter (which seems a punishingly high charge to pay for inadequate postage). Her letter five years later, 25 March 1883, suggests her son was still mindful of those he had left behind. She gratefully appreciates the ten shillings (£62) he has sent, which was much needed 'in the time of their adversity'. He also

---

254 1880 infant mortality rate in England and Wales was approximately 150 per 1,000 live births, OU Open Learn: https://www.open.edu/openlearn/ocw/mod/oucontentview.phpid=28151&section=2.2. Accessed 29 June 2020. 2020 UK rate is 4.13, http://www.geoba.se/country.php?cc=GB&-year=2020 Accessed 29 June 2020.

255 Stated in the *Form of Application for the Admission of a Child*, 8 January 1898, that formalised Edward's entry into Reverend Dr Stephenson's *Children's Home and Orphanage*, Bethnal Green, London. Finlayson Family Archive. For wage rates of agricultural labourers 1850-1914: http://www.geoba.se/country.php?cc=GB&year=2020 Accessed 29 June 2020.

sent her over a piece of his wedding cake. 'I assure it was amazing and also strange to think that it would have last so long', she wrote. While undertaking new obligations as husband and father, he did not forget his obligation as a son. Edward's recollection of his childhood in Folkestone foregrounds the chapel and the Methodist community.

[My] family found its whole life centred in its Church and being a happy family there was no need for compulsion to attend church services or to take part in the Church's activities. The children had their Sunday School and the parents their Church and for them the Sunday was _the_ day of the week.[256]

As well as the Sunday School the church also ran the Folkestone Wesleyan School for infant and primary pupils. Part of the state sector providing compulsory education on weekdays, it was intermittently criticised by government inspectors for the poor quality of both buildings and instruction.[257] It had no playground, maybe an additional reason why Daniel and Alice chose not to enrol Edward and his siblings. However, during the academic year 1893-4 they did train their Standard IV pupils to recite Henry Longfellow's 'The Slave's Dream', which begins

Beside the ungathered rice he lay,
　His sickle in his hand;
His breast was bare, his matted hair
　Was buried in the sand.
Again, in the mist and shadow of sleep,
　He saw his Native Land.
Wide through the landscape of his dreams
　The lordly Niger flowed;
Beneath the palm-trees on the plain
　Once more a king he strode;

Its theme of a stolen West African captive reimagining their free condition back home suggests that what the school lacked in physical resources was compensated somewhat by the quality of texts studied.

256 Edward Tull, _The Film that Will Never Be Screened_, Finlayson Family Archive.
257 Folkestone Wesleyan School, September 1893-February 1909, M13/6/5/4.

The emotional, psychological and physical support provided by the Methodist community and their extended families would be much needed in the relatively short but fertile marriage of Daniel and Alice. Between February 1881 and November 1891, they produced six children, a pregnancy period for Alice of fifty-four months. After Bertha and William, Cecilia Sarah Ann was born, 14 March 1884, Edward James Alexander, 28 June 1886, Walter Daniel John, 28 April 1888 and Elsie Alice Elizabeth on 7 November 1891. It was a strenuous decade for the 'tender plant 'culminating in the death of her mother a few months before Elsie's birth. The 1891 Census lists the Tulls at 51 Walton Road, a small terraced house in a working-class neighbourhood.[258] They had moved there sometime after Walter's birth at 16 Allendale Street.

The three addresses traceable to Daniel and Alice are in the Hythe district of Folkestone and very close to one another, all connecting to Black Bull Road. Moving to different residencies in the same neighbourhood was common practice. Failure to pay rent through unemployment, the need for more bedrooms after birth and cheaper rent were common reasons for loading up the handcart and pitching up five minutes away.

The arrival of the South Eastern Railway in 1843, using the port as its railhead for boat services to France, revived the ancient town in such spectacular fashion that by the end of the century the population had grown by a factor of ten to forty-thousand. With fast trains to and from London, it reinvented itself as a fashionable resort.

The speed of this expansion is even more remarkable when considered alongside the population growth from the Domesday Book figure of six-hundred in 1086. In the seven hundred and fifty-seven years to 1843 it rose only by a factor of seven. 'On Bank Holidays,' observed *Blackwood's Edinburgh Magazine*, 'it is swamped in excursionists.' The discrete monthly journal also noted extreme differences in the physical qualities of a disproportionate number of its residents, there being large numbers of elderly and soldiers. The former coming for the sea air and the vivifying ingredients of its spring water; the latter stationed at Dover, Hythe and Shorncliffe barracks. There was also a military hospital at Sandgate. 'On the seafront, amid the khaki and the bathchairs', continued *Blackwood's*, 'there are German bands but

---

258 N.A., London, 1891 Census, Folkestone north, column 1, schedule 50. Living in the street nearby were a harness maker, three general labourers and two gardeners.

few nigger melodists in gaudy raiment' implying in its default superior manner Folkestone was not downmarket enough for showy Blacks to earn a living from entertaining the promenaders. It is not like Margate, Ramsgate or Hastings, it continued, but superior to them all.[259]

A less elitist, local view is presented in the *Folkestone, Sandgate and Hythe Pictorial* of 1890 which talked of a variety of entertainment on offer, from military bands that 'discourse sweet music to itinerant companies of minstrels and harmonious brothers' that perform at the Exhibition Building and Pier Pavilion. Folkestone of the eighteen nineties was growing, attractive to outsiders, relatively prosperous and a gateway to the continent. It was a place where Edward would, almost certainly, have seen other people of colour outside his family. In the 25 March letter from his brother in Barbados, Samuel identifies a Bajan whom Daniel had met in Folkestone.

> The gentleman whom you were in conversation with from Barbados to the railway station as you mentioned in your letter Mr Jones his name is, his business is well known by the caracter [sic] of J. B. Barrow & Co., Roebuck St, Bridgetown. He is my employer a very good gentleman I believe he would have done you any favour withy [sic] perfection.

Favour in this context implies he could be trusted to deliver letters, presents, documents, etc., between the UK and Barbados. JB and JH Barrow had been trading from 138 Roebuck Street since at least April, 1848. Mr Jones may well have been an expatriate White Briton with business interests in Barbados, rather than an African-Caribbean with whom Daniel could share common cultural experiences. However, the latter did meet him in the UK, and by chance.

Samuel concludes by sending 'love' [from] 'James and Girdy... to their little cousin'. The latter is most probably Marian Gertrude, born at Station House, Bridgetown, 8 February, 1882. He also had an eponymous son, Samuel James, who was buried 6 October, 1874, aged four months but no record as been found of another son with the forename James.[260]

---

259 *Blackwood's Edinburgh Magazine*, no. 943 (May 1894), vol. 155, pp. 660-73.
260 Samuel James and Elvira Tull (nee Nurse) had, possibly, seven children. As well as Marion Gertrude and Samuel James, there was: Edward Nathaniel,

However, a James Thomas Daniel Tull was born on 16 September, 1880 to an Elizabeth Tull.[261] It is not known if there is a family relationship.

Living at 51 Walton Road, Folkestone, the Tull children attended the North Board School – now Mundella Primary School – Black Bull Road. At the top of their street, the playground and classrooms visible from their front windows, it was near enough to troop home for dinner before returning in the afternoon for more of the characteristic practice of education for working-class Victorian children: monitor-supervised rote instruction.

Daniel seems to have been in constant employment. This conclusion is supported by his remittances back to Barbados alongside information given in an application form to the Children's Home and Orphanage (CHO) stating Daniel worked for a Mr R. Webster, 6 Claremont Road, once his employment with Justice of the Peace Holden and his son had terminated. Family tradition has it that Daniel's carpentry skills were contracted also by Liberal MP and campaigner for safer ships, Samuel Plimsol, who retired to Folkestone in 1892. He is best remembered for his invention of a line around the outside of ships, its submersion indicating overload.[262]

This consistent income gave him the financial means to rent houses and pay rates, qualifying him to vote in General Elections under the 1884 Representation of the People Act. Those men without purchase upon some form of evaluated property were denied the right to choose who should govern them. Daniel was part of an enfranchised minority. Just over a quarter of adults were eligible to vote and women not at all. It was a political status denied his parents. Yet, of the five elections in which Daniel was eligible to vote, the parliamentary candidate was returned unopposed three times.

---

baptised 28 April, 1878; David Emmanuel, born December, 1880; George Irving, born 1st June, 1886; Daniel, baptised 11 December 1887; Donald St Clair, born 22 November, 1890.

261 Barbados Baptisms, 1739-1891, https://www.familysearch.org/tree/person/details/KL8J-8ZP accessed 5 November, 2020.

262 Thanks to Edward's granddaughter Pat Justad for the oral history about Daniel and Samuel Plimsoll. For further information on Plimsoll's tireless campaigning to make ships safer for seamen see: https://spartacus-educational.com/TUplimsoll.htm and https://www.brh.org.uk/site/2020/07/hero-samuel-plimsoll/ Both accessed 25 November 2020.

Sometime in the autumn of 1893, Alice was diagnosed with breast cancer and the brightness of 51 Walton Road suddenly, unexpectedly, dimmed. Her treatment over the next seventeen months at best slowed her painful decline. During this period Grace Hill Chapel made payments to Daniel of £1 (£131) on 2 October 1894, the same amount six weeks later with a further ten shillings in the Spring of the following year.[263] The record does not show the reason for the payments but it would be possible that they were to meet medical expenses – doctors bills and drugs to ease Alice's pain – while also helping Daniel meet household costs if caring for his wife was preventing him working. It was an example of the conscious commitment of the Methodist faith community to welfare outside the spiritual domain and became a more regular feature in the lives of the Tulls. The darkening shadow shrouded completely the family, Easter Sunday, 14 April 1895.

The only photograph that exists of Daniel with his children was very probably captured on the day Alice was buried. All are wearing mourning black except his youngest daughter Elsie, resplendent in a white dress and hat, sitting on her father's knee. Daniel and eldest son William are both suited and wearing bowler hats. Second daughter Cecilia is dressed in a ribboned hat, caped coat and fashionable boots. The hats of Edward and Walter are flat and their white collars outside their suits. The four eldest children looked as though they have something in the side of their mouths, a soothing sweet – maybe a favourite of children of the day, a gobstopper? In the background is what could be a bird cage. Quite likely taken in the back yard of Walton Road, it shows a 'respectable' working class family able to afford 'Sunday best' clothing and footwear. It also exhibits a desire on Daniel's part to provide for his children what most Barbadian youngsters growing up in the eighteen-sixties were denied: clothes that allowed a sense of pride in appearance. For hundreds of years sartorial choice had been denied his ancestors, a recognition of which Daniel was no doubt aware, in contrast to the educated writers of *Blackwood's Magazine* who were reassured by the absence of 'nigger[s]... in gaudy raiment'.

Alice dictated her last wishes to Daniel who recorded them in his Journal. Elsie was to have her 'rings and keeper'. Cissie would inherit 'her

263 Poor Stewards Cash Account, Folkestone, M13/6/2/8, Kent Archive and History Centre.

grandmother's ring and silver thimble and keeper. The babies clothes to be equally divided amongst the two girls'. Her first thought for her 'cloak and bonnet was to leave it to 'Miss/Mrs (?) Palmer' (her niece/sister in law?). However, this is crossed out and replaced with unclear script. It could be the coat and hat that Cissie is wearing. On the assumption that by making the equivalent of a will just over two months prior to her passing, Alice was aware her cancer was terminal and that discussions were current within the extended family about a maternal replacement, is it possible that it was her desire for them to be passed on to the future Mrs Tull?[264]

Mourning his wife of fourteen years and responsible for five children under fourteen, Daniel's in-laws offered help. The niece of Alice, twenty-six-year-old Clara Alice Susanna Palmer, daughter of her brother William and wife Sarah, married Daniel at the Grace Hill Chapel on 17 October 1896, 'largely to mother the children'.[265] Like her Aunt Alice, Clara was born at Elms Farm, Hougham, Dover. Imposing such an all-embracing familial obligation while practical, given her single status, and socially acceptable, given the norms and values of the period, was nonetheless burdensome. On marriage this young, unworldly woman became stepmother to five children. Yet, it also reaffirms the close ties that existed between the Tull and Palmer families. The birth of Miriam Victoria, 11 October 1897, while providing a physical refutation to the inference that the union of Daniel and Clara was wholly one of practical convenience, the additional responsibility of an extra mouth to feed if it did not cause worry at the time, certainly did just two months later.

While the gradual withering of Alice had been tortuous for both families, the death of Daniel from heart disease, 10 December 1897, so soon after the birth of his fourth daughter, must have been crushing for his children and Clara. His death certificate, signed off by J. Murray LRCP, records the cause as 'disease of the aortic valve 3 years syncope'.[266] This illness produces dizziness and fainting and today would be dealt with by valve replacement surgery. If Daniel's condition had been known for three years this raises the possibility that Clara was

264 *Journal*, Saturday 2 February, 1895.
265 *Form of Application for the Admission of a Child* to *The Children's Home and Orphanage*, Walter Tull, 8 January 1898, Finlayson Family Archive.
266 *Certified Copy of an Entry of Death*, HC 318811, 3 November 1995, the original issued in the Registration District of Elham, Folkestone, Kent, 11 December 1897.

aware before she married him. It was a debilitation of which Alice may also have been cognisant. If so, it reaffirms the selfless nature of his second wife's commitment.

Thrust into the all-consuming role of single-parent, stepmother of five and parent of a baby daughter, though just over a decade older than stepson William, Clara was now head of a family of six. As brown-skinned Others the loss of their caring and protective shield must also have left the children feeling incredibly vulnerable, physically and emotionally.

Below Alice's last wishes in his Journal the author entered his, 11 November, one month before his death. Willie was to inherit his tools

unless one of the other boys are carpenters then they shall be equally divided between them & that the things in the house be sold & equally divided among the children. The effects of my first wife to [sic] and my Lodge be sold the silver and plates and rings to go to the girls all these things to be sold such as furniture and Lodge accept [sic] Willie can arrange to keep a home together for all of them in any case Bill [Beer] is not to neglect the two girls especially Elsie.

Requesting the Lodge to be sold, it is unclear to what Daniel is referring. Another general term for the contents of 51 Walton Road? In Clara's application to the CHO she explicitly states the rental amount, clearly indicating Daniel did not own their terraced house. Was it his carpentry workshop?

His final instructions reveal a father and husband vitally concerned about the future situation of his family once his is no longer alive. He both acknowledges the identity of his wife's next partner and supports the extended family's efforts to do what is necessary to try to keep them together. By naming his wife's next husband, Bill (Beer), it suggests family discussions were current over the future welfare of Clara and children.

Daniel had paid into a life insurance policy with the Prudential Assurance Company from which his widow received £16 (£2,095), most of which, presumably, was spent on medical and funeral expenses.[267] It was a relatively large sum of money, equivalent to six months wages for an agricultural labourer like Clara's father William, the uncle of

267 *Form of Application for the Admission of a Child* to *The Children's Home and Orphanage*, Walter Tull, 8 January 1898, Finlayson Family Archive.

her stepchildren and grandfather to Miriam. It would be reassuring to think Clara did have some cash under her mattress for emergencies. In such a desperate and difficult situation – poor, female, young, five dependents – it would have made rational economic sense to be cagey about financial circumstances. The day after his death, she was awarded £1 *G.A.* (general assistance?) by Grace Hill, bringing the total amount paid to the family over the previous three years to £3.10s (£458).

The ability of the extended Palmer families to assist further was spent: they had neither financial nor physical resources spare to offer. Getting by on farm labourers' wages meant poverty was always a foreboding vista on the horizon. William, fifteen years old, earning seven shillings a week as an apprentice carpenter, was the only member of the Tull family employed. The rent at Walton Road was six shillings a week. This did not allow 'Willie to keep a home together for all of them' as Daniel had wishfully conjectured. In the absence of a widow's pension, Clara had no option but to beg for parish relief from the Poor Law Guardians of the Elham Union, a recourse usually taken only in the most desperate of situations. Turning to the taxpayers of her community for money to live would entail a demeaning scrutiny of person and home by local worthies ultra-sensitive to their obligation of keeping to a minimum the rate burden upon their fellow members of the propertied class.

Inspecting applicants in the misery and discomfort of their home, the guardians would distinguish those exhibiting characteristics of the 'deserving poor' – God-fearing, teetotal, law-abiding and obedient – from 'undeserving poor' – non-church going, criminal, anti-authority, free-thinking and class conscious. If categorised as the latter and marked for indoor relief, families would be fragmented and scattered to the dreaded Workhouse a harsh, regimented, emotionally cruel institution, sub-divided by gender and generation.

In light of their attendance at chapel and Daniel's active involvement in the wider Methodist community as Visitor and choir member, alongside his proud record of consistent provision, the Tulls were considered 'deserving' and granted outdoor relief of five shillings ten pence per week. It helped, no doubt, that John Holden was chairman of Guardians of Elham Union with councillor Kingsmill also a member.[268] Though a meagre sum, for the time being it meant they could continue living as a family at Walton Road. The donation from parish funds

268 Elham Union Minute Book, 3 March, 1898, p.250. G/EL/AM 22. Kent History and Library Centre.

contributed toward a total weekly income of twelve shillings and ten pence. However, after rent, six shillings and ten pence was left for food, fuel and clothing for seven, one of whom was baby Miriam. Unsurprisingly, the figures did not add up and the family could not make ends meet. Despairing, Clara sought help from her last remaining port of call, the Methodist community. The resident minister of Grace Hill, the Reverend George Adcock, took pastoral control of Clara's plight and recommended Edward and his younger brother Walter to the CHO, personally sponsoring their application.

The Grace Hill Chapel had a financial and spiritual connection with the orphanage – motto, 'seek and to save that which is lost' – in Bonner Road, Bethnal Green, London. It raised money on behalf of Folkestone Methodist Circuit in support of the missionary activities of principal Reverend Dr Thomas Bowman Stephenson among London's young poor and homeless. Born at Newcastle-upon-Tyne in 1839, he had been motivated to work among destitute children by his experience as a young Methodist minister in Manchester and Bolton during the Lancashire cotton famine of 1861-65. Inside the mills, children laboured in brutal, de-humanising conditions that disfigured their minds and bodies. On the streets and in hovels pretending to be homes he saw hunger, starvation and malnutrition.[269]

Appointed in 1868 as minister to Waterloo Chapel, Lambeth, in London, he witnessed further child deprivation, most notably abject poverty, parental absence and homelessness:

Shoeless, filthy, their faces pinched with hunger and premature wretchedness, and I began to feel that now my time was come. Here were my poor little brothers and sisters, sold to hunger and the devil, and I could not be free of their blood if I did not do something to save some of them.[270]

The increasing demand by Capital for below subsistence-cost labour and an acute shortage of housing affordable are not economic and social phenomena unique to our century. However, their Victorian

269 For description of the horrendous living conditions of the Manchester proletariat see Friedrich Engels, *The Condition of the Working Class in England in 1844*, (London, 1892 edition).
270 NCH/Action for Children online history: https://www.theirhistory. co.uk/70001/info.php?p=13&pno=0 Accessed 22 October 2020.

manifestation was coupled with an absence of state support for poor families and mothers. These systemic processes that did much to create a growing underclass of homeless children.

Despite the Tull's Methodism and Folkestone Methodist Circuit's voluntary contribution to CHO funds, entry for the boys would not be a simple formality. The orphanage was consistently full.

> We receive children of all creeds and none. We deal with babies of a few days and with young men and women passing out of their teens. We are continually appealed to by Boards of Guardians, the Society for the Prevention of Cruelty to Children, the Reformatory and Refuge Union, the Ragged School Union, the Royal Patriotic Fund, and other Societies for dealing with soldiers' orphans; by ministers of all denominations, by police court, city and town missionaries, deaconesses, parish visitors, rescue workers, and by all sorts of social and philanthropic organisations.[271]

The older Tull girls, Cecilia and Elsie, argued Adcock, could stay in Folkestone and help Clara with baby Miriam and other domestic responsibilities; while William was essential as the sole breadwinner. Initially, Elsie was due to go with Edward and Walter until a rethinking of options envisaged Cecilia going into service and Elsie becoming Clara's main help.

Adcock knew Stephenson personally and was not shy of reminding him, when advocating the boys' case, of the financial assistance Folkestone Methodists had consistently provided the CHO. In an exchange of letters, Adcock emphasised the need of the seven-member Tull family for outside help is 'more urgent that I've already described.' He also pointed out Grace Hill Chapel is helping with funds for 'rent for the present [and] a mangle' so Clara could take in washing to supplement the family's meagre income.[272] Under 'special circumstances in the Form of Application', Adcock explained:

> His first wife's protracted illness (cancer) exhausted his little earnings.

---

271 'The Story of Forty Years, 1869–1909, for the Children of Sorrow' *Highways and Hedges,* July and August, 1909, p. 104.
272 Tull file *Epitome of Correspondence* (hereafter *Epitome*). Letters between Adcock and Stephenson, January–February 1898. Action for Children Archive, Watford, Hertfordshire.

Step-parent mother was related to the first wife & married largely to mother the children. She has had a hard struggle to meet... disbursements occasioned by first wife's long illness. She is far from strong but if relieved of two children. . . she might with help keep a home for the remaining four children – three of which not being her own.[273]

Edward is described as being 'honest, truthful, good natured and obedient' and in 'very good' health. (Though maybe this state of physical wellbeing was not always so. One Tull boy, possibly Edward, is reported in May, 1894 to 'have lately returned after a long illness'.)[274] The North Board School provided a report on his academic progress: in July, 1897, aged eleven, he had been examined in standard four and was subsequently taught to standard five.[275] (An 1861 government commissioned report into implementing a system 'of cheap and elementary instruction' for working-class children in England suggested a payment-by-results structure.[276] Elementary schools were subsequently arranged with a regime that concentrated on teaching literacy and maths. Pupils were examined in Standards I to VI, approximating ages seven to twelve.)

This statement of Edward's achievements in relation to national requirements are significant in helping to understand his emotional durability. Despite the protracted illness and death of his mother, the remarriage of his father, a young stepmother replacing his biological parent and the birth of Miriam, his development was still meeting expected levels.

273 *Form of Application* , section 13, Action for Children Archive.

274 *Folkestone Board School (Boys) Log Book*, 29 May 1894, C/E/S/148/2/1, Kent History and Library Centre. Thank you to Rod Illingworth at Kent Archives for bringing the *Log Book* to my notice. An outbreak of Scarlet Fever in 1899 forced some children to be quarantined in their home for a week in November.

275 Report on Edward's academic achievement from North Board School headmaster, J. Arthur Mummery to CHO, 15 February 1898, Action for Children Archive. Walter is recorded in the *School Log Book*, as having received a medal for his studies in Scripture and being awarded second place in Standard III Geography, 23 March 1896 and 15 July 1897, respectively.

276 *The Royal Commission on the State of Popular Education in England*, (London 1861), p.1. Gillard, D (2018) *Education in England: a history* www. educationengland.org.uk/history.   http://www.educationengland.org.uk/history/chapter06.html Accessed 29 June 2020.

Headmaster Mummery encouraged sport, particularly football. In this he was a pioneer. Organised competitive sport at and between state elementary schools was still in its developmental infancy. It was not until 1904 that the English Schools Football Association was formed. On two occasions in 1895 afternoon instruction was suspended 'to enable boys to see an important football match'. Whether this involved the school football team is not made clear but a visit by a Mr Vaughan in October which resulted in him subscribing to the School Football Club, confirms its existence. A couple of years later a Mr George Peden presented them with a new football.[277] Given both Edward and Walter's proven abilities it would not be surprising if they were key members of the school team.

Both Adcock and Stephenson were keen to see the boys enter the CHO. The former could see first hand Clara's distress and burden. It is reasonable to assume the local Methodist minister thought it his Christian duty to prevent decline into chronic poverty long-standing and active members of his congregation. If that meant sending away Edward and Walter so the rest of the family could stay together, so be it.

Stephenson, as principal, had a fiduciary duty to the CHO alongside his pastoral role as guardian of the orphanage children. These two responsibilities were not always compatible, though without close watch upon finances, there would be no CHO. He was anxious Elham Union contribute toward the boys' upkeep until maturity. To this end there was negotiation of a financial contract through a round robin of letters between Lonergan, the clerk and superintendent registrar of the Union, Stephenson and Adcock. If I did admit them, writes Stephenson, 20 January, 1898, would the Union continue their support? Holden, Kingsmill and the other guardians acquiesced. A missive of 22 January, sees Lonergan asking if further funds, additional to the weekly contribution of the boys' maintenance, would be expected for 'clothing, emigration or outfit when the children leave your home?' He also voluntarily pointed out 'the father of these children was a negro and they are consequently coloured children. I do not know if you are aware of this or whether it will in any way affect the application?'[278] Stephenson replied, characteristically, that it made no difference. In

277 *Folkestone Board School (Boys) Log Book*, 16 January, 6 March, 24 October, 1895 and 26 October, 1897, C/E/S/148/2/1, Kent History and Library Centre.
278 22 January 1898, *Epitome*. See also *Elham Union Minute Book*, p.224 (20 January, 1898), p.235 (3 February, 1898), p.245 (17 February, 1898), G/EL/AM 22, Kent History and Library Centre.

respect of the weekly contribution, he adds, though any reasonable offer would be considered, he suggests a sum representing the cost of maintenance in a Workhouse school would be acceptable.

Grace Hill Chapel made periodic donations to the CHO: in 1899 a total of twenty-three pounds fifteen shillings (£3,074); between 1903 and 1909, nine pounds seventeen and seven pence (£1,203).[279] No more are recorded up to 1915. The larger amount corresponds to Edward and Walter's entry and residence, while the lower aggregate spans the latter's sole occupation until his maturity at twenty-one when he would be responsible for his welfare.

The financial settlement agreed through the three-way postal exchange resulted in the Elham Union subsidising the maintenance of the boys at the rate of four shillings per week (20p) each plus outfits on maturity at eighteen. This combined sum of eight shillings (40p) per week was two shillings and two pence (11p) more than was paid to Clara for the upkeep of herself and five dependent children. Had they agreed to pay such a figure to the stepmother it may have been possible for the family to remain together. With William's weekly contribution of seven shillings (35p) the total would have been one shilling (5p) more than the weekly wage of Clara's father William or Uncle Robert.

The Agreement between Clara and the CHO stipulated there was to be 'no interference in any way' by her while the children were in the Home. Further, if the children (or child) were taken back 'without the agreement of the committee', the sum of eight shillings per week per child, multiplied by the length of duration in the Home, would have to be repaid. This was twice the sum the Elham Union allocated and was prohibitive. These economic circumstances determined the CHO's de facto rights over the children. Another clause gave the orphanage the right to send the children abroad. These conditions had to be agreed before the case for acceptance could be considered.

From 1869 until retirement in 1900 – when he was replaced by Dr A.E. Gregory – Stephenson was principal of the CHO. Described by one biographer as a man 'singularly free… from any social pride or caste feeling of any description', photographs from *Highways and Hedges*, the house journal of the CHO, and the Action for Children Archive

---

279 *Grace Hill Folkestone Wesleyan Methodist Offertory Book* 1899-1915, entries for 28 February March 25, 27 December,1899, December 1903, 10 January,1905, 1 January, 27 December, 1906, 31 December,1908 and 28 December 1909. M13/6/2/13, Kent History and Library Centre.

show children of varying ethnicities at Bonner Road.[280] Tolerance of difference courses through Stephenson's Methodism as bright as the tail of a meteorite. His comparatively enlightened feelings on 'race' and colour were both confirmed and galvanised through his trips abroad to South Africa and the USA. An accomplished organist possessing a fine baritone voice, in both countries he preached, worshipped and sang at Black churches. He was overwhelmed by the singing in Cape Colony and Natal. A dulling effect upon this generally progressive persona was his sectarian attitude to the Roman Church: he was 'fervently anti-Catholic'.[281]

The substantial terraced houses that ran along one side of Bonner Road comprised the greater proportion of the orphanage residencies. 'The families number in the aggregate 330 children'.[282] Stephenson wanted to recreate the feel and dynamic of a large family in each house under the supervision of a surrogate mother trained by the CHO. This relatively unique and enlightened approach to childcare was inspired by the care of homeless children he had witnessed in Germany during a visit to the newly unified country in the aftermath of the Franco-Prussian war, 1870-71. His pioneering work was not unnoticed:

Dr Stephenson's Children's Home, at Victoria Park, is… engaged in giving a fresh start in life to many a destitute and friendless boy or girl… In these Homes everything that can be done is done to enable the children to overcome their bad habits, and to fit them for some useful occupation when they leave the Home. Industry and intelligence, order and cleanliness, cheerfulness and activity, are encouraged; religion is inculcated; and the whole discipline through which the children pass cultivates and improves them so much, that it is difficult to recognise in these sturdy, active intelligent boys and girls leaving the Home, the pale-faced, poor, neglected ones who entered it some years before. Many more lives would be brightened, if people, seeing how much we are all benefited by this work of rescue, would give of their charity.[283]

---

280 William Bradfield, *The Life of the Reverend Thomas Bowman Stephenson* (London, 1913), p. 153.
281 Gordon E. Barritt, *Thomas Bowman Stephenson*, (Peterborough, 1996), p. 22.
282 *The Story of Forty Years*, p. 108.
283 Uncle Jonathan, 'Walks in and around London' (1895) in Lee Jackson,

Stephenson had constructed and implemented an ethos in pursuit of four pastoral aims: to provide the love, care, discipline and stability of a surrogate family; to inculcate a moral code based upon Wesleyan Methodist principles; to provide a basic education in core subjects such literacy, numeracy and religion in the orphanage's elementary school; and to provide vocational skills. In seeking these objectives the Home would also play its role in the imperial mission, providing viable human resources for the Empire, home and abroad.

After medical examination at which the boys' history of illness and vaccination was recorded, alongside descriptions of their intelligence and general health, they were cleared to be admitted on 14 February 1898. Adcock had made arrangements with his chapel for money to cover expenses for Clara to travel to Bethnal Green with her 'two dear sons, the little dark boys'.[284]

Leaving their loved ones on St Valentine's Day could have been interpreted by the boys in their more melancholy moments as poignantly ironic. Yet Clara, Adcock, Stephenson and Lonergan had conspired in an arrangement motivated, in differing degrees, by love and concern. Their hope was that the sacrifices made would be repaid by long-term gain in the shape of an albeit atomised family but one saved from poverty and the necessity of vice. In fact, the return was far greater than could have been imagined.

A few days prior Adcock received a telegram from Pendlebury, Stephenson's deputy and governor of the Home, saying there was *no room*. A flurry of heated exchanges followed. Adcock was 'amazed'. Had not Stephenson told him the boys could come up 'at any time?' 'A misunderstanding' replied the Reverend Dr 'they may be sent for at any time'is what I believe I said'. It was finally settled that the boys should come on the original date:

> In all the circumstances of the case, however, I feel it much better that the children should come at once. There are no vacancies, but we can temporarily make arrangements by sending two other children to another branch where the numbers are not so strictly limited as here. We will, therefore, receive the children on Monday as you are aware.[285]

The Victorian Dictionary at http://www.victorianlondon.org/childhood/drstephensonshome.htm Accessed 22 October, 2020.
284 *Epitome.*
285 Ibid.

The date seems to have been jinxed. They did not enter that Monday bcause Clara was ill. Action for Children records imply Edward and his younger brother, chaperoned by Adcock, were handed over to a member of the CHO staff at Cannon Street Station, London on 24 February. However, a handwritten recollection by Edward states a 'kindly . . heartbroken' Clara took them to Bonner Road.[286]

Within the walls of Walton Road was a portrait of paternal grandmother Anna. Staring directly at the camera she is dressed in a high-necked dress with embroidered trimmings and bonnet typical of a mid-Victorian British woman wearing her Sunday best. Except, of course, that the photograph was captured in a Bridgetown studio where outside temperatures in the shade would have been around thirty degrees Celcius making the clothing swelteringly inappropriate. The image speaks to an absence of the absolute poverty forced upon her parents. Were Edward and siblings aware of her death at eighty-one from 'chronic congestion of the brain and iffusion', 17 March 1896, in the Lunatic Asylum?[287] If Daniel was informed, there is no record of it or mention in his Journal where the last entry is dated 11 November, 1897. That his mother died from a heart related illness that frequently has a genetic causation may suggest an explanation for Daniel's early death from heart disease. Anna had been a patient in the asylum for one hundred and nine days. The institution's nomenclature is misleading. Its medical function was to socially isolate patients with long-term and incurable illnesses relating to the whole body. Daniel's father, William, outlasted both passing away 16 September, 1900 his burial solemnised in the Moravian Chapel, Roebuck Street, Bridgetown by Brother CJ Oehler. Daniel's sister, Sarah Elizabeth also died in the year her mother passed, 23 April 1897.

For both the Folkestone and Bridgetown wings of the diasporic Tulls, the last five years of the final decade of the nineteenth century was extraordinarily devastating.

---

286 Edward Tull, *The Film that Will Never Be Screened*, Finlayson Family Archive.
287 Entry for Tuesday, 16 March, 1896, *Asylum Records,* Barbados Archives. It is possible that this condition would now be labelled pulmonary arterial hypertension, propensity to which is believed to be genetic. https://www. webmd.com/lung/pulmonary-arterial-hypertension accessed 10 July 2020.

Chapter Eight
Trauma, Shock and Awe?

TOUGH LOVE

The non-residential departments of the Bethnal Green orphanage were contained within foreboding iron gates defending a large open space – 'The Big Yard' – behind which a row of terrace cottages provided further living quarters. The site now hosts a primary school while the opposite side of the road remains much as it was, a terrace of mid-Victorian step-ups speculatively built for an enlarging middle class. In Edward's essay 'The Film that Will Never Be Screened'[288] he describes, with a sprinkling of characteristic dry humour, their induction into the orphanage, its geography, daily routine and the attempt at replicating an organisation of families.

At the entrance, which was situated in Bonner Road, London NE, you would be shown over the offices. Here the Governor's Room and Offices for the workings of the Home occupied a fairly large block of buildings. Carrying on past this building you would come to the Chapel which occupied the corner of a great big square or quadrangle... paved with wooden blocks and all around it are fairly big houses... There are names over each house, [each] gifted by the various people whose name they bear... [the] one in which... we... finished [our] stay in the Home is called Sunday School House. This house was gifted by the Methodist Sunday Schools of the country. Another is called Wakefield House... after Lord Wakefield... first treasurer of the Home.

In one corner [of the quadrangle] the noise of machinery and. . . printing presses. Through another door... cooking and baking. Another shows us a dining hall for the staff whilst another shows us a gymnasium. There is a little stairway at the side of the gymnasium... leading to a room that every boy and girl aspires to. . . the choir room. This Home had a famous choir of boys and girls conducted by a famous musician and it was the ambition of every boy and girl to become a member... a queer room, [it had] a series of desks which rose tier on tier at which one could only stand.

288 Finlayson Family Archive. It is thought it was written around 1937.

Let us go back to the quadrangle... set apart... in a lesser quadrangle of its own... the girls' Houses.

One corner I must mention – for cleanliness is next to Godliness. There is a big communal bath, something like the big football clubs have today and adjoining it is a swimming pool.

Highfield House was [our] very first house... as junior members... the Sister, as she was called, had fifteen boys in her charge and her accommodation consisted of three bedrooms, her sleeping room and her sitting room, a dining room, a play room and a washing room with lavatories... Each house was constructed on the same plan, but and it is a big but, each house was a home. Sister was the mother and the head of the house... All the work of the house had to be done by its occupants with the exception of the two oldest boys and girls. They were working girls or boys. Each boy or girl had his or her duties no matter what age and it was the Sister's duty to see that the house was perfectly run.

[We] had... been provided with clothing and unlike many Children's Homes... kept these clothes. Each child in the National Children's Home had their own distinctive clothing, which is important. Dr Barnardo's did not follow these lines. Our boys were given their separate lockers to put their own possessions in and shown where to place their separate clothing. They each had their separate beds in a room that slept six.

A bell rings... it is 6.20 a.m.. All the boys in their room rise and dress, after which they make their beds. In the Reception House... boys have been shown what to do, so they fling off all the bed clothes, turn the mattress and make the bed leaving the top sheet with the correct six inches turned down and the night gown carefully folded. Following the other boys downstairs they go to their locker to get their own towel, brush and comb to proceed to the washing room to wash in cold water... They proceed to the play room and stand in line. Sister makes her appearance and sees that every boy is present and then the boys proceed to their various tasks before breakfast. Being newcomers [we] start at the bottom and naturally the bottom is cleaning of boots or rather shoes. Not one pair, but all the pairs of the household... the Sister's especially. No fancy pastes such as Ki-wi in those days, it was the good old fashioned blacking that was lubricated with, I can find no better word, water. Having finished fifteen pairs of shoes, an inspection by the Sister was enacted and if favourable, put away in various lockers. Breakfast came as a happy relief, but what had the other boys been doing?

The two eldest boys, who were called Working Boys, had gone off to the printing shop and bakehouse, but as the house has to be cleaned, as your house has to be cleaned, the other boys had various tasks. The three older boys had the bedrooms to scrub and the bedrooms were bare boards. This was the procedure: each took a bucket, scrubbing brush, cloth and soap with pail and cold water, and each took a strip of those boards. At every fourth patch the water had to be changed until the room was finished. One boy was set to clean the brass taps of the washing room, not with Brasso but with Globe Polish, whilst another scrubbed the floor (concrete). Another had to scrub the playroom, which was tiled, whilst another set the breakfast table. Every boy had a task that kept him occupied until breakfast time and no task was finished until Sister had passed it satisfactorily. Breakfast consisted of bread and magarine with cocoa. That meal finished and the dishes washed the whole house walked in order accompanied by the Sister to the Chapel for morning prayers.

Each house was fully represented in the Chapel and the prayers were conducted by the Governor. The choir was made up of about 40 boys and girls. A hymn, a prayer, a bible portion and the Benediction was the usual order of Service but on Monday morning instead of the Reading a boy or girl from each house had to stand and repeat a Text that had been chosen by the Sister. There was no Chapel on Sunday because the Home went to the Methodist Church in Bonner Road about 200 hundred yards away and the Home Choir led the Priest at morning and evening services.

After prayers came school for the majority of children. The school was beside the Chapel. Two boys aged 13 proceeded back to the house. They were house boys and only went to school in the afternoon. The senior house boy had the Sister's quarters to clean and look after whilst the junior had to dust, clean and prepare downstairs. . . the boys' quarters. Dinner was a one course meal – soup one day, meat pie another, fish another. Plain wholesome feeding one would call it but the boy with taste would call it many things. The boys whose duty it was to wash up after dinner had to stand by 'til the Sister inspected the dinner dishes. This duty rotated – two boys were [picked] each week to do the dinner dishes.

School again in the afternoon and tea at 5 pm, but before tea a thorough personal washing. The boys stripped to the waist and washed from there upwards. That didn't finish it. Sister required every boy to appear before her for inspection and that inspection was no careless thing. Hands and nails were first looked at, then under the armpits and finally the ears. I remember one small boy who had difficulty with his ears. Strive as he would he would never seem to get his ears clean. Tea consisted of the same course as breakfast, bread and margarine with cocoa.

For two hours after tea the boys could use their time as they liked in the play room except the choir boys who might have a choir practice, but no noise was allowed and at 8 pm the boys stood in line preparatory to going to bed in an orderly manner and with the common greeting of 'Goodnight Sister'. No talking was allowed in the bedrooms.

In the summer time the leisure hours were spent in the quadrangle just as you boys or girls spend your time out of doors, marbles, skipping ropes, spring tops, etc.

His fascinatingly detailed account privileges us (almost) with the taste, feel and smell of his turn of the century orphanage. While the daily routine of order, hierarchy and discipline are typical of such out-of-the-ordinary, enclosed institutions be they prisons, boarding schools, monasteries or barracks, he is keen to emphasise the CHO's concession to individual identity in allowing boys to wear 'their own distinctive clothing'

As well as worshipping at the Bonner Road chapel, Edward writes ,each Sunday members of the Home would attend Approach Road Methodist Church, of which Stephenson was superintendent. It was nearby and, importantly, part of the wider Methodist community. While only a short walk once a week, the effect of meeting with people not connected to the Home was refreshing, vital and a large step in helping the institutionalised children feel part of the world outside. It would afford each child an entry point to, and reminder of, a society from which they had been torn or left behind but to which they would return at some point in the future.

Beyond the CHO's imposing gates in middle-class Bonner Road was picturesque, leafy Victoria Park with bandstand, boating lake and manicured gardens. A verdant refuge in one of the poorest, most densely occupied boroughs in the world's largest city. Walking down Bethnal

Green Road toward Shoreditch, Edward and Walter would have skirted the southern border of the Nichol, a working-class ghetto of around six thousand fictionalised by Arthur Morrison in his much publicised and widely read novel, *A Child of the Jago*, published in 1896. Criticised for sensationalising its deviant sub-culture, the author responded he wrote as he found after eighteen months of participant observation. A real-life child of the Jago was Arthur Harding whose oral recollection of growing up in what was considered London's most feared slum is contained in Ralph Samuel's *East End Underworld* (1981). Harding tells of a close-knit community with intense tribal loyalty where gangs, guns and prison were as much a feature of life as overcrowding, vermin and incursions by middle-class missionaries. A rival firm from nearby Commercial Road was named after their leader, Darkey the Coon, a flamboyant 'man of colour',[289] also known as Ikey Bogard, awarded a Military Medal in the First World War.

THE EAST END, POLITICS AND PEOPLE OF COLOUR

Growing-up fast was a necessary consequence of the rapid change which had occurred in Edward and Walter's short, eventful lives. Protected from its roughest, harshest quarters Bethnal Green in the late eighteen nineties and early nineteen hundreds was no place for the naïve. Poverty was endemic. Situated at the heart of the working-class East End, it was dotted with the pock-marked features of capitalism's victims. Especially vulnerable were children.

> Everywhere in the crowded thoroughfares and street markets would be seen bands of homeless children, orphaned or cast out, pathetic recruits from the gutter in the battle for survival.[290]

It could be argued that the iconography of Victorian urban poverty – overcrowded cottages in narrow streets spilling over with weary mothers cradling malnourished infants and shoeless, grubby, thin, children wearing rags - is archetypal Bethnal Green. Associated with these conditions are the smells of poverty: sweat and waste, animal and human. Odour and discharge and prevailing westerly winds are the reasons why affluent

---

289 *East London Observer*, 29 August 1914, p. 3, in Ralph Samuel, *East End Underworld* (London, 1981), p. 321.
290 William J. Fishman, *East End 1888*, (Nottingham, 2009), p.160.

Londoners moved west, upwind, while the poor had to settle in the east, downwind. Mixing with these were the stinks produced by the predominant trades.

For seventy years, the people of Bethnal Green and the surrounding area were the support for London, the makers of clothing, boots, shoes, furniture, and other products which required hard labor but produced little income. Each had its own distinctive smell, adding to the miasma of unwashed bodies and cheap food. Tanners and leatherworkers had the smell of urine, feces, [sic] alcohol, and lye. Weavers and dyers carried the distinctive smell of their product, whether wool and silk or chemical and natural dyes. The sweet smell of pine, tar and sweat pervaded the area around a furniture maker's workspace, but inside, it smelled also of grease, rosin, ash, coal, and sulfure [sic]. Each tradesmen, artisan, factory worker, or food worker carried home that smell in their clothes, which might be worn for as many as six days straight between washings.[291]

Those suffering from the noxious cocktail of poverty, homelessness and unemployment were forced toward the only shelter on offer, the workhouse. Overcrowded and under-funded these prisons of the poor were desperate to offload those that could not work and earn their subsistence keep. Many orphans and discarded young were transported to the colonies so they would not represent a cost to local rate-payers. The clerk of neighbouring Whitechapel Union of Poor Law Guardians, William Vallance, proudly boasted of his strict workhouse regimes, their low cost and discharging over two thousand children into sea service.[292] For his pecuniary skills he was rewarded both in cash additional to his salary and having a road named after him upon which stood a workhouse infirmary under his command. (In later years it would become legendary for housing the Kray family).

There were movements, philanthropic and political, that were active in Bethnal Green. Hygiening the poor, morally and physically, preoccupied and obsessed social engineers. The destruction of the Nichol and its replacement with the Boundary Estate by the newly-created London County Council was the city's first municipal slum clearance scheme

---

291 Audrey Gray, *The 'Happiest Corner' of London: Bethnal Green 1881-1951*, M.A. dissertation, Louisiana State University, 2012, p.8.
292 Ibid., p.162.

under the 1890 Housing for the Working Classes Act. The 1911 Census suggests overcrowding decreased by around three per cent. Providing decent housing, children with compulsory instruction in state-funded schools and siphoning waste underground was a bourgeoise attempt at configuring an aesthetically acceptable and comparatively civilised urban environment.

For socialists and communists who congregated – alongside numerous other belief groups – each Sunday in Victoria Park such solutions masked the uncomfortable truth that poverty was created by an economic system the liberal reformers were attempting, fundamentally, to sustain.

On the big central lawn are scattered numerous groups, some of them very closely packed. Almost all of the religious sects of England and all the political and social parties are preaching their ideas and disputing...The anarchists, who are rare, declare the uselessness of all government, demand the absolute liberty of all citizens, will not admit any intellectual differences... but affirm, on the contrary, that we were all born with equal facilities... At last here we are in the midst of a strong group in socialistic discussion... 'we ask our friend where he sees the liberty of a workman who works ten hours a day for a morsel of bread... we are curious to know what he thinks of the poor girls who are reduced to sell themselves in our streets. Does not our friend know that labour is the source of all riches.'[293]

A frequent Sunday speaker at Victoria Park was Dominica-born Celestine Edwards. If not railing against another man of colour, Mancherjee Bhownagree and his aspiration to become Bethnal Green's MP for the Conservative Party or condemning the imperial theft of Uganda this well-known orator attacked domestic injustice alongside proselytising for abstinence and Christianity.

Edwards's concern with the liberties and rights of people of colour helped prepare the way for the 1900 Pan-African Conference in the metropolis which another Black Londoner, Sylvester Williams, was instrumental in organising. This meeting in the metropolis of international anti-colonialists was an important milestone in the struggle for self-emancipation. Williams, along with Edwards's Antiguan mentor, Reverend Henry Mason Joseph, convened in London in 1897 the

293 J.H. Rooney, *Harper's Magazine*, February 1888 quoted in Fishman, (2009), pp. 331-2.

inaugural meeting of the possibly the first Black civil rights group in Britain, the Africa Association.

There was much to fight for and against. A Black resident of London at the turn of the century described the experience of another while out in the West End.

> Recently, [one of] three white men, of gentlemanly appearance…
> going in the opposite direction to that of a coloured man… called
> the attention of his comrades to the presence of the coloured man,
> and then said 'Look at that thing'… This laceration of the feelings
> of coloured people, which has now become a practice in England,
> is partly due to the fact that Englishmen, having adopted the notion
> that they are superior to coloured men, have found rudeness and
> incivility to be the best supports of the imposture.[294]

Radical and revolutionary political groups promoting a reshaping of society to meet the needs and interests of all, whatever their ethnicity, were a feature of nineteenth century London. People of colour, such as William Davidson, Robert Wedderburn and William Cuffey played leading roles.

Jamaica-born Davidson – a mixed-heritage son of the attorney general and an African Caribbean woman – secretary of the shoemaker's union, was hanged in 1820 for his part in the Cato Street Conspiracy. The plan was to assassinate prime minister, the earl of Liverpool and his reactionary Cabinet as they dined in Mayfair, instigating a popular revolution. Davidson's group had been profoundly shocked and angered by the previous year's Peterloo Massacre in Manchester. Cottonopolis, as it was known because of it ubiquity of mills, had a population of nearly two hundred thousand. It had no members of Parliament with the vast majority of adults having no right to vote in any election. A peaceful demonstration of some sixty-thousand people in support of parliamentary reform at St. Peter's Field was brutally attacked by the Manchester and Salford Yeomanry. At least eighteen were killed by shot, sabre and being trampled upon by horses of the charging militia. The youngest was the unborn child of Elizabeth Gaunt with the first victim

---

294 Theophilus E. Samuel Scholes, *Glimpses of the Ages: or the superior and inferior races, so-called discussed in the light of science and history'*, Vol.II in Fryer, (1984), p 439.

named as William Fildes, aged just two, who was crushed by a horse while in his mother's arms. Over seven hundred were seriously injured. The government and Crown's response was to congratulate the militia and the Manchester magistrates for their decisive action. Following the carnage, Liverpool's regime ensured the quick passage of the Six Acts, legislation designed to severely limit political gatherings by working class people and prevent literature being printed and distributed which called for democratic change. The inflamed Cato Street rebels were betrayed by government spy and infiltrator George Edwards.

Revolutionary preacher, printer, essayist, publisher and freeman of colour Robert Wedderburn, a political associate of fellow Jamaican Davidson in the Society of Spencean Philanthropists in 1824 published his autobiography, *The Horrors of Slavery*. He detailed witnessing as a child his mother, Roseanna and grandmother mercilessly flogged, almost to death. He was imprisoned in 1819 for, among other demands, asserting the right of enslaved people to kill their oppressors. Though not a Cato Street participant he foreshadowed Marx in arguing the desperate plight of the chattel slave and the industrial working class had a common origin and solution in capitalism and revolution. Imprisoned again after the failure of the Cato Street plan and the brutal executions of Davidson and four others, he was held captive in Dorchester prison – much of the time in solitary confinement – for two years.

The Chartists, the first mass working class political movement, collectively embodied the vision of Davidson, Wedderburn and Marx. They demanded the right to vote for adult males along with other democratic reforms. Inspired to join the National Charter Association after being sacked for going on strike, mixed-heritage tailor William Cuffay was eventually elected to the Chartists' five man national executive. A few years later, in 1845, *The Times* described the London-based Chartists as 'the black man and his party'. Through the use of spies and agent provocateurs the government ensnared Cuffay and other leading Chartist militants, convicting them in 1848 of attempting an armed uprising. The London tailor demanded to be tried by his peers, as designated in the Magna Carta.

I say you have no right to sentence me... It has not been a fair trial, and my request to have a fair trial – to be tried by my equals – has not been complied with. Everything has been done to raise a prejudice against me, and the press of this country – and I believe of other countries too – has done all in its power to smother me with ridicule. I ask no pity. I ask no mercy. I expected to be convicted, and I did not think anything else... After what I have endured this week, I feel that I could bear any punishment proudly, even to the scaffold.[295]

Cuffay was transported to Tasmania where he died in workhouse poverty July, 1870 after continuing his struggle for working-class rights. Two other notable Black Chartists, David Anthony Duffy and Benjamin Prophitt were also arrested, convicted and transported.

The proletarian East End was fertile territory for disseminating ideas of social and economic improvement though collective action. The groundbreaking resistance by women workers to the extremely punitive and life-threateningly dangerous working conditions at the Bryant and May match factory in Bow, even by the harsh norms of Victorian capital, resulted in the Matchgirls' Union victorious 1888 strike. The successful Dockers' Strike the following year invigorated previously non-unionised workers, instigating growth in workplace organisation known as New Unionism. Leading actors in the strikes and in the subsequent raising of class confidence and consciousness – building upon the foundational courage and determination of the workers involved – were socialists Annie Besant, Eleanor Marx, Ben Tillet, John Mann, James Keir Hardie (founder of the Labour Party), HM Hyndman and John Burns. Between 1892-99 membership of trade unions increased from one million five hundred thousand to over two million.[296] At the conclusion of the Dock Strike, involving thirty-thousand stevedores and the same number working in associated industries, Engels wrote to Eleanor Marx, his partner in the translation of her father's work's into English.

I envy you your work in the dock strike. It is the movement of the greatest promise we have had for years, and I am proud and glad to have lived to see it. If Marx had lived to witness this! If these poor downtrodden men, the dregs of the proletariat, these odds and ends of all trades, fighting every morning at the dock gates for engagement, if they can combine, and terrify by their resolution the mighty Dock

295 Peter Fryer (1984), pp.407-9.
296 Thanks to John Simkin and his excellent educational resource, Spartacus Educational, for much of the information on working class political movements of the nineteenth century and the individuals involved: www.spartacus-educational.com

Companies, truly then we need not despair of any section of the working class. This is the beginning of real life in the East End, and if successful will transform the whole character of the East End.[297]

Edward did not stay in the East End long enough to evaluate Engel's hope. Some thirty years after their relocation to the CHO he did reflect Walter was hardier and better equipped to cope with the initial shock of entry and subsequent emotional acclimatisation. '[I was] homesick and a little frightened. [Walter] being of a sturdier mould seemed ready to sample new ways and new means'.[298]

LOVE AND LONGING

If applicable, it was usual practice to allow new boarders visits from their families. Letters arrived frequently from Clara, William, and Cecilia – Cissie – requesting to see the boys. Two months after their entry, Clara sends a postcard asking to see her stepsons. By the end of the year, writing from her new home at Little Singledge, Coldred, Dover where she was now living with Elsie and Miriam, her affection remained undiminished:

I should like to come and see the to [sic] little boy [sic] tomorrow Thursday as I am in Tottenham My to [sic] dear little sons the dark boys. I hope it will not put you out and in any way as I have not been able to write before so shall be up about 3 o'clock tomorrow afternoon. Yours truly Mrs Tull.[299]

Her request coincided with preparations for her marriage the following year to Bill Beer. The 1901 Census registers all four living at Little Singledge. It also records living at this hamlet her brother Henry, his wife Constance, their daughter Constance (and the Taylor family of Frederick and Susan and nine children. Taylor was the maiden name of Edward's maternal grandmother, Sarah-Ann, though it is not thought they were related). Henry's given occupation is tractor engine driver,

297 Friedrich Engels to Eleanor Marx, August 1889. Published in the *Labour Elector*, Vol.II, No. 35, 31 August 1889 in Marx and Engels, *Articles on Britain*, (Moscow, 1971), p.401 and footnote 214, pp.441-2.
298 *The Film that Will Never Be Screened.*
299 Letter from Clara to CHO, 8 December 1898, *Epitome*.

(while Frederick's is 'waggoner on farm', identical to Bill Beer's).

Clara's maternal love and obligation towards her adopted sons continued throughout her life. Letters in the Action for Children Archive reveal a stepmother and siblings ever-concerned for the boys welfare and development, determined not to let the seismic, emotional upheavals break their family bond. Working as a domestic maid in her home town, Cissie asks to visit her brothers. During the summer of 1899 William pens at least four letters asking if he can spend time with his brothers. A few months later in November he requests to visit again.

William's inarticulate but profoundly heartfelt letters reveal his unsettled feelings. His father, writing in his *Journal*, had made a death-bed plea that Clara's proposed new partner 'not neglect' his two youngest daughters, recognising his surviving family would experience, again, a period of emotional trauma, transition and adjustment. His eldest son, who formally registered his death, was undoubtedly disturbed by yet another parental figure entering his life, however benign Bill Beer's impact may have been. Yearning for his brothers, the seventeen year old embarked upon a nomadic journey, skirting the edges of South London. The year Clara and Bill married, he moved to 10 Thanet Road, Erith, Kent. A few months later he rented lodgings at 99 Gresham Road, Brixton,(then in the county of Surrey) less than 10 miles from the orphanage. While at these addresses he requested his younger brothers visit him for holidays. On occasion, when permission was refused for the boys to leave the grounds, they would alternatively allocate a brief time-slot for William within.[300] However, the three were allowed to spend time together on two occasions in 1899 and 1900 at William's lodgings at 53 Medara Road, Brixton. They sang in his local church where a collection for the CHO was taken. His desire to host them for two weeks in August 1900 was turned down because they were on a choir trip. (This has additional poignancy. It was during this tour that the Warnocks initiated their adoption of Edward, ultimately taking him even further away from William.)

Stephenson's love of music, his belief in its therapeutic and evangelical influence, had inspired him to form an orphanage choir and band in the eighteen seventies. Each year on Temperance Sunday, celebrating the joys of abstinence, they would be led through the streets of Bethnal Green by 'Black Bob, a converted drunkard' who would put on a show

---

300 Ibid., Letter from William, received by CHO 28 June, 1900. Across the top is written 'can see them briefly'.

of dexterous gymnastics by tossing an iron bed-leg high above his head, catching it and following up with a quick, neat exchange of hands.[301] (It is not known if Bob's nickname was a reference to his ethnicity.) Stephenson's beloved solo was Blind Bartimaeus, from the 'Negro Spiritual' tradition. He may have picked it up on his visits to African-American churches or heard it performed in a repertoire of enslaved spirituals by the African-American Fisk Jubilee Singers when they toured Britain during the same decade. His excellent baritone voice was a crowd puller, initially at the Waterloo Road Chapel, Lambeth and later at the Approach Road Chapel, Bethnal Green. A working man standing outside the former, listening, commented 'it's worth half a crown any day to hear a parson sing like that'.[302]

The first choir and band tour was in 1878, with twenty-six musicians aged between ten and fourteen and an unspecified number of singers. Performed favourites were hymns *Onward Christian Soldiers; Stand Up, Stand Up for Jesus; Mine Eyes Have Seen the Glory* and *O Safe the Rock*. The dual purpose of the tours was to raise much needed money for orphanage running costs and showcase boys and girls for adoption.

With their caps as much in their hands as on their heads, during the late summer and autumn of 1900, the choir and musicians, including Edward and Walter, once more toured the country. Performing at Glasgow's main Methodist church, St John's, as well as singers the ensemble had an impressive array of instruments including dulcimers, drums, mandolins and bells.

The children sang The Bells of the Joyous Morn… and the Lord's Prayer, beautifully chanted… an orchestra… dulcimer, xylophone, mandolins… [all] betokened careful training.[303]

Edward was noticed by a Glasgow couple, James and Jeannie Warnock. Through an intermediary, J.W. Butcher of Claremont Street Wesleyan Church, their place of worship, the Warnock's offered to adopt.

---

301 Cyril Davey, *A Man for All Children: The Story of Thomas Bowman Stephenson* (London, 1968), p. 91.
302 Ibid., pp. 195-6.
303 Morag Cross, Blog 20: *The Tull Brothers* https://www.firstworldwar-glasgow.co.uk/CHttpHandler.ashx?id=25685&p=0 Accessed 20 December, 2017.

I have what I consider to be an excellent offer for Eddie. His host is a dentist whose clientele is mainly among the poorer people. He is willing to take Eddie – treat him as a son, teach him a profession & if the boy proves worthy eventually work the connection into his hands.[304]

The 'connection' was Mr Warnock's St Vincent Street dental practice.[305] Butcher finishes his letter to the new principal of the CHO, Dr Gregory – Stephenson having retired some months earlier – with a persuasive flourish.

Your children on this trip have in power of behaviour surpassed all my former experiences & they were good. I think I shall when all cheques are to hand be able to send you between £65 and £66 nett [sic].[306]

Echoing Adcock's communication with Stephenson over the boys' application, those who rely on charity are often reminded of their vulnerability and Butcher was not slow in making Gregory aware who was doing who a favour in this exchange.

Both Butcher and Gregory accepted the role of money in the saving of souls: for the orphanage to accept more children it needed both funds and to place in the community – home or abroad – those in its care. Devising ways and means of attracting income was an integral feature of the institution's culture. Public collecting boxes were distributed; subscription adverts bought in newspapers. In 1899 the Young Leaguers Union (YLU) was established to encourage fundraising by children inside and outside, especially ex-residents (like Edward, who became a member).

The thirteen year old was fortunate in not crossing the sea in order to step over his new threshold. Sending children abroad to anglicise Britain's expanding empire was annual practice. By 1909 it had sent two

304 Butcher to Gregory, 11 October 1900, *Epitome*.
305 James Warnock was not a registered dentist and was unable to call himself as such but he could remove teeth and make false teeth. There was a trade association for such practitioners: *The Incorporated Society of Extractors and Adaptors of Teeth*. I am indebted to dentist and relative of Jean Warnock, Mike Gow, for the information about Jean and James Warnock.
306 Butcher to Gregory, *Epitome*. The value of £65 in 2019 is over £8,000.

thousand children to Canada alone. In 1894 thirty-three boys and one girl were shipped on the *Labrador* to Hamilton, Newfoundland. Three years later another thirty-four boys arrived.[307] (Elham Union was also sending families and individual children to Canada. In May, 1906, it agreed a sum *not exceeding* £12 to be paid towards the expenses of orphan Bertie Holmwood's emigration.)[308] Migrating to an unfamiliar environment was a feature of working-class and rural communities. An estimated ten million people from England and Wales boarded ships to try their luck elsewhere between 1861-1900.

Clara − now Mrs Beer − delighted Edward had the opportunity to move to a domestic and social milieu in which his life chances would be greatly improved, sent a basket of food for a celebratory last supper at Bonner Road.

Her subsequent actions in writing to, and visiting Walter, suggests her gift, while accentuating the positive step for Edward, was not an insensitive ignoring of her youngest stepson's increased vulnerability.

THE WARNOCKS

James Kay Warnock married Jane 'Jeannie' Cooper 31 December 1880. They had one child, daughter Elizabeth − Lizzie − some seven years older than Edward. Little is known about her. She was born the year before her parents' union, disappearing from view on maturity. Jeannie was sixteen years old when she had Lizzie, James twenty-three. She lived with them until at least 1901.

Jeannie had grown up in the Kirkintilloch Poorhouse with her older half-brother, James Cooper. Their mother, Mary Cooper, died of phlebitis at Kirkintilloch in 1866, when Jeannie was four years old. James Warnock had worked as block printer (1881 Census) and calico printer (1891 Census). It seems likely he became a dentist − mechanical (1901 Census) after meeting his brother-in-law who was already a practitioner.[309]

Jeannie was a singer and performed at The Incorporated Society of Extractors and Adaptors of Teeth Annual Dinner in 1912. (In front of her adopted son?) Watching and hearing Edward sing for the orphanage

307 *The Story of Forty Years, 1869–1909*, p. 98.
308 Elham Union, 16 May 1906, G/EL/ACa 4, Kent History and Library Centre.
309 See Mike Gow, *Dental History Magazine*, vol. 1, no. 1, 2007 and vol. 5, no. 2, Autumn 2011.

choir she may have felt empathy with this brown-skinned boy in a sea of White faces. She knew what it was like to feel an outsider and shared a love of music. Listening to his melodic voice made an irrepressible impression.

> His fine baritone voice was heard on many occasions as a singer of sacred music and also on the concert platform. In this sphere he excelled with rendering of negro spirituals.[310]

Possibly, for Jeannie, Edward represented an opportunity to give love – a scarce commodity in her deprived, institutionalised childhood – to a young child from an environment with which she empathised. Her impoverished background helps an understanding of how she and James may have approached taking the very difficult decision to bring Edward into their family and away from his brother (whom they very likely saw also singing in the choir). As a unqualified teeth extractor James Warnock could not charge dentist rates, instead his fees had to be pitched at a level affordable to his working class patients from the tenements surrounding his practice. It is unlikely that they had the financial wherewithall to care for both boys.

When formally adopting Edward, the Warnocks promised to regard him as their son. Despite their limited means the couple appear determined to act in his best interests.

> Some of the conditions we have not complied to as we do not intend putting the boy to work at present. We consider him smart and intelligent and would like to send him to school, in order to fit him better for the occupation we desire him to follow.[311]

A range of competing and conflicting emotions would have coursed through Edward as, in the cool of a mid-November morning, he walked out of the gates of the orphanage. He had spent thirty-three months institutionalised. Now, once more he was embarking on a new beginning with his third set of parents leaving behind in the 'harsh and disciplined but not unbearable'[312] environment his beloved young brother. As

---

310 *Carrick Herald* (Girvan), December 15th 1950.
311 Mr and Mrs Warnock to Mr Pendlebury, principal of Bonner Road, undated (c. October 1900), *Epitome*.
312 Edward Tull-Warnock, *The Film That Will Never Be Screened*, Finlayson

children of colour in an overwhelmingly White society life may have presented itself as a wildly unpredictable. The emotional turmoil and conflict caused by this rupture was not new or abnormal but its intensity probably was. Walter would very likely have been pleased for Edward, going to a relatively affluent family home where he would have his own room and fire and the opportunity to study for a profession. Yet, for each, the person on whom they relied most was no longer within touching distance.

Chapter Nine
One of Us?

GLASGOW

Writing to his prospective son-in-law during the troubled, austere summer of 1942, Edward discussed what Duncan should call him. He revealed that as a fourteen year old he chose to call his new parents mater and pater rather than mother and father 'and funnily enough all their friends adopted my mode of address'.[313] He references an adolescent of growing confidence and self-assuredness that was replacing the frightened youngster that had entered the orphanage in the shadow of his sturdier younger brother.

The Warnocks' ground floor tenement at 465 St Vincent Street was an improvement on the austere frugality of Bonner Road. Edward would not now have to share his bedroom with five others. The fourth member of the household was their twenty-one year old daughter Lizzie. The flat doubled as James Warnock's dental practice. Also resident was Robert Adamson, his apprentice dental mechanic.

Stepping out of his tenement close, Edward would find a city with an appearance not too dissimilar to London. While the population of just over three quarters of a million was much smaller, it was the second largest city in the British Empire with an underground railway system, opened in 1896. It was also a proletarian industrial conurbation whose inhabitants suffered disproportionately from ill-health. The most common causes of death in nineteenth century Scotland were tuberculosis, typhus, scarletina, whooping cough, smallpox and measles. In Glasgow respiratory diseases and tuberculosis were particularly widespread and fatal, with children especially vulnerable. During the eighteen nineties, infant mortality was one hundred and twenty-nine per thousand live births but in the deprived, poverty-stricken Gorbals it was two hundred.

THE CITY AND THE SLAVE TRADE

Glasgow had grown exponentially through the industrial revolution. An economic and social transformation energised by the blood of

---

313 Letter from Edward to Duncan Finlayson, 7 July 1942, Finlayson Family Archive.

his enslaved ancestors, its relationship with the triangular trade and plantation enslavement, while not as universally infamous as the other port cities London, Liverpool and Bristol, is a developing narrative. Until recently Scotland's historiography tended to play down or ignore its people trafficking past. T.M. Devine's (2015) collection of essays notes the Glasgow firm of Alexander Grant Junior and Co among a number in the city that profited.[314] The pro-enslavement Glasgow West India Association was formed in 1807 the same year, significantly, as the slave trade abolition legislation was enacted. The influential *Glasgow Courier* newspaper unapologetically opposed any government interference in the right to profit from enslavement. Nicholas Draper, whose groundbreaking work on making widely accessible extrapolated data from the slave compensation records at the UK National Archives has raised enormously the quality of the debate. His contribution to Devine's collection focusses upon Scotland's links as evidenced by his University College, London team's prolonged research into the records at Kew.

These excavations and analyses are a solid foundation from which to work backwards to the fundamental role in the transatlantic trade of Scotland's most renowned royal dynasty, the Stuarts. Prior to James VI claiming the English throne at the beginning of the seventeenth century, the dynasty had ruled Scotland for over three hundred years. Without the creation of the Stuart initiated and controlled RA in 1660 and its rededication to slave trading above all else three years later it is questionable whether the industrialisation of people trafficking would have been characterised by such wide-ranging intensity. Royal patronage - with all the protection and privilege this status entailed - propelled forward at a rapid pace the commercial momentum of both the trade and settler colonisation during Restoration. Though the Navigation Acts discriminated against the involvement of Scotland-registered ships, Devine's essay collection suggests Scottish ship owners, captains, doctors, plantation owners, overseers and agents were numerous. The Port of Glasgow was established in the sixteen-sixties as were the city's first sugar houses. Both developments, in great part, an outcome of the rapidly expanding Barbados sugar industry built on enslaved labour supplied by the Stuart family firm. It is estimated there were between four and five thousand Scottish settlers in the Caribbean during this

---

314 T.M. Devine, *Recovering Scotland's Slavery Past. The Caribbean Connection,* (Edinburgh, 2015).

decade, though many were forcibly transported.

The 1707 Act of Union legally entitled Scotland-based companies to enter without restriction the triangular trade. Petitions from merchants in Glasgow, Edinburgh, Montrose, Dundee Aberdeen and Inverness were sent to Parliament soon after demanding the opportunity to exercise the right and complaining of the monopoly of the RAC. However, it was not until a decade after the union that the first registered enslavement ship set sail from Scotland. Most of the vessels in the trade embarked from Greenock or the Port of Glasgow. Unable to profitably compete with the English slave trading ports of London, Liverpool and Bristol, Glasgow instead established itself as the premier location for the import and export of plantation-grown tobacco-leaf. Consequently, a thriving merchant quarter grew, centred around Miller Street. St Vincent Street is nearby. The Oswald family in Stockwell Street formed one of its most influential and affluent companies, dealing as well in sugar and wine. They financed vainglorious building projects, including St. Andrews by the Green church. When plutocrat Richard Oswald died in 1784 his *Glasgow Mercury* obituary was obsequious and deceitful.

Perhaps there are few men, whose loss will be more generally felt, or more sincerely regretted, than that of Mr Oswald, for few had a finer understanding, more liberal sentiments, or more extensive information. Blessed with affluence, his principal study seemed to be to employ it in acts of kindness and generosity.

He was buried in Ayrshire despite his kin having a vault in Glasgow Cathedral, uniquely the sole merchant family to be granted such hallowed resting space. Another of the tobacco barons, the Buchanans, had to be content with a plot at the entrance.

In 1748, partnered by other London-based Scots, the Oswalds bought the RAC's former enslaved holding pen of Bance Island in the Sierra Leone River. It allowed European slave traders to do business with other Europeans rather than stealing bodies from the mainland or negotiating with local chiefs through cabashiers (middlemen). To anaesthetise grim reality, they laid out a miniature golf course – with tartan uniformed African captives as caddies – facilitating pleasurable respite from the dangerous necessities integral to their business.[315]

315 *It Wisnae Us. The Truth about Glasgow and Slavery*, https://it.wisnae.us/glasgow-and-the-slave-trade/ Accessed 16 February, 2021. The *Glasgow*

Like other Scottish merchants the Oswalds were absentee plantation owners, owning four estates. Draper's study of the compensation records suggests Scots accounted for fifteen per cent of absentees while comprising ten per cent of the UK population. Of these awards, Glasgow accounted for twenty per cent while having ten per cent of Scotland's population.[316]

Memorials and other markers to (absentee) planters, enslavers and triangular traders are visible in the city's public space. The cathedral has stained glass dedicated to noted tobacco lord, Alexander Speirs of Elderslie. It also displays a memorial to former Lord Provost, Andrew Cochrane, a Virginia planter. The Gallery of Modern Art is housed in the Royal Exchange building, financed by tobacco lord, William Cunninghame. The sole surviving mansion of another, Robert Findlay's Tobacco Merchant's House, built in 1775, is at 42 Miller Street. Outside there is a Merchant City Trail plaque proclaiming 'Tobacco Exchange. Tobacco and Sugar were traded here in the eighteenth century.' Buchanan, Ingram, Glassford and Dunlop Streets are all named after tobacco barons.

EDUCATION

Edward was enrolled at Allan Glen's School[317] in North Hanover Street – just north of Merchant City – an elite (but not elitist) fee-paying school. The institution emphasised sport and science as essential pillars of education, an ethos categorised as Muscular Christianity, summarised in the maxim 'healthy body, healthy mind'. Its innovative headmaster, John Guthrie Kerr, on taking over in 1890, transformed the learning environment from one of dour academic effort to the pursuit of intellectual and physical excellence through rigorous endeavour. The

Mercury obituary is dated 14 November.

316 Nicholas Draper, 'Scotland and Colonial Slave Ownership: The Evidence of the Slave Compensation Records' in T.M. Devine, (ed.), *Recovering Scotland's Slavery Past. The Caribbean Connection,* (Edinburgh, 2015), pp.174,179.

317 Allan Glen's will stated that his Trustees were to invest his estate to build and endow a school, the purpose of which was 'to give a good practical education and preparation for trades or businesses, to between forty to fifty boys, the sons of tradesmen or persons in the industrial classes of society'. http://www.allanglens.com/index.php/allan-glen-s-school Accessed 16 February, 2021.

formula nine parts perspiration plus one part inspiration, he believed, equalled success.

No obstacle – no progress; no fight, no joy of conflict... It is in personal effort and a sense of contest, in the things of the mind or the muscles, that youth will best attain to intellectual manhood, moral courage and physical fitness, and so promote efficiency for service to the world.[318]

For a period in the early nineteen hundreds, Allan Glen's sports days were grand social events held at iconic Hampden Park. Edward 'played [football] with distinction'[319] for his school, which may have included a few games on this revered turf trodden by many greats of Scottish football, such as Guyana-born Andrew Watson. The first man of colour to captain Scotland – or any national football team – a few decades earlier. His father's nativity was Kiltearn, Ross and Cromarty.[320]

The growing reputation of the school amongst Glasgow's enlarging middle-class was witnessed by the prestigious captains of industry who delivered annual Speech Day addresses. John Ward, president of the Institution of Engineers and Shipbuilders, was guest of honour in 1903. Edward would have heard him proclaim the integral role of Allan Glen's in maintaining the preeminence of British capitalism.

We who belong to the engineering or allied professions feel proud in having been pioneers in much good work; but we must recollect that there is no standing still among nations, and the race for industrial supremacy. Our rivals represent many nations, and their efforts to outstrip us in technical and industrial science are steady and continuous. Our hope for maintaining our supreme position lies

318 Quoted from *Pleasure, Profit and Proselytism: British Culture and Sport at Home and Abroad, 1700–1914,* J. A. Mangan (ed.) (London, 1982), chapter 5, 'Catalyst of Change: John Guthrie Kerr and the Adaptation of an Indigenous Scottish Tradition', p. 101. The mature Edward was living proof of the efficacy of his school's philosophy: a practitioner of medical science and keen amateur sportsman.
319 Obituary, *Carrick Herald,* 15 December 1950.
320 Tony Talburt, *Andrew Watson. The World's First Black Football Superstar,* (London, 2017). Watson was the first man of colour to captain a national football team.

largely in the fact that young men, like yourselves, in every town and city, are being specially trained to efficiently master their professions, both scientifically and practically.[321]

Ward's enthusiasm in sharing the anxious preoccupations of his class in preserving their ability to continue profit maximisation by dominating global markets, in hindsight, has a chilling resonance. Many historians of the Left argue the primary motivation for Britain declaring war on Germany in 1914 was inspired by the very fears Ward articulated eleven years earlier.[322] While Edward survived the carnage, his two brothers did not and one wonders how many of the adolescent audience also perished because of the predominance of Ward-like rhetoric. Poignantly, John Guthrie Kerr resigned as headmaster in 1917 to nurse victims of the war.

The embodiment of a muscular Christian, Edward was voted president of the Old Boys' Association in 1936. If this science and sport academy concentrated and focused Edward's intellectual and physical predilections, a nod must also be given to the necessary discipline required for single-minded success which was forged in childhood and early adolescence. Daughter Jean remembered her father taking a cold bath each morning and when off-duty doing household chores such as washing-up and lighting of the evening fires. These qualities of methodical routine, galvanised at the orphanage and Allan Glen's, were a legacy initiated by his biological parents. The Kent Palmer's and the Barbados Tull's would both have been supremely aware of the consequences of lethargic indiscipline: starvation. For the plantation-based Tulls, however, any indiscrete expression of emotional or physical indiscipline, however slight, could have had fatal consequences.[323]

Edward's positive experience at the school – where he made life-long friends such as Rangers and Scotland footballer James Bowie, naval designer and engineer James McNeill and brother-in-law Fred Reid[324] – assisted in acceptance in 1906 by the Incorporated Glasgow Dental

321 J. A. Mangan (ed.) (London, 1982), p.95.

322 Eric Hobsbawm, *The Age of Empire 1875-1914*, (London, 1995), p.54.

323 Interview with Jean and Rev. Duncan Finlayson, Appin, Argyle, 20 February 1995.

324 Ibid. For more information on McNeill see Andrew McCance, 'James McFadyen McNeill' *Biographical Memoirs of Fellows of the Royal Society*, Vol.11 (Nov., 1965), pp.126-134.

Hospital, Dalhousie Street. Within walking distance of St Vincent Street, he proved himself an 'outstanding student and won prizes for his operative work and general duties at the hospital', [325] taking second prize in both Dall and Ash Awards. The first named was funded by a bequest from William Dall, 1855-1932, 'for expertise in laboratory and porcelain techniques';[326] the second, a reward of three guineas, was for written work on a dental subject funded by Ash and Sons, dental manufacturers.

Subsequently, Edward undertook a course in anaesthesia from the Royal Infirmary, graduating with a Licence in Dental Surgery (LDS) from the Royal Faculty of Physician's and Surgeons, Glasgow, 1910. It had been empowered to issue the diploma via the reforms of the late eighteen seventies and was located conveniently at 242 St Vincent Street. Scotland's higher education institutions had a pioneering and proud record of educating people of colour during the nineteenth century. Edward's successful completion of his training ensured continuity into the twentieth. His ability to watch and learn from mater Warnock and James Adamson no doubt contributing.

The Warnocks had now relocated a little further along St Vincent Street to 419, continuing the dental practice at their new address. Having remained true in their vision for a professional future for Edward, laid before Stephenson in 1900, it is unclear why their adopted son – who had now added Warnock to his surname out of respect for his adoptive parents[327] – did not begin his career at the home in which he lived. Was it James's wish that Edward should be initiated by a professional with formal training and qualifications and then return as a registered dentist in order to legitimise the St Vincent Street practice?

DENTISTS AND DENTISTRY

It is also unclear if Edward was Britain's first licensed dentist of African Caribbean heritage.[328] Joseph St Clair, who stowed away to Bristol from

325 *A story of courage and achievement in early dentistry: Edward Tull-Warnock,* https://www.bda.org/library/history/bame-in-dental-history Accessed 30 July 2019

326 http://www.historyofdentistry.group/index_htm_files/1998Oct4.pdf Accessed 25 July 2020.

327 Interview with Jean and Rev. Duncan Finlayson, Appin, Argyle, 20 February 1995.

328 Evans (1995), p.215 names three dentists of colour, all Ghanaians, in

Barbados in 1876, became an unregistered dental practitioner in that city. Using herbs to create his unique concoction of tooth powder he extracted teeth at Bristol Bridge and county fairs.[329]

Dentistry during the second half of the nineteenth century had been under scrutiny and transformation.

As a recognised 'profession' dentistry didn't get status until the late 1800s – in 1858, the Dental Hospital of London opened, the first clinical training establishment for dentists in Britain and the Medical Registration Act permitted the College of Surgeons to grant licences in dental surgery, with the first ones being awarded in 1860 ... Prior to this, dentistry could be carried out by anyone who claimed to have the skills, leading to some interesting techniques and barbaric practices! Scotland was slightly ahead of the curve when it came to taking qualifications seriously, in 1856, Dr John Smith, a surgeon-dentist, and later President of the Royal College of Surgeons of Edinburgh, was the first person to conduct a course on dentistry with instructions for medical students.[330]

Progress was slow. The 1871 Census reveals a paltry two hundred and forty-four dentists serving Scotland, with few having recognised qualifications. One dentist was available, on average, to thirteen thousand seven hundred and seventy-one people. The Dentists Act 1878 and the expansion of university-based courses and qualifications envisioned unlicensed practitioners being eradicated by natural attrition through securing the learning of dentistry within academia. This institutional gatekeeping of dental knowledge would embourgeoisify a hitherto unlicensed trade and raise both the exchange value of that knowledge and the cultural capital accrued through transformation to a profession.

---

immediate post-Second World War Scotland: Mr Neizer, Mr Oddoye in Fife, and Mr Tetteh-Larteh in Dalkeith.

329 Joseph St Clair married Bristolian Maisie Stallard and their family have lived in the West Country for generations. His father William Robert St Clair was a tailor in Barbados. The family's biography is available at https://www.sgsts.org.uk/SupportForVulnerablePupils/EMTAS/Shared%20Documents/The%20St%20Clair(e)%20Family.pdf Accessed 19 January 2021.

330 *BAME in dental history. A story of courage and achievement in early dentistry: Edward Tull-Warnock,* https://www.bda.org/library/history/bame-in-dental-history Accessed 19 August 2020.

A register of dentists would be created to distinguish accredited bona fide dentists such as Edward from self-taught teeth extractors such as pater James. The first published Dentists Register of 1879 reveals one hundred and four dentists for Glasgow attending to a population of over half a million. By the end of the century, while the population of Scotland had increased by nearly twenty per cent, the number of dentists on the Register had risen by less than three per cent. Glasgow had just ninety-eight dentists serving three quarters of million inhabitants with an even split between formally qualified and self-taught.[331] It was a sellers market... if you were White.

Twenty-four year old Edward had been appointed by post for his first job as an assistant dentist in Birmingham. He had applied by letter enclosing the required testimonials and, voluntarily, a photograph. Eagerly travelling south by train, he arrived in the Midlands the evening before. The following morning new-suited and clean-booted, gold watch and chain adorning his waistcoat – a present from his proud, adoptive father – the expectant novice tapped on the front door of the practice. What met him clawed the shine from his enthusiasm. With an expression of uncomfortable surprise, bordering on shock, the dentist spluttered, 'my God, you're coloured, you'll destroy my practice in twenty-four hours!' before, without ceremony, closing the door in his face.[332] Devastated, he caught the train back to Glasgow the following morning.

While cruel and bigoted, it was a serendipitous rejection. He found alternative employment with a more enlightened member of the profession and, more importantly, met his future wife.

In a revealing talk given to a Girvan Methodist Guild meeting some two decades later he humorously recalled his first successful operation as an assistant-dentist on a

plumber who had come to the workshop to mend the pipes. Work being a secondary consideration and the boss being absent, I commenced to tell him all that there was to know about dentistry. He,

331 Much of the information on dentistry during the nineteenth century is from: Ross, Rufus Myer *The development of dentistry: a Scottish perspective circa 1800-1921*. PhD thesis, University of Glasgow, 1994. http://theses.gla.ac.uk/3218/1/1994RossPhD.pdf Accessed 25 July 2020.
332 Interview with Jean Finlayson (née Tull-Warnock) and Rev. Duncan Finlayson, Appin, Argyle, 20 February 1995.

on his side, proudly showed me three loose teeth that a Dentist could not extract. THAT was asking for it. There were some old forceps in that workshop that were used for anything but the extracting of teeth and assuring the Plumber that I was the man for the job I got busy. The Plumber for all I know is still living...[333]

Successfully completing his apprenticeship period, Edward registered as a fully-fledged dentist on his twenty-sixth birthday, 28 June 1912. Soon after James 'pater' Warnock died, aged fifty-nine from chronic nephritis. On the day Britain declared war on Germany in 1914, he took over the management of the practice under his name. This elevation of the surgery to one now headed by a qualified professional would have given James great satisfaction, both as father and practitioner. It was also fortuitous. Seven years later another Dentists Act closed off the profession to the unregistered. Recognising that 'dentistry is practically a new profession'[334] and 'applauding the move to professionalise the service and acknowledging the need for formal qualifications',[335] while in its passage as a Bill, Edward wrote a letter of support to the *Glasgow Herald* that was republished in the British Dental Association's (BDA) house journal.

I am one of the qualified dentists who believe that much good will come to the dental profession and to the public by the passing of the Dentists Bill now before Parliament. The great thing in this Bill is prohibition of practice by the unqualified. In other words, after the passing of the Bill any person who wishes to join the dental profession must qualify. I keep asking myself, 'Do the present qualified dentists realise this great fact?' From many of the letters that have appeared in your paper one would come to the conclusion that their text is, 'What we've got we'll hold.' I will admit that the qualified dentist of the present is asked to make a big sacrifice for the qualified of the

333 Edward Tull-Warnock *Types of Humanity to be Seen in a Dentists Chair* (undated) Finlayson Family Archive, p.4. Mater Warnock and Cissie were active members of the guild.
334 Ibid. p.1.
335 *BAME in dental history. A story of courage and achievement in early dentistry: Edward Tull-Warnock*, https://www.bda.org/library/history/bame-in-dental-history My thanks to Helen Neild, head of the BDA Knowledge and Library Services for bringing Edward's letter to my attention.

future, but surely the granting of what is asked is not beyond us. The qualified dentist of the present day has a good chance of raising the dental profession to the level of the medical for the future, and if we do not take the chance we shall be condemned in the future, and justly so, as we have condemned those who have shelved this question in the past.[336]

It is conceivable that Edward's public thoughts on the issue of legally restricting dentistry to the professionally qualified were arrived at through practical experience, his moral compass and personal politics. He had been inducted into the dental environment by unqualified James Warnock and had witnessed the need of poorer people for dentistry. His egalitarian Methodism upheld the principle that all human beings were deserving of dignity in the essential necessities of life. Health care must surely feature in this list. His socialism emphasised the systemic delivery of these necessities. So, it was not as a rejection of the social worth of unqualified practitioners, such as his adoptive father. It was in the hope of raising the applied quality of the profession which should then be socialised and available to all, irrespective of means. The practical realities of having an inner-city surgery where the family dining room was the waiting room and those in oral pain but on low pay or unemployed could not pay for treatment, kept Edward's professional feet on the ground.

Glasgow's pioneering mixed-heritage dentist embodied the Protestant work ethic. Because the practice and apartment were in the same building, Betty and Jean would see him briefly over lunch. This would be followed by a twenty minute nap before he returned to the surgery in the front room. His one full-day off, Sunday, revolved around the Methodist church and community, a tradition reaching back to childhood in Folkestone. Soon after the 1926 move to the Randolph Road family home, Friday mornings would be reserved for golf at the Hilton Park Golf Club on Stockiemuir Road, Milngavie. His workaholic schedule seems to have relaxed a minute fraction by Jean's early twenties when, after 'arriving home late tired after a good day's work [10 hours], it's my custom to supply my daughter Jean with a glass of Horlick's.'[337]

---

336 The *Dental Surgeon*, 5 February 1921 reprinted from the *Glasgow Herald*, 14 January, 1921 from *BAME in dental history. A story of courage and achievement in early dentistry: Edward Tull-Warnock.*
337 Edward to Duncan Finlayson, 25 March 1942, Finlayson Family Archive.

A life-long campaigner for a national health service, Edward recognised poverty as the primary cause of ill-health. He was a member of the Socialist Medical Association (SMA). Formed in 1930 after a meeting at the National Labour Club, the annual conference of May, 1936, agreed a constitutional change allowing dentists and other health professionals, such as nurses and midwives, to join. Later that year a meeting organised in Glasgow discussed 'the possibilities of a complete state medical service'.[338] Four years later a branch was officially established in the city.

The association encapsulated Edward's outlook, fighting for medical reform through the prism of socialist politics. It had an international perspective. At least sixteen SMA members travelled to Spain as part of the celebrated International Brigade to oppose General Franco's fascist insurrection against the elected republican government. Volunteering their medical support, they helped finance a hospital and facilitated the supply of staff and equipment.

In the month the UK government declared war on fascist Germany, the SMA reminded parliamentarians of the domestic enemies produced by vast inequalities of wealth, health and income: infant mortality in green and affluent Coulsdon, Surrey was thirty-two per thousand live births while in Stockton-on-Tees in north-east England it was one hundred and thirty-four; Scottish mums were twice as likely to die in childbirth than those in England, with malnutrition prevalent in over two million out of a population of just under five million. It led a deputation to the minister of health to highlight the desperate plight of civilian sick in wartime. Describing the conflict as an imperialist war, it protested the internment of anti-fascist refugees, especially doctors.

Aneurin Bevan, minister of health in the 1945-50 Labour government that introduced the National Health Service (NHS), acknowledged the formative and pioneering role the SMA had played by consistently arguing for tax-funded universal health provision free-at-the-point-of-delivery.

Post-war the SMA continued its internationalist agenda questioning the British government's support for fascists and right-wingers in Greece after it had been liberated from the Nazis by communist-led partisans.

---

338 *Glasgow Herald*, 9 October 1936, newspaper cutting held in Socialist Medical Association archive, U DSM/6/1-25, Hull History Centre.

The membership list now included another dentist of colour, Nigerian OA Ajose, a fellow Glasgow graduate. With more people of colour as members and the growing racialisation of British politics the executive committee in 1950, in co-ordination with the League of Coloured Peoples (LCP), agreed a resolution condemning the prejudice 'coloured students face in Britain and urged they be shown more friendliness.'[339] The resolution, calling for tolerance and fraternity, represented the intersection of class and ethnicity that defined Edward's life. That his professional organisation should work with another pressure group with which he supported and was friends with its founder, Jamaican doctor Harold Moody, was significant. It integrated and combined his personal and professional concerns as a man of colour within a socialist agenda.

Moody's passion for the rights and civil liberties of people of African descent was shaped by his Christian beliefs that, unlike Edward, moulded a more conservative outlook. His influence within the LCP was dominant with the organisation eschewing radical politics and favouring a more collaborative approach with representative institutions of the ruling class, such as the Colonial Office. Formed in 1931 after its founder had lived in London for over twenty-five years, the primary objectives were social justice and racial harmony.

Despite Moody's personal antithesis to revolutionary politics its executive included Ghanaian communist, Desmond Buckle. Another, Barbadian Cambridge University graduate Cecil Belfield Clarke, like Moody practised as a GP in London for over forty years and served on the British Medical Council. Early LCP members comprised a selection of Britain's most notable activists of colour such as Una Marson, CLR James, Paul Robeson and Jomo Kenyatta. There were also many White members.[340]

They produced a newsletter, *The Keys*, publicising their work. A March 1940 edition contains a correction from Edward to the assertion that Moody's son, Charles Arundel, had recently become the first Black infantry officer. He reminded members that his brother Walter had achieved that status some twenty-three years earlier. Another (eponymous) son of Moody's, Harold Ernest Arundel, was a regular

339 SMA archive, U DSM 1/1-3; 2/1; 6/1-25, Hull History Centre.
340 A detailed synopsis of Harold Moody and the LCP: https://www. encyclopedia.com/history/encyclopedias-almanacs-transcripts-and-maps/moody-harold-arundel and https://spartacus-educational.com/ SLAmoodyH.htm Both Accessed 22 December 2020.

visitor to the Tull-Warnock's Randolph Road home for tea while studying medicine at Glasgow University. Sharing with Duncan a love for pugilism, the two would train together at a local boxing gym.

A fine specimen, Harold would lie on a mat and say 'hold me down'. We would jump on his back and finish up with the life squashed out of us.[341]

The Church of Scotland minister recalled a story of Harold Ernest Arundel's when in India. Getting into a car two White GI's foolishly grabbed him saying 'that's our taxi Nigger'. They ended up in the gutter with the reminder 'this is not the States, boys'. The same arm that floored the racist Americans was used to put the shot for Britain at the 1948 Olympics in his hometown of London where he was a member of South London Harriers. Now also a GP, two years later he represented England at the 1950 British Empire Games in New Zealand where he won a silver medal. Falling in love with the country he emigrated, serving as mayor of Glen Eden, Auckland for six years.[342]

Edward's political activism was ingrained into his daily life. He practised it in his family, with daughter Jean being instructed to make available her unwanted toys and clothes for distribution to impoverished residents of nearby tenements. At work he would not refuse treatment if the patient was poor and unable to pay. While members of the SMA felt fulfilled and overjoyed when health care, including dentistry, became free to all on 5 July 1948, some medical professionals saw the establishment of the NHS as a threat to their income and quality

341 Interview with Reverend Duncan Finlayson, 2 June 2008.
342 The inaugural British Empire Games were held at Hamilton, Canada 1930. Represented were Newfoundland, Bermuda, British Guiana, Australia, New Zealand, South Africa, Wales, Ireland, Scotland, England and the hosts. A report by the Council for Great Britain observed: 'At Hamilton, where Britons alone were concerned, there was a warmth of comradeship, a spirit of cordiality and even self-sacrifice which will assuredly bear fruit among those young men and women of the British race'. Quoted in Katharine Moore,' 'The Warmth of Comradeship', The First British Empire Games and Imperial Solidarity', International Journal for the History of Sport, vol.6, September 1989, No2, p.249. Perhaps it was the colour bar in British boxing that channelled Harold Ernest Arundel into athletic competition. Black pugilists had not been allowed to fight for British titles since 1911. It was not until 1948 that mixed-heritage middleweight, Randolph Turpin, was allowed to contest a domestic title.

of life. It was introduced in the face of overwhelming opposition from the British Medical Association and Conservative MPs. Edward had fought a personal battle with pneumonia in 1942, necessitating a retreat to the countryside for fresh air, rest and recuperation. He would have been aware how fortunate he was in having the resources to do what he and Betty felt was necessary to overcome the illness. Experiencing the beginnings of an era where individual luck and chance as the main weapons in fighting ill-health were being replaced by a standing arsenal of collectively-owned medical munitions designed for the sole purpose of saving lives must have been both satisfying and reassuring.

In his entertaining professional revelations to the Girvan Methodist Guild Edward relayed a poignant story.

At a meeting of Dentists sometime ago I heard a gentleman who practices in a very populous but poor district relate the following. A little girl walked into his surgery and holding out a sixpence said, 'my mother said you were to take out as many as you can for that.'

For the benefit of his audience he made some pertinent suggestions about dental hygiene: visit the dentist and eat fruit and vegetables, regularly.

No Pure Food Campaign was needed... 50 years ago... Chocolate: Iced Cakes: manufactured jams: concocted puddings of the custard type &c were unknown then and bad teeth were the exception rather than the rule. It is only by going back to the simpler diet that we can hope to keep our stomachs right and our teeth healthy... Medical Science has decreed, that the most important factor in regard to the health of the body is that we must have a plentiful supply of Vitamins... They are to be found in fresh vegetables and fresh fruits.[343]

Ironically, nearly a century later amongst the plethora of guidelines, instructions and advice bombarding the UK public, official and unofficial, on building immunity against illness, is a very similar argument and message: the relevance of diet.

---

343 For both quotes, Edward Tull-Warnock *Types of Humanity to be Seen in a Dentists Chair* pp. 6 & 9, respectively.

Chapter Ten
Families and Politics

Edward's conscientious adoption of the role of family patriarch – growing in importance over time – and his commitment to the preservation of material relating to his family's history is arguably his greatest legacy. His accumulation represents the foundation of the collection now formally known as the Finlayson Family Archive. Much of its content made its public debut during the National Museum of Scotland's 2008 exhibition about Black Scots. The archive represents a unique documentation of characters and episodes from a Black Atlantic family over four centuries from enslavement to twenty-first century acknowledgement in the *Oxford Dictionary of National Biography*.

Edward's decision to add Warnock as a hyphenation in his surname signifies his attitude to the family as an institution and the values that flow from it. He cherished his, working throughout his life to nurture its maintenance and durability. His letters to the CHO of May and July, 1903, requesting Walter be allowed to have his summer holiday in Scotland, illustrate an early, physical manifestation. Some years later, with Edward inheriting responsibility for the care and well-being of mater Jeannie Warnock on the death of James in 1914, we once again witness this preoccupation with Cissie invited to live at the Warnock's summer home, Bloomfield Cottage, Garelochhead, Helensburgh. Surrounded by a picturesque countryside of lochs and inlets, served by a railway station the cottage perched close-by the shore of Gare Loch. (The last photos of Walter, newly-commissioned as a second lieutenant, were taken there in the spring of 1917 before he returned to France.)

During the nineteen twenties and thirties, Cissie lived at 5 Daisy Bank, Henrietta Street, Girvan. With a comforting sea-view reminiscent of home she acted as carer, housekeeper and dental receptionist.

The residence also became a welcome refuge for sisters Elsie, Miriam and step-mother Clara and Bill Beer, especially during the Second World War when the threat of invasion was a wearisome preoccupation for the population of England's south coast. Edward would try to find work for market gardener Bill. This sense of responsibility for his extended family was a role, Jean observed, he enjoyed and was grateful for the privilege, even if it did entail additional duties and expenditure.

It is not beyond the imagination to envisage the legacy of his father and grandparents having influence. It was an incessant battle of the enslaved to build and keep a family. While the eradication of their chattel status enhanced their ability to remain physically close to their kith and kin, their unchanging poverty continued to act as a counterforce. Edward's personal experience of emotional rupture and geographical relocation, together with his father's perceived injustices and lack of paternal support as recited in his *Journal,* may have provided the ingredients that fuelled his determination to use whatever means were at his disposal to strengthen familial bonds.

Understandably but unfortunately, his financial resources did not allow him to physically pursue and explore his Barbadian family. They may have been closer in proximity that he thought. In the spring of 1916 ten stowaways from Barbados were discovered on the *Savan,* sailing from the West Indies to London. One was a 'S. Tull.' The reason for their travel is not recorded but it was not unknown for men from the island to secrete aboard UK-bound ships in order to enlist in the British Expeditionary Force. A year previous, nine men from Barbados stowed away on the *Danube* in order to volunteer. When they were discovered, they were arrested and appeared at West Ham Police Court. Ridiculing their misguided patriotism, they were the victims of taunts from the magistrate.[344] S. Tull and his companions were sentenced at Thames Police Court to fourteen days hard labour. Following the journey that his namesake Daniel had made forty years earlier this particular Tull did not have such a fortuitous outcome. In the *Returns of Passengers* the writer records the date of their conviction, 5 May, concluding '[I] have not heard of them since'.[345] The diasporic journeys of both Tulls, some forty years apart, illustrate the extremes of fortune awaiting those brave enough to try.

Several members of Edward's extended family left Barbados for other Caribbean islands – as his father had done initially – and the North American mainland. John Richard Finlay Tull, whom Daniel's sister Sarah Elizabeth cites in her Will as her nephew, died a Methodist

---

344 See Larry Burchall, *The Rise of the Faceless and the Internet Warrior?*, (Victoria, Canada, 2002), p.49.

345 *Incoming Passengers. Returns of Passengers brought to the United Kingdom in ships arriving from Places out of Europe, and not within the Mediterranean Sea,* 2 May 1916.

minister in Antigua. Another nephew of Daniel, Edward Nathaniel, son of Samuel James, is listed in the 1930 USA Census as a single, fifty year old sugar plantation labourer living in Christiansted, St. Croix, Virgin Islands. Discussed below is Samuel's fourth son, Daniel, who spent at least the last seventeen years of his life Harlem, New York much of it during its vibrant, confident, revolutionary, renaissance era.

LOVE AND MARRIAGE

Having been denied the dental assistant post in Birmingham because of his prospective employer's racism, Edward experienced the nitty-gritty of daily surgery at his adoptive father's unregistered St Vincent Street practice. In 1912 he found employment as assistant to registered dentist Mr Cruickshank at Aberdeen.

In this north-eastern fishing town characterised by its grey granite buildings, while attending Crown Terrace Methodist Church Edward met and fell in love with Elizabeth Elliot Hutchison. She was the daughter of Jane Elliot and Alexander Burnett Hutchison (ABH), prominent members of the city's business and civic community, their Central Bakery business having numerous retail shops about the city.

Edward's welcome into this influential family of practising Wesleyan Methodists echoed the reception his father had received from the Palmers in Folkestone. (Daniel and Alice had also first met at chapel.) Adoption by the Warnocks transformed Edward's quality of life: emotionally through their love and care; physically through having his own bedroom; and culturally through his piano lessons and education at Allan Glen's and the Glasgow Dental Hospital and Royal Infirmary. The cultural capital acquired through betrothal to Elizabeth represented yet another development in his social transformation: being son-in-law of the Hutchison's required the private and public deployment of social skills expected and demanded by the bourgeoisie.

Jean's family reminiscences suggested her illegitimate maternal grandfather had not always been accustomed to the relative affluence her father encountered when joining the family.

A.B.H. served his apprenticeship as a baker in Dundee at a fairly early age (12-14?) & there must have met my grandmother Jane Elliott who lived in Downside, Dundee. Gran died about 1923 & grandpa must have remarried about 2 years later – a R.C. [Roman Catholic] whom

I knew as 'Aunt Agnes' – a rather imposing and handsome woman, – not very popular with the family, but that is another story! It was said (by then) that grandpa would possibly have been Provost of Aberdeen (he *was* Senior Bailley) if he had not married Agnes. Gran was very well liked and people took badly to his 2nd marriage. Thank goodness none of this bothered me. I remember a fun grandpa who called me 'Maggie Clart' (wonder why?) – I can still smell the home-made tomato soup & steak pie, served by maids at his dining table. Dear maids Maggie Glenine & Cathy? who tolerated me wonderfully in their domain in the basement. They had a sitting room, I think, as well as [a] large kitchen there was a 'lift' from kitchen to butler's pantry – all this in 19 Queen's Road… There was a dining room, library, morning room & drawing room on the ground floor – bedrooms next floor, & attic rooms above that. Grandpa had a Minerva car, driven by Webster, the chauffeur who had a house at the bottom of the garden.[346]

Edward and Elizabeth – Betty – married at Crown Terrace Church, 28 September, 1918. Edward was still grieving the death of Walter six months earlier and encouraged his fiancé and her parents not to have too grand an event. Some members of his immediate family attended including Cissie who was caring for mater Warnock at Garelochead. William, a sapper in the Royal Engineers and wife Gertrude, sent a congratulatory telegram signing off 'Gert and Bill.'

After a reception at the Hutchison family home, they honeymooned at the coastal hamlet of Kippford on the shore of the Solway Firth in Dumfries and Galloway. A notice was posted in the Marriages column of the *Aberdeen Weekly Journal,* Friday 4 October, informing readers the 'adopted son of the late James K. Warnock, Glasgow, and Mrs Warnock, Bloomfield, Garelochhead' had married 'Elizabeth Elliot, youngest daughter of Baillie A.B. and Mrs Hutchison, 70 Hamilton Place, Aberdeen. The family home would be at 419 St Vincent Street,

---

346 Jean Finlayson, *Tales of Grandfathers (and Grandmothers),* (undated), pp.1-2, Finlayson Family Archive. The office of senior baillie approximates in England and Wales to chief magistrate with Provost comparative to mayor. The observation that by marrying a Roman Catholic ABH unofficially disqualified himself from elevation to Provost would have been consistent with contemporary discriminatory practices - sectarianism - towards Catholics and/or those married to them.

Glasgow. Jean was born two years later, their only child.

If the celebration of the marriage had not been the grand affair culturally expected of the daughter of the baillie of Aberdeen, the death of Betty's father ten years later certainly was with Edward undertaking conspicuous roles now considered a familial duty. Having already carried an obituary, the *Aberdeen Press and Journal* devoted two columns to the Civic Funeral of Late Ex-Baillie Hutchison. The detailed report describes how he was 'laid to rest... with full civic honours'. Following a private service at the Hutchison residence, 19 Queen's Road, a public commemoration was held at Crown Terrace Church. Attending were senior representatives of Aberdeen's most dominant institutions, the town council, Harbour Board and Incorporated Trades. One of eight pall-bearers alongside the deceased's three sons, Edward helped 'carry the beautiful oak coffin, with its lid hidden from site by a wealth of floral tributes', into the church. After the service, as a designated chief mourner with the sons he followed the cortege – headed by the civic dignitaries – through the streets to Springbank Cemetery, 'the crowds of onlookers who lined the route [paying] silent tribute to the passing of a respected citizen.'[347] The total value of his estate was valued at over £14,645 (£926,947).

Jean's depiction of her great-grandmother in 'Tales of Grandfathers' has a romantic tinge.

> Great Gran Hutchison had a wee shoppie that sold pies in Rose St. Aberdeen and they lived above it, I think. At least it was in central Aberdeen & when my mother was a young lass, I think her gran lived in Rose St.

She probably would not have known her grandfather's involvement in one of Aberdeen's biggest court actions of the mid-to-late eighteen-nineties, dubbed the Nellfield Scandal, involving a cemetery owned by the town's bakers. As first master of the Baker Trade in Aberdeen he and two other trustees of the cemetery were sued in a class action claiming desecration. Large numbers of graves had been opened, the interred remains destroyed, burned, moved or damaged and the *lairs* (plots) resold for up to four pounds (£536) each. The claimants were successful in alleging that this had been done for profit and gain and that they should be compensated. ABH and the other trustees professed ignorance

347 *Aberdeen Press and Journal,* 22 February 1928. Obituary, 18 February.

blaming their employee and manager of the cemetery, superintendent William Coutts. The case only came to light, the newspaper reports stated, because gravediggers Raffan and Hay laid to rest the ghosts of their consciences by speaking out.[348]

Despite the time demanded by his high-profile civic roles and business commitments, Jean writes her maternal grandfather found time for Saturday cycle rides down the coast to Banchory with Betty and sister May – who formed a close, platonic relationship with Edward. All were rewarded with a boiled egg tea. There was also summer holidays on the coast at Forres, north west of Aberdeen where a substantial portion of the time would be spent at Forres Golf Club.

At her grandparents home in Queen's Road in the nineteen twenties and thirties Jean enjoyed playing in the attic and writing on the old bakery ledgers stored there. 'The Queen's Road house was fun for me, even if not all that homey for mum and her brothers and sisters'.[349] Was this an oblique reference to the changed domestic environment occasioned by the death of grandma Jane in 1924 and the new regime of Aunt Agnes after her marriage to ABH in 1925?

Jean does not explain why her grandfather's second wife was not popular with some members of the Hutchison family. Her good looks, being a late-coming heir to a substantial family fortune and replacing a much loved mother and wife would be the successful ingredients of a captivating drama. In real life such situations of competing family dynamics tend toward outcomes of tension and mistrust.

Edward's granddaughter, Pat Justad, recalled her mother commenting she was blessed with grandparents. Some she had not had the privilege to meet, such as Alice and Daniel. Others were geographically distant but sometime visitors and residents, such as Clara – 'Nanny Beer' – and Bill Beer. Once married, still more came into her life from husband Duncan's lineage, such as the McLeans.

Edward was conscious it would have been a wrench for twenty-four year old Betty to leave her (pre-Aunt Agnes) home and family in Aberdeen, a town in which she had lived all her life. Jean described how her father would bring back to Glasgow sweet-peas grown the garden in Girvan, alongside fresh-caught salmon and other local foodstuffs for his 'quiet, reserved, thoughtful and utterly dependable' wife.[350] His

348 *Aberdeen Press and Journal,* 18, 22 June 1896 and 6 October, 1899.
349 *Tales of Grandfathers…* p.2
350 Interview with Jean and Reverend Duncan Finlayson, 20 February, 1995.

upbringing by three mothers perhaps allowed him an insight unavailable to most.

JEAN'S CHILDHOOD AND EDUCATION

Jean talked of her 'very happy and spoilt [early] childhood'[351] in St Vincent St. Characterised by contentment, security and relative affluence it compared favourably to the desperately poor William and Richard Streets close-by. The latter was 'a dreadful tenement with one hundred folk to one stair'.[352]

Her recollection of this first childhood home was framed by a sense of largeness. Their sitting room looked out upon the yard, 'a vast grassless rubbish filled space surrounded on four sides by tenements'. In the basement was the kitchen, maid Bella's bedroom and a workshop in which dentures were made and repaired. The workshop mechanic was 'Wee Ferguson', whom the Reverend Duncan Finlayson remembers possessing a wry humour. Just after the Second World War recruitment posters offering twenty pounds a week with all found for police work in troubled Palestine were scattered about Glasgow. 'Nae bloody likely, twenty poonds a week and nae foond' was the dental mechanic's wary response.[353]

In her memoir Jean stresses Bella, from Port Charlotte, on the Isle of Islay in the southern Hebrides, 'was very much part of the household and my confidante'. This bond may have galvanised while she cared for the infant Jean embedded with double pneumonia. The young Gael even tried to teach the younger Lowlander her language, without success. She stayed with the Tull-Warnocks most of her life, living-in until she married in 1939, thereafter working as a daily helper. Yet she still 'had to fight for an increase in wages from £3 to £4 per month' for a six-day week, commented Jean, a touch sacrilegiously. Her work would begin at half past six in the morning with preparation of Edward and Betty's morning tea, after which breakfast would have to be on the table before eight in order the pupil not be late for school, the dentist on-time at his practice.

Jean attended Glasgow High School for Girls. Founded in 1894 it also

351 Interview with Jean Finlayson, 20 February 1995.
352 Jean Finlayson *Tales of Grandfathers (& Grandmothers)* (undated), Finlayson Family Archive. p.4.
353 Interview with Reverend Duncan Finlayson, 2 June 2008.

had a primary department and was situated on two sites in Garnethill and Kelvindale in the West End. Her father thought there might be a greater propensity for racist bullying at a local school.

> By my blood my daughter will have problems of the kind that I have had and if I can do anything to give her confidence and a bit of status, I know it's wrong but I am going to do it.[354]

There was also a personal connection that eased Edward's anxieties. The head, Flora Webb, was formerly his Latin teacher at Allan Glen's. In 1936 she had an additional reason to be proud of her formative contribution with Edward taking presidency of the alumni association. It was a prestigious position conferred through a vote of members thereby carrying authoritative weight. It was also cultural equity that would help, if needed for instance, in enforcing his resolve that no harm should come to daughter while Ms Webb's current – and equally prestigious – institution was in loco parentis.

Jean's fond memories of her Glasgow upbringing as 'very cushioned 'suggests Edward's paternal vigilance over her welfare as a child of colour paid off. She felt her mixed-heritage ethnicity was, in stranger's eyes, fluid: Maltese, Greek, South American. Mirroring her father's experience she suggested that, 'until recently' [the mid-nineteen nineties], Scotland was less hostile toward people of colour.[355]

Despite school fees absorbing a substantial portion of his earnings, Edward did his best to adhere to Charles Dickens' Micawber principle (from David Copperfield): 'Annual income twenty pounds, annual expenditure nineteen nineteen and six, result happiness. Annual income twenty pounds, annual expenditure twenty pounds nought and six, result misery'. He lived up to his income but not over it. The stable and secure learning environment allowed Jean to develop her academic faculties and eventually study for an MA in History at Glasgow University.

Preventing unnecessary worry and anxiety in the life of his daughter, caused by ignorant others, was a driving passion. His workaholic lifestyle, allied with an irrepressible enthusiasm to enjoy earned moments of leisure, was his leitmotif. He also ensured for those loved ones around him opportunities more abundant than he had time to share.

354 Interview with Rev. Duncan Finalyson, 2 June 2008.
355 Interview, 1995.

Jean and Betty spent most summers in Girvan where, devoid of the company of a brother or sister, she would often invite a friend from Glasgow. Before mater Warnock became unwell, she and Cissie would swap their home in Girvan, keeping Edward company in Glasgow during August while his wife and daughter enjoyed the Ayrshire coast.

Jean retained a mental album of vivid memories, like the town crier announcing the sailing of the *Lady Ailsa* to Ailsa Craig, a volcanic plug of two hundred and forty acres ten miles offshore. Then a renowned holiday destination, now colonised by puffins and gannets. During its human habitation Edward's visits, while not vocally and publicly proclaimed, did merit mention in the local press.

> Mr E. Tull-Warnock, dentist, Girvan and Glasgow, crossed over to Ailsa Craig last week in the 'Lady Ailsa' and extracted fifteen 'crunchers' out of the mouths of two Craig residents. The journey was made in a choppy sea, but the painless extractor enjoyed the trip.[356]

His professional duty was often rewarded by the captain of the vessel with friendship and free passage. Jean sometimes accompanied him and recalled the delicious goat's milk scones made by three sisters who ran the tearoom.

Girvan harbour was a child's playground of funfair rides and stalls. At the open air bandstand on (nearby) Stair Park, the omnipresent Pierot Concert Party, a franchised clown-attired sextuplet, amused and entertained with comedy, song and impersonation. And, the most essential element of any child's summer holiday, ice creams, were on sale for half a penny, one penny and three pence. Is it significant that Jean remembered the prices? The town also had 'flea-pit picture houses and community singing around the piano'.[357] Yet, even with all of these attractions, the most satisfying treat was meeting her father off the train on Tuesday and Friday evenings, arriving for his surgeries the following day.

In 'Tales of Grandfathers' Jean recalls another father-daughter activity involving trains: Saturday afternoon excursions by subway to watch Rangers FC. They had the best seats in the stadium, sitting in the director's box alongside club president James – Jas/Jimmy – Bowie. 'No wonder I still recall the name of the Rangers players

356 'Vale of Girvan Notes', *Ayr Advertiser*, p.6, 13 September, 1934.
357 Jean Finlayson, *Tales of Grandfathers*.

in the 30's!' Duncan was not so sure she was a willing participant.

My wife, Jean, attended many games at Ibrox with her father in the directors' box and grew quite bored of it – she would far rather have been at the pictures with her mother. Dad was of course in Girvan doing his dentistry on Saturdays, so there were only certain occasions when they could make it along to games. However, in later years if ever we needed tickets for international matches or big fixtures they were always made available through Jimmy.[358]

A compensatory factor that may have diluted Jean's reticence was the collective excellence of those she was watching. Bowie's boys won the league title season after season, missing out on only three occasions between 1930-39. She may have been at the traditional New Year's Day Old Firm match, 2 January 1939, when a UK league attendance record of 118,567 was set.

While Betty chose not to participate, it was one of the few activities involving the Bowies from which she excluded herself. That the couples enjoyed time in each other's company is evidenced not just by Jean and Duncan's reminiscences but surviving letters. Dated only by the day and month but probably written in 1937, Edward gently prods his missed daughter to write.

You must be enjoying your holiday… Everywhere I am asked 'What sort of time are you having in Paris? Well' I have to reply 'There is no news so far but there is hardly time'. So Monday should bring some news of your journeyings…

He then supplies his daughter with the commodity of which she has starved him.

When I got back to Glasgow [from Girvan] I found mummy had been for a walk round Southbrae so I at once set off. We will call at the Bowies / Which we did / We walked there and stayed until 11.40 P.M. Just Mr and Mrs Bowie and ourselves / They have been in Paris and entertained us with their doings. Today, Sunday, has been a lovely

358 Reverend Duncan Finlayson quoted in Paul Smith, *Aye Ready, Rangers War Heroes*, (Edinburgh, 2011), p.16.

day. All your friends wanted news of you – which I couldn't give them... Mummy sees by the paper that Mary Pickford has arrived in Paris today. Perhaps you will see her... Make the most of your time I know you are like me and will do so. [359]

FRIENDSHIPS

Edward's worked hard to build and maintain family and social relationships. He knew through experience the importance of having and keeping close trusted people who reciprocated love. His psychological and emotional durability, his inherent humour and the moral guidance provided by his Methodist faith and socialist beliefs, equipped him with life skills that facilitated a clarity of thought and feeling. His son-in-law, the Reverend Duncan Finlayson, emphasised the profound effect of Wesleyan values.

He and his brother... were the kind of people they were because of their basic Christian faith which was a motivating force in both their lives. It was a faith nurtured in the Methodist Church – the significance of which was absolutely critical at every important time and turn of the Tull family story from splendid 'Granny' Anna in Barbados – right through to my wife Jean.[360]

The friendship with Jas Bowie began while pupils at Allan Glen's school. It continued for the rest of their lives, galvanised by their unified efforts on the football pitch. His friend's excellence is remembered in several alumni newsletters by former pupil and football historian Bill Murray. Despite its contemporary reputation as a rugby-playing institution,

Dr Kerr loved football and the school had a special relationship with

359 Edward to Jean, Sunday 28 March. Assuming Jean did not go without her parents before she was sixteen, there were two possible Sundays, 1937 and 1943. The latter date is disqualified because civilian travel abroad was severely restricted and Paris was occupied by the Nazis. It could have been a sixth-form trip with Glasgow High School for Girls. May Pickford was the highest paid female film star of the silent movie era and a founder of United Artists. She was in Paris in 1937.

360 Letter, Reverend Duncan Finlayson to Ruth Caleb, Finlayson Family Archive.

The Royal Adventurers of England. Trading into Africa was created by the Stuart royal family on Restoration. It was the first joint stock company dedicated to trading in enslaved people: 'to furnish his Majesties American Plantations with Negroes at certain and moderate rates'.

Cape Coast Castle, Gold Coast (Ghana) was a notorious holding fort for captured West Africans before they were transported as enslaved chattle to the Americas.

Detail of a seventeenth century map of Barbados showing the names and locations of plantations including 'The tenn thousand Acres which belongeth to the Merchants of London.' As well as camels, donkeys and boar the map features, in the top left hand corner, two enslaved persons running away and chased by a horse rider who has opened fire on them.

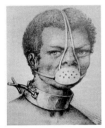

Anna Lashly. Edward's grandmother born into plantation enslavement c.1815. (Copyright Finlayson Family Archive)

Clifton Hall Slave Register, 1817. Edward's grandfather, William Criss, is listed (seventh down) as a nine-year-old field labourer who was born in Barbados.

A collar and iron mask. These barbaric restraints and shackles illustrate planter ideology that the enslaved, as property, were equal to animals rather than humans.

An eighteenth-century sugar plantation. Some historians have argued that the precise division of labour provided the template for the factory system in the UK that was the organisational foundation of the industrial revolution.

Calvary Moravian Church, Roebuck Street, Bridgetown is where the Tulls worshipped after they moved to My Lord's Hill in the 1860s. Daniel Tull attended the church school.

Clifton Hill chattel/peasant shacks. These shacks in Clifton Hill housed the enslaved such as Anna Lashly and William Tull who laboured on the Clifton Hall plantation.

Alice Palmer, Edward's mother, born Hougham, Kent 19 March 1853, died Folkestone, Kent 14 April 1895. (Copyright Finlayson Family Archive)

The Tull family in Folkestone. Edward is standing next to his seated father Daniel who is supporting sister Elsie on his knee. Brother Walter is sitting in front of Edward and next to sister Cissie. Eldest brother William, like his father, is wearing a bowler hat. The occasion is probably the funeral of mother Alice, April, 1895. (Copyright Finlayson Family Archive)

Bonner Road Orphanage, Bethnal Green. Edward entered the orphanage with his brother Walter in February, 1898. A comparatively progressive Methodist institution, it had a gymnasium and swimming pool. Both were members of the choir which toured Britain to raise funds and showcase members for adoption. (Copyright Action for Children)

The Children's Home and Orphanage choir, c.1900. Edward is seated front row, furthest left. Edward's brother Walter is seated front row, third from the right. (Copyright Action for Children)

James Warnock who, with his wife Jean, adopted Edward in 1900 after hearing him sing at St. John's Methodist Church, Glasgow as a member of The Children's Home and Orphanage choir. (Copyright Mike Gow)

Edward was pupil at the fee-paying Allan Glen's School between 1900–1906. With a muscular Christian ethos it is where he met lifelong friend, Rangers and Scotland footballer James Bowie. He was elected president of the Old Boys Association in 1936.

Girvan Athletic FC c.1908-09. Edward is fifth from the left, front row. Edward's schoolboy friend Queen's Park FC player, James Bowie, who signed for Rangers in 1910, is third from left, back row. (Thanks to Ritchie and Lorna Conaghan of Girvan for sourcing this photo)

Elizabeth 'Betty' Hutchison, Edward's wife, daughter of the baillie of Aberdeen. (Copyright Finlayson Family Archive)

The last photo of Edward with his brother, Walter, Garelochhead, May 1917. Edward standing left. Seated are, left, Edward's adoptive mother, Jean Warnock and right, his sister, Cissie. (Copyright Finlayson Family Archive)

Edward in his dentist's attire, possibly taken at Girvan, c.1920s (Copyright Finlayson Family Archive)

Edward was a member of Turnberry Golf Club in an era when the colour bar was widely practiced. In 1928 he won the club's prestigious Weir Trophy and the Naysmyth Cup, competed for by dentists in Glasgow and the south-west of Scotland. (Copyright Finlayson Family Archive)

Edward was protective of his brother Walter's historical legacy, writing to the *Glasgow Evening Times* when Harold Moody of the League of Coloured People claimed his son was Britain's first Black army officer. (Copyright Finlayson Family Archive)

Edward and Betty's daughter, Jean, married proud Highlander Duncan Finlayson in 1943. (Copyright Finlayson Family Archive)

Edward, daughter Jean and son-in-law Duncan Finlayson. (Copyright Finlayson Family Archive)

Glasgow dentist Mike Gow and children, relatives of Edward from the Warnock side of the family, capturing the moment the city publicly acknowledged Edward's brother Walter as one of the first Black officers in the British Army. (Copyright Mike Gow)

Edward's grandchildren after receiving their £5 coins from the Royal Mint commemorating the life of their great uncle Walter, Edward's brother, killed in action at the Second Battle of the Somme, 1918. From the left: Iona, Edward, Duncan and Pat (Copyright Finlayson Family Archive)

Crown disclaimer Bridgetown boardwalk. While the UK government persistently dismisses the claim from Barbados for reparations for enslaving the antecedents of its population, the British Crown persistently lays claim to its territory. This sign is located at Carlisle Bay where slave ships landed their captives from West Africa.

Queen's Park FC, even being allowed to use its famous stadium foathletic meetings before Bishopbriggs took over in 1923. Arthur F. Murray, who played for Queen's Park and became club president from 1921 to 1923, was a Latin teacher at that time. He took over the football and among his many talented players the most outstanding was James Bowie, who was signed by Rangers from Queen's Park in 1910 and went on to play with the 'Gers until 1922 (including two appearances for his country just after the War); three years later he joined the Board, on which he served and presided for many years until ousted by Bill Struth in 1947.[361]

In a letter addressed to newly-weds Jean and Duncan, a contented Edward relays news occurring after the couple had departed the reception for their honeymoon at Bridge of Orchy. Particularly worthy of record was how James Bowie had entertained some of the guests and kept them in 'continual giggles'. The Rangers chair and president of the Scottish Football League was also 'hung on to' by Wee Ferguson to perform another entertainment duty: a ticket for the Glasgow FA Cup final played at Hampden Park that day between Rangers and Clyde. The persistence of Edward's workshop mechanic paid off. Taxied to the ground, he watched the match as a guest of his illustrious sponsor.[362] Wee Ferguson was fortunate in his timing, a quality the Ranger's chairman was accused of lacking after being controversially deposed a few years later (referred to in the quote above by Murray).

The following Wednesday, Betty, her mother and Edward visited the Bowies 'to sort of sum up the wedding festivities'.[363] Other members of the extended family, Betty's sister May and husband Fred Reid, were also there.

Reading the runes from the most devastating crisis he had faced in football career, that caused him never to set foot in his beloved Rangers again, Bowie was progressive in his politics. After playing nearly three hundred senior games, serving as director and then chairman over a period of twenty-seven years, he would soon need his friends' wise counsel and shoulders to lean on after being told by shareholders he was no longer wanted. 'The Battle for Blue Room' erupted in 1947 after

361 Allan Glen's School Club *Newsletter,* October 2009, p.3; July, 2010, p.6.
362 Letter to Jean and Duncan Finlayson, 10 October 1943, Finlayson Family Archive.
363 Letter to Jean and Duncan Finlayson, 15 October 1943.

Bowie suggested to manager Bill Struth that at seventy-one years of age he might need the help of an assistant who would succeed him on retirement. This angered the legendary boss.

The League Flag, which was up for grabs 'officially' for the first time after WWII, was flying proudly over Ibrox for the 26th time. The inaugural League Cup was won after a 4-0 trouncing of Aberdeen at Hampden. The Iron Curtain had been draped over a Rangers goal that conceded only 34 goals in 43 games as the Rangers fans flocked to Ibrox in their tens of thousands to follow their team which had just delivered a 9th League Title in a row. All was Red, White and Blue in the garden of Rangers. That summer, those loyal fans had no reason to believe that all was not well within Ibrox.[364]

Bowie's mistake was to voice his statement two months before the Annual Meeting at which positions on the board would be voted upon, including his. This gave Struth the time to canvas support among shareholders for a chair with a different perspective on his future. Despite Bowie's background as a player, Struth had a view of chairmen common amongst club managers: if I'm successful on the pitch, keep your nose out of my business. Internecine warfare broke out and Edward's close friend lost. It broke his heart and ultimately the consequences of what some saw as a boardroom coup had fatal consequences.

The power went to the big battalions. No longer would the board be made up of former players with a particular love for the club they had served. A watershed moment in the history of the club. Rangers was no longer a football club - it had become a commercial entity. The revolution of 1947 was the first step that took Rangers along a road that led to ownership by the John Lawrence Construction Group in 1985, in 1988 to David Murray and in 2011 to Craig Whyte. The position we now find ourselves in has its roots in the Battle of the Blue Room in 1947. The fall out from then resonates into the modern era.[365]

364 Gary Havlin, 'The 1947 Battle for the Blue Room and its consequences today', *The Rangers Standard* https://www.therangersstandard.co.uk/index. php/articles/club-history/261-the-1947-battle-for-the-blue-room-and-its-consequences-today Accessed 10 November 2020.
365 Ibid. While under Craig Whyte's control Rangers became bankrupt and

Another Allan Glen's old boy, Fred Reid, shared Edward's political beliefs and was close friend of future Labour leader Hugh Gaitskell. He had grown up in the slum tenements of William Street, close-by St Vincent Street. His father was infamous as the 'drunken [horse drawn] cabbie' whose notoriety was not so much his capacity for alcohol but that his children had no shoes. One studious and determined son, however, used his poverty as a spur and won a school scholarship. This was Fred's backstory as told by the Finlayson's in our 1995 interview. They believed he graduated from Aberdeen University[366] after which he married May Hutchison. Achieving a senior position in the General Post Office in northern England, the couple understood Gaitskell wanted him to head the institution nationally. (The Labour leader died in 1963 one year before the party won power. Some historians of politics argue the cause of his passing is still contentious.)[367] He also had a career in the Territorial Army. Fred and May's son, Edward was, said Jean, the nearest she had to a brother. A lifelong friend, she and Duncan attended his funeral at Hitchin, Hertfordshire.

Edward and Betty's local friendship network saw the elision of various separate but intermingling constellations: family, faith (religion and politics), school, work and leisure. Active in this universe included chartered accountant and former Allan Glen's pupil Menzies Anderson, an active member of the Old Boys Club; Dr Sked from Girvan; the McDonalds from Randolph Road and from the Methodist Church, renowned artist Wilfred C Appleby. Some characters would appear in more than one constellation, such as the Reids and the Bowies. It was heavily populated, with many calls upon their time. Sometimes the strain of such a packed calendar took its toll, as Edward outlined to Duncan.

Her [Jean] mother and I are going our 'Dingers'. We went to the Alhambra on Monday, we visited on Wednesday, Pictures on Friday and D'Oyle Carte Saturday / That's some going for us / I don't know

were relegated to the fourth tier of Scottish football in 2012 for financial mismanagement.

366 No record of Fred's graduation can be found in the *Roll of Graduates of the University of Aberdeen, 1901-1925*, https://abdn.primo.exlibrisgroup.com/view/delivery/44ABE_INST/12153374700005941 Accessed 10 November 2020.

367 John Simkin, 'Hugh Gaitskell', *Spartacus Educational*, https://spartacus-educational.com/TUgaitskell.htm Accessed 10 November 2020.

whether our constitutions will stand another such week.[368]

Unless Edward's fitness had suffered a sharp decline since the previous year – possible given he was a drinker and a smoker but not probable given his participation in golf, table tennis and walking – it might be argued he was positing a rhetorical question. This is supported by a holiday story recounted to Duncan. A Highland rest and recuperation break to recover from the effects of pneumonia with Betty at Carr Bridge/Drochaid Charr in July 1942 was memorable for one mishap after another. Incredibly, given the reason for the sojourn, it included involuntarily walking seven miles blind in one hundred frantic minutes.

We had one of the many delightful walks after breakfast that are famed around Carr Bridge and regretted we had not purchased a Section Map that we saw on the station stall at Aviemore. Mum decided on bed for the afternoon and I decided I would get that map / I had 1 1/4 hrs to do 5 miles as I thought and catch the Train we should have got the previous day back to Carr Bridge by 4 o'clock… I went along that road in my best old time training manner / Having done 2 1/2 miles by the clock and to my mind half way I enquired as to how far it was to Aviemore / 4 1/2 miles was the reply / I panicked mentally / Should I go back or forward, If I went back I had no map [defeated] if I went forward I could get the Map but no train till 7. / I decided on the forward movement and put more into it than ever / After a further spell I asked again / 2 miles to go after another bit I enquired again 3 miles to go / Ach what was the use / Just keep going and hope that the train was even later than yesterday / I put still more into my effort and when I met 3 of the landed gentry I enquired once more / Oh you are about there, a half a mile will do it / I said Thank God. I crashed into the Station / drenched with perspiration having done the 7 miles in 1hr 40 minutes… How is that for a washed-out professional man of 56 years… However, I had set up a record I shall never attempt to break… when you are 56 try it and I'll probably congratulate you on the other side.[369]

---

368 Sunday, 14 September 1943. Finlayson Family Archive. *Dingers* possibly refers to the busy, energetic schedule. See *Dictionary of Scots Language* https://www.dsl.ac.uk/entry/snd/dinger Accessed 14 November 2020.
369 Edward to Duncan, *Monday 20th*, Finlayson Family Archive. A 7 July,

Edward's reference to 'landed gentry' suggests he recognised their social background by their accents and additional markers, such as clothing and bearing, and saw fit to identify them. This contrasts with the others to whom he had enquired where no description is offered. This encounter between a Black Scot of enslaved grandparents and those representative of a class which enslaved is a discussion to which we will return.

Not everyone was captivated by Edward's ability to tell a funny story. In our 1995 interview Duncan, once Jean was not in hearing distance, was keen to point out that some in Randolph Road, situated in the affluent West End of Glasgow, consciously ignored Edward and his family. Another resident who had great affection for the Tull-Warnocks confided to Duncan that 'some of them scarcely speak to Ed in the street'.

SPORT AND LEISURE

Between 1904-12 Edward played football for Scottish Football League second division Ayr Parkhouse FC and non-league Girvan Athletic FC and Ballantrae FC. 'A tricky inside forward and a menace in the goalmouth' [370] he turned out for Girvan alongside James Bowie. Building a relationship with the community, he soon provided what the town lacked, a dental practice. Not owning a car travelling by foot, taxi or public transport he would make the two hour train journey in a first class carriage twice a week for his Wednesday and Saturday surgeries, located first at Ailsa Street and then at 29 Henrietta Street[371] administered by Cissie. Reverend Duncan Finlayson recalls

Edward played football with James Bowie, who would later go on to become chairman of Rangers after first playing for the club. The two were very close friends. I don't know how that friendship began but

---

1942, letter to Duncan mentions 'going on holiday shortly' to the Strathspey region in which Aviemore and Carr Bridge are situated, inferring it was not in the too distant future. There were no other twentieths of the month falling on a Monday in 1942 other than in April which would not fit the chronology of the letters.

370 Obituary, 'Death of Mr Tull-Warnock', *Ayrshire Post*, 15 December 1950.
371 Ibid.

I do know that when [he] moved into the west end of Glasgow there were a few neighbours who would not speak to him on the grounds of the colour of his skin. Through all of that adversity, he also struck up some wonderful friendships with those who did welcome him.

He] was a very fine footballer in his own right. He could have played for Rangers himself, I'm sure. Dad, as I always called Edward, turned out for Ayr Parkhouse in the days when the club was the equivalent of a senior team and also for Girvan at the same level. He always had a close connection with Girvan, so much so that when he went into practice in Glasgow he also established a practice in Girvan and bought a house in the town. He was already well known in the area through his football and for many years he was the only dentist in Girvan. When his sister Sissy [sic] moved up from England, to look after his adoptive mother after she had suffered a stroke, it was the house 'in Girvan that she lived in, so the family had strong links to that area'.[372]

Edward made his debut for Ayr Parkhouse, 6 March 1909 away against Cowdenbeath scoring in a two-one defeat. Meanwhile, that season his brother Walter was turning out both for Clapton FC and Tottenham Hotspur. It is possible that this is the first time two brothers of colour were playing for professional clubs simultaneously on both sides of the border.

The game at North End Park between Cowdenbeath and Ayr Parkhouse was not of a very high standard. The pitch was hard, and with the ball travelling fast, and a strong wind blowing, the play was somewhat haphazard ... Ends had just been changed when Warnock secured the ball in an advantageous position, and without the least hesitation, drove home the equaliser... The Ayr team were unlucky to lose both points... the forwards were nippy in their movement ... Riddell (Clydebank Juniors) and Warnock (Rockbank Juniors) each made a successful debut.[373]

---

372 Paul Smith, *Aye Ready, Rangers War Heroes* (Edinburgh, 2011), pp.14-15.
373 *The Scottish Referee*, Monday 8 March 1909, p.3. My thanks to Daniel Morris for bringing this report to my notice. Brother William was also a footballer, playing for two Kent clubs, Folkestone and Dover St Mary's, according to the 20 March 1909 *Football Star* feature article on Walter.

Walter's game for Clapton that day was postponed because of snow. Instead he pulled on the white shirt of north London's biggest club and played for their 'A' team at home against Shaftesbury Athletic. In a five-two win, he 'often caught the eye' matching his brother's performance with a goal.[374]

Table tennis, golf and bowls were Edward's other sports. His actions on the bowling green have not survived posterity, other than an obituary mention.[375] 'The ping-pong gang' comprised four couples who, during the winter, took it in turns to host sessions. Edward had his legendary 'haunted bat' so called, no doubt, because it scared the living daylight out of his opponent. During December and January they also metamorphosed into an amateur dramatic group that performed annually, for invited friends and family, at the Princess – later the Citizens – Theatre. Usually the same players enacted the same roles in the same pantomime, Peter Pan. Jean, in 'Tales of Grandfathers', asks, tongue in cheek, if she was indoctrinated. This January event followed the tradition of the Christmas visit to the panto at the Theatre Royal.

Dentists in Glasgow and the south-west of Scotland had formed in 1925 the Western Dental Golf Club (WDGC) whose members would compete twice a year, in Spring and Autumn, at Turnberry Golf Club. The overall winner of the two meetings was awarded the Nasmyth Cup, a sliver rose bowl. Edward triumphed three years in succession between 1928-30. In recognition of his status as victor ludorum he was given a miniature silver replica of the cup which remains proudly in golfing grandson Edward Finlayson's possession. There was also an annual Glasgow versus Edinburgh match. Another Glasgow dentist and fellow member of the WDGC, Albert W. Grimson, provides a taste and flavour of what the game entailed, what meaning it had, to devotees like Edward.

Friday the 14th May 1920 was one of those beautiful Spring days; so welcome after a long dreich winter. The sun shone and with a jaunty step I made my way northwards from Carlton Place across the Suspension Bridge. I carried a week-end bag and a set of golf clubs. Golf bags were light and slim in those days with only a small ball pocket and no hood. I examined the clubs which were all hickory

374 *The Weekly Herald (Tottenham and Edmonton)*, Friday 12 March, 1909, p.3.
375 *Carrick Herald*, 15 December, 1950.

shafted (steel shafts did not appear until 1929). They consisted of a driver, a baffy (a sort of No.4 wood), a mid-iron, a jigger (a No.4 iron with a rather narrow face), a mashie-niblick and a putter. We had spent an hour or so in the work-room polishing the wrought iron heads with emery cloth and treating the leather grips with a touch of castor oil; all set for the week-end. The golf balls were Silver Kings, Birdie Colonels and Dunlop Maxflys. My errand was to deposit them in the Left Luggage Office at St Enoch's Railway Station for my boss, Dr James Mason Noble. He was due to catch the 5.05 pm train for Turnberry and the first post-war meeting of the Glasgow Odontological Society Golf Section and the golfing members of the West of Scotland Branch of the BDA. What a delightful way, I thought, to spend a week-end!![376]

From the late nineteen twenties Friday mornings were also reserved for walking the greens of the new Hilton Park Golf Club. His partner would usually be a fellow dentist.

Writing to Glasgow University student Duncan a few weeks before his wedding to Jean, Edward acknowledges the stress of his intensive revision. Sitting by the radio and listening to the Brains Trust, he offers the 'wisdom' of his experience, 'I trust you are reading hard for your exams. I once went off to a place to read a bit where the golf championship was being played'.[377]

The Turnberry course in Ayrshire was convenient because of its proximity to his second practice. He officially joined in 1924, giving his address as 5 Daisy Bank, Henrietta Street, Girvan. His friend, Dr Alan Sked, was a member. His proposer was appositely named Malcolm J. Finlayson, a founder member in 1902 and former headmaster of Girvan High School. Lord Ailsa, the biggest landowner in Ayrshire with seventy-six thousand acres, was president of the club while another aristocrat, old Etonian Lieutenant Colonel North Dalrymple Hamilton was captain. The club bar would be dotted with the social elite of western Lowland society. The prestigious fraternity held a summer competition

376 A.R. Grimson, *Memorial Album of the Western Dental Golf Club* from 'Dental Golfing Memories. A.R. Whitelaw reviews Albert Grimson's Memorial Album of the Western Dental Golf Club.' Thanks to Edward Finlayson and Mike Gow for bringing this to my attention. The Glasgow Odontological Society Golf Section was a forerunner of the WDGC.
377 Sunday, 14 September 1943.

for the Weir Trophy. Exclusively for players with handicaps of fourteen and over, Edward won it in 1928 – his annus mirabilis – becoming the undisputed champion of Turnberry links.

Edward's ability to win the acceptance of the club's influential members is illustrative of his learned skills in the development of a double consciousness. He was, like his brother Walter, able to mix comfortably both with people from different socio-economic backgrounds and right-wing politics while not compromising his identity as the proud grandson of enslaved people of African descent. Jean and Duncan emphasised how family friend Menzies Anderson was 'quite conservative'. Jean recalled how friends of her parents, during the era of apartheid in South Africa, brought their Afrikaner visitors to Randolph Road. The customary hospitality of Edward and Betty being quickly extinguished by Mr Voisey's White supremacist attitudes. Though she stressed her parents did manage to keep their cool.

Edward had acquired sufficient cultural capital – enough to offset the negative equity others placed on the value of his skin colour – through education, marriage and profession to traverse with confidence the consciously-placed obstacles, adroitly dodge the verbal grenades and pick himself up and dust himself down as many times as necessary. His experience as a man of colour in White bourgeoise society did not diminish him (or prevent him from walking home with the trophies).

In golf he was unique. The vast majority of golf clubs in the UK during the twentieth century operated colour and gender discrimination. Brown-skinned men and women whatever their complexion were not welcome. Applicants needed validation by current members to be accepted and those that did not reflect the internal demographic were usually rejected. This negative exclusivity gradually became an historical burden as the attraction of golf declined. A report from this century observed:

> Specifically in golf… historically embedded systems of private member governance and clandestine admission procedures enabled the middle classes to preserve their superior social status and increase their social mobility through the golf club. Being a member… enabled gentlemen (usually) to develop relationships and conduct business with like-minded individuals whilst simultaneously demonstrating their superior taste and social standing.[378]

378 David Piggott, Gary Leslie & Greg Poller, *Widening Participation in Golf.*

Edward's legacy in this arena is the fascination of golf for his eponymous grandson who, while he declines to accept he is on a par, nevertheless has a similar handicap range.[379]

The cultural dimension to Edward's involvement in the Methodist Church is witnessed through his singing and love of negro spirituals in particular. This inheritance from his father, who was a member of the Grace Hill Methodist Chapel choir, was a tradition embedded into plantation existence as an instrument of survival. This method of resistance and expression was in turn borrowed from the enslaved's ancestral origins where music held a primacy in West African cultures. A fund-raising evening of choral entertainment hosted by Glasgow's Temple-Anniesland Wesleyan Methodist Church in 1908 had Edward opening, singing the hymn *Face to Face With Christ My Saviour* followed later in the evening by another solo performance, *Queen of Angels*. He was called upon again in the second part of the programme to fulfil the bass role in the choir's rendition of *Saul of Tarsus*. 'Unfortunately for the financial success of the concert, the audience was not by any means so large as the programme merited'. Nevertheless, Edward and others performing key roles were given votes of thanks.[380]

At his Claremont Street Chapel, Edward sang and conducted the choir. He also held other official roles, such as Circuit Steward. Jean remembered the choir coming to her home to practice. The church and its music 'intertwines in all our lives'.

A tongue-in-cheek tale of musical woe involving Jean and her mother Edward humorously recounts in his characteristic dry style to future son-in-law Duncan.

Tonight I thought I would look up some old songs that might be suitable for my daughter, my day being past. I selected Two. The first of which was a poem from 'The Quiver' – for your benefit apply to Mother and Father. The music was by Frederick Cowen. Whether

Barriers to Participation and Golfmark, (English Golf Union and University of Lincoln, undated), p.6. https://core.ac.uk/download/pdf/29018735.pdf Accessed 11 November, 2020.

379 Many thanks to Edward Finlayson for the material he provided on his grandfather's golfing achievements and history. Thanks also to Tom Paterson who researched the Minutes of Turnberry Golf Club to reveal the details of Edward's membership application.

380 *Milngavie and Bearsden Herald,* Friday, 24 April 1908.

my rendering was at fault or Mrs W's playing somewhat sketchy, Jean didn't seem impressed, so I produced my 'Piece de Resistance' 'O Divine Redeemer' which I had mentioned to you. It starts with a recitative and the music being by Gounod I need say no more. Admitting that Mrs W had not played it for 20 years there was no excuse for the scene which followed. I put all I knew into it almost bringing tears to my own eyes but I ask you what would you think if you saw the Audience hanging helpless on to the door handle with tears streaming down her face and the pianist unable to continue in a like condition / Not mark you because of the sentiment of the song but purely because their visible faculties had been over stimulated. I have never been so insulted in my life. I did the only thing possible, I refused to continue and left the room.[381]

Proof that daughters and sons ridiculing parents' attempts to foist upon them music of their taste is nothing new. Within Edward's self-deprecation is illustration of the centrality of music in the Tull-Warnock family. In his letter to his teenage daughter while she was busily exploring Paris, he includes a drawn musical notation with a request for her thoughts after he had described a Sunday at home and in chapel, immersed in song.

We started the morning with 'Christ the Lord is Risen Today' but as [Wee] Willie [Ferguson] was in bed I had to sing Tenor, not so good. The start of the hymns were punk [flat] / We sang 'God so loved the World' not too good but tough. Mr Evans was there and I've never heard him better and told him so, he said it was due to John's decision to join the ministry. So your 'group' has done something.

Fast forward fifty-two years and with no tears in her eyes and not feeling the need to hang on to anything but her train of thought, Jean felt the cultivation of friendship and kinship groups, particularly the latter, had a lineage and resonance that extended back to their African genealogy. When in trouble, needing help or assistance the extended family reached out to her father 'and he was very glad they did'.[382] Family records and oral history proved many examples. Seventy years after his

381 Letter, Edward to Duncan Finlayson, 25 March 1942, Finlayson Family Archive.
382 Interview with Jean Finlayson, 20 February 1995.

death more are surfacing. Glasgow dentist Mike Gow, a relative from the Warnock side of the family, noted that in September, 1911, Edward was witness to the marriage of his great-grandparents Leonard Gow and Mary Aitken. The groom was his adoptive cousin.

JEAN AND DUNCAN'S WEDDING

Revealed through surviving letters his most blushingly proud moment of fulfilment as family patriarch was at another wedding, of Jean to Duncan, at the University Memorial Chapel, Glasgow, 9 October, 1943. A student at Glasgow University Duncan was captivated by her singing as a member of the choir. An English, Philosophy and Theology scholar, it was love at first sight. (This scenario – a heart being captured through the combined attraction of voice and appearance – had a curiously poetic resonance with her father's unconscious seduction of the Warnock's.) The presiding minister was Reverend James Clarence Finlayson.

Edward put his heart and soul into ensuring his daughter's memorable day was not spoilt by bad planning and organisation. This went as far as exchanging letters with prospective son-in-law Duncan, over a year prior, discussing by what names the latter should address Betty and himself (alongside details of Duncan's past of which maybe his daughter should remain ignorant).

If it were not for the fact that I am going on holiday shortly I should say that your letter should have been severely censored. All reference to lotus eating life ought to be deleted. However you have only whetted my appetite and as anticipation is really a part of pleasant reality I thank you for your very interesting letter / The opening strikes me as somewhat formal / Mr & Mrs Warnock / Surely with your young original mind you can strike on something that will meet the case.

Edward then cites his choice to call *his* Mr and Mrs Warnock, pater and mater, rather than father and mother. He continues

I don't know the Greek for parents but that might be considered, only one drawback / if it sounded something like a god I don't fancy the part ... I called Mrs Warnock's Parents Dad and Ma but I did that as one of the family long before I had any great notion of making the thing proper by marrying one of their Daughters. / Old Man is no good … I find all our Methodist Parsons greet each other that way and I've no desire to be classed with them. 'Sir' is the way I've always addressed my elderly friends and I did quite naturally *not* deferentially or even respectfully really friendly like just to acknowledge the difference in age. But if you and Jean don't strike on something shortly I shall have to reconsider the position for I will not have my Wife and myself addressed by our prospective son-in-law, as Mr & Mrs W.[383]

Fortunately for Duncan this life and death issue of acceptable nomenclature – with references to classical mythology – was resolved and Edward did not have to reconsider the position and call off the wedding. In his next letter to Duncan, he signs himself off as Dad or Pop and after that, Dad, with references to Betty as Mum.

There had been another, serious, subject of importance that Edward raised of which he really did need to be fully satisfied before he gave his agreement. When Duncan asked for Jean's hand he both comforted and forewarned the noviciate minister of the Church of Scotland:

I can see there is no question of colour matters affecting you. You do realise your children may be Black… They may be blacker than me. And don't underestimate what that means.[384]

Proud runner-up in the university boxing championship, Duncan reassured Edward he felt equipped with the requisite skills to deal with the most extreme of situations should they arise (such as the Bridge of Orchy incident on their honeymoon).

The wedding gathered extended family and friends from all parts of the UK: the disparate Tulls from Girvan and Kent; the Finlaysons from Ardrossan, Ayr and the Vale of Leven; the Magillivrays from Inverness-shire; James Warnock's sisters, Aunts Georgina and Maria from Bonhill; the Tull-Warnocks from Glasgow; the Hutchisons from Aberdeen. Edward was determined that in these trying times of war, austerity and loss the ritualised transition between the conclusion of his and Betty's guardianship of their daughter's life-journey to one of romantic love and partnership, would be joyous and memorable.

Following tradition, to begin their honeymoon in the western Highlands the bride and groom left the wedding before other guests.

383 Edward to Duncan, 7 July, 1942.
384 Interview with Reverend Duncan Finlayson, 2008.

The next day Edward reported-in. Taking his letter to the General Post Office so they received it promptly, he wrote proudly

> After you had left the Battle Ground, everybody voted Your Day a complete success and Dr Stocker or Uncle Tom as you have known him all your days asked me if I couldn't arrange a wedding once a fortnight... Having seen you off the premises we all went back and sat down to Afternoon Tea.

For Duncan's particular benefit, his pleasure at spending time with his son-in-law's clan was spelled out.

> It was a further chance to speak to the Folk and I don't think I missed anybody. Your Ayr contingent, Duncan, really did enjoy your Wedding and they all gave Mum and I a warm welcome to Cathcart St. which we shall certainly avail ourselves of once we get settled down. The Vale folk were a bit surprised I knew the Beautiful Vale[385]... We sang 'Auld Lang Syne' at 4p.m. prompt and 'For They Are Jolly Good Fellows' with Mr and Mrs Tull-Warnock in the ring and the Folk left to get ready for their final Do's.

Some of the guests accompanied Edward and Betty to 21 Randolph Road before setting out for the theatre in the evening.

Concluding the letter by complimenting Duncan on the speeches Edward confesses 'I felt relieved everything had gone as we had planned and it will be a day I'm quite sure our guests will remember'. However, there was one blemish that he was endeavouring to eradicate: the Sunday Mail named Duncan as 'the Reverend D. Rutherford in some issues... I have written to the editor to point out the mistake.'

Revealingly, in this letter, Edward makes light of a departing comment by his long-time friend and brother-in-law, Fred Reid.

> Mr Reid made his usual smart exit by saying he would have to go home and take his 'Coloureds' out of the Water.

It provides a graphic moment testifying to the all-pervasive conceptual presence of skin colour as a cultural instrument of perception and

---

385 Edward may be referring to the Vale of Leven celebrated in the song *Beautiful Vale of the Leven.*

analysis. Fred was part of the family and remained close to Edward throughout his life in Glasgow. Yet, even on this best special day a remark alluding to colour was not thought inappropriate. There is no suggestion by Edward that Fred uttered it maliciously. Yet, it was said and provides a glimpse of the unpredictable and chaotic cultural environment that people of colour experienced in early twentieth century Britain. In all dimensions of life – social, cultural, political and economic – they were never allowed to forget the symbolism of their complexion.

As well as the letter above, composed between morning and evening services at Claremont Street Chapel, there were two more over the next five days with Edward reaffirming the success of the occasion, filling in details of omission and catching up with issues raised.

He begins his Tuesday missive with a quote from Rudyard Kipling's *Recessional* (1897, to which he may have been introduced at school). 'The tumult and the shouting dies: The Captains and the Kings depart'. A jingoistic paean to Empire, the poet's verse pits 'lesser breeds without the Law' against God-backed Gentiles who 'hold Dominion over palm and wine.' However, pacifist Edward was not allying with the sentiment of the piece but making literal allusion to the departure in particular of May and Fred's son, his nephew Captain Edward Reid, serving in the armed forces for whom he had great affection.

> Today... the captain departed and we were sorry to see him go / Edward has a place in the team too / He plays a game on his 'leave' and never lets the team down / Those yearly visits in his early days has made him a part of our Home and I'm sure Jean looks upon him as a brother rather than a cousin / A sound lad.

Edward's ability to call upon a network of influential contacts allows him to reassure the couple that he has done his best to limit the fire damage caused by a naming error in the *Sunday Mail*. You are 'such important people' that the print run was stopped with only two editions carrying the mistake. He congratulates Jean for using a sporting term to describe her husband's induction into the Tull-Warnock team.

> That is how I look at it. I've signed on a new player / I'm the centre-half of the team but I can't last for ever and a wise manager always tries to have a good one in reserve... if ever the time comes when I can't go the 90 minutes / well it is comforting to know that there is

a better in reserve. About 1968 you might get an occasional game in the 1st Eleven.

Alongside the football metaphors, Edward also finds space on the page for his other passion of golf. If, as previously discussed, wedding and football should not mix, nor should golf and honeymooning. With characteristic self-deprecation he reminds the couple that the best holiday he had with Jean was when 'I had to leave my golf clubs at home / I was 100% happy'. Concluding, he offers some fatherly advice to his son-in-law along the lines of 'your wife is always right'. He promises in his next letter – where he reiterates this principle – to include observations of the *Girvan contingent* sisters Cissie, Elsie and Miriam, stepmother Clara and husband Bill Beer.

Cissie was no longer looking after mater Warnock. She had died three years earlier from a series of strokes after a long illness in which she had been virtually bedridden for seven years. Even so, she still managed to play a good game of dominoes daring Cissie – 'a more devoted 'daughter' she could not have had' [386] *Sunday Mail* Edward or any other visitor to take her on. Before her incapacitation, Cissie and mater Warnock had been active in Girvan's Methodist community. Duncan in 2008 described the former as being a pillar of the congregation. Clara, Bill, Elsie and Miriam had moved from Kent temporarily to escape the bombing and invasion threat felt more acutely on the south coast. Edward helped farm worker Bill find a job at a local horticultural nursery.

Headed *The Final Report* Edward begins by responding to a letter, informing Duncan he was wrong: the announcement of the wedding had been inserted into *Evening News*. He then mollifies with the revelation he had bagged two tickets for the boxing event about which Duncan had told. (Both went together to promotions in Glasgow with Duncan particularly impressed by Belizean welterweight Selvin Campbell, known professionally as His Satanic Majesty Lefty Flynn, who had beaten on points Jake Kilrain at St Andrews Hall the previous year.)[387] He continues

> At Girvan everyone seemed to know of your wedding. The local reporter came in to get detail and knowing the Press you ask me and I will do my best to oblige... I knew I should be caught out sooner or later / It came much sooner than I expected / The Dress. I said

386 Jean Finlayson, *Tales of Grandfathers.*
387 Interview with Rev. Duncan Finlayson, 2 June 2008.

the Bride was a White Bride and that stated I appealed to Auntie [Cissie?] but apart from suggesting Victorian she wasn't much help so I phoned Mrs Wight and got her to speak to Auntie whilst Auntie Elsie stood by with paper and pencil. Broche Poult and Limouges are not basic English so I pass... I got a report from our Girvan contingent's subsequent activities following 'Auld Lang Syne'... they went on the skite ... to the Pictures before making for Girvan / Well you know what Saturday is for Pictures / They landed... in the middle of a French Picture and had to leave before they could see the beginning to catch the 8 o'clock train / By the time they got home they were famished and being Tulls they indulged themselves and Auntie had a Nightmare / But all voted your wedding day in their fives.

Edward concludes this string of letters with contentment that the hospitality had satisfied and the photographs secured, except 'Bill's effort '(Bill Beer). Before signing off he once again admits error in questioning whether the couple should take their bikes to the Bridge of Orchy Hotel.

My objection was due to the fact that I thought you both needed a physical rest but if your cycling has toughened you for a Winter's Work then you were right and I again wrong.[388]

Edward's endearing willingness to hold his hands up when mistaken was perhaps a necessary consequence of his matching propensity to say as he saw.

FINLAYSONS AND THE GÀIDHEALTACHD

His son-in-law's family, the paternal Finlayson's and maternal MacLean's, had lived in and around Inverness-shire for generations. Duncan was born at the (ruined) cathedral town of Elgin, on the River Lossie some forty miles east of Inverness, 10 September, 1917 to Catherine MacLean and Duncan Finlayson. Raised in Marybank and Strathpeffer, he was

---

388 These wedding-related letters from Edward to Jean and Duncan are dated 10, 12, 15 October 1943 courtesy of the Finlayson Family Archive. Thanks to Pat Justad for pointing out Mrs Wight is Hannah, the mother of vet James Alfred Wight, who gained fame as the novelist James Herriot.

schooled at Marybank Primary and Dingwall Academy. As well as boxing, his other sports, shinty and fishing, reflected this Gàidhealtachd heritage. At his funeral service at Fodderty and Strathpeffer Parish Church, conducted by Reverends Alan Watt and Gordon MacLean, 12 October 2012, there was little space so numerous were family, friends and local people offering their love and condolences for the last time. The final reading was of Duncan's writing where he eulogises, with dazzlingly vibrant imagery, his idyllic childhood. It reveals the essence of what the Highlands meant to him.

The Conon, where it flows under the Bridge at Moy, is a noble, broad and impressive river. It is none of your rollicking Highland burns, but broad and powerful and of a telling personality, at least with personality for those of us who knew it in its many moods and changing aspects and levels.

The Conon, flows from the long waters of Loch Luichart, which fingers its way to the west, being fed in turn by the Fannich River. But the splendour of the Conon owes much to its far longer tributary the Meig and the Blackwater with its spectacular falls at Rogie, where the salmon leap gloriously for the delectation of the crowds of summer visitors. I write these river names because to write them is an act of love. All these rivers mean all kinds of human things to me – Meig and Blackwater, Fannich and the beloved Orrin – this last named pouring itself into the Conon beyond the Moy Bridge area of which I chiefly write as the settings of my early youth – childhood indeed. The Orrin it is that traverses magnificent Highland moorland from its birthplace far in the wild vastness of the north Monar Forest. It is by the name Conon that the river finally flows ever wider into the Cromarty Firth near Dingwall.

The river, then, in its calmness and dignity and quiet power was very significant to my early life. The word 'picnic' for example meant just one thing to me. It was a trip, usually with the Fraser boys, the schoolmaster's sons from across the road, and perhaps young Doris their sister, to an area half a mile or so down from Moy Bridge where there was accessible green islands with trees and quiet eddies of water ideal for sailing model boats. They were quite ingenious these model boats, cleverly adapted clockwork engines. The engines came from cheap clockwork cars, purchased in Woolworth's Inverness. The designing, of course, was done by the very clever Fraser boys, Willie and Alister, who were a little older than me and marvellously tolerant of me then and later. Down there then, in the shade of the trees by the river, with quiet pools and gently gliding runs, the pleasure of a long sunny afternoon included lemonade – a luxury for rare occasions only, with the spring top so hard for young fingers to push off and pull on, and a packet of Abernethy biscuits. Occasionally the day might be set off with a bar of chocolate, halfpenny bars of immensely chewy toffee called 'Rocket', or even by one of us having a bag of acid drops, all stuck to each other but richly sharp and satisfying to the mouth.

His maternal great-great grandfather fought at the 1746 Battle of Culloden in which Highland clans pledged their support to Charles Stuart (Bonnie Prince Charlie). The defeat of their Jacobite army by George II's forces, led by the Duke of Cumberland, resulted in over two thousand killed or wounded compared to around three hundred soldiers of the Crown. This mass slaughter of Dirk-wearing men rushing into battle carrying swords facing a ranked wall of gun-firing redcoats was followed by a reign of terror. Highland communities were systematically dispossessed of their property and heritage, with the eventual emigration of some forty-thousand to North America. Seen crossing the river the following day Duncan's ancestor was never heard of again, 'having doubtless perished along with so many other brave men on the Duke of Cumberland's ruthless raid after the victory on Culloden Moor'.[389]

Fortunately his grief-stricken but defiant family managed to stay put. The grandson of the Culloden veteran, Duncan's maternal great-grandfather and Gaelic speaker, John Macgillivray, becoming a renowned teacher at Culloden School. Dutifully occupying the post for forty-six years he schooled two generations. His commitment had been foreshadowed: he had walked over three hundred and sixty miles in the hope of securing his appointment.

---

389 Obituary, 'A Schoolmaster of Olden Time', *Inverness Courier*, Tuesday 29 December, 1891, p.5. Finlayson Family Archive. Individual thanks to Duncan Finlayson, the son of the Reverend Duncan Finlayson and grandson of Edward, who loaned the informative booklet, *A Living History of Balloch*,(Balloch Village Trust, 2009) citing part of John Macgillivray's obituary. Interestingly, a school photo of 1950-51 pupils at Balloch - formerly Culloden - primary school on page 55 includes one of colour, Douglas Gray.

After leaving Aberdeen [University] Mr Macgillivray taught a school at Daviot for eight or nine years, and then, a vacancy occurring in the school at Culloden, he offered his services as teacher. The successful candidate required to pass an examination at Edinburgh, and thither, accordingly, he went, performing the journey there and back on foot. He left Edinburgh on the return journey on a Tuesday morning, and arrived at Inverness on the Thursday evening having walked fifty miles the last day. He carried in his pocket a sealed letter approving of his appointment, and he attributed the rapid journey northward to his anxiety to learn whether the letter he carried was favourable or otherwise.[390]

His Herculean strength as a pedestrian may have had its origins in his daily fourteen mile round trip from his home village of Daviot to Inverness as a young school pupil in the early years of the nineteenth century. (If virtual races between deceased people were creatable, he certainly would be a contender to break Edward's proud Aviemore walking record.)

Commencing his Culloden teaching career at twenty-nine he lived near an elderly Mrs Geddes. Her memories of the infamous battle and recollection of Prince Charles Stuart at Culloden House the day before, no doubt made vivid the exploits of his grandfather and his companions. John Macgillivray lived until his nineties, as did the Reverend Duncan who prospered until his ninety-fifth year. Tenacity and longevity seem to be familial traits. His mother, Catherine MacLean, the granddaughter of John, lived to one hundred and one.

This social history of class struggle and conflict, at times disguised in nationalist attire, provides some understanding of why Duncan, as a Highlander, may have been able to convince his father-in-law that he understood the discrimination Jean faced. Disavowal of prejudice is a characteristic people of colour have remarked upon in their written experiences of the Highlands. Trinidadian William Besson, of African Caribbean and Chinese heritage, while a medical student at Edinburgh University in the nineteen-twenties, with a friend

> made a cycle tour from Edinburgh to Fort William... we took tents with us and cooking materials so that we didn't go to any hotels... as far as possible we cooked on the road and fed ourselves from farms.

390 Ibid.

We travelled all the way through Argyll up to the Caledonian Canal and we found nothing but hospitality among the farming community. As a matter of fact they overwhelmed us with hospitality. The only time we found a little rudeness was on one occasion we stopped at a certain farm and we heard two voices talking to each other and saying, referring to us, 'Here are two Chinks coming'. But those were young men, they were people on tour, and I didn't know where they came from.[391]

Twenty years later the UK government recruited Belizean forestry workers (of African descent) from what was then British Honduras for lumberjacking at various locations in the Highlands. Despite many complaints directed at the government and its officials about their treatment, the feeling amongst the workers was positive towards local communities. At Golspie, Sutherland, forty-five miles north of Strathpeffer, Belizean forester Theo Lambey described:

The people were grand; the village was like our own… In the public houses the people were treated like special guests. They were really good to us. Of course most of the people were old and not too suitable for military service, the local womenfolk, children and the uniformed soldiers with whom we got on well.[392]

Mrs Harrison of Kildonan, who grew up in Golspie, was interviewed by historian Marika Sherwood in the nineteen-eighties. She had fond teenage memories of the time the men from Central America populated her small village.

I used to serve in my father's sweet shop and I remember studying Omar Khayyam [for sixth year examinations] and being most surprised when this black man spoke and quoted lines from this poem. He was Bill Lightburn and was to become one of our many friends… The men came to the village of Gospie in 1943. Very soon these lads were accepted by us… Thy had their own football team and played against

391 William W. Besson, *Caribbean Reflections. The Life and Times of Trinidad Scholar (1901-1986). An Oral History. Edited and introduced by Jean Besson. Foreward by C.L.R. James*, (London, 1989), p.70
392 Amos A. Ford, *Telling the Truth. The Life and Times of the British Honduran Forestry Unit in Scotland (1941-44)*, (London, 1985), p.58.

the Golspie boys. They regularly attended church services... I can vividly recall the Sunday morning when they left Golspie by special train – I could say the whole village was at the station to bid them farewell and sorry to see them go.[393]

My first meeting with any members of the Tull-Warnock-Finlayson family was in the Highlands in 1995. Catching the West Highland line train from Glasgow Central to Oban I was nervously excited at meeting Jean and Duncan.

After leaving Dumbarton, crossing the River Leven at Craigendoran, we met the West Highland Line proper. From this point the hills were bigger, the lochs more numerous. Gare Loch was the first, its blue-grey expanse supporting numerous colourful sailing boats. Once out of Garelochhead station – I then had no idea of the significance of this settlement to Edward – soon a slither of water, the aptly named Loch Long, caught the eye. Here the geography of snow-capped hills metamorphoses into mountains reaching further into the white-blue sky. As these enlarged so did the expanse of the lochs they created, with Ben Lomond and Loch Lomond dwarfing the snaking diesel train.

We passed about five more lochs, all backdropped with imposing mountain terrain, before reaching the station of Oban, a port town for ferries to Mull and the Uist isles. I was met by Duncan. The village of North Shian, in Appin, Argyll, where he and Jean lived, was some twenty-three miles north. Driving along the A828, following the contour of Loch Creran, listening to him breaking the ice, I realised my mischievous, charming host was not the archetypal straight-laced clergyman. Taking a narrow track left we arrived at Rhugarbh Cottage, a caber-toss from the loch shore. Edward's smiling, diminutive daughter welcomed me into their bungalow in this beautiful, quiet, treescaped village.

They quickly produced numerous boxes, files and albums of material he had conscientiously kept and protected to which both had added their oral and written reminiscences. Then just a treasured heirloom, these primary sources of a family embodying the triangular navigational circuit of the Black Atlantic are now properly recognised as a precious national resource.

While Jean was aware of the historical presence of people of colour

393 Marika Sherwood, *Many Struggles. West Indian Workers and Service Personnel in Britain (1939-45)*, (London, 1985), p118.

in Scotland it is unlikely that she knew the forced migration of her West African kith and kin led to another woman of colour, Eliza Junor, settling in the Highlands with her brother, William, a year after the end of the Napoleonic Wars. They were brought to Fortrose, a Black Isle village on the Moray Firth coast, by their plantation owning father, Hugh Junor, who had migrated from Scotland to Guyana. Returning with wealth accumulated from enslaved labour, he also brought his children who had been born to a local woman of colour.[394]

The entry of the Junors into this history allows a segue into a story which involves the Macgillivrays, MacLeans, Finlaysons and Tull-Warnocks: the daughter of John Macgillivray, Katie, inherited a renowned and coveted needlework tapestry depicting a map of the world. It had originally been created by her husband William Grant Junor's sister, Margaret Ross. This piece of cloth artwork was, according to Ed Finlayson, 'much admired and envied by other members of the family – including my dad's mum and her sisters – who hoped that they may inherit the piece when Auntie Katie died'.[395] However, newcomer Edward suggested the beauty of the craftwork deserved special care, a wider audience and public access. The most suitable institution able to meet these criteria was, he suggested, the local museum in Inverness. The special affection Aunt Katie had for Edward, made her deaf to pleas for keeping it in the family. It remains in the museum and, as his grandson astutely observes

It illustrates something of the personality and I imagine charm Edward must have exhibited. Here he is – a mere in-law – meeting a close knit Highland family – apparently making a significant impact.

---

394 Many thanks to Ed Finlayson, grandson of Edward, for alerting me the link for this story. For more information on Eliza, William and their father Hugh and research into the Highlands' link with enslavement see the excellent work undertaken by Dr David Alston: https://www.spanglefish.com/slavesandhighlanders/index.asp?pageid=222591 Accessed 10 October 2020. Dr Alston has also made a short-film about the Junors, *Eliza: https://www.bbc.co.uk/news/uk-scotland-highlands-islands-55001490* Accessed 23 November, 2020.
395 Email correspondence, Tuesday 24 November 2020. Katie's husband was banker William Junor. They lived in the Inverness area, close to the Black Isle where Fortess is situated.

Unfortunately, there were influential Highland chiefs who were not content with the locals offering indiscriminate, welcoming hospitality, whether to in-laws or migrant workers. The Duke of Buccleuch thought the Belize foresters work-shy. He was particularly upset at the close proximity of these Black men to White women. 'The people in the neighbourhood were encouraged to be friendly to them and the girls have interpreted this rather widely'.[396] The underlying concern of the aristocratic landowner was miscegenation, the obsessive preoccupation of eugenicists and White supremacists. The irony was, as Ford notes with dignified anger, he and his fellow Belizeans were in Britain to assist in a conflict that was headlined as a war against fascism, an ideology that has racial struggle and Aryan (White) supremacy at the heart of its authoritarian ideology.

Married to a member of the Lascelles dynasty, notorious Barbados enslavers that were ennobled, Buccleuch, sometime Lord Steward of the Royal Household and close to George VI, was one of a number of fascist senior aristocrats and anti-Semites that included the king's brother, Edward VIII and Prince George, Edward VII's son. With Lord Brocket, Buccleuch attended Hitler's fiftieth birthday party in 1939. All were keen to see the UK ally with Nazi Germany against the Soviet Union.

The Marburg papers confirm this wish of Edward VIII. Initially secreted in the German countryside by a high-ranking Nazi officer, uncovered the collection of documents reveal close, fraternal contact between the abdicated king, Hitler and influential members of his regime. After being suppressed by successive UK governments the file was begrudgingly released into the public domain in 1996. The contents were explosive. It exposed the Nazis' trust in Edward believing he would be able to persuade the most influential sections of the British Establishment – government, Crown, City of London and Church of England – to reach a peace agreement and leave Hitler free to attack the Soviet Union. If this condition was achieved, Edward would be restored to the throne. Whilst they occupied Paris he asked the Nazis to place a protective guard around his residence.[397] He also requested the

396 Amos A. Ford (1985), p.75.
397 While Edward was colluding with the fascists occupying Paris, resident Christos and his friend Freddie Knoller a Vienna Jew who, to evade capture, was provided with the gentile identity of Robert Metzner by Christos.

Luftwaffe continue its arial bombardment of London to break the will and confidence of the people. There were other damning revelations that caused severe embarrassment to the House of Windsor who immediately sought to distance themselves from their exiled relation. Edward VIII, Prince George, Buccleuch, Brockett and other elite Nazi supporters such as the dukes of Westminster, Wellington and Hamilton, the 22nd earl of Errol, the marquess of Graham and Lords Darlington, Redesdale and Londonderry (Churchill's cousin) viewed communism as the greatest threat to their wealth and power. These were not disaffected upper-class outsiders, they were powerful members of the ruling class with keys to the doors of the most exclusive portals of power in Britain.

The Anglo-German Fellowship was an organisation that existed between 1935-39 with the aim of fostering friendship between Britain's governing elites and Nazi Germany. As well as being populated by many of the names listed above, it also had individual and corporate members of the City of London and Fleet Street such as Montagu Norman, governor of the Bank of England, Geoffrey Dawson, the *Times* editor, Price Waterhouse, Unilever, the Midland Bank and Lazard Brothers. Financier Norman played a key role in opening channels of credit for Hitler's rearmament and economic stimulation programmes.

A fatal and tragically ironic consequence of this was the use of British-made ordnance by the Wermacht. As an adolescent schoolboy in 1940 James Arthur Taylor of Little Lever, Bolton went one morning into a field near his home to investigate with his brothers the impact of the night's bombing by the Luftwaffe. Firms in the vicinity, such as Dobson and Barlow and Mather and Platt, were making aircraft parts and weaponry for the war effort. These were the probable targets of the raid. James Arthur found metal parts of exploded bombs, one of which was inscribed 'Made in Sheffield'.[398]

Fascist sympathisers, the dukes Buccleuch and Hamilton, the marquesses of Graham and Zetland and the Earl of Galloway were amongst the largest landowners in Scotland. A month after the Britain

---

Working as pimps they supplied intelligence to the French Resistance. I was privileged to meet nonagenarian Freddie and his wife Freda at their Barnet home in 2015. He confirmed Christos was my uncle Christophe, my dad's eldest brother. See Freddie's biography, written with John Landaw, *Living with the Enemy. My secret life on the run from the Nazis,* (London, 2005), pp. 98-128.

398 Related to the author by James Arthur's daughter, Elaine Taylor. The bomb fragment was kept in the Taylor family garden shed for many years.

declared war Hamilton wrote to the *Times*.

> I look forward to the day when a trusted Germany will again come into her own… We do not begrudge Germany Lebensraum, provided that Lebensraum is not made the grave of other nations… We shall, I trust, live to see the day when… a healing peace is negotiated between healing men.[399]

Some historians believe Hamilton and others were active in seeking to bring about a truce which would leave Germany to pursue it primary political aim of destroying the USSR. With echoes of John Buchan's spy thriller, *The Thirty Nine Steps*, John Simkin presents a convincing argument in support when discussing the clandestine night flight to Scotland of the second most powerful member of Nazi government, Deputy Führer Rudolf Hess, 10 May 1941. He landed twelve miles from the Duke of Hamilton's estate after reputedly being escorted on the final part of his journey by the RAF. Captured by Home Guarder David McLean and handed over to Sergeant Daniel McBride and Emyr Morris, he asked: 'Are you friends of the Duke of Hamilton? I have an important message for him'.[400]

Government intelligence agencies, such as MI5 and MI6, had been aware of the collusion of senior royalty, aristocrats, City of London merchants with Nazi officials and influential supporters. One UK resident of particular concern was Princess Stephanie von Hohenlohe. A file of her activities noted in 1938:

> She is frequently summoned by the Führer who appreciates her intelligence and good advice. She is perhaps the only woman who can exercise any influence on him. [She is] actively recruiting these British aristocrats in order to promote Nazi sympathies.[401]

---

399 James Douglas, *The Truth about Rudolf Hess*, (London, 2016).

400 ohn Simkin, *Rudolf Hess*, https://spartacus-educational.com/GERhess. htm Accessed 18 November 2020. Hess's use of 'middleman' Hamilton to access senior members of the British Establishment would be consistent with his pre-war connections with fascist and pro-Nazi organisations and his intimate relationship with influential figures in palace and government.

401 File KV2/1696 NA, London, cited in https://spartacus-educational. com/2WWkentD.htm Accessed 29 December 2020.

Simkin continues:

According to MI5 the list of people she had been associating with over the last few years included Prince George, the Duke of Windsor, Wallis Simpson, Ethel Snowden, Philip Henry Kerr (Lord Lothian), Geoffrey Dawson, Hugh Grosvenor, 2nd Duke of Westminster, Charles Vane-Tempest-Stewart, 7th Marquess of Londonderry, Ronald Nall-Cain, 2nd Baron Brocket, Lady Maud Cunard and Walter Rothschild, 2nd Baron Rothschild. In August 1938 French intelligence, the Deuxième Bureau, told MI6 that it was almost certain that Princess Stephanie was an important German agent.[402]

While ruling class collaboration continued long after war had been declared, the father-in-law of Edward's granddaughter Pat, Thorleif Emil Justad, was working for the Norwegian secret service doing what he could to defeat the fascists. A notable venture was the Shetland Bus, a secret special operations group that operated a clandestine link between the Shetlands and Norway. It assisted Norwegians fleeing from the Nazi occupiers and undermined, through sabotage and raids, the latter's ability to operate.[403]

PEOPLE OF COLOUR AND FASCISM

People of colour had a personal interest in working towards the defeat of fascism because the triumph of this racially motivated ideology would mean at best a return to slavery and forced labour, at worst arbitrary execution. World War Two RAF navigator, Guyanan Cy Grant, for a brief period in the summer of 1943 achieved notoriety throughout Germany. Shot down in Holland and captured, his photo was featured in the official newspaper of the Nazi party, the *Volkischer Boebachter*. Underneath the illustration of the squinting, weary, young, African Caribbean officer was printed 'Ein Mitglied der Royal Air Force von unbestimmbarer Rasse' [A Member of the RAF of Indeterminate Race]. His ethnic categorisation was proudly displayed as propaganda by the Nazis to illustrate the miscegenist tendencies of the British in the 'race' war: we are the only people fighting to protect the purity of

402 https://spartacus-educational.com/2WWkentD.htm
403 My thanks to the son of Thorleif and husband of Pat, Tor Justad, who kindly provided details of his father's exploits.

Whites, was the message. A prisoner of war for two years 'during which time he had to reflect on the irony of having fought to defend a country that had, in former times, enslaved one line of his ancestors'.[404]

African Germans Hans-Jurgen Massaquoi and Theodore Michael suffered as men of colour under Hitler's fascist regime. While former friends and neighbours deserted, disowned and disappeared, theirs was a daily battle to stay alive. It is estimated between ten thousand and twenty-five thousand resident people of colour were murdered by the Nazis. One of Hitler's first decrees was to racially classify the population into Aryans and non-Aryans, immediately creating an apartheid state. Life subsequently became a living nightmare. As an eight year old Massaquoi was violently assaulted by fascist soldiers. Michael was imprisoned in a concentration camp and endured years of forced, hard labour. It was a miracle both survived and were able to publicise their experiences when the vast majority of brown-skinned Germans perished.[405]

German international footballer, Otto 'Tull' Harder, star centre-forward for Hamburg during the inter-war years, was for some time in charge of security at Neuengamme concentration camp. Joining the Nazi party in Autumn 1932, by the following Spring he was a member of the elite and notorious black-uniformed militia, the SS. Under the control of Heinrich Himmler it was their responsibility to ensure the core fascist policy of racial cleansing was ruthlessly implemented at all levels of German society. Harder took his nickname from Walter Tull whom he played against in 1911 when Spurs toured Germany. After the war he was sentenced to fifteen years imprisonment. He served less than a third.

The absurd inconsistencies characterising Harder's story illustrate the seminal contradiction that plagued Edward, brother Walter and people of colour: the dissonance between subjective identity – character – and objective identity, defined by attitudes of the powerful to them. Harder willingly embraced Walter Tull as role model footballer while energetically collaborating in the destruction of all who did not fit the Aryan profile, the untermenschen. In his few months supervising the guards at Neuengamme, at least two hundred captives were murdered.[406]

404 Cy Grant , *A Member of the RAF of Indeterminate Race*, (2006).
405 Hans J. Massaquoi, *Destined to Witness: Growing Up Black in Nazi Germany*, (London, 2001). Theodore Michael, *Black German: An Afro-German Life in the Twentieth Century*, (Liverpool, 2017).
406 Ulrich Hesse-Lichtenberger, *Tor! The Story of German Football* (London,

The fascist ideology of White supremacism was a bourgeoise response to the crisis in industrial capitalism during the inter-war decades of the nineteen twenties and thirties. It built upon the ideas of eugenicists and their practical manifestation, Scientific Racism, a psuedo-Darwinist distortion of the evolution theory that categorised the world's populations by distinguishing between 'races' of varying biological, intellectual and cultural maturity. Developed in Europe and the United States during the middle and second half of the nineteenth century, it attempted to infuse racial theory and discourse with the irrefutable authority of scientific legitimacy. By applying the methodology of the natural sciences, through physiological and philological analysis an objective re-evaluation of the ascribed characteristics of the White, Yellow and Black 'races' would decide their worth to human civilisation once and for all.

The fount of Scientific Racism in Britain was the Anthropological Society of London, organised by James Hunt. Its members developed the concept of the Aryan master 'race'. The Society, building upon the works of Count de Gobineau, Robert Knox and others asserted the primacy of 'race', with its human profile of colour and shape and its social profile of class and culture, as a determinant of behaviour. The writings of de Gobineau, Knox and Hunt attempted to revive the theory of polygenesis: each 'race' of humanity having separate beginnings, there being no common ancestry. In this hierarchical formulation black and brown skinned people were being shoehorned into a vision of distinct human evolutions that devalued non-whites and their past and elevated the European to the summit of human development. The polygenists asserted that Blacks, and the Yellow 'race' just above them, were unable to reach European levels of civilisation because of their natural inferiority. It was the duty of Whites, therefore, to act as permanent guardians over their dark, child-like charges. Such views were given credence by contemporary repositories of wisdom like the 1884 edition of the *Encyclopaedia Britannica* which stated authoritatively that

no full-blooded Negro has ever been distinguished as a man of science, a poet, or an artist, and the fundamental equality claimed for him by ignorant philanthropists is belied by the whole history of the race throughout the historic period.[407]

2002); Kevin E. Simpson, *Soccer Under the Swastika,* (London, 2016).
407 (Cambridge), p. 318.

This statement was published a year after Francis Galton published his thesis on eugenics – a term he coined, borrowing from the Greek word eugenes defining superior hereditary endowment - which added to the canon of Scientific Racism. The anthropologists held physical appearance to be a signifier of one's position in the racial hierarchy. The phenomenon of increasing European dominance, influence and hegemony in the affairs of more and more of the world's peoples was explained quite simply as the unstoppable march of history; of the former's natural – therefore cultural – superiority. Twenty-seven years after it had dismissed the possibility of African peoples having histories that had advanced humankind, the *Encyclopaedia Britannica* discussed in great detail the (atavistic) characteristics of the Negro. It confounded the uninitiated reader with an array of obscure terms: *prognathism* (projecting jaw); *brachycephaly* (short headed); *platyrrhine* (short, wide nose); *hypertrophy* (enlargement); *zygomatic* (facial bone). This was not an editorial oversight. The barrage of unintelligible semantics was designed to underpin the validity of the thesis of African inferiority by locating the intellectual source of knowledge within the well-spring of scientific enquiry. It concluded

mentally the Negro is inferior to the white... The mental constitution... is very similar to that of a child ... after puberty sexual matters take the first place in the Negro's life and thoughts. [However, because of their] dog-like fidelity ... given suitable training, the Negro is capable of becoming a craftsman of considerable skill.[408]

From being stripped of their histories and their territories, they were now stripped of their status as members of humanity. The practical de-civilising of the African through the imposition of foreign economic, social and political systems – commodity production, wage labour,

408 (Cambridge), pp. 344-345. Footnote 1, p.344 explains how Negro hair is 'unlike true hair and like true wool'. This racial hierarchy didn't preclude sub-types within groups. The Catholic Irish – Celts – were considered to be closer to the Negro than the Anglo-Saxon. See *Nothing But the Same Old Story. The Roots of Anti-Irish Racism, Information on Ireland*, (London, 1986). For a more positive view of this connection, Ahmed Ali and Ibrahim Ali, *The Black Celts*, (Cardiff, 1992). There is little doubt that the ideas cited above are highly dangerous when allied with sovereign political power – Apartheid Israel and South Africa being the most recent examples.

private ownership of land, monogamy, centralised autocracy etc – reached its climax with the animalising of the 'Negro' persona. With no past, no inalienable territorial rights and their membership of the civilised 'races' of humankind rescinded, no holds were barred in their mistreatment. Legal enslavement may have had ended in most countries and continents, but the project of economic enslavement of of Africa to the needs and wishes of European capital was fully underway during these closing years of the nineteenth century. Britain was a leading player. Its ruling-class believed that they were destined, either by divine command or as the most evolved branch of humanity, to re-create and re-order the uncivilised world in their own image. And if this was not possible because of the poor genetic quality of the indigenous people, just to govern.

The cultural reconfiguration of the ruling class as the biologically superior master race was propagated, amongst others, by influential Scottish writers: anthropologist Robert Knox, phrenologist George Combe and Thomas Carlyle who, after Emancipation, advocated the return of enslaved labour to the Caribbean. Suffused with the legitimacy of scientific methodology, this Caledonian endorsement of innate White supremacy chimed with arriviste Highland landowners who had made their wealth through the enslavement of Africans and creole Caribbeans. The intellectual outpourings of the Scientific Racism trio allowed the plantation-owning Highlanders to whitewash their blood-drenched wealth.

HIGHLAND CLEARANCES
AND ENSLAVEMENT WEALTH

The identity of the region was, as part of this shapeshifting, also undergoing reconceptualisation. A brutal deracination of indigenous communities by some powerful aristocratic landowners, such as the Sutherlands who benefitted through marriage from wealth acquired through enslavement, entailed forcing tenants off farming land and reconstituting its use with sheep-grazing, grouse-shooting and fishing. There is a direct relationship between wealth acquired through Caribbean plantation ownership and enslavement, the revolution in landownership that occurred in the first half of the nineteenth century in the Highlands and these mass evictions.

Significant direct and indirect beneficiaries of slavery made at least 63 estate purchases in the west Highlands and Islands of Scotland in the years between 1726 and 1939. The majority of those purchases (37) took place between 1790 and 1855… the main years of the Highland Clearances. The peak of slavery related sales occurred in the late 1830s – in the years following the slavery compensation pay-out.[409]

MacKinnon and Mackillop estimated that more than half of the land of the West Highlands and islands and around a fifth of Scotland's total acreage has been owned by families that accumulated wealth through enslavement.

In 1854 Glasgow University mathematician Hugh Blackburn and his wife, Jemima, bought the Roshven Estate, Moidart with wealth accumulated from the plantation economy of Jamaica and the sugar trade in Glasgow by his father, John, who left over £100,000 (£10,264,000) in his Will. Another inheritor of slave-derived wealth was Mary Hanbury, wife of Baronet Sir Francis Mackenzie of Gareloch (where the Warnocks had a cottage), who independently bought Inverewe and Kemsary estates for her son, Osgood Hanbury Mackenzie.[410] Mackenzie's eponymous relative was Lord Seaforth, governor of Barbados between 1801-06 and chieftain of the Clan Mackenzie who owned plantations of enslaved people in Guiana. The twenty-fourth chief of clan Maclean, Lieutenant General Sir Fitzroy Jeffreys was an enslaver of at least one hundred and eighty-five men, women and children in Barbados for which he was paid £3,676 (£481,387) in 1834.

Jean and Duncan Finlayson enjoyed their retirement for many years living in Argyll, the ancestral domain of the Dukes of Argyll, historically one of Scotland's most influential families. The seventh Duke, while Lord John Campbell, acquired through two marriages tens of thousands of pounds in cash and over one and seventy enslaved on the island of Jamaica. Redcastle Estate in the Black Isle some fourteen miles south east of Strathpeffer – the location of Jean and Duncan's final home and the domicile of three of their children Pat, Iona and Duncan – was bought by Colonel Hugh Baillie, of the Dochfour family, with the

---

409 Dr Iain MacKinnon & Dr Andrew Mackillop *Plantation slavery and landownership in the west Highlands and Islands: legacies and lessons. A Discussion Paper* (Scotland, 2020), p.8.
410 Dr Iain MacKinnon & Dr Andrew Mackillop, (Scotland, 2020), p.5, footnote 3.

£22,500 (£2,946,466) compensation received in 1834.

It is unlikely Edward and Jean knew the depth of detail about this incursion of wealth into the Highlands acquired from the enslavement of their African and Barbadian ancestors. They would not have had the benefit of recent illuminating work by Tom Devine, Iain MacKinnon, Andrew Mackillop, David Alston, Geoff Palmer, Chris Bambery and others. Organised by Nathan Rothschild of Rothschild Bank, heading a syndicate of financiers, they 'underwrote the issue of three new series of securities to raise £15 million'[411] (£1,964,310,345) for the government to finance the total compensation fund of twenty-million. This national debt burden, forty per cent of Britain's national budget in 1834, was paid off in 2015.

The Windrush generation and their descendants would have also contributed. This cruelly ironic scenario is contextualised by the actions of successive governments during the last four decades who have placed legal obstacles in front of people of colour applying for British citizenship and/or permanent residence status from the two key regions of the triangular trade, West Africa and the Caribbean, adding to the miasma of moral contradiction and political shame. The vast majority of Africa-origin people in the Caribbean were forcibly placed. Their ancestors had no choice. One voluntary migration journey for which they – as a diasporic group – had chosen to undertake was to work in the UK. Only to find that their 'welcome' was subsequently replaced by a hostile environment in which descendants of enslaved people were being chained once more – by the same ruling class that had shackled and enslaved their predecessors – and sent on yet another unwanted journey this time labelled, without irony, deportation.

Some sixty-six miles south of Strathpeffer is Glengarry Forest. During the late eighteen nineties the Reverend Norman Maclean of the Church of Scotland was sent as minister to the parish of Glengarry and Glenquoich. He could not help noticing the lack of people compared to his previous incumbency on Skye.

There you had two of the most beautiful glens in Scotland, and except for the scattered village of Invergarry and a handful of cottages at Glenquoich, the whole land was empty and desolate. [It had become] a sportsman's paradise... emptied of life to become playgrounds for

411 Nick Draper in https://fullfact.org/economy/slavery-abolition-act-loan/ Accessed 27 January, 2021.

aliens.[412]

MacKinnon and Mackillop argue that clearances by landlords representing the new slavery elite were some of the worst examples. Over two thousand nine-hundred people were forced by John Gordon of Cluny off land in Uist and Barra that these indigenous bailtean communities had lived and farmed for generations. The Gordon family had plantations in Tobago. One of the most brutal mass evictors was the aristocratic Sutherland family, who wanted more rental income from their land.[413] Karl Marx devoted an 1853 article to their callousness.

The person who stood at the head of this economical revolution was… the Countess of Sutherland, alias Marchioness of Stafford… When the Countess of Sutherland inherited these estates, which she afterward brought to her husband, the Marquis of Stafford, afterward Duke of Sutherland, the population of them was already reduced to 15,000. My lady Countess resolved upon a radical economical reform, and determined upon transforming the whole tract of country into sheep-walks. From 1814 to 1820, these 15,000 inhabitants, about 3,000 families, were systematically expelled and exterminated. All their villages were demolished and burned down, and all their fields converted into pasturage. British soldiers were commanded for this execution, and came to blows with the natives. An old woman refusing to quit her hut was burned in the flames of it. Thus my lady Countess appropriated to herself 794,000 acres of land, which from time immemorial had belonged to the clan. In the exuberance of her generosity she allotted to the expelled natives about 6,000 acres – two acres per family. These 6,000 acres had been lying waste until then, and brought no revenue to the proprietors. The Countess was generous enough to sell the acre at 2s 6d on an average, to the clan-men who for centuries past had shed their blood for her family. The whole of the unrightfully appropriated clan-land she divided into 29 large sheep farms, each of them inhabited by one single family, mostly English farm-laborers; and in 1821 the 15,000 Gaels had already been superseded by 131,000 sheep.[414]

412 Quoted in MacKinnon & Mackillop, (2020), p.17.
413 Chris Bambery, *A People's History of Scotland*, (London, 2014), pp.109-111.
414 *The People's Paper*, No 45, 12 March 1853. https://www.marxists.org/archive/marx/works/1853/03/12.htm Accessed 1 December 2020.

Marx argued the Highlands Clearances follow a similar sweeping away of peasants in England during the sixteenth, seventeenth and eighteenth centuries, usually to enable sheep grazing. Indeed, the collective exercise has been depoliticised to a geographical phenomenon: Lost Villages. He links these dispossessions to a continuum that goes back to the Conquest of 1066 and the subsequent Domesday Book, 1086, used by successive Norman kings to calculate potential tax revenues and ensure they had control over land ownership claims.[415]

FAMILY PATRIARCH

Though normally domiciled in Kent, youngest sister Miriam – Aunt Mirrie – intermittently visited Glasgow and Girvan. She stayed for a prolonged period during the Second World War. Married to Leslie Kingsland they had one son, Walter (named after her brother?). He married Rose Browning. Duncan suggested Miriam's marriage was punctuated with periods of Leslie's enforced confinement at Her Majesty's Pleasure. With striking looks and an outgoing nature she attracted attention from a local Girvan vet who may have been interested in more than platonic friendship. To Cissie's embarrassment, annoyance and disapproval, the two would meet for drinks at local hotel.

Cissie took her Methodism seriously and attempted to live by its strictures. Her sister was not so keen. It was a clash of life-styles, morals and values reflective of the different paths their lives had taken. Cissie, born in 1884, had eleven years of her devout mother's influence and thirteen years of her equally God-fearing father's. Going into service during her teenage years she had a life serving temporal and spiritual beings. In 1901 she is recorded in the Census as living at 6 Cambridge Gardens, Folkestone and working as domestic servant for retired boarding house landlady, Mary David. Her formative cultural and social development as a child and adolescent was an experience forged by a family life that, according to Edward, revolved around Grace Hill Methodist Chapel. This shaped their values and outlook, creating a moral compass by which they could navigate life. Cissie's surviving letters in the Finlayson Family Archive have numerous religious references and

---

415 8 August 1845 Parliament passed the Enclosure Act allowing appointed commissioners to confiscate common land. Between the seventeenth and the twentieth centuries nearly seven million acres of land belonging to the people has been privatised and enclosed. See Working Class History (2020), p.159.

allusions.

Miriam was born in September 1897. She knew only her mother Clara, Daniel dying just a few months after her birth in December. Her step-father, Bill Beer, was a farm waggoner. After leaving Folkestone when her mother remarried, she and sister Elsie grew up in the villages of Coldred and Kearsney, both adjacent to Dover. She married Leslie Kingsland, a Deptford-born railway clerk, at River Parish Church in October, 1924. Given away by her step-father Elsie's husband, motor mechanic Alfred Seward, was best man and one of the witnesses. They honeymooned in Penzance.[416] Apart from her stay in Scotland during the war she remained in the south of England, dying two years after Edward. Leslie died in Kent 1981, their son Walter four years later.[417]

After Edward's death Cissie returned to the county of her childhood and the Rochester home of widowed sister Elsie. Alfred died during the Second World War. Mater Warnock passed away in 1940. With Jean and Duncan starting a family – their first child Patricia was born in 1946 – and Betty living with them, circumstances configured a new era for Daniel and Alice's eldest daughter. She spent the rest of her life assisting Elsie in running the tea-bar at St Bartholomew's Hospital in the town. Such was her devotion to this unpaid vocation that Elsie received a British Empire Medal in November 1977. In a typical expression of Tull obstinacy, she refused to travel to the palace and instead forced

the Queen's representative Gavin Astor, second Baron Astor of Hever, to come to her. He awarded it in the boardroom on her eighty-sixth birthday. Writing to her niece Pat and complaining of arthritis in her knee, she reveals how overjoyed she was at the family's response (hopefully it also eased the pain).

416 *Dover Express*, 17 October, 1924. Marilyn Stephenson-Knight, *'Who did He Think He Was?' Walter Tull's Family History in Dover and Folkestone,* (Dover War Memorial Project, undated). My thanks also to Sally Hough, curator of the Tull exhibitions at Folkestone, Manchester United F.C. and Barbados Museum and Historical Society in September 2018, March 2020 and November 2020, respectively for information about Edward's extended family, in particular his sisters, Cissie, Elsie and Miriam.

417 Immigration and passenger lists record a Walter Leslie Kingsland of Dover, Kent travelling to Canada in 1953 with the given occupation as steward. On his return in 1954 his occupation is miner. The National Probate Calendar 1985, p.4926 states Walter Leslie Kingsland of Dover died 18 January 1985 leaving an estate valued at £27,775 (£84,791).

It was lovely to get cards from my own folk. I had over one hundred cards and letters but I still treasure a line from my own people. I also had a surprise letter from Rita, Mildred's niece which was lovely. Now the great day is on my birthday Lord Astor is coming to the hospital to present it to me.[418]

There was a tenuous family connection with the peer. The Eton-educated Oxford graduate was married to Lady Irene Haig, daughter of Field Marshall Douglas Haig, commander of the British Expeditionary Force, 1915-18, in which Elsie's brother Walter had served. Nicknamed 'Butcher Haig' for his willingness to pursue military strategies that involved an enormous loss of life, over two million casualties were suffered under his command. Walter was one of them. Perhaps there was a modicum of poetic justice in Hever travelling to Elsie to honour a member of the Tull family. As well as having her be-medalled portrait immortalised by artist J. Thomas, TV South featured Elsie and her award on their *Day by Day* programme, presented by Fred Dineage.

After marriage William and his family also stayed close to their Kent roots, apart from a brief sojourn in Nottingham during the first decade of the twentieth century. After being widowed in March 1920 when William died of tuberculosis – the effects of World War One gas poisoning while serving as a sapper in the Royal Engineers – Gertrude lived at their married home in Greenfield Road until her death in March 1952. As well as daughters Mildred, Doris and Gladys they had one son, Frederick who predeceased his mother and sisters, aged sixteen in 1926. Mildred, 'a nice, nice soul' [419] remained a spinster. Duncan wrote

Of the girls, the one with whom we have had close and continuing contact to the present (March 1990) is MILDRED. She did not keep well in younger days (TB – her father Bill had TB trouble at one point). She has been up north and stayed with us on several occasions. when her health improved she went to work for a Rector and his wife in a local Rectory but later had a useful working life with Pfeiffer the Chemists. She is now… aged 82 and still living in Folkestone. We are in regular communication. She suffers badly from tinitus but keeps cheerful.[420]

418 Elsie to Pat Justad, 30 October 1977, Finlayson Family Archive.
419 Interview with Reverend Duncan Finlayson, Strathpeffer, June 2008.
420 Reverend Duncan Finayson, *Story of a Family*, (1997), p.1. Finlayson

Through Jean and Duncan I was hoping, in 1995, to meet Mildred – Millie. She was the only member of the Tull family alive who had met all her grandparents children, her aunts and uncles. A good friend of the latter, Mrs Daniels, acted as go-between.

This afternoon I went to see Millie & I could not believe she would be so bright again – it was wonderful to be able to really chat & she was so pleased to talk about her family and the past.[421]

Unfortunately, her health deteriorated and the meeting did not take place. She died in 1999.

Mildred's sisters married two Georges, Hopkins and Hoskins. The daughter of Gladys and George Hopkins, Rita Humphrey is now the oldest surviving Tull relative. She lives in Maidstone, Kent with husband Charles having had four children. Their son, Graham, appropriately a Spurs fan, has taken a keen and supportive interest in the development of his extended family's wider exposure. Blond haired and blue-eyed he was due to travel to Barbados in the spring of 2020 only to have his roots exploration frustratingly postponed because of Covid travel restrictions.

At many events celebrating Walter Tull numerous members of the extended family have attended. A groundbreaking 2019 exhibition at Folkestone Museum, curated by Sally Hough, highlighted the achievements of Walter but also documented the wider family. Coming together for its memorable opening was not just the former Spur's captain and England international Ledley King but four generations of Alice and Daniel's descendants from Strathpeffer to Kent.

Cissie was the peripatetic step-daughter, sister and aunt. Soon after Edward and Walter were domiciled in London she began earning a wage as a live-in domestic servant in Folkestone. Serving God and those close to her was what she did for the rest of her life. Spending her sunset years alongside her younger sister she would have been delighted about the public recognition of Elsie's selfless dedication. Her own devotions in

Family Archive.
421 Mrs Daniels to Jean Finlayson, Friday 10 March 1995, Finlayson Family Archive. It is not known when Mildred worked for the pharmaceutical firm. The 1939 England and Wales Register has her living at Flat 1C, 123 Chariton Road, Folkestone, working as a domestic servant. https://www.ancestry. co.uk/discoveryui-content/view/16305299:61596?indiv=try Accessed 17 December 2020.

this vein – caring for mater Warnock and running her adored brother's surgery – had been returned with the currency that mattered most to her, the love of her family. Fittingly but tragically, it was while on holiday in the Monifieth, Angus home of Jean and Duncan – while the latter was minister of St Rule's Parish Church – that she died. Victim of a stroke, she could not remember where she was and fell out of a window. Both had great affection for her. Duncan, over forty years later, remembered her as though 'quite correct yet' having many endearing characteristics. One was her storytelling which was *rarely* straightforward, often veering off at a tangent, Ronnie Corbett style. Their daughter Iona recalls a warm, friendly aunt who was a good listener and would spend time, while she was a child, combing and brushing her hair.

Cissie had a close and tender and relationship with Walter. For Christmas 1913 he presented her with a book of poetry by E.W. Wilcox dedicated 'To Cis, with love from Walter'. To celebrate this important festival in the Christian calendar, three years earlier he gave her *The Ingoldsby Legends* – humorous re-workings of medieval poetry and folklore – with a similar inscription. Does it suggest one, other or both had fondness for verse?

War and peace characterised the last decade of Edward's life. The first half of the nineteen forties was turbulent, traumatic and profound. People lost loved ones because of the war, normal life was disrupted. It transformed the social and political outlook of the majority. Working class people, emerged more confident and assured. The General Election result of July, 1945, saw the unashamedly socialist manifesto of the Labour Party endorsed with a landslide victory, winning three hundred and ninety-three seats. The new government promised no return to the Depression and widespread poverty of the nineteen thirties. The guiding manual of this new beginning was the 1942 Beveridge Report, a body of ideas that in their implementation laid the foundation of the Welfare State. Its debate in the House of Commons in 1943 inspired George Orwell to comment favourably in a radio broadcast. If Edward, a member of the SMA, had been listening he would have been jumping for joy. His professional life embodied a commitment to the principle and practice of free healthcare for all, financed by taxation.

A pacifist, he was excused military service because of his occupation. The carnage of 1914-18 took numerous members of his extended family, including two of his brothers. Now the killing fields had reappeared with the excuse this time that it was a war for democracy against fascism. However, for many socialists this reasoning had many flaws. Most glaring was the continued existence of the fascist states of Spain and Portugal. They were left alone throughout the conflict, both surviving as dictatorships until the nineteen seventies. Yet, out of the 1939-45 maelstrom emerged a Britain that Edward had dreamed of but, at the beginning of the decade, probably thought unrealisable in his lifetime.

Personally, he had done what he could to mitigate the bleakness. Amidst the dark days of the Blitz, blackout and rationing he had facilitated a protective coming-together of the extended family, its bonds strengthening, its size enlarging.

He had been proactive in protecting the welfare of Jean in many ways, not least in introducing to her tools of political analysis in order she better understood the confusing and contradictory realities of the world outside. Together they visited the National Children's Home in Harpenden, Hertfordshire to colour with realism his fatherly recollections. The least it would have done was allow Jean to value the material and emotional security of her relatively privileged upbringing. As well as adopting both her father's rejection of physical force as having a legitimate place in politics and his love of Paul Robeson, Jean was a supporter of the Peace Pledge Union, the most diverse and eclectic of groupings resisting militarism and war. Created in 1934 members signed a commitment stating

War is a crime against humanity. I renounce war, and am therefore determined not to support any kind of war. I am also determined to work for the removal of all causes of war.

Quaker groupings comprised the most numerous of the religious anti-war alliances, while Wesleyan's gravitated towards the Methodist Peace Fellowship. Pacifism as a principle Jean was keen to affirm during our 1995 interview. The creation of Save Europe Now by publisher Victor Gollanz half a century earlier presented an opportunity for Jean and Duncan to do something practical towards the rebuilding of mainland Europe, in particular Germany after its internal poisoning by fascism and external destruction by allied forces. Gollanz appealed for a collective effort to provide food parcels to counter the growing hunger epidemic in Europe. It was a campaign to which they both devoted time and energy.

Duncan's attendance at Robeson concerts and communist rallies with Edward where, presumably, lively discussions would have preceded and proceeded was an invigorating infusion into his progressive theology. As a minister, particularly in Glasgow where in the early nineteen-fifties he was appointed as associate secretary to the Foreign Mission Committee, he would organise debates and discussions themed around the social role of the church. To put his money where his mouth was, he often chose to concentrate his work in areas of economic deprivation, apportioning ten percent of income to community projects. His subsequent posting as warden of the Church of Scotland's Pearce Institute in Govan, an initiative dedicated to providing social and cultural resources for the benefit of working men and women, testifies to his reputation as a minister dedicated to improving the lives of the communities he worked with. A previous incumbent, George Macleod, was founder of the Iona Community – 'an ecumenical Christian community of men and women'[422] originating on the island of Iona – that has embedded and continued through successive generations of the Finlaysons, inspiring the name of one of their children.[423]

By the time they had moved to Monifieth in 1963 Jean had given birth to four children: two, Patricia Elizabeth (1946) and Duncan MacLean (1948) when the couple – with Boots, their cat[424] – were residents of Stonefield Manse, Herbertson Street, Blantyre while Duncan was minister of Stonefield Parish Church, Glasgow Road; their second boy, Edward James (1951) while in Glasgow and second daughter, Iona Catherine (1961) in Musselbrough where Duncan ministered to the parishioners of St. Ninians. Yet, the mother of four still found time to be an active member of Amnesty International. Their anti-war passion was given hip status by John Lennon and Yoko Ono's globally publicised bed-ins for peace in 1969.

In that year Duncan was appointed principal of St. Colm's College,

422 https://iona.org.uk/movement/ Accessed 28 December 2020.
423 For a short biography of the Reverend Duncan Finalyson's career as a minister in the Church of Scotland: https://blantyreproject.com/2017/08/rev-duncan-finlayson-1917-2012/ Accessed 21 December, 2020.
424 Boots' predecessor, Socks, was the principal villain of a story related to Duncan in a letter from Edward, 16 December 1942, where he confesses taking one of its nine lives 'by squashing in the front door as it tried to get out' before sparring with it for the rest of the evening until 2 a.m. when tired and exhausted he admitted defeat and went to bed.

Edinburgh, the first male to hold the post. Established seventy-five years earlier to train female missionaries for the Free Church of Scotland it had evolved into a mixed gender, pan-Christian institution collaborating with other academic bodies offering a range of courses while still retaining its original focus.

In his letter of 12 October, 1943 Edward used the language and terms of football to, tongue-in-cheek, analogously lay out a plan of succession for patriarch of the extended family which he hoped and expected Duncan to inherit about 1968. It was an unofficial honour that now could be defined as chauvinistic and archaic. It reflected prevailing socio-economic circumstances and cultural norms. Simply, men had more access to more and better paid jobs and therefore, like it or not, generally had more economic and cultural capital – more power. It is transparent that Edward used his benignly and with approval of those around him.

Edward succumbed, after a series of strokes, on 3 December 1950 while still registered as a practising dentist. He had been ill for some while and his death had not been unexpected. He was cremated at Glasgow's Crematorium Western Necropolis two days later. Numerous newspaper obituaries were posted, including the *Glasgow Herald*, *Ayrshire Post* and *Carrick Herald*. 'An Appreciation of the well-known dental surgeon' in the latter remembered:

> On qualifying as an L.D.S. he had a short spell in Aberdeen (where he met his wife) and later returned to the Overnewton district of Glasgow where he was well known and respected. He fixed at this time his first surgery in Girvan, and henceforth on Wednesdays and Saturdays he visited our town. In Wesleyan Church circles he was an ardent worker and a singer possessing a rich voice, he was well-received everywhere in South Ayrshire. On the Turnberry Golf Links or on the Bowling Green he was a 'stout' opponent and enjoyed nothing better than a fighting finish. His professional colleagues in the City [Glasgow] and here in Girvan appreciated him for his cheerfulness and the high quality of his work. The greatest compliment and tribute paid to Warnock was when the Allan Glen's Old Boys' Club elected him as their President in, I think, the year 1936. To one who knew him intimately it can be said he truly loved his Girvan and his many friends in the town. He has passed on, leaving in our hearts a lasting and fragrant memory. 'He was a man take him for all in all: I shall not

look upon his like again'.[425]

Betty received many letters of condolence from friends, fellow Christians, dental patients and others extolling her husband's virtues. Malcolm and Agnes Duncan from Blantyre, writing to Jean, recalled:

Your father had endeared himself to us with his bright, cheery ways, and his eagerness to teach us how to sing well. Especially do we think of him at this time with the carol singing. Whenever I hear them, I am reminded of that Xmas eve when he so gallantly led the singing in our church.

Edward's preeminence at that carol service had also made an ineradicable impression upon another Blantyre couple, Jennie and Cliff. Addressed to Jean and Duncan one of them writes

My own associations with him were of the happiest and I know there are a great many people who will miss him for he was a Christian gentleman and the world is a better place because he has been here. I personally will remember him, as will many Stonefield folks, at the Christmas eve service for I will always carry the memory of that small dark figure leading that huge congregation in the singing of the carols he loved so well.

Menzies Anderson, a pal of many decades, confessed

I have lost a very good friend of many years standing, and my circle of friends is very much poorer for his passing – His tireless zeal for the causes which he held most dear was most marked – not only was he having new ideas, but he was always prepared like so many, to back these ideas with more than his share of hard work. Above all else he had a broad humanity which manifested itself in many ways…

Jean and Duncan told that one of the ways he mischievously proclaimed his more controversial causes was while his muted audience, mouth stuffed with cotton wool, was immobilised in the dentist's chair.[426] Edith K Neil of Glasgow, for many years on the books of the St

---

425 15 December, 1950.
426 Interview, 20 February, 1995.

Vincent Street surgery, wanted to relay to Betty not just her sympathies but also emphasise the quality Edward's dentistry (with or without such comedic sideshows).

He introduced me to you once as one of his oldest patients and in all my dealings with him he was most kind and considerate besides giving excellent workmanship. My brother boasts of a filling that still holds after thirty years... he was so much appreciated by a wide circle of friends & acquaintances and we who are left may be worthy of having associated with so noble a person.

Thom M. Hunter remembered Edward's earliest days in the city as an adolescent and also praised, among other attributes, his professional skill.

Mr Warnock was a first class practitioner, and as such all admired him: but he was far more than this, for we all loved him as a friend. My memories of him go back to the time when he came as a boy to Claremont Street. Ever since then I have been in close touch with him, as a scholar, a teacher, an office bearer, and a musical expert. Everything he did, he did well; he made friends of all and enemies of none.

Edward's qualities were felt by many and, in light of their eulogies, if it could be proven that the only immortal part of one's self is reputation, the shining star of Edward's temporal existence would forever burn bright. Granddaughter Pat Justad's memory of her grandfather, though sparse, was profound.

I only have snapshot memories of him, his surgery, Girvan, Tuttie Frutties, his laughter. Mum told me that when I was a baby & 'Truby King' was all the rage, you were not supposed to pick up crying babies just because they were crying?! Idea I think [to] build up tolerance to frustration!! I am sure mum would not adhere to this, but what she did say [was] that grandad certainly did not & and he would pick me up when crying... I had an odd experience a few years ago. I was flying Inverness to Gatwick... on my own. I am a *very* nervous flyer & very anxious on plane in window seat of 3 seats. Apart from the anxiety about flying I was also anxious about being blocked in by two people if I had [a] panic attack. As [the] plane filled up 2 large black men, professional looking in suits took the two outside seats. I did not speak to them but I immediately felt safe. I could not work out why on earth & then thought of grandad! Only thing I could think of that could make me feel immediately safe & flight no problem.[427]

Duncan foregrounded his political influence and quality of character.

My late-father-in-law Edward Tull-Warnock was, and is very dear to me. I owe him a great deal. We did all kinds of things together. We shared our left wing socialism. He was simply one of the finest men I have ever known. With a tremendous sense of humour and unique sociability he also had a passion of concern for the poor, the disadvantaged and the shut out people of society.[428]

Though eighteen years earlier than predicted his son-in-law's elevation to the1st eleven would not cause a break-up of the team. It did, however, necessitate a movement of the family furniture once Betty had moved in. The Girvan and St Vincent Street properties were sold and Cissie moved back to Kent, Edward's wife and sister not sharing the closest of friendships.

During the mid-nineteen nineties a number of Scottish newspapers kindly ran articles appealing on my behalf for information about Edward.[429] Forty-five years after he stopped practicing I received numerous letters from former patients and acquaintances.

Allan Loudon of Glasgow recollected as a ten year-old in 1925: 'My parents were caretakers and I lived there [419 St Vincent's Street]. He was indeed a gentleman'.

Isobel McDonald of Aberdeen wrote that Edward was her family's dentist in Glasgow.

---

427 Pat Justad, *Grandad Warnock*, (undated), Finlayson Family Archive. Eugenicist Frederic Truby King advocated a routinised, disciplined approach to infant welfare and upbringing. See https://spartacus-educational.com/Frederick_Truby_King.htm Accessed 8 June 2021.
428 The Reverend Duncan Finlayson to Ruth Caleb, Finlayson Family Archive.
429 *Aberdeen Press and Journal*, 9 January, 1995, p.12; *Aberdeen Evening Express*, 16 January, 1995, p.9.

The last time I remember an appointment at Mr Tull-Warnock's is 1948. I was expecting my first daughter so the treatment was free. Until my husband left for Aberdeen in 1954, a Mr Godfrey had taken over the practice. I can remember the daughter's wedding photo in the waiting room, if I remember correctly, the groom was a minister.

A letter from Mr James Jack of Troon, an old friend, told of Edward's Girvan practice.

The daughter you refer to was called Jean. I know her quite well & indeed visited her & her husband Duncan Finlayson in the early part of the war when he was a minister in Blantyre, Lanarkshire. Mr Tull-Warnock practiced dentistry in Girvan twice a week, Wednesdays and Saturdays but I don't remember him ever staying there, although Jean did, in the summer. I don't think the house belonged to him but to a relative. Regarding his football prowess I am sure he told me at one time he played for Glasgow Rangers... Regarding playing for a team [called] Girvan Athletic... I don't remember a team of that name unless it was pre-1920. There was a Girvan Corrmitans [?] and a Girvan Juniors in the 20's-30's.[430]

In only one letter was there mention of the colour of Edward's skin.

---

430 The Loudon, McDonald and Jack letters are in the author's possession: Allan Loudon's letter is dated 16 January 1995; Isobel McDonald's, 11 January 1995 and James Jack's, 24 January 1995. Girvan Athletic F.C. ran from 1892-1939, see http://girvanfc.co.uk/history/ Accessed 3 August, 2020. Mr Jack may have been referring to mater Warnock when suggesting Daisy Bank belonged to a relative.

Chapter Eleven
Edward and Walter[431]

PULLING WALTER NORTH

On enlisting in the 17th Middlesex Regiment First Football Battalion, December 1914, Walter named Edward as next of kin. They had needed each others qualities during the emotional tornados that had whipped through their childhood: Edward's outspoken humour and beautiful voice, Walter's quiet strength and humility. Their character traits complimented and produced a whole greater than the sum of its parts. Their lives post-Folkestone reflected a yearning to be together again.

When Edward left his kid brother behind, 14 November 1900, each step upon the Bonner Road pavement, each clip of the horses hooves upon the cobbles, each puff of locomotive steam, each rhythmic clickety-clack of the train's wheels as it speeded north was a reminder that the inseparable had been sundered. It would have been a profoundly discomforting thought for Edward knowing Walter's isolation would now be more acute than ever.

He resolved to maintain as much and as close contact as possible. On reaching 465 St Vincent Street he immediately sent off a postcard reassuring Mr Pendlebury, principal of the CHO, he had 'arrived in Glasgow tonight at quarter to seven quite safe'.[432] The following day Edward again put pen to paper saying he felt 'happy and quite at home'and that he would be learning French and Latin and 'piano for pleasure' and that his adoptive parents had instructed 'that if I study hard I will one day be an LDS'.[433] (Addressing his correspondence to Pendlebury rather than Walter was adherence to protocol rather than preference. His words would have been relayed to his brother.)

The Warnock's actively encouraged a continuance of the brothers' relationship by putting their hands in their collective purse beyond what was required and expected. Toward the end of May, 1903, Edward once more communicated with the CHO.

---

431 Much of the material for this chapter is derived from Phil Vasili, *Walter Tull, 1888-1918, Footballer and Officer,* (London, 2018).
432 Edward to CHO, 14 November 1900, in *Epitome*, Action for Children Archives, Watford.
433 Ibid.,15 November 1900.

I again take the liberty of writing to you concerning my brother's holidays. We should be very pleased if you would permit Walter to visit us for a fortnight. We will send his return fare on receiving a letter from you, I may also add that although I cannot be with you on Founder's Day yet I think of you and hope you will have a happy time. I keep in touch with the Home affairs by collecting and being a member of the YLU. I hope you will see it convenient to allow Walter to visit us and oblige with an early reply.

At the end of the letter, Edward adds a postscript, requesting that if possible his brother be allowed to come up 'straight from conference making the fare lighter as he had done the last time'.[434]

Initially the orphanage was reluctant. Walter was going through a difficult time emotionally. The consecutive traumas he had faced from the age of seven, culminating in Edward's departure for Glasgow alongside the psychological, emotional and biological disruption caused by adolescence and puberty, were surfacing in his behaviour. He reacted to these devastating losses and internal changes and developments with anger and frustration. In his July letter, written on headed letter-paper – 465 St Vincent Street, Glasgow – and signed E. Warnock, Edward enclosed Walter's train fare, equivalent to two weeks' wages for a manual worker.

We were sorry to hear that Walter had gained your displeasure, but we were pleased to see by your letter that he has so far improved as to allow him to visit us. Enclosed you will find 52/– which you stated would be req'd for his fare. I shall await your letter containing arrangements.

Notes written upon it after it was received at the orphanage suggests Walter was initially allocated a fortnight between Saturday 11 and Saturday 25 July but then amended to Tuesday 21 to Thursday 8 August. His ticket was to be tourist class.[435]

Walter's ability to travel north during the school holidays would

434 Ibid., 27 May 1903.
435 Ibid., 4 July, 1903. A fatal buffer stop collision at Glasgow St Enoch station in which sixteen people lost their lives and many more were injured occurred while Edward hosted his brother. It was one of Scotland's worst rail accidents to date.

have been severely restricted once his apprenticeship in the printing department had begun. The orphanage produced much printed material in the form of plain and graphic postcards, including one which features an aproned, adolescent Walter, shirtsleeve rolled-up partially hidden behind a compositing machine in the workshop. It is unclear how frequently he visited Edward and the Warnock's in the latter part of the decade, if at all. What is transparent is that less contact did not diminish their inseparability.

The visits of Walter to Glasgow, Garelochhead and Girvan inspired an affection for Scotland that endured. In some respects his trajectory was following a path not too dissimilar to his loved and loving brother: both playing for (Scottish and English) Football League clubs, Ayr Parkhouse and Tottenham Hotspur, both training for careers, dentistry and printing/professional football, both eager to constantly reinforce the emotional bond with the extended family that now ranged from Folkestone to Glasgow. When Walter made his debut for Spurs, Edward received a portrait postcard of him standing proudly in his kit in front of the newly built stand at White Hart Lane. Untypically, given the meticulous attention Edward gave to keeping letters, postcards and other material documenting family history, no record survives of him watching Walter play.

FOOTBALL AND THE COLOUR PREJUDICE

As one of Britain's first generation of professional footballers of colour Walter was unique: the first for Clapton (as an amateur), Spurs, Northampton Town and Rangers. He was also the first Black professional to play on the continent of South America, when Tottenham toured Argentina and Uruguay in the close-season of 1909.

> Early in the tour [Tull] installed himself as favourite with the crowd...
> [He] took his punishment well, not afraid to have a fair tussle with the opposition... He is the latest convert to the team and will improve in such good company.[436]

On returning to England Walter experienced another version of away fans 'welcome'. The racist abuse mercilessly and viciously spat at him in

436 *Buenos Aires Herald*, 8 June 1909, p.9 in Phil Vasili, *Walter Tull, 1888-1918, Footballer, Officer*, (London, 2018), p.65.

a game at Bristol City in October so incensed London match reporter, *DD*, that he demanded the off-field bullying of the home crowd be sub-headed in bold ink in his match report. Never before had the colour prejudice against footballers – or any sports person – been highlighted and prioritised above the activity itself.

> He is the Hotspurs' most brainy forward. Candidly, Tull has much to contend with on account of his colour. His tactics were absolutely beyond reproach, but he became the butt of the ignorant partisan. Once, because he 'floored' Annan with a perfectly fair shoulder charge, a section of the spectators made a cowardly attack upon him in language lower than Billingsgate. Let me tell these Bristol hooligans (there were but few of them in a crowd of nearly twenty thousand) that Tull is so clean in mind and method as to be a model for all white men who play football whether they be amateur or professional. In point of ability, if not in actual achievement, Tull was the best forward on the field.[437]

To have racial abuse reported and headlined was a quantum leap forward. During the career of world sprint champion and professional footballer, Arthur Wharton, during the last two decades of the nineteenth and early years of the twentieth centuries, racist shouts and comments were commonplace. Yet never, as far as we can see, did a report introduce its commentary with reference to the insults, let alone headline the abuse. At best it was alluded to in code inferring disproportionate attention without providing detail. If it is the case that this report in 1909 was the first of its kind, we owe a great debt to the anonymous *Daily News* hack with the nom de plume 'DD'. He began a journalistic tradition that took another eighty years, at least, to consolidate.

The history and political geography of Bristol as a port whose wealth, growth and importance was a consequence of the slave trade may explain, in part, the vociferous prejudice of a minority of City's supporters. To this potent cocktail of local, cultural factors we should add an event that occasioned a free-for-all against people of colour: the assassination in London, 1 July 1909, of Sir William Hutt Curzon Wylie, a member of the colonial government in India by nationalist Madan Lal

---

437 *The Daily News*, 4 October 1909. The 'Billingsgate' reference alludes to the swearing and slang reputedly common amongst porters in London's Thames-side fish market.

Dhingra.

A public show of grief by the political establishment engendered a primitive mood of racist hostility to non-Whites. Dr James Jackson Brown, living in the same east London borough as Walter and one of the few medical practitioners at Whitechapel's London Hospital, commented 'every coloured person had a hell of time.'[438] Dhingra's life expired at Pentonville Prison, 17 August, with a punitive drop and retributive tug of the hangman's rope.

It may have reassured Edward - and other members of the family - to know that his brother, while the lone player of colour at Spurs, was not alone. Numerous team photos taken between 1909-1911 picture him sitting next to Jabez 'Dorando' Darnell who, in all images, has an eye-catching handle-bar moustache. Known affectionately as the India Rubber Man,[439] they are often the only teammates smiling, suggesting the sharing of a joke or banter. It occurs too often to be coincidence and speaks to a firm friendship that lasted over seasons. His great granddaughter Karin Darnell confirmed that a close bond between the two was part of family folklore. Bedfordshire-born Darnell played left-half and joined Spurs from Northampton Town. His nickname 'Dorando' is said to have been a reference to the Italian runner Dorando Pietri who won the 1908 Olympic marathon at White City – but was later disqualified for being helped across the line – sporting a similarly extravagant moustache. It is not known why he was also called the India Rubber Man. His great granddaughter feels it could be a reference to his dark hair and swarthy complexion.

THE FIRST WORLD WAR

Walter spent nearly a year training in various parts of England as an enlister in the civilian army, the British Expeditionary Force (BEF), created for the First World War. This lengthy period of acclimatisation to military life and discipline may have been a consequence of the celebrity status of the battalion comprised in great part of professional

---

438 Jeffrey Green, 'Brown, James Jackson' in *Oxford Dictionary of National Biography* (Oxford, 2004).

439 Email exchange with the great granddaughter, Karin Darnell, 25 February, 2021. Frustratingly, Jabez Darnell's house was burgled soon after his death and much of his football memorabilia that could have added detail to his relationship with Walter was stolen.

footballers. The Army Council – the political executive of the army, its ruling body – and War Office, it seems, were in no haste to ship this idolised section of the working class to the killing fields of France and Belgium.

As a Britain-born man of colour, Walter's admittance to the BEF was problematic. The success of people of colour in enlisting often depended upon lightness of pigmentation and the whim of the recruiting officer. Walter managed to defuse and neutralise the institutional racism faced by men of darker hue through his status and reputation as a nationally-known professional footballer. The usual bureaucratic mechanisms used to filter out 'undesirables', such as 'failing' the medical examination, being difficult to justify.

However, national gatekeepers were ever vigilant. On the very day, 21 December 1914, Walter signed his Short Service Attestation form B.2505 at Fulham Town Hall, Gilbert Edmund Augustine Grindle, head of the West Indies Department, Colonial Office, warned: 'I hear privately that some recruiting officers will pass coloureds. Others, however, will not, and we must discourage coloured volunteers'.[440] Had the dutiful bureaucrat received an inquisitive telephone call or telegram from an anxious registration officer in west London?

Bonfire Nightl 1915, the 17th Middlesex assembled at Folkestone harbour for transportation to France. Maybe there is more than a little poignancy in Walter leaving from his hometown – waved off by stepmother Clara, her husband Bill Beer, brother William, sister-in-law Gertrude, nieces Mildred and Gladys and sisters Elsie and Miriam? – in the shadow of an annual commemoration foiling a sectarian seventeenth century plot to create political mayhem with gunpowder? He was embarking to, what we know in hindsight, was a conflict characterised by the unprecedented deployment of weapons of mass explosive destruction; a blood-stained fireworks show that would soon have a devastating effect upon the twenty-seven year old.

Lance Sergeant Tull – promoted three times during training – a member of Major John Pretyman-Newman's 'A' Company reached the wet, cold, mud-clinging front line between Le Basseé and Loos, near Annequin Fosse on 9 December. Still officially MP for Tottenham's

440 CO 318/333/50043, West Indian Contingent, minute by Gilbert Grindle, 21 December 1914, quoted by David Killingray, 'All the King's Men? Blacks in the British Army in the First World War' in Rainer Lotz and Ian Pegg (eds.), *Under the Imperial Carpet: Essays in Black British History*, (Crawley, 1986) p.170.

neighbouring constituency of Enfield, a seat he had held since 1910, it is likely that Pretyman-Newman would have known of Tull. The battalion suffered their first casualty two days later with the death of 21-year-old Private James MacDonald from Fife, killed by machine gun fire while on sentry duty.

Walter and the 17th spent the next fortnight in the killing zone. In a moment of respite he wrote to the new principle of the orphanage, describing the terrain. 'At no period of the year [could it] be termed beautiful & just now it is looking very bleak and desperate, with a super-abundance of mud on all roads'.[441]

When enlisting the common refrain to reassure hesitant volunteers was it would be 'over by Christmas'. Two had passed by the time of Walter's letter to Hodgson-Smith. Despite a constantly mounting death toll, he writes with the characteristic naivety of the civilian-soldier.

For the last three weeks my Battalion has been resting some miles distant from the firing line but we are now going up to the trenches for a month or so. Afterwards we shall begin to think about coming home on leave. It is a very monotonous life out here when one is supposed to be resting and most of the boys prefer the excitement of the trenches to the comparative inaction whilst in reserve.

Within a couple of months 'the excitement of the trenches' paralysed him with acute mania[442] known more commonly as shell shock or what today would be diagnosed as post-traumatic stress disorder (PTSD). After nine continuous days on the front line he was admitted to Lady Hadfield's Anglo-American Hospital at Wimereux, 28 April, his twenty-eighth birthday. Transferred back to England on hospital ship *St. Denis*, 9 May, he had served over five months without leave throughout this cold, snowy winter in northern France.

Folkestone had the Bevan Military Hospital at Sandgate. If a patient, visits from family would have been a welcome aid to recovery. His nerve-shredding experience on the Front Line would have contrasted like hell to heaven with the sight, sound and touch of brother William and family and sisters Clara, Elsie and Miriam. (William was conscripted as a sapper in the Royal Engineers sometime after March 1916 so may have been

441 To Mr Hodgson-Smith, exact date unclear, 1916, Walter Tull Archive in Finlayson Family Archive.
442 Military Service Record, WO 339/90293/175466, N.A, Kew, London.

actively assisting the war effort elsewhere.) Walter's extended family of Palmers and Taylors were also nearby and within visiting distance. It is not known if Edward took the sleeper train down from Glasgow but given the closeness of the brothers it would have been highly probable. Unfortunately, the records of the hospital were lost in bombing during the Second World War and no other documents – military record, letters, diary, notes, medical reports – have surfaced revealing further insight on Walter's hospitalisation.

Ben Shepherd (2002) argues that as many as fifty-thousand men were treated for nervous complaints during the second half of 1916, a period roughly corresponding with the notorious first Battle of the Somme in which over a million combatants died. Richard Smith (2004) notes that approximately two hundred-thousand soldiers were discharged from the Army on psychiatric grounds during the war, by the end of which there were twenty specialist Army hospitals dealing with shell shock compared to one in 1915. Medical staff did not fully understand the cause, effect or treatment of the epidemic of neuroses. Writing to a friend in that year, the Oxford Professor of Medicine commented

> I wish you could be here in this orgy of neuroses and psychoses and gaits and paralyses. I cannot imagine what has got into the central nervous system of the men.[443]

Various explanations were constructed, ranging from cowardice to damage of the brain caused by nearness to heavy shell explosions. Often ignoring patient pain, treatment could involve electric shock. Proselytised by practitioners as groundbreaking the response was as brutal as the cause.

Some medical staff suggested that nervous complaints were signs of degeneracy, the complainants lesser individuals unworthy of equal treatment. This eugenicist view legitimised any medical response, however brutal, because the recipients were defective members of the human race.

The War Office and its contemporary incarnation, the Ministry of Defence (MoD), for decades refused to accept that war could inflict lasting psychological damage. After the 1991 Gulf War, termed Operation Granby, the resultant mental illness diagnosed in many veterans was labelled Gulf War syndrome rather than PTSD. It was not until a 2003

443 Ben Shepherd, *A War of Nerves* (London, 2002) p.2.

class action in the High Court brought by over two thousand British military personnel who had served in operations before 1996, that the MoD accepted the condition was genuine and to which any soldier could be susceptible as consequence of participating in military conflict.[444]

Lance Sergeant Tull returned to France, 20 September, posted to the 23rd Middlesex (2nd Football). Despite yet another debilitating trauma he had the strength and will to return. On leaving the south coast his step may have overlaid with boyhood memories of happier, peaceful times as he embarked from his hometown once more. When he and Edward had left Folkestone making that difficult, unwanted journey to Cannon Street station and the orphanage two decades earlier, neither had known what to expect. An innocent to war, he had been beaten to breaking point as punishment for his gullibility. Now, there was no mystery about the reality. Stepping ashore at Boulogne later that day in the fading autumn light, at the mid-point of the first Battle of the Somme, his eyes were wide open, his mind aware, his sensitivity hardened, his self scarred. Once again he would face the unprecedented horror of the front-line trenches. And day-to-day racism. There was a respite from the former; there was no escape from the latter.

Remarkably, just over three months later, on Boxing Day, Walter arrived back in England. After an initial period of six weeks leave he was to report for officer training at No.10 Officer Cadet Battalion, Gailes, Ayrshire. Graduating Second Lieutenant into the Special Reserve of Officers at the end of May 1917 he became the first working-class man of colour born in the UK to be commissioned an infantry officer in the British army.

Driven by expediency, his promotion violated army rules and regulations. He had fought in the last months of the Somme where his battalion had lost well over half its men resulting in a severe shortage of officers. Uniquely, in this conflict the army was forced to seek out men of officer material from its mass ranks of civilian combatants. Respected as a soldier that had not only recuperated from extreme illness but used the restful months to renew and rebuild, Walter was marked out by his commanding officers as dependable, brave and a popular leader.

Leave allowed time to visit the Tulls, Beers and Palmers in Folkestone before catching-up with Edward. While in Glasgow, Walter attended his

---

444 Tristan McGeorge, Jamie Hacker and Simon Wessely, 'The MoD PTSD decision: a psychiatric perspective', *Occupational Health Review*, 122. July/August, 2006, pp.21-28.

brother's Wesleyan Church in Claremont Street before catching a train to the Ayrshire coast to spend time with Cissie and mater Warnock at the cottage in Garelochhead. It was during this sojourn north that Walter signed for Rangers FC of Glasgow, 2 February, making his brother very happy.

Professional football in Scotland continued throughout the war and Rangers were adapting to the changed environment with difficulty. Their main Glasgow rivals, Celtic, had won the league title the last three seasons ending Ranger's pre-war dominance. A key player at the club was Edward's close friend James Bowie and it would not be stretching credulity to argue he had a hand in the signing. He knew of Walter's qualities as a footballer but having had the chance to meet him on his numerous visits to Glasgow would have been acquainted with his attributes as a human being. As a senior player his recommendation to the manager and the board on the added quality Walter brought would have carried weight.

The last photographs of the two brothers together were taken in the garden at Garelochhead during the Spring. The family group picture of a seated mater Warnock and Cissie, with them standing behind, appears to frame a moment of gloom: no one is smiling. The newly-commissioned officer was soon to return to France. The black and white image presciently captures forever a second from his last moments with his family. Ever.

Yet, there was an alternative reality, one which recognised the success of both brothers to actively shape the direction of their lives. They had arranged between them a future, war permitting, in which they would be once again be living in the same city after separation spanning decades and hundreds of miles. Edward was also accepting his de-facto responsibility as patriarch of the extended family, facilitated by his relative affluence compared to other members of the extended family. Only Walter, with his officer's pay of ten shillings and six pence per day and prewar income of around four pounds per week, was on a par financially.

During the summer, back amidst the explosive tension of war, Edward's pioneering brother found some precious down time in which he chose to share his feelings.

23rd M'sex Rgt

B.E.F.

Y.M.C.A.

Officers' Rest House,

France, August 10th 1917.

Dear Eddie.

I'm once more enjoying life some miles distant from the front line &
if that jade 'rumour' doesn't err, we shall be a few miles still further
away by this time next week. Our crush are expecting some weeks
rest to re-organize, so if that comes off I shall be very lucky. I joined
the Battalion on Saturday when they came back from the line & was
posted to 'D' Coy. On Monday at noon my Coy. Cmndr detailed me
to go up & inspect the portion of the trench 'D' Coy were to hold
as we were to go up that night. Three other subs & myself started
off about 1.30 but Fritz was shelling the back areas like a demon &
after dodging about from trench to trench we got fed up & struck
across country. We were lucky & got to a tunnel which would help us
on our way considerably. Unfortunately the outlet was flooded & we
got soaked up to our hips, but H2O is less dangerous than shrapnel
or HE. From the flooded place we had to go along a track knee deep
in mud, but Fritz let us alone & we reached retired HQ safely, where
the Adj't of the Batt. to be relieved made us welcome & gave us
tea. From there our way lay across open ground formerly no man's
land, now one mass of shell holes. It was impossible to proceed in a
straight line anywhere of more than one to two yards. Our guide did
his best & after being on our way about 5 hours from the time we left
camp, we reached our destination a distance of about 3 miles taking
a direct line. My Coy. arrived soon after 1 am & then I was informed
I would not be wanted. You can guess I wasn't long in getting a move
on, but by the time I was back in the tunnel I was well knocked &
begged a seat amongst some RE Signallers. I found they were all from
Scotland. Didn't Glasgow Corporation form a Coy? This was the
crowd. Anyway the Serg't was from Burntisland & had been at school
with Manning of Northampton. They refreshed me with a good tot
of rum, & sat talking until nearly 5 am when I pushed on for the
nearest village. I must have been within 200 yards of the place when
I nearly collapsed, & suddenly realised I'd had nothing to eat since
lunch, about 17 hours since. A YMCA Canteen was my salvation & I
succeeded in persuading the orderly to cook some sausages & make
a cup of tea. The meal revived me & after a rest I proceeded on my
journey, reaching the transport lines about 8 o'clock. I had a good tub
and got into bed, but couldn't sleep, so dressed again & walked into

a small town nearby for lunch. Didn't I sleep that night through! All the guns in France couldn't wake me.

   This morning one of our chaps arrived from the line after taking part in a good piece of work. Keep your eyes on the papers & perhaps you will read about it. Anyway, he's bound to get a decoration. Enclosed is a 1 mark note which he gave me as a souvenir. You can guess where it came from. I'm also sending a label which I cut from a box. Note the date! Cannot stop to write more now. Have had all your letters. Love to all. Yours affectionately,
Walter.
PS I am applying for transfer to the BWI when the Batt. come out tomorrow.

This understated letter is one of two surviving Walter penned from the Front. The first to Hodgson-Smith at the orphanage was optimistic and lacking information about action. In this YMCA missive he recounts a very dangerous assignment and talks of reorganisation after the decimation of his battalion in the Battle of Messines. In letters that have not survived, written to Cissie, Edward's daughter Jean believed her uncle, by this time, hated the war.[445]

Arguably the most significant part of the letter is the postscript, where he informs Edward that he wants a posting to the BWI (British West Indies Regiment – BWIR). Its place as a footnoted afterthought belies its significance. Why would the recently commissioned 2nd Lieutenant want to switch regiments after serving two and half years with soldier comrades with whom he also shared a vocational affinity? Was he conscious of his 'otherness' as a Black officer in a White battalion? Did he face hostility even among his brother footballers? Did he feel he would be more at ease in a force that had as its uniting element the common experience of racism?

Culturally, the BWIR would be a varied mixture. Officered by Whites, recruits could come from any part of the British ruling class's Caribbean Empire. It speaks to Walter's political maturity that he felt his presence would be of more use and better received among those with whom he shared an ethnic and political affinity rather than a cultural and professional commonality. He may have thought his chances of promotion to Captain and posting to a less intense theatre of war would also be enhanced by the transfer.

445 Interview with Jean and the Reverend Duncan Finlayson, 1995.

After the killing fields of Flanders his battalion, the 23rd Middlesex (2nd Football), were posted in November to the less frenetic beauty of alpine northern Italy. Their brief was to stop the southern advance of Austrian and German troops now threatening Venice, Padua and Rome. After detraining at Isola Della Scala, 22 November, they marched the one hundred and five miles to their allotted sector around Montello in the lower Dolomites overlooking the eight-hundred metre-wide River Piave.

In the south, at Taranto, the BWIR was working as labourers, a posting that would eventually erupt into mutiny and rebellion over their status and treatment.

The indefatigable enemy was the winter weather. With the ice-cold River Piave as the front line, this natural foe was ever present. Holding firm against enemy forces on the eastern bank necessitated reconnaissance and raiding parties, designed to capture prisoners and intelligence. Missions, more often than not led by subalterns, meant traversing fast-flowing chest-high waters, usually at night, often bare-chested with a smothering of whale oil or thick grease. Wearing minimal clothing and kit, various methods were used to ford the river including ropes, linking arms, piggy back, thumb-sticks with wrist loops and long sticks. Boats and rafts had been tried but were either unsuitable or unmanageable. Wading tended to be the preferred option. To pre-empt hypothermia and frostbite, sodden soldiers returning from missions would be wrapped in warm blankets or hauled into barrels of hot water in specially constructed steam rooms resembling Turkish baths.

WALTER'S MILITARY CROSS

On Christmas Eve, Walter led a raid through the numbing rapids under cover of darkness. It is recorded in his battalion's War Diary: '2/Lt Tull & fighting patrol cross river, short reconnaissance raids, no sign of enemy'.[446] This is the first known, documented occurrence of a working-class Black officer leading White, British Army infantry troops on a wartime mission.

At 6.10pm on New Year's Day, 1918, under the stars once more, Walter commanded troops on another life-threatening foray. He and twenty-six men from his 'C' Company crossed the river again to attack

446 War Diary, 23rd Middlesex Regiment, 24th December 1917. WO 95/4243, N.A., London.

the enemy and destroy their forward positions. After his party had waded through, reconnoitred and given the all-clear, following behind them would be three hundred colleagues led by his friend, 2nd Lieutenant Pickard. As the advance guard, enemy opposition would be met first by Edward's brother and his men.

Major General Sidney – Swanky Sid – Lawford, commanding the 41st Division of which the battalion was part, visited two days later to congratulate this mass incursion and capture of prisoners, officially citing the Black Second Lieutenant for his bravery:

> I wish to place on record my appreciation of your gallantry and coolness. You were one of the first to cross the river prior to the raid on 1/2 Jan. 1918 & during the raid you took the covering party of the main body across and brought them back without a casualty in spite of heavy fire.[447]

So doing, Major General Lawford acquiesced in formally defying Army regulations prohibiting men of colour from 'exercising any actual command or power'.[448]

It was probably to this mission that regimental commander Major Poole and colleague on the raid, 2nd Lieutenant Pickard were referring, in separate letters, when they informed next-of-kin Edward that his deceased brother had been recommended for the Military Cross.

Poole:
[Walter] was very cool in moments of danger & always volunteered for any enterprise that might be of service. He was recommended recently for a Military Cross. He had taken part in many raids. His courage was of a high order and was combined with a quiet & unassuming manner.

Pickard:
Allow me to say how popular he was throughout the Battalion. He was brave and conscientious; he had been recommended for the Military Cross & had certainly earned it; the Commanding Officer had every confidence in him & he was liked by his men. Now he has made the supreme sacrifice pro patria; the Battalion and Company have lost a

447 Lawford's citation can be viewed online in the Walter Tull Archive, item 37. https://waltertullarchive.com/archive/ Accessed 1 October 2020.
448 *Manual of Military Law*, (London, 1914), p. 471.

faithful officer; personally I have lost a friend. Can I say more! Except that I hope that those who remain may be as true & faithful as he.[449]

In writing both broke military rules:

> The subject of recommendations for honours and rewards is to be treated as strictly confidential and officers are forbidden to divulge at any time the nature of the recommendations they have made. In no case should the relatives or friends of an officer or soldier be informed that he has been recommended for reward.

This quote is taken from *Instructions Regarding Recommendations for Honours and Rewards* (1918), a detailed and comprehensive booklet laying out the regulations and procedures for military awards. Major Poole, DSO OBE, was a career soldier and high ranking officer. Responsible for submitting medal recommendations he would have known the protocol, aware his disclosure to Edward was prohibited. Yet, he still chose to inform him. It could be argued that Pickard, as a junior officer, may not have known but unlikely given his status as Company commander. What is certain is that both had first-hand experience of Tull's soldiering skills. On the raid Pickard had trusted his life and that of his men to their Black comrade. It is highly significant that both took time and trouble to let Edward know that his brother had been put forward for a medal. It begs the question: did they know a little more, especially Poole? Had he been notified of the decision regarding the recommendation? Did his frustration spur him to let Edward know a recommendation had been made? If the rules had been rigidly followed only Walter, the officer who submitted the application on Army Form W.3121 and personnel at the Military Secretary's Office and General Headquarters, who received the original and copy, would have known.

Did Poole and Pickard hope Edward would pursue the injustice? Major General Sidney Lawford, as commander of the 41st Division, would also have been involved in the recommendation process. Is it likely that, having personally cited him for his 'gallantry and coolness', he would have then rejected a call for a Military Cross? What were the odds of an officer mentioned in his battalion's War Diary for a leading

---

449 Major Poole to Edward Tull-Warnock, 12 April 1918; 2nd Lieutenant Pickard to Edward, 17 April, 1918, Walter Tull Archive in Finlayson Family Archive.

part in a much publicised and applauded raid, formally congratulated by his Brigade commander, not receiving any medal or award? I do not have the statistics – if they exist? – but I guess the probability would be very low. We do know officers were decorated for their persistent valour rather than a single act of bravery. Yet, Walter was not decorated as an officer despite having 'certainly earned it' by being 'brave and conscientious; popular; liked by his men'; leading a raiding party that did 'excellent work'; being 'true and faithful; a great player of 'both games' and having a very high reputation for courage and devotion to duty'. That these qualities, recognised by Pickard and Poole, men working closely with him, did not merit any award or decoration whatsoever, goes against the normal practice of the time.

Why?

It cannot be argued the higher echelons of army command were unaware of the significance of the missions led by Walter. A secret report of the raid for General Headquarters by Lieutenant Colonel Haig Brown, Commanding Officer of the 23rd Middlesex, praised Walter's group: 'The covering party established themselves in a forward position 300 yards after crossing without any opposition, and did excellent work until withdrawn'.[450] His account provided the substance for 14 Corps GHQ Intelligence Summary for 2 January 1918 which stressed the success of all elements of the raid:

> Our patrols crossed the Piave… opposite Fontigo without difficulty. On the far bank hostile patrols were met with and considerable rifle and machine gun fire encountered. Our patrols withdrew after inflicting casualties on the enemy… Our casualties were insignificant.[451]

This dent in the enemy's defences was much publicised by the British government, eager to propagandise early British successes in their assistance of the Italians. A *New York Times* article, 8 January 1918, was headlined

> British Are Active on the Piave Front. British patrols have once again crossed the Piave River, the War Office announces. They forced

450 WO 95/157/633 War Diary, 123 Brigade, 'Report on raid carried out by the 23rd Middlesex Regiment on the night of 1st/2nd Jan. 1918', Lt. Col. Alan R. Haig Brown. N.A., Kew, London.
451 WO 95/157/633 'Italy, GHQ, Intelligence Summaries, January 1918'. N.A., Kew, London.

passages at various points, causing alarm in the enemy lines.

Despite this substantial contemporary evidence in support of the medal recommendation, the MoD still, as I write, refuse to posthumously award Walter his Military Cross.

WALTER IS DEAD, WALTER IS DEAD

After making headlines in the Alps, Walter and his battalion headed back to France, arriving 8 March. They found a changed mood amongst rank and file troops. The socialist revolution in Russia in which the feudal, autocratic regime of the Czar had been over-thrown by a popular uprising led by the Bolsheviks, was inspiring rebellion among many young conscripts forced to fight. The government of soviets (councils) in Moscow immediately pulled their military out of the carnage and convened peace talks. This fuelled a growing discontent by ordinary soldiers on all sides who, by 1918, realised they were disposable resources in an internecine conflict between rival representatives of imperial capital.

> The future seemed to be an endless vista of battles, each one worse than the last... the morale of the army had settled onto a bottom of fatalistic despair, in which the majority carried on mechanically, waiting for their next wound, while the weaker members went under, either to lunacy, desertion, or self-inflicted wounds.[452]

The German army's high command, no longer having to fight on the Eastern Front, launched the first phase Operation Michael. The aim of this Spring offensive – the second Battle of the Somme – was a decisive, final, war-ending victory. Two days later, on the morning of 23 March the 23rd Middlesex was heavily bombarded. In the Front Line at Beugny they suffered large casualties, before being attacked by incessant waves of determined enemy infantry. The battalion retreated, bivouacking the night at Favreuil aerodrome, a village held by the BEF since the previous March. The day's losses amounted to four killed, thirty-nine wounded and twelve missing.

452 Captain Desmond Allhusen, 8/King's Royal Rifles, quoted from Malcolm Brown, *1918: Year of Victory* (London, 1998), p. 4, in 'The Best Football Team, the Best Platoon', p. 33.

The aerodrome fell the next day necessitating further retreat. Again casualties were high: thirteen killed, fifty-seven wounded, six missing, six missing believed killed and twenty-two missing believed wounded.

On 25 March, after two days and nights of blood-drenched, ear-splitting hell, Walter and the remnants of his battalion woke – if sleep was possible – once more to the sound and impact of shellfire, followed by further waves of grey-clad enemy soldiers surging towards them bayonets first. Abandoning their position, they reformed behind a railway embankment. The day was characterised by further chaotic regroupings, symbolised by the abandonment of their 41st Division HQ at Aichiet-le-Grand.

Our Brigades and Battalions were very mixed up and, in addition, troops of many other units, including old Labour Company men and other oddments of that sort in were intermingled in the constant stream which poured through.[453]

It was in this defensive action that 2nd Lieutenant Walter Daniel John Tull lost his life. His death is officially recorded as 'somewhere in France or Belgium'.[454] Lieutenant Colonel Alan Haig Brown, commander of the 23rd Battalion, who recommended him for his commission, was also killed. The War Diary entry reads:

Monument [sector] March 25 8 am: Shelling of our line commenced. Enemy attacked shortly afterwards compelling the troops to withdraw... The enemy continued to push forward in massed formation. It was not until the units on both the left and right had retired that the Battn commenced an orderly withdrawal by platoons. Casualties were heavy and the enemy reached the trenches in considerable numbers... The Battalion assembled at GOMMECOURT 25/26th. 13 Killed. 61 Wounded. 30 Missing. 1 Missing believed Killed. 7 Missing believed Wounded. Killed – 2nd Lt W. D. Tull, 2nd Lt T. J. Petty. Wounded – a/ Capt W. Hammond MC, Lt R. A. Green, 2nd Lt G. Barton. Missing believed Killed – Lt Col. A. R. Haig-Brown DSO. Missing – a/Capt. B.

453 *The Journal of Arthur Nugent Acland*, p.88, Imperial War Museum, London, 03/29/1.
454 Military historian Andy Robertshaw suggests Walter may be buried in an ummarked grave at Heninel-Croisilles Road cemetery.

T. Foss MC. Evacuated Sick – 2nd Lt J. Jennings.[455]

Jean told of the day, 17 April 1918, her watery-eyed father received the dreaded telegram. 'The worst moment of my life, he tearfully sighed, continuing I just couldn't believe it… the thought kept going through my head, Walter is dead, Walter is dead'.[456]

In his state of shock Edward had to pull together and finalise the various threads of his late brother's life. Executor of his Will, he was obliged to have the document legally confirmed and ensure the instructions carried out.[457] He wrote to Major Poole asking how he could retrieve Walter's effects; to Northampton Town FC informing them of their former player's passing; and, dutifully as next-of-kin, tortuously broke the tragic news to the extended family.

THE BRITISH ARMY AND RECRUITS OF COLOUR

Adherence to an ideology of White supremacy characterised the Army Council. From the outset of the war, it had resisted Black recruitment and the use of Black troops. While Section 95 (2) of the Army Act allowed people of colour to enlist, the consensus among military chiefs was the morale of White soldiers would deteriorate serving alongside those of colour. Additionally, the majority of soldiers would not readily accept orders issued by officers of colour.

An official colour bar on non-regular officers in the armed forces, explicit in the *Short Guide to Obtaining a Commission in the Special Reserve of Officers,* existed. To qualify for a commission, 'a candidate must be of pure European descent, and a British born or naturalised British subject'.[458] This was reaffirmed in the Manual of Military Law (1914)

455 War Diary, 23rd Middlesex Regiment, 25th March 1918. WO 95/4243, N.A., London.
456 Interview with Jean Finlayson, 1995. The telegram can be viewed on the Walter Tull Archive: https://waltertullarchive.com/archive/ accessed 12 October 2020.
457 The Will was confirmed at Glasgow, March 1919 with Walter's address given as 419 St Vincent St. Glasgow. His estate was valued at £229 and sixpence, equivalent to approximately £13,111 in 2019. Details of his Will are registered in the National Probate Calendar, Scotland, 1919, p.1116. My thanks to Lorna and Ritchie Conaghan of the Girvan and District Great War Project for bringing this document to my notice.
458 *Short Guide to Obtaining a Commission in the Special Reserve of Officers,*

which authorised 'alien soldiers, including any negro or person of colour to hold honorary rank but they must not exercise any actual command or power'.[459]

This contradicted the British Nationality and Status of Aliens Act 1914 which defined 'the status of all those born within the British Empire as 'natural born British subjects".[460] The legislation gave Empire subjects equivalent status to those born in the UK. The ambiguity over ethnic criteria required to become an officer was clarified by a ruling in the 1914 Manual (confirming the regulation contained in the Short Guide):

> Commissions in the Special Reserve of Officers are given to qualified candidates who are natural born or naturalised British subjects of pure European descent.[461]

It did not matter where you were born in the Empire but it did what colour you were. However, if you were of light brown-skin, from an upper middle class background and prepared to say yes on your application form to the question 'whether of pure European descent?' exceptions could be made. This was the case for Jamaica-born and Dulwich College educated Second Lieutenant George Bemand of the Royal Field Artillery, killed-in-action Boxing Day, 1916 in France, aged twenty-five. (His brother Harold, denied a commission because of his darker complexion, remained in the ranks as a gunner. He was killed-in-action, 7 June 1917 aged nineteen.) Compatriot David Clemetson, an alumnus of Clifton College, Bristol and Trinity College, Cambridge, a

scion of one of the richest plantation-owning families on the island, was also commissioned a Second Lieutenant in the Pembrokeshire Yeomanry.

(London, 1912), p. 8.

459 *Manual of Military Law*, (London, 1914), p. 471.

460 Richard Smith in *The Oxford Companion to Black British History*, (Oxford, 2007), p. 176.

461 *The Manual of Military Law* (1914) defines the Special Reserve of Officers as 'a branch of the Reserve of Officers… designed to ensure that all units, services and departments of the regular forces shall be complete in officers on mobilization; to make good wastage which will occur in the regular forces in war, and to provide officers for special reserve units', p. 198. Immediately below is the paragraph instructing officers must be of 'pure European descent'.

He was killed-in-action on the Western Front, 21 September, 1918, aged twenty-five. Second Lieutenant Euan Lucie-Smith, of the 1st Battalion, Royal Warwickshire Regiment completes the trio of Jamaica-born officers. A pupil at two public schools he was the son of the Postmaster for Jamaica. He was reported killed at Ypres, 25 April 1915, aged twenty-six.[462] Mixed-heritage John Albert Gordon Smyth, born in Blaby, Leicestershire, was commissioned a temporary Second Lieutenant and killed in France on 29 June 1918, aged thirty-three. Son of a clergyman on his first application for a commission he answers yes to the pure European descent question. Across the form is the annotation '*a horrible bounder. Reject*'. Did this condescending dismissal betray the prejudice of an irritated adjudicator when confronted with a well-spoken brown-skinned person who formerly worked as a bank clerk in Civvy Street?[463]

Recruitment of British subjects in the US was under the management of General White. Secret cypher telegrams between White, his boss – the UK ambassador – at the British War Mission and the War and Colonial Offices in London detail the anxiety the Army Council had about accepting men of colour into combat roles.[464] By March 1918 over 2,000 had registered to enlist. Continuous delay in their induction and deployment led to growing discontent. In a secret telegram dated 19 February, 1918, he asks what he should do with these 'Wooly [sic] headed niggers'.[465]

Simultaneously, men of colour were prosecuted for not heeding their conscription notice. Robert Reubens, a South Asian from Singapore, was tried at Brighton Magistrates Court in 1917 for failing to report for military service. His defence was that he was in the UK to study, thus exempted. Despite the Ministry of National Service stating he should not have been served with a conscription notice, he was convicted.

In the summer of 1918, four years into the war and desperate for fighting men, the Army Council officially sanctioned 'British subjects of colour' in the British Army.

The intention of the Army Council was, and is, to provide a place

462 For details of all three Jamaican officers see: Frank Cundall, *Jamaica's Part in the Great War 1914-1918*, (London, 1925); Bemand, WO 339/30835, Clemetson WO 374/14274, Lucie-Smith WO 339/10918, NA, London.
463 Smyth's military record can be accessed at WO 339/69930, NA, London.
464 WO 32/4765, NA, London.
465 General White to War Office, 19 February 1918: WO 32/4765.

in the combatant arms of the British Army for British subjects of colour resident in Great Britain and the United States and also for the better class British subject of colour or half caste resident in the Colonies for whom no appropriate combatant unit exists in the colony in which he resides.[466]

Political expediency now displaced moral chaos.

The regulation affirming ethnicity more important than natality was not officially lifted until the Second World War when Charles Arundel Moody was commissioned into the Queen's Own Royal West Kent Regiment.

WALTER'S LEGACY

Walter's legacy is built upon the foundation laid by Edward. Without his care and diligence in preserving both his existential being and his physical memory through preserving letters, medals, photographs, newspaper cuttings and other memorabilia, his deserved revival would not have occurred with such force of detail. Edward's love for his brother assumed a protective appearance as time progressed. He was determined that the achievements and respect Walter humbly accrued during his short, momentous life would not be forgotten. A memorial plaque at Claremont Street Wesleyan Church of worshippers killed in the war contained Walter's name.[467] In 1940 he corrected information contained in Harold Moody's LCP newsletter that his son, Charles Arundel, was the first Black infantry officer in the British Army. He also further ensured his adopted city's prominence in Walter's legacy was publicly recognised by writing to the *Glasgow Evening Times* who subsequently ran a story headed 'First Coloured Officer in the British Army' alongside a photograph of a smiling Walter in his officer cadet uniform.[468]

---

466 War Office to Under-Secretary of State, Colonial Office, 24 August 1918, CO 323/782/41475 in Richard Smith, *Jamaican Volunteers in the First World War* (Manchester, 2004), p. 68.

467 Claremont Street Methodist Church closed in 1950. The memorial plaque is now displayed at Partick Methodist Church, 424 Dumbarton Road, Glasgow G11 6SN. My thanks to Ed Finlayson for bringing this to my attention.

468 *Glasgow Evening Times*, 12 February 1940. The sub-heading read: 'Glasgow

The Pages of the Sea initiative was part of the commemorations of the hundredth anniversary of the First World War armistice. Coordinated by film-director Danny Boyle, it invited coastal communities around Britain to remember those that did not return. A dramatic, stunning and emotional profile of Walter, designed by sand artists Sand in Your Eye, was carved on Ayr beach. It represented recognition of his links to: Ayr, where he trained as an officer at Gailes; his brother's dental practice at Girvan; and to Scotland to which he had pledged his future by signing for Rangers in February, 1917. Respectful but fittingly angrily, Carol Ann Duffy's 'Wound in Time', was specially written for the event.

It is the wound in Time. The century's tides,
chanting their bitter psalms, cannot heal it.
Not the war to end all wars; death's birthing place;
the earth nursing its ticking metal eggs, hatching
new carnage. But how could you know, brave
as belief as you boarded the boats, singing?
The end of God in the poisonous, shrapnelled air.
Poetry gargling its own blood. We sense it was love
you gave your world for; the town squares silent,
awaiting their cenotaphs. What happened next?
War. And after that? War. And now? War. War.
History might as well be water, chastising this shore;
for we learn nothing from your endless sacrifice.
Your faces drowning in the pages of the sea.

'War, war', that machine-gun repetition of bloodletting that marked and scarred Edward's life and millions of others, was the motivation of his pacifism. *Walter is dead, Walter is dead,* three words of mustard gas intensity that seeped poison – the real effect of war – into his being. Both brothers had bequeathed from their mothers and fathers a mature moral compass built from the precepts of the Moravian and Methodist faiths and the lived experience each had as progeny of the enslaved and dispossessed. It guided Edward, who added his ingredient of left-wing socialism, helping him deal not only with the devastation of his brother's death but the subsequent disrespect heaped upon memories of the lost. The disregard for the sanctity of life shown by the ruling class with their

Man Who Signed for Rangers FC.' *League of Coloured Peoples Newsletter,* no.6, March 1940.

predilection for armed force whether at home against striking workers, in the colonies against freedom and liberation movements or generally in arms production and expenditure was consistent throughout his life. Those that did return did not come home to a land fit for heroes but under-employment, poor housing and inadequate medical care. Those that owned and controlled society seemed devoid of a moral compass in their relationship with working people.

CLAIMING WALTER

Scotland's growing assertiveness in its reclamation of Walter's legacy was boosted by the Ayr beach sand sculpture and the decision of the Royal Mail to dedicate a pillar box in his honour in Byres Road, Glasgow in recognition of Black History Month, 2020. Painted black with gold trim it featured the same head and shoulder's profile of the Second Lieutenant that the organisation had used when issuing postage stamps in his commemoration two years earlier. Summarising, the postbox bio read he 'also signed on to become the first black player for Rangers'.

It would be comforting to conclude this chapter by arguing that Walter's achievements as the first Black working-class officer in the British Army and first man of colour to sign or play for Clapton, Tottenham Hotspur, Northampton Town and Rangers football clubs broke down barriers in which others followed, but it would be a distortion of reality. There was not another Black British officer for another twenty-two years after Walter's death; Chris Hughton was the second man of colour to play for Spurs, signing in June 1979, sixty years after Walter's recruitment; New Year's Eve 1987 was the occasion of Rangers securing the signature of their next player of African-Caribbean heritage, Mark Walters.

With the resurgence of fascism, racism is polluting matches more frequently. When Millwall FC hosted Derby County for a Championship game on 5 December 2020 players of both teams, in common with other clubs in professional football in the UK, knelt on one knee. It is an agreed gesture of support for Black Lives Matter's (BLM) campaign against racism and arbitrary and unfair discrimination. In response, despite having players of colour representing their club, a small number of home fans booed. Antigua and Barbuda international Mahlon Romeo, at the club since 2015, commented

I'm almost lost for words, I don't know how they thought that would make me feel. I don't know what they thought taking a knee stood for.

But I think I've explained it simply enough.[469]

Derby County's manager, Wayne Rooney and assistant manager, Leroy Rosenior, both publicly condemned the booing. The latter posted on his Twitter page:

Proud of the team. Proud of the players. Proud of the staff. Proud of the result. Proud of the club. Proud to be Black.[470]

However, Conservative politician and government minister, Environment Secretary George Eustice, on a Sunday morning talk show, felt it was more important to rubbish – without, it seems, a hint of self-awareness – the anti-discrimination movement as 'political'.

My personal view is that Black Lives Matter, capital B, L, and M, is actually a political movement, which is different from what most of us believe in, which is standing up for racial equality.[471]

This dismissal of both the booing and validity of BLM by Eustice angered Rosenior:

What hurt even more than the booing is the response of George Eustice this morning. Being a cabinet minister and conflating a positive, unifying message as a message of activism, and politicising something that every single person on this planet should be supporting. It's not a political message, let's make this absolutely clear. This is a message about unifying our country. When top political figures are creating division, how difficult is it at ground level? [472]

In criticising, Rosenior has history on his side. BLM began as

469   https://soccer.nbcsports.com/2020/12/07/wayne-rooney-millwall-players-react-to-fans-booing-players-for-taking-the-knee/ Accessed 12 February, 2021.

470 @rosenior_liam23, 8.13pm, 5 December, 2020.

471   https://internewscast.com/cabinet-minister-wades-into-row-after-millwall-fans-boo-players-taking-the-knee/ Accessed 12 February, 2021.

472 Rosenior to Radio5 Live, 6 December 2020, quoted in https://www.belfasttelegraph.co.uk/sport/football/we-must-not-accept-actions-of-mindless-few-wayne-rooney-on-millwall-booing-39832981.html   Accessed 12 February, 2021.

a grassroots formation by people of colour in the US responding collectively to police violence. It has grown organically into a global phenomenon bringing together activists primarily to oppose racism but also to resist negative discrimination generally. One if its key demands is a defunding of non-law and order responsibilities of the police - such as mental health crises, homeless encampments and begging - in order to transfer resources to agencies more capable of dealing with them.

Home Secretary Priti Patel also undermined the movement and its aims in an LBC radio interview:

> I don't support protests... there are other ways in which people can express their opinion... Those [BLM] protests were dreadful... Protesting the way in which people did last summer was not the right way at all.[473]

I marched on both London demonstrations protesting the murder of George Floyd 28 May and 3 June, 2020. They each attracted tens of thousands, a rainbow of ethnicities, ages, genders and beliefs. They were defiant, peaceful, determined marches of solidarity led by BLM activists of colour.

The actions and words Eustice, Patel and prime minister Johnson who also refused to condemn booing of England players taking the knee, can have an enormous and often wildly disproportionate negative social impact.[474] The achievements of people of colour like Walter Tull in overcoming discrimination can be sabotaged overnight. There was no organised anti-discrimination group within football to which he or his club could complain about the racism he endured. It was another seven decades before they would appear, the outcome of localised club initiatives by fans. There is an unbroken historical link connecting the prejudiced and discriminatory treatment of Walter Tull at Bristol, the principled response of journalist 'DD', the nineteen-seventies anti-racist fans' initiatives and BLM: injustice occurred and people took positive, peaceful and progressive action. It is a necessary and fundamental right

---

473   https://www.independent.co.uk/news/uk/politics/priti-patel-take-knee-blm-protests-b1801326.html   and   https://morningstaronline.co.uk/article/b/anti-racists-outraged-patels-blm-comments Both accessed 13 February, 2021.

474   https://morningstaronline.co.uk/article/s/prime-minsiter-cant-bring-himself-condemn-booing-england-fans Accessed 30 July 2021.

of human existence. Discussing Walter Tull's legacy – a battleground of competing narratives – and protecting his core values of tenacity, self-belief, faith, tolerance and humility is a collective endeavour. Edward's love for his brother ensures we have the materials to sustain this focus and not be sidelined or overcome by malignant forces.

The first campaign to publicly recognise the achievements of Walter Tull was a fan-led initiative to embed Walter's legacy into the cultural fabric of Northampton Town FC. It culminated in a collaboration between club and supporters that, on Sunday, 11 July 1999 saw the unveiling, outside the Sixfields Stadium, of an inscripted memorial sculpture within a Garden of Remembrance. Designed by Paul Mason and funded by donations from fans, the public and organisations such as the Football Unites, Racism Divides, the Professional Footballers' Association and Kick It Out, the ceremony was coordinated by Brian Lomax an elected supporter-director who spearheaded the project.

Edward's grandson, Ed Finlayson, represented the extended Tull family and spoke about the growing acknowledgement his great uncle was now receiving. It was a well-attended event that warmed the soul as much as the sun of that hot summer day warmed the body. One side of the memorial detailed Walter's footballing achievements. The other read:

> Through his actions, Tull ridiculed the barriers of ignorance that tried to deny people of colour equality with their contemporaries. His life stands testament to a determination to confront those people and those obstacles that sought to diminish him and the world in which he lived. It reveals a man, though rendered breathless in his prime, whose strong heart still beats loudly.[475]

For many years Ed has performed the public role of the family's Tull ambassador. National recognition of Walter and growing awareness of Edward has necessitated a sharing of this duty with siblings and relatives. While working as a social worker in north London during the nineteen seventies and eighties he would often pass White Hart Lane where just half a century earlier his uncle had entertained. Incredibly, it was not until Spurs invited him did he first step inside. In a filmed event

---

475 It was an honour to be asked to write the inscription for the memorial. See Appendix 5 for a list of subsequent educational projects and initiatives inspired by Walter Tull with relevant website links. Compiled by Daniel Morris for which I'm extremely grateful.

for a documentary on Black History he was given, in Walter's memory, a team shirt named *Tull* presented and signed by midfielder and England international Dele Ali. Tears in his eyes, Ed's patience in waiting for the right moment to foot the turf of his great uncle's stage was timed to perfection.

Chapter Twelve
Edward, Paul and Politics

COLOUR, CLASS AND MUSIC

Jean described her father as 'very left-wing'.[476] Duncan referred to his 'left-wing socialism'. In Edward's orbit, alongside Methodists and other non-conformist Christians of similar political hue, such as Moravians, it was socialists, communists and the Left in general who campaigned against racism, colonialism and war. The fusion of these anti-Establishment ideologies and beliefs alongside his lived experience as a mixed-heritage Briton moulded his pacifist, Christian socialism.

> It is my firm conviction that the Church acting up to her highest ideals, and functioning as she is intended to function, always stand for the material welfare as well as the Spiritual welfare of the Human Race.[477]

During the 2010 World Cup in South Africa I was involved in *Offside,* an exhibition of the contribution of African footballers to the professional game in the UK. It was hosted by District Six Museum and Home Coming Centre in Cape Town and co-produced with Football Unites, Racism Divides, Kick It Out and the British Council. Also working at the inspiring venue – dedicated to retaining the memory of a community of colour forcibly evicted from central Cape Town during nineteen-sixties apartheid – were volunteers from a university in the USA. During an afternoon coffee break I chatted to one. He was interested in politics, a reason behind his decision to volunteer at the museum. He had not heard of fellow African American, Paul Robeson, described as 'the most famous living American' by the *Daily Worker* in 1950.[478] We discussed his accomplishments. The young student was: amazed by Robeson's achievements; angered at the price he paid for them; and outraged at the confiscation of a history and cultural heritage denied him.

Fortunately, the actions and words of Paul Robeson have reached

476 Interview, 1995.
477 Edward Tull-Warnock *Paul Robeson* (undated) Finlayson Family Archive, p.4.
478 30 May.

millions of people around the world. Edward was one of them. He was determined that the legacy of this iconic warrior's praxis would be passed to his family. The towering North American inspired on a number of levels: politically, in his willingness to voice the concerns, anger, preoccupations, dreams and hopes of Black people; culturally, through his international profile and acclaim as a ground-breaking actor and singer of Negro spirituals; in sport where, as an excellent (American) footballer suffering at the feet and hands of White opponents – often brutally – he refused to be bullied, eventually winning representative honours.

Robeson's tussles lasted a lifetime. Edward, in a public talk, commented: 'He was battered in every scrimmage but he fought on'.[479] He was never allowed to fully leave behind the segregated sidewalk of his Princeton, New Jersey childhood. However profound and enriching his social contribution as a scholar, actor and sportsman the eagerness of powerful opponents to demean him and his achievements never wavered. Slavery may have been abolished with the defeat of the confederate army but the viciously gratuitous degradations of the plantation continued. (His father, a preacher, was born into chattel slavery and remained chained to that status until he escaped at fifteen years of age.) In his eulogy to Robeson Edward also dwelled on the importance of Negro spirituals to the enslaved. He quotes the song, 'Sit Down', its simplicity and clarity summarising the essence of such an existence.

I'm going up to heaven and sit down
Goin up to heaven and sit down
Oh! sit down sister, sit down child
Sit down and rest a little while.

I'll see my Lord, he'll say 'sit down'
See my Lord, He'll say 'sit down'
Oh, sit down sister, sit down child
Sit down and rest a little while.[480]

Edward's admiration for the Princeton, New Jersey-born Rutgers University graduate flows through his piece, the information for which he draws from Eslanda Goode Robeson's biography of her husband,

479 Edward Tull-Warnock, *Paul Robeson*, Finlayson Family Archive.
480 Edward Tull-Warnock, *Paul Robeson*, pp.6-7.

Paul Robeson, Negro. The title captures the twin themes of her book and the dual consciousness of the subject. From the nineteen twenties her partner had determined that he would not leave unchallenged any consideration of his life that attempted to separate out his existences as a citizen of the United States and a man of colour in a segregated society. Forty years before John Carlos and Tommy Smith raised proudly their black-gloved fists on the medal winners' podium at the Mexico Olympics, claiming their success for all African-Americans rather than the USA, Robeson was demanding symbolic evaluation of his accomplishments. His life's work must be seen as a refutation of Jim Crow segregation and the White-supremacist ideologies that attempted to justify it. For people of colour, worldwide, his intellectual, artistic and sporting faculties embodied an existence and respect denied to the vast majority.

His passionate affection for the UK, 'I have found perfect freedom and peace',[481] contrasted with his experience of overt racism in the USA. He compared the oppressive colour prejudice of Princeton to a southern plantation town. Negroes lived in daily fear of their lives being stolen. 'We had no rights and one might be shot for objecting to being pushed off the pavement'.[482] The eruption of the Spanish Civil War in 1936 while Robeson was living in Britain, reaffirmed his belief in the necessity of class unity as the instrument to defeat ethnic and national divisions that capitalism and fascism fostered.

> The miners of Wales, who gave great support to the anti-fascist movement, welcomed me when I came to sing on behalf of aid to Spain and invited me into their union halls and into their homes. The Welsh miners and other workers whom I met throughout England and Scotland, made it clear there was a closer bond between us than the general struggle to preserve democracy from its fascist foes. At the heart of the conflict, they pointed out, was a class division, and although I was famous and wealthy, the fact was I came from a working-class people like themselves and therefore, they said, my place was with them in the ranks of Labor.[483]

---

481 David Dabydeen and Shivani Sivagurunathan in *Oxford Companion to Black British History* in David Dabydeen, John Gilmore and Cecily Jones (eds) (Oxford University Press, 2007), p. 417.
482 *Daily Worker*, 18 April 1949 in N.A. KV2/1829.
483 Paul Robeson, *Here I Stand*, (Boston, 1988 edition) p.54.

In the UK-produced film, *The Proud Valley*, set in a Welsh pit village, he played heroic collier David Goliath, his nomenclature encapsulating the movie's theme. Giving his life to save his colleagues, his character illuminates the liberating potential of class solidarity and the ultimate irrelevance of colour difference. Goliath is a Black hero, a role unavailable in nineteen forties Hollywood with its ethnic typecasting and formulaic narratives. To play roles that had the imagination and political will to go beyond mainstream stereotypes of simple and obedient or rebellious and destructive, African Americans had to create a parallel cinema industry with the Micheaux Film Corporation – for whom Robeson worked – and the Lincoln Motion Picture Company, prominent. While blessed with a constant supply of talent, they were forced to worked with a poverty of resources, producing films with lower production values as cruel pay-back for their independent spirit.

His residence in Britain during the nineteen twenties and thirties witnessed a clarification and maturity of his political beliefs. Leaving the theatre after performing a matinee performance of *Show Boat,* he delayed returning home to Hampstead after hearing anonymous voices singing with a perfection of harmony and timing. Emerging into view he saw what seemed, in the first instance, at odds with the beautiful, captivating music: working men marching with political banners. In solidarity he walked alongside and learned they were Rhondda Valley miners blacklisted by mine owners after the 1926 General Strike some three years earlier. Impoverished and hungry, they paused for rest. The comparatively well-dressed, well-fed and considerably larger African American sang 'Ol' Man River' and other spirituals in empathy. He knew from experience these men would find solace in the words and music from a genre that voiced their plight. This cultural intersection made a lasting impression upon Robeson and the miners and forged an unbreakable bond to which *Proud Valley* bears testament. 'It's from the miners in Wales, [that] I first understood the struggle of Negro and White together'.[484] The singer also paid towards their food, clothing and fares home.

This common experience of exploitation by workers on both sides

484 Robeson quote from Jeff Sparrow 'How Paul Robeson found his political voice in the Welsh Valleys' *Observer,* 2 July 2017 https://www.theguardian. com/books/2017/jul/02/how-paul-robeson-found-political-voice-in-welsh-valleys#comments Accessed 21 August 2020.

of the Atlantic that was the foundation for the bond between Robeson and the working class of Britain has, over time, been the inspiration for other forms of shared culture. The Northern Soul phenomenon is possibly the most popular and obvious example. The nineteen sixties and seventies saw these up-tempo creations of African-American singers and groups became the exclusive playlists of DJ's at all-night soul clubs, mainly in the North and Midlands of England. Venues such as Manchester's Twisted Wheel, Stoke's Torch, Blackpool's Mecca, Wigan's Casino and Market Harborough's Lantern on a Saturday night would be packed with working-class young people bursting with the desire to athletically dance away the previous five days of mundane toil. Working in jobs that demanded repetition and suppressed creativity they could empathise with the singer from the car factory production-line in Detroit desperately searching out love as a compensatory escape or the beautifully crafted sound of the gospel-singing chanteuse from the Jack Crow southern states demanding *Respect!* from deep within her heart. These lyrics and music from oppressed people of colour in the United States appealed to, and chimed with, the sensitivities and lived experience of young, working class urban Britons. However, what gave the music its magic was its upbeat positivity that spoke to an unbreakable, defiant spirit. This was the unique ingredient in what was already an incredibly attractive art form. The shuffling, spinning, somersaulting, springing dancers of the all-nighters could also take spiritual inspiration from a rhythm, beat and sound that made their bodies *rock* – as Edward, borrowing from Eslanda Robeson, three decades earlier, described the relationship between African-American church congregations and Negro Spirituals – with balletic movement.

The against-all-odds, emotive output of their state-side soul heroes, a joy-inspiring cultural production despite the seemingly unending burden of racial discrimination, consequently acted as super-glue to an already strong bond. *Keep the Faith*, the Northern Soul movement's motto wrapped around the graphic of a closed fist, was taken from the signing-off phrase of pioneering *Blues and Soul* journalist Dave Godin, who coined the term northern soul. Godin consciously chose politicised language, *Right on Now, Keep the Faith,* drawn from the US civil rights struggle, as his signature closure to his bi-monthly columns. Gospel, for Godin, was the mother of soul.

Edward's admiration and affection for the African American – 'it is as a singer of Negro Spirituals that I love and admire Paul Robeson' –

whom he credits for popularising, alongside Roland Hayes,[485] the gospel genre, by osmosis seeped into his wife and daughter. Edward's habit of conjuring inspiration born of excellence for his Sunday morning choir duties at chapel involved playing a vinyl recording of his singing, a fond and indelible memory of Jean's. Betty wrote to the giant African-American and was delightedly surprised at receiving a signed card in response.

ROBESON AND SCOTLAND

Reverend Duncan Finlayson fondly recalled attending with his father-in-law 'the big communist meetings'. On at least one occasion Robeson topped the bill. His deep baritone voice – akin to slowed-down, harmonious thunder – mesmerised his audience of Glaswegian working people. The repertoire of Negro Spirituals, folk ballads and polemical oratory enthralled audiences who incessantly demanded many encores. The searing impression Robeson made upon the young Highlander was obvious, with the ninety-one year old interviewee still vividly remembering the encore finale of 'Love Will Find a Way' sung seven decades earlier.

Robeson was popular in Britain – the springboard for his global acclaim – not least because he was deeply knowledgeable about British culture. Gaelic was among the many languages he studied. As early as 1938, The Scotsman reported that he had a 'working knowledge of Gaelic.' But what made Robeson unique was that he strived to connect national streams of culture to an all-encompassing global culture. 'When I was in Scotland,' said Robeson, 'I was reminded of how near the Gaelic folk songs are to our own. When I sing them I feel that they express the same soulful quality that I know in Negro music. Indeed, they contributed no small part to the development of our music and the Gaelic speaking Negro was not uncommon in the Southern States two centuries ago.' [486]

485 For more information on Roland Willsie Hayes see Kwame Anthony Appiah, Henry Louis Gates Junior (ed.) *Africana: The Encyclopaedia of the African and African American Experience, Volume 3* (Oxford, 2005) pp.184-5.
486 Gerald Horne, *Paul Robeson. The Artist as Revolutionary,* (London, 2016), p8.   https://library.oapen.org/bitstream/id/150bde08-bbe5-4eb3-a1f8-d2d668134b14/650017.pdf Accessed 20 August 2020.

Robeson spoke and sang at Kelvin Hall, Glasgow, 12 May, 1949. It could be this now-iconic event to which Duncan was referring. Organised by the Communist Party of Great Britain (CPGB) but hosted by the Scotland USSR Society, four thousand turned out for an evening of musical entertainment and political inspiration. Preparations had been ongoing for some months prior, monitored by City of Glasgow Police Special Branch who wrote to the director general of MI5 in April warning them that the Negro singer would be appearing at a public meeting in early May with the Dean of Canterbury.[487]

Robeson had toured Scotland as a musical entertainer over ten years earlier after the stage play in which he starred, *Plant in the Sun,* completed its London run. It dramatised the necessity for black and white unity in workplace struggles. The intervening years saw a philosophical transition in Paul's attitude to his dual persona of musician and activist. Three experiences made deep impressions: a pre-war visit to Nazi Berlin which he described as akin to experiencing a Klu Klux Klan government; the horrendous outcome of the Spanish Civil War, leaving a million dead and a fascist dictatorship; and a second global conflict which laid waste many more millions. All confirmed his belief that art and politics could not be separated. This conscious reconfiguration is captured in the short film of his Edinburgh performances, *A Star Drops In,* directed by David Pickering and commissioned by the National Union of Mineworkers (NUM). Before his evening at event Usher Hall, hosted by the Scottish Area NUM who bussed and railed-in miners from all over the country, Paul sung in the afternoon the poignant and apposite 'Ballad of Joe Hill' to workers at Woolmet Colliery, on the south-eastern edge of the capital. Passing through the pit gates two years earlier they would have seen a notice which read: 'This colliery is now managed by the National Coal Board on behalf of the people'. That union organiser and song-writer Joe Hill had his life terminated because of his persistent and dogged struggle in pursuit of collective goals was not lost on Robeson, who sings with profound feeling to an enamoured audience. Captured on black and white film is this solemn, vindicatory musical epitaph to an executed comrade.

Historian of the Black Diaspora in Britain, Marika Sherwood, in 1998 recorded interviews in Glasgow with some who had attended Robeson's

487 Chief Constable W. Ewing to Sir Percy Sillitoe, 6 April, 1949. File KV 2/1829, p.91a, National Archives, London. This secret service file on Robeson is available online.

post-war concerts and rallies. The speakers testify to the high regard in which he was held. They were eager to emphasise the eight year campaign of Scottish communists and miners, alongside their Welsh comrades and colleagues, to have the African American's passport returned after it was confiscated by the USA government in 1950.

—In factories where I worked, even if people were a bit critical of his politics, there was a lot of admiration for his singing.
—I just fell in love with his voice at seventeen. I wanted to marry him so he could sing to me alone.
—I go the sack from my job in New Zealand for taking around a petition in the factory to get Paul Robeson his passport back.
—What a wonderful thing to get sacked for! [488]

Contributors to the forum felt the love for Robeson originated in identifying with his struggle as an African American. His fight for emancipation carried echoes of their battles of class and culture as working class Scots. The love was reciprocated, Robeson learning traditional Gaelic folk-songs and singing them in their original form; walking at the head of May Day rallies in Glasgow and Edinburgh, culminating in speech and song. In an interview with the *Edinburg Evening Dispatch* in November 1958 he reminded readers 'I am very pro-Scottish, but [aware that his affection could be misinterpreted as prioritising bourgeoise patriotism over the primacy of international class unity] don't let them draft me into your Scottish nationalist movement here'.[489]

Legendary Glaswegian communist Jimmy Reid became a friend of Robeson. An active trade unionist his rousing workplace platform speeches were on a par for their oratorical force and power with the timbrous clarity and impassioned beauty of Robeson's singing. A tactical masterstroke was his visionary 'work-in' which defeated the Conservative government's attempts to close down Upper Clyde Shipbuilders in the

---

488 Unnamed contributors to a forum discussion organised by Marika Sherwood, Glasgow 11 February 1998. Those taking part were Marion Eastdale, John Tonner, Alex Cunningham, John Kay, Helen King, Marion Caldow, Robert Caldow, Ruby McLean, Peter McLean, George Bolton, Iain McLeod, Pat Mulligan. My thanks to Marika Sherwood for sharing these tapes from her extensive archive.
489 Horne, (2016), p175.

early nineteen seventies. At Reid's 2010 funeral, Robeson's rendition of Beethoven's 'Ode to Joy' was played, honouring the former's wishes.

The African American recognised the unremitting solidarity and support shown by communists and working people in Scotland. Not just in his personal struggles, but to other African Americans such as the Scottsboro Boys. Nine youths of colour, ranging from thirteen to nineteen, were arrested in March 1931 in Paint Rock, Alabama for allegedly raping two White women. Despite one later withdrawing the accusation, all were sentenced to execution, except thirteen year old Andy Wright where a hung jury suggested life imprisonment rather than the electric chair. The case immediately became a cause celebre with the International Labour Defence (ILD), the legal aid section of the Communist International, using its organising power to support the families in building a campaign. News of the injustice spread rapidly. In London, two thousand people braved a cold winter's day in February to march from the Thames embankment to Hyde Park. The speedily convened London Scottsboro Defence Committee included Jomo Kenyatta and Vera Brittain. In Wales, the communist member of parliament for Battersea, Shapurji Saklatvala spoke to a rainbow audience at the Barry Colonial Social Club, Cardiff where two hundred signed a resolution condemning the boys inhuman treatment. India-born, Saklatvala had been elected the first communist MP in 1922 for north Battersea. His election agent, Black Briton John Archer, was the second man of colour to hold the office of mayor – of Battersea – in 1913.

The ILD facilitated a European speaking tour assisting Ada Wright, whose other son Roy was on death row. This was a courageous undertaking by the forty-two year old domestic servant who had barely been out of Tennessee. It would also have reassured this distraught middle-aged African American a long way from home – and whose overwhelming life-experience of White people would have been as purveyors of bigoted misery – that people of colour such as Arnold Ward of the Negro Welfare Association and George Padmore, editor of the *Negro Worker,* would be part of her team.

Wright arrived in London in June 1932 and was met by Shapurji Saklatvala, Bob Lovell, head of the British ILD and 'a large number of white and coloured workers.'... She spoke in London, Manchester,

Dundee, Kirkaldy, Glasgow and Bristol along with ILD organizers.[490]

The *Daily Worker*, 7 July 1932, featured Ada's Glasgow campaigning on the front page, along with her photo. She was met at Queen Street Station by a large number of working people before heading a procession to Springburn, accompanied by a flute band. There, and at Gorbals and Bridgetown, Ada addressed open-air meetings relaying the scheduled killing of her sons and their friends by the US state. Posters and banners advertising her solidarity tour in Britain carried the slogan, 'Stop the Legal Lynching'. Another edition of the paper described her meeting in Dundee.

> Cries of indignation rent the air as she told in simple, poignant language of the brutal savagery of the drunken, lynching mob outside the Court House, demanding death for the boys... The Dundee workers will not quickly forget the visit which has forged new bonds of unity between British workers and their coloured comrades.[491]

Throughout the nineteen thirties, Robeson ensured the Scottsboro nine would not be forgotten. He dedicated music and theatre performances, made personal donations and spoke at public meetings. In June 1938 when German, Italian and Iberian fascism was rampaging across Europe and Ethiopia, he joined with author H.G. Wells and lawyer DN Pritt in issuing a statement to the press.

> Despite the present tragic turn of world events and the constant war rumours which are spreading, there are still some people who are determined to press for the recognition of human rights [and who] appeal to draw folks to the case again... How is it that five can still be guilty if four are innocent? Justice should be international and we ask British opinion to show its practical sympathy.[492]

---

490 Miller, James A., et al. 'Mother Ada Wright and the International Campaign to Free the Scottsboro Boys, 1931-1934.' *The American Historical Review*, vol. 106, no. 2, 2001, pp. 403–04. JSTOR, www.jstor.org/stable/2651612. Accessed 17 Aug. 2020.

491 *Daily Worker* 5 July 1932 in James A. Miller, 2001, p.21.

492 Quote from Susan D. Pennybacker, *From Scotsboro to Munich: Race and Political Culture in 1930s Britain*, (Woodstock, 2009), p.61.

If unable to attend the Glasgow meetings, Edward's political and moral support for their cause would nevertheless have been absolute. While appreciative of the qualitative difference with the lived experience of people of colour in apartheid-practising USA, he had no blindspot when it came to the presence of discrimination in Britain. While legally-defined separate development was a ubiquitous characteristic of all states in the republic, differentiated only by the degree to which economic and social discrimination was imposed, Britain too had a long history of directives aimed at specific ethnic and religious communities. In the thirteenth century, Edward I issued a decree expelling Jews from England. Elizabeth 1 through her Privy Council authorised three documents instructing the removal of African-heritage people of colour from England. One, the 1596 open letter to the City of London and civic authorities in other towns complained: 'There are of late diverse blackamoores brought into these realms, of which kind there are already here too manie… Her Majesty's pleasure therefore ys that those kinde of people should be sent forth of the land'. This was followed a week later by her open warrant demanding public officers hand over 'Negroes and blackamoors' to merchant Casper van Senden for banishment. In 1601 a third proclamation was dispatched saying how upset she was that 'great numbers of negars and blackamoores [have] crept into the realm'.[493] Cromwell virtually outlawed Gaelic culture and practice in Ireland in the mid-seventeenth century, a suppression replicated in the Highlands after the Battle of Culloden.

In the twentieth century this tradition continued with the 1905 Aliens Act – aimed mainly at working class Jewish immigrants – and the Alien Restrictions Act 1914 resulting in over sixty-thousand 'non-British' people being interned in prison camps. Its amended 1919 version enforced differing rates of pay on British shipping dependent upon colour and ethnic origin of the seamen. Alongside discriminatory legislation there was also corporate rules and regulations which were prejudicial to people of colour.

---

493 Fryer (1991), pp 10-12; Peter Ackroyd, *London: The Biography* (London, 2001), p. 711; Emily Weissbourd. ,'Those in Their Possession': Race, Slavery, and Queen Elizabeth's 'Edicts of Expulsion." *Huntington Library Quarterly*, vol. 78, no. 1, 2015, pp. 1–19. *JSTOR*, www.jstor.org/stable/10.1525/hlq.2015.78.1.1. Accessed 10 Feb. 2021.

Edward would have been aware of the historic cultural and economic sectarianism – a form of racism – faced by Catholic residents in his city, particularly Irish Catholics. Despite a sizeable presence there was no St Patrick's Day parade. Employment in the preeminent industries of shipbuilding and engineering were subject to the NINA – No Irish Need Apply – rule, as was access to housing. Celtic Football Club was formed with the purpose of raising funds to make less brutal the squalid lives of the migrant Irish poor.

As a British man of colour, the psychological anxiety produced by the physical horror of the post First World War 'race' riots in Glasgow – and other port cities – would have been a ferocious reminder that the presence of people of colour was only as safe as the intensity and concentration of their collective vigilance.

The Alien Restrictions (Amendment) Act had the effect of reaffirming the divide and rule tactics of the Establishment.

> The 1919 Aliens Act was introduced against the background of fervent nationalism and anti-German feeling created by the First World War… and was renewed every single year between 1919 and 1971.[494]

The violence of 23 January 1919 broke out at a shipping company's yard in James Watt Street, half a mile from Edward's dental surgery. Lots of demobbed sailors were chasing few jobs. As was the practice with Irish labour in the nineteenth century, ship owners and their agents used Black British and colonial seamen to drive down wages and were allowed by law to pay them less than White sailors. This inevitably caused friction between desperate workers. Fighting broke out and spread to the street. It soon escalated to housing and hostels used by sailors of colour. Under siege and in fear of their lives at a boarding house in Broomielaw Street they fired shots at an angry and aggressive crowd. The violence resulted in one West African and two White seamen being injured. The local press blamed the 'coloured' seamen for the shipping company's policy of hiring at the lowest rates possible.

The trouble began because the blacks were being given preference

---

494 Ruth Brown, 'Racism and Immigration Controls', *International Socialism*, Autumn 1995, p.8. The 1971 Immigration Act, aimed primarily at making entry difficult into the UK for migrants of colour, negated the necessity for renewal.

over the whites in signing on for a ship about to sail. The whites resented this, especially as it is well known that coloured men are paid lower wages.[495]

Workers in Glasgow and Clydeside were in an insurrectionary mood. Veteran soldiers and sailors – Black and White – were returning not to the promises of 'homes fit for heroes' and their old job back but an economic environment where wartime profiteering continued. Such was the angry, collective, class conscious response to these parasitic machinations of capital, that the region was christened Red Clydeside.[496] However, the outrage of one group of needy workers attacking their comrades over scarce resources brought dishonour to that name and tradition. To add further shame, the two most influential trade union leaders, Willie Gallacher and Manny Shinwell, exacerbated tensions by reaffirming the dominant narrative that 'alien' seamen were responsible for the systemic inadequacies of the shipping industry in the recruitment of labour. The former was admired by Lenin as an influential anti-war activist amongst the Glasgow proletariat where he headed the Clyde Workers' Committee while working tirelessly to build a revolutionary communist party in Scotland. (He was a founder member of the Communist Party of Great Britain in 1920.)

Addressing a large crowd of seamen in the yard immediately prior to the disturbance a local journalist reported Shinwell as highlighting the great number of British sailors who were without work and their thousands of colleagues who would find it difficult to secure employment aboard ship once they had been released from the armed forces:

This he attributed to the refusal of the Government to exclude Chinese labour from British ships, and it was essential, he said that action should be taken at once.[497]

---

495 *Evening Citizen* (Glasgow), 24 Jan. 1919, p.3 in *Black Sailors on Red Clydeside: rioting, reactionary trade unionism and conflicting notions of 'Britishness' following the First World War*, Jacqueline Jenkinson, University of Stirling.

496 The brave militancy of Glasgow suffragettes contributed to this tradition. On 9 May 1914 they physically battled with police who tried to break up their meeting. When the police tried to storm the platform and arrest speakers they were foiled by hidden, protective barbed wire.

497 *Evening Times*, 23 January 1919, p.1 in Jacqueline Jenkinson, Black Sailors on Red Clydeside, p.12.

Shinwell, Gallacher and other prominent members of the labour movement were agitating for a General Strike demanding a forty hour week. The cause had wide support, especially in the docks, transport and mining industries. Later that month, over seventy-thousand downed tools. Other Scottish workers joined in along with those in Tyneside and Belfast. The class conflict escalated when, in a strategy echoing the Manchester bourgeoisie's Peterloo Massacre of peaceful workers one hundred years earlier, mounted and foot police charged the rear of a supporting protest of sixty-thousand in George Square, injuring thirty-four. The workers fought back with Gallacher punching the chief constable. A sheriff tried to read the riot act, enacting martial law, but had it torn from his hands. Gallacher and Shinwell were arrested. (They later received three and five month prison sentences, respectively.) The uprising continued throughout that Friday with the war cabinet meeting in London. The Secretary for Scotland feared the Scottish Bolshevik revolution had begun. Twelve thousand troops, one hundred lorries and six tanks were deployed to the city from other parts of the country and northern England. The government shied away from using the soldiers stationed at the local Maryhill Barracks anxious that they would side with their working class comrades.

On Sunday morning the military took over the city centre in a massive show of Establishment power: machine gun placements dotted George Square; power stations were surrounded; tanks parked in the Cattle Market. 'The city chambers is like an armed camp. The quadrangle is full of troops and equipment, including machine guns'.[498]

Edward lived in the central Overnewton district of the city. At one end of St Vincent Street was George Square and city chambers. This military occupation would have dominated talk at Claremont Street Chapel morning service. It may have been the decisive factor in his commitment to pacifism. War had not solved the problems faced by working people, home or abroad, as the Russian Revolution and the events on (Red) Clydeside testified.

Gallacher felt it was a missed opportunity to establish a workers' soviet (council).

Had there been an experienced revolutionary leadership, instead of a

---

498   https://www.theguardian.com/uk-news/2019/jan/06/100-years-on-the-day-they-read-the-riot-act-in-glasgow Accessed 3 February, 2021. See also Kenny MacAskill, *Glasgow 1919: the Rise of Red Clydeside*, (Hull, 2019).

march to Glasgow Green there would have been a march to the city's Maryhill Barracks. There we could easily have persuaded the soldiers to come out, and Glasgow would have been in our hands.[499]

The paradoxical juxtaposition of these two events was not lost on the *Workers Dreadnought*, newspaper of the Workers' Socialist Federation: an attack by a large group of workers on a smaller group over the use of the latter to drive down wages and deprive the former of employment; followed by an outburst of real and symbolic violence by the uniformed state against workers seeking to restrict the working week (thereby creating additional employment).

Do not you know that if it pays to employ black men employers will get them and keep them even if the white workers kill a few of the blacks from time to time? [500]

It was a summer of violence directed at people of colour in maritime communities: Arab seamen were attacked in South Shields; Negroes stabbed in the Port of London docks; Bermuda-born ship's fireman, Charles Wotten, murdered in Liverpool; three people killed in Cardiff.

The Socialist Labour Party felt impelled to speak out. It pleaded with workers, failed by their trade union leadership, to cease fighting each other and recognise the systemic cause of their economic and social problems.

The Trades Unions have prided themselves on having ousted coloured labourers from certain occupations... The very existence of capitalism depends upon driving all the elements of present day pugnacity, a trait always in prominence after a great war, into racial or national avenues. By forcing the workers to ease off their pugnacity over lines of colour, this blinds them to the class line which forms the focus of the struggle of the modern international proletariat.[501]

---

499 Ibid. So worried was Glasgow Corporation about the revolutionary potential of working class Glaswegians that in April 1916 it introduced a by-law restricting the right of free assembly. Coming into force in 1922 it was widely ignored. See Working Class History, *Working Class History. Everyday Acts of Resistance and Rebellion*, (Oakland, 2020), p.81.
500 *Workers Dreadnought*, 7 June 1919 p.1354 in Jacqueline Jenkinson, *Black Sailors on Red Clydeside*, p.19.
501 *Socialist* (Glasgow), 10 July 1919, p.264 in Jacqueline Jenkinson, *Black*

Having coped with the death of his brother the year previous the destructively murderous summer of 1919 was not the introduction to married life Edward – and Betty – had imagined. Sporadic, racialised animosity and violence was a motif that that was emblematic in the lives of people of colour living in Britain. In the decade Edward was born imperial Britain fought no less than three wars of conquest in Africa. It was a major beneficiary at the 1884 Conference of Berlin where European powers mutually agreed rules governing their rape of the continent. Second wars in Sudan and South Africa closed the century. The geopolitics of colonialism and imperialism with its justificatory ideology of racial hierarchy poisoned popular consciousness. The White working class were instructed to perceive the world as rationally structured by 'race' and ethnicity. However tranquil Edward and Betty attempted to make their lives they could not escape this pervasive narrative which consistently sought to demean people of colour, home and abroad.

Seamen of colour were again officially cast as unwanted Others with a 1925 addition, the Special Restrictions (Coloured Alien Seamen) Order which gave the police and immigration authorities greater powers of deportation. By the nineteen thirties the lives of Black sailors had been so consistently precarious and threatened, the LCP lobbied government to take ameliorative action.

In his Robeson talk Edward recounted Eslanda's homage to New York's Harlem as the one locale in that country where people of colour could live, work and walk out safely.

[Paul] naturally settled in Harlem, the negro quarter of the city. Here he soon found himself among friends... To them, Paul Robeson was a Hero... Negroes were glad that in appearance, colour and features, he was typically Negroid... He soon became Harlem's special favourite... His many friends always felt that he was one of themselves, who was doing great things, rather than that he was some far-off celebrity... It takes him hours to negotiate ten blocks.[502]

In quoting her description of the public affection Harlem's favourite son received traversing 143 Street to 133 Street, Edward would not have known that this may have included his cousin, Daniel, who lived at 26 West 136 Street. Born in Barbados in 1887 the son of uncle Samuel James

Sailors on Red Clydeside, p.20.
502 Edward Tull-Warnock, *Paul Robeson*, pp.21-22.

and aunt Elvira and named after his father, he had lived in the US for at least seventeen years by the time of his death July, 1941. Unmarried and working as a lift operative in an apartment block he succumbed to chronic pulmonary tuberculosis while a patient at Seaview Hospital. His passing was registered with the authorities by cousin Lilian Nurse. Just over twenty years earlier Edward's eldest brother had died of the same illness.

The hospital on Staten Island was the largest tuberculosis sanatorium in the country and is credited with pioneering treatment of the bacterial infection that attacks the throat and lungs. The 'white plague' was so deadly and contagious that one in four people in the USA died from it a century earlier. A survivor treated during the same decade as Daniel recalled

> I was a patient at Seaview Hospital from 1949 to 1952. The nursing staff (bi-racial after 1947) and housekeeping staff (almost all African-Americans) were very good to the small patients (of mixed ethnicities); so were the doctors (mostly white). My parents got to see me once a week – they had to come from Brooklyn by ferry and bus. Most of the patients in my ward were Puerto Rican so those of us who wanted to make friends with our nearest neighbors learned Spanish or English (or Spanglish) as soon as possible. The real trauma was when one of the patients was really sick. Most of us were ill, but responding to treatments. Those who were really sick were not responding.[503]

COMMUNISM AND COLOUR

While it is accepted, but not acceptable, that revolutionary activism will more often than not attract the attention of the secret police, the combination in Robeson's case of colour and communism made covert surveillance on both sides of the Atlantic inevitable. At the height of his popularity in the nineteen forties, FBI chief J.E. Hoover illegally placed him on the Custodial Detention List. 'In an emergency he would be gathered up and put in a concentration camp as a dangerous subversive'.[504] Under Hoover's direction the FBI hounded Robeson. His

503 Diane Scillia, 14 December 2014 https://forgotten-ny.com/2000/03/hospital-of-the-damned/ Accessed 30 August 2020.
504 The National Security Archive interview with Paul Robeson Junior,

son suspects they may have tried to murder him.

He made a tour through the South on behalf of the Progressive Party in 1948 and on the way there, there was a car accident in which he fortunately was not injured, but the left front wheel came off the car. Fortunately, it didn't swerve, it would have gone into the on-coming traffic, it was on a highway. And there's little doubt in my mind that the FBI was responsible for it, because the surveillance shows that they had the car under surveillance and the driver under twenty four hour surveillance, so it's difficult to assume that they didn't know about the sabotage. So by 1948, the FBI was trying to not only neutralise him, but if an accident happened to him, so to speak, they would be very happy.[505]

Hoover also bullied his UK counterparts in Special Branch and MI5 to make Robeson's life as difficult as possible. MI5's representative at the Washington Embassy, R. Thistlewaite, wrote to his boss Sir Percy Sillitoe, in February 1949 passing on information from the FBI about Robeson's imminent visit to Europe. The agent requests that his colleagues in London feed back his activities to Washington. Sillitoe responds

With reference to your letter W.1076 date 18th February 1949, we should have let you know earlier that we are collecting information on ROBESON's visit to this country and propose to let you have a summary when his visit has come to an end. He is expected to leave for the United States immediately after the Easter holiday. For the present, you may care to know that, as expected, he has been in frequent touch with members of the British Communist Party who appear to have made themselves responsible for arranging his list of engagements. Details will be included in the summary. C.I.A. also have asked for information about ROBESON's activities in the United Kingdom and on the Continent. We propose to let them have a note separately, so that they may pass our information on to Washington, while you keep the F.B.I. informed.[506]

---

published 1 November 1998 https://nsarchive2.gwu.edu/coldwar/interviews/episode-6/robeson1.html accessed 11 August 2020.
505 Ibid.
506 Sillitoe to Thistlewaite, 2 April, 1949 File KV 2/1829, p.88a National Archives, London.

The immediate post-war years saw the USA government and its allies, particularly the UK, ratchet up their anti-communist rhetoric and propaganda. Churchill's Iron Curtain speech of March 1946 signalled the beginning of the Cold War in which the destruction of the Soviet Union was to be the primary focus of western powers. Being a member or supporter of the Communist Party was now a politically legitimate reason for covert surveillance and tracking. One example was the illegal instruction issued to local government electoral officers in the UK that the voting slips for communist candidates be kept to identify supporters to Special Branch and MI5. Gordon Winter, an officer of the South Africa security service, BOSS, boasted in 1981 that the apartheid government knew the names of all who had voted for the Communist Party of Great Britain via these two agencies.[507]

Robeson's initial visit to the UK was as an actor, starring in the Eugene O'Neil play, *Emperor Jones*. While a resident of London in the nineteen thirties the political department of the Metropolitan Police, Special Branch, and MI5 assigned people and resources to spy. However, shadowing him for his political views was a waste of public money for two primary reasons which became widely and publicly known: he was never found to be engaged in illegal activities; like most communists, he was active in battling fascism. Yet, like the Prussian secret service report[508] on communism's most influential revolutionary, Karl Marx, while he was living in Soho in the eighteen fifties, it did reveal information that

507   https://www.theguardian.com/notesandqueries/query/0,,-1051,00. html Accessed 1 September 2020.

508 Prussian spy, Wihelm Stieber, visited Marx living in dusty, smoky, cramped rooms in Dean Street, Soho with his wife Jenny and children, Jenny, Laura and Edgar. 'There is not one piece of good, solid furniture in the entire flat… Here is a chair with only three legs, there the children play kitchen on another chair that happens to be whole; true - it is offered to the visitor, but the children's kitchen is not removed; if you sit on it you risk a pair of trousers. But nothing of this embarrasses Marx or his wife in the least; you are received in the friendliest manner, are cordially offered a pipe, tobacco and whatever else there is; a spirited conversation makes up for the domestic defects and in the end you become reconciled because of the company, find it interesting and even original'. From Rachel Holmes Eleanor Marx, A Life (London, 2014), p.8. In confirmation of the Marx's child-centred approach to parenthood, Holmes (p.12) also relates Eleanor's tale of Jenny, Laura and Edgar being pulled around the room on chairs attached to their father in imitation of a train and carriages.

some independent-minded historians have found useful and informative in corroborating deconstructions of the very stereotypes upon which such surveillance was predicated and commissioned. The Robeson file records bugged phone calls with the CPGB's London office, his friendship with fellow activists of colour, Ghanaian Desmond Buckle – who acted as his unofficial secretary for his 1949 visit – and Barbadian Peter Blackman; his attendance at the LCP; his anti-fascist resolve; his commitment to the peace movement, amongst other detail.

Reading the clandestine surveillance reports on this communist anti-fascist, collected when the UK and USA were fighting fascism alongside the USSR, lends their insights a surreal quality. One observation from June 1943 is particularly revealing.

> Paul Robeson is known to be rather gullible… He is rather strongly anti-white and slightly anti-British as a result of an insult sustained at the Savoy Hotel in London. He is a crank on the colour question.[509]

It was precisely because he was not politically gullible in accepting the myth of the American Dream that he was hounded: successive USA governments had refused to uphold for people of colour the principles of the constitution promising 'justice, domestic tranquility and 'general welfare'. The two other accusations are equally absurd. He lived contentedly in Britain for many years. It was where he felt he could be most politically useful, expecting to live out his days on the island.

Robeson is considered by veterans of the USA Civil Rights movement of the nineteen fifties and sixties as their inspiration. Rosa Parks, Malcolm X, Martin Luther King, Sidney Poitier et al, stand upon his shoulders. BLM has direct lineage to this tradition of resistance in which the revolutionary singer, actor, sportsman and intellectual was profoundly influential and prescient. He consistently fought police violence, the drift into fascism and for acknowledgement of the genocide of people of colour by slavery and racism. Today these poisons are still destructive forces in the body politic of capitalist societies.

POST-WAR PROTECTION OF FASCISTS AND FASCISM

In August 1945 Robeson visited war-devastated Europe. A covert FBI report revealed he was horrified by the 'anti-Negro and pro-German

509 SIS report, 10 June 1943 N.A. KV 2/1829 51a.

attitude of our [White] American troops. [US officers] he found to be anti-Russian and convinced that war with Russia was inevitable'.[510] He was astonished to find State Department officials and military officers working with fascists and ex-Nazis in Czechoslovakia. While Jews, Slavs, communists and Roma had been the Nazis primary targets for extinction, Robeson was conscious that their concept of Aryan racial supremacy also had Black folk in their sights.

According to Nazi ideology racial struggle was the motive force of history. Competition at its most naked was not over the control of material wealth and the means by which a society creates that wealth, but between 'races' for purity, survival and dominance. Only the unadulterated and non-miscegenised would endure. The salvation of the human 'race' - in effect, for Hitler, the biological struggle for Aryan pre-eminence - was only possible through the elimination of all other (sub-) species. Thus the apparatus of racial oppression and destruction so characteristic of Nazism: official denigration of minorities; ethnic ghettoisation; forced and slave labour; concentration camps and the application of eugenic and ethnic cleansing genocidal in scale.[511]

The sight of US government and military officials openly collaborating with the defeated warriors of this ideology must have shocked and shaken. He was right to have been concerned. The cooperation he witnessed matured into a secret right-wing terror network known as Stay Behinds and Gladio.[512]

Research has revealed secret armies have existed across Western Europe during the Cold War. Coordinated by the North Atlantic Treaty Organization (NATO), they were run by the European military secret services in close cooperation with the US Central Intelligence Agency

510 Horne, *Paul Robeson*, (2016) p.98 and footnote 105, p.217.
511 Phil Vasili, *The First Black Footballer*, (London, 1998), p.190.
512 See BBC Timewatch *Operation Gladio* broadcast summer 1992 https://www.youtube.com/watch?v=1YhRBxxyRqs; and *NATO's Secret Armies, Operation Gladio* https://www.youtube.com/watch?v=rbrGvwiG9b8 Both accessed 3 September 2020. For additional material on the clandestine work of secret groups to undermine democracy see also David Teacher, *Rogue Agents. The Cercle and the 6I in the Private Cold War 1951-1991*, (UK, 2013).

(CIA) and the British foreign secret service Secret Intelligence Service (SIS, MI6). Trained together with US Green Berets and British Special Air Service (SAS), these clandestine NATO soldiers, armed with underground arms-caches, prepared against a potential Soviet invasion and occupation of Western Europe, as well as the coming to power of communist parties. The clandestine international network covered the European NATO membership, including Belgium, Denmark, France, Germany, Greece, Italy, Luxembourg, Netherlands, Norway, Portugal, Spain, and Turkey, as well as the neutral European countries of Austria, Finland, Sweden, and Switzerland... In order to guarantee a solid anti-communist ideology of its recruits, the CIA and MI6 generally relied on men of the conservative political Right. At times, former Nazis and right-wing terrorists were also recruited... General Giandelio Maletti, a former head of Italian counterintelligence, in March 2001, confirmed the CIA might have promoted terrorism in Italy. After the so-called Piazza Fontana massacre, which in 1969 had killed sixteen and wounded eighty, parts of the bomb had been planted in the villa of well known leftist editor Giangiacomo Feltrinelli in order to blame the terror on the Communists. 'The impression was that the Americans would do anything to stop Italy from sliding to the left,' Maletti explained. He concluded, 'The CIA, following the directives of its government, wanted to create an Italian nationalism capable of halting what it saw as a slide to the left, and, for this purpose, it may have made use of right-wing terrorism.' [513]

These terrorist attacks in Western Europe against civilians included the August 1980 Bologna Railway Station bombing which killed eighty. Each murderous outrage was blamed on a left wing group. Named the Strategy of Tension, the intention was to push public opinion towards the idea that socialism represented chaos while the status quo, with NATO as its military arm, offered stability. After the Bologna massacre the police and secret services lassooed as many activists as their ropes could encircle.

A secret report of the clandestine Bilderberg gathering at Bad Aachen, Germany in 1980, released into the public domain by Wikileaks,

---

513 Daniele Ganser 'Terrorism in Western Europe: An Approach to NATO's Secret Stay-Behind Armies' in *The Whitehead Journal of Diplomacy and International Relations,* Winter - Spring 2005, pp.69-73. See also Daniele Ganser, *NATO's Secret Armies: Operation GLADIO and Terrorism in Western Europe,* (London, 2004).

suggested a nuanced relationship between NATO and the leader of the popular Italian Communist Party (PCI): 'In Italy the will to defend the country was relatively strong within the Communist party, as Berlinguer realised that without the Atlantic alliance a fate similar to that of Dubcek was likely to befall him'. This suggests that Berlinguer, who was distancing the PCI from the Soviet Union, relied upon NATO for his political survival. The detail of this unlikely alliance is not known but the political context, as outlined above, is. The Cold War preoccupation with a perceived communist threat, whether from the Soviet Union or domestically from Eurocommunism, had real consequences for Italy. In July 1948 a right-wing assassin attempted to murder the PCI leader, Togliatti. Thirty two years later Bilderberg attendees, some of whom may have known of the Stay Behind networks, Operation Gladio and the Strategy of Tension, concluded 'while Eurocommunism is less fashionable as a topic these days, it and other internal political developments are just as important over the long run'.[514]

The deceptive, covert activities of Robeson's government in west and central Europe was mirrored domestically in the victimisation and imprisonment of communists spearheaded by senator Eugene McCarthy. Under constant surveillance wherever he went, home or abroad, the African-American nevertheless had his passport confiscated in 1951. A spiteful act, it was also a testimony to his global popularity. His political profile was illuminated further when he and fellow activist, lawyer and friend, William Paterson, laid a petition – *We Charge Genocide: The Crime of Government Against the Negro People* – before the UN, on behalf of the Civil Rights Congress, charging their government with the systematic destruction of African-American life and culture. It was signed by many respected members of that community, including Jamaica-born Ferdinand Smith, co-founder of the National Maritime

---

514 Dubcek was reforming first secretary of the Czechoslovak Communist Party in 1968 who was ousted by the Soviet Union. For the 1980 Bilderberg Report see https://file.wikileaks.org/file/bilderberg-meetings-report-1980.pdf. UK 1980 attendees included General Sir Harry Tuzo, deputy supreme allied commander Europe; merchant bankers John Baring, Lord Roll of Ipsden, Judith Maxwell, Andrew Knight, Sir Ronald Grierson; politicians Dennis Healey, Douglas Hurd, Sir Frederic Bennett. My thanks to Alan Harman for researching this list. For other Bilderberg reports see https://file.wikileaks.org/file/?fbclid=IwAR2U_Evqah_Qy2wxNY12FMqFC5dAFUcZL5Kl4FIfQuMFMp8ssbM46oHXWMI Both accessed 15 January 2021.

Union and Trinidadian and Claudia Jones who was exiled from the USA to Britain in the 1950s. (A serendipitous banishment, Jones was instrumental in creating the Notting Hill Carnival.) While the petition received widespread publicity and support outside the US, in that country it was largely ignored by the mainstream media. Yet, despite Establishment attempts to cancel its message its legacy persists. At a review of USA practices during the 2014 UN Convention against Torture eight Chicago activists presented an eponymous report charging the Chicago Police Department with coordinated acts of terror against the city's African Americans.

RESPECT

Edward's profound respect for Paul Robeson as a colossus of the African Diaspora runs through his talk. Edward cites Robeson's experience at his university in trying to win a place on the American football team.

> When Robeson first reported for practice, the players were surprised. There had never been a black man in the Rutgers Eleven. That was bad enough, but when the black boy showed them he could play, the fat was in the fire. Bad enough to lose your place in 'the Team' but to lose it to a Negro was not to be thought of, for it would be a disgrace never to be lived down.[515]

This political football which had a lace of many threads holding it together, could have been written about his illustrious brother and the obstacles he faced as a professional footballer at the highest level in England. It was an experience Edward may have encountered playing for Scottish second division Ayr Parkhouse FC and as a golfer. That Robeson faced up, overcame and recounted, with millions watching and listening, was inspirational to people of colour. It shone light on their hidden stories and common experience. This was the African American's mission in life, Edward argued, to evocate the Negro experience. The cultural references Edward uses in his talk to emphasise or add definition also provide insight into his life and leisure as a mixed-heritage Glaswegian. He compares: the antebellum Negro journey North to the (post-famine) migration of Irish people to Scotland, also looking for work. (The Ireland-born population in 1931 was 124,296); the vast

515 Edward Tull-Warnock, *Paul Robeson*, p.16.

crowds of college football in the US to the paucity of Clyde FC's gate; the 'harmony of the cheering, singing and shouting at American university football fixtures to that at Ibrox as rendered in 'The Wells o' Weary". He alludes to his close friend James Bowie, a director of Rangers FC and chairman, 1934-47, as witness to the 'blind referees' stateside.

Edward was a participant observer in Robeson's most influential decades. That their personal interests in sport and music – as both scholars and practitioners – converged was a fitting harmony to the commonality of their lived experience as men of colour. The Glaswegian died the year before the American had his passport confiscated. However, he would have been heartened by the international support and campaigning that followed for its return, much of it in Scotland. In 1958 the US government lost a court case that decided such action illegal. As soon as possible Robeson was back in Scotland, singing, orating and campaigning.

Chapter Thirteen
Changing Colour of Narratives

IDENTITY

Edward was content with who he was and had become. He was proud of his mixed heritage. He asserted the African Caribbean dimension of his origin. He spoke publicly about the enslavement of his paternal grandparents. It was fitting, therefore, that the writer of his *Carrick Herald* obituary, 'JM', should finish with the words of Scotland's most celebrated poet, Robert (Rabbie) Burns – a favourite of Edward's – from his revolutionary verse, *A Man's a Man*.

Is there for honest Poverty
That hings his head, an' a' that;
The coward slave-we pass him by,
We dare be poor for a' that!
For a' that, an' a' that.
Our toils obscure an' a' that,
The rank is but the guinea's stamp,
The Man's the gowd for a' that.

What though on hamely fare we dine,
Wear hoddin grey, an' a that;
Gie fools their silks, and knaves their wine;
A Man's a Man for a' that:
For a' that, and a' that,
Their tinsel show, an' a' that;
The honest man, tho' e'er sae poor,
Is king o' men for a' that.

Ye see yon birkie, ca'd a lord,
Wha struts, an' stares, an' a' that;
Tho' hundreds worship at his word,
He's but a coof for a' that:
For a' that, an' a' that,
His ribband, star, an' a' that:
The man o' independent mind
He looks an' laughs at a' that.

A prince can mak a belted knight,
A marquis, duke, an' a' that;
But an honest man's abon his might,
Gude faith, he maunna fa' that!
For a' that, an' a' that,
Their dignities an' a' that;
The pith o' sense, an' pride o' worth,
Are higher rank than a' that.

Then let us pray that come it may,
(As come it will for a' that,)
That Sense and Worth, o'er a' the earth,
Shall bear the gree, an' a' that.
For a' that, an' a' that,
It's coming yet for a' that,
That Man to Man, the world o'er,
Shall brothers be for a' that.

Written in 1795, in the wake of the Haitian, American and French Revolutions that drew upon Norfolk-born Tom Paine's *The Rights of Man* for intellectual affirmation, Burns demands virtues and qualities be assigned to action and character not rank and appearance. Iconic African American anti-slavery activist Frederick Douglas recognised this humanity, buying an edition of Burns' poetry on his successful escape from chattel bondage. He was excited to visit his Ayr birthplace and sister, Isabella, while on a speaking tour of Scotland in 1846.

I am now in the town of Ayr. It is famous for being the birth-place of Robert Burns, the poet, by whose brilliant genius every stream, hill, glen and valley in the neighborhood have been made classic. I have felt more intense in visiting this place than any other in Scotland, for, as you are aware, (painfully perhaps) I am an enthusiastic admirer of Robt. Burns... On our way to the [Burns] Monument we enjoyed a pleasure and a privilege I shall never forget. It was that of seeing and conversing with Mrs. Beggs, an own sister of Robert Burns, and also seeing and talking with the poet's two nieces, daughters of Mrs Beggs. They live by the road side in a small thatched cottage, humble but comfortable. When Mr. Renwick made them acquainted with the fact that we were from America they received us warmly. One of the nieces said her uncle was more highly esteemed in America than in Scotland… Burns lived in the midst of a bigoted and besotted clergy – a pious but corrupt generation – a proud, ambitious, and contemptuous aristocracy, who, esteemed a little more than a man, and looked upon the ploughman, such as was the noble Burns, as being little better than a brute. He became disgusted with the pious frauds, indignant at the bigotry, filled with contempt for the hollow pretensions set up by the shallow-brained aristocracy.

He broke loose from the moorings which society had thrown around him. Spurning all restraint, he sought a path for his feet, and, like all bold pioneers, he made crooked paths. We may lament it, we may weep over it, but in the language of another, we shall lament and weep with him. The elements of character which urged him on are in us all, and influencing our conduct every day of our lives. We may pity him but we can't despise him. WE may condemn his faults, but only as we condemn our own. His very weakness was an index of his strength. Full of faults of a grievous nature, yet far more faultless than many who have come down to us on the page of history as saints. He was a brilliant genius and like all of his class, did much good and much evil. Let us take the good and leave the evil – let us pursue his wisdom but shun his folly; and as death has separated his noble spirit from the corrupt and corruptible dust with which it was encumbered, so let us separate his good from his evil deeds – thus may we make him a blessing rather than a curse to the world.[516]

This call from Douglas to respect the common woman and man of whatever complexion, exemplified by Burns, was a sentiment and tradition of which Edward was part. Throughout his life his brown skin was infused with values chosen by influential others. His objective appearance – the perception of him in the minds strangers – had a pre-determined meaning over which he had no control or input. This abstraction changed according to time and place. It was not fixed. The fluid identity of an earlier Glasgow resident and man of colour, Henry Wharton, provides an historical parallel.

The son of a freeborn African Grenadian mother and a Scottish

---

516 Letter from Douglas to Abigail Mott, 23/24 March, 1846 published in the *Albany* [New York] *Evening Journal* in *https://www.bulldozia.com/douglass-in-scotland/douglass-burns-and-scott/douglass-letter-from-ayr/* Accessed 1 February, 2021.

merchant and sea captain, Wharton was born in Grenada, 1819, in the main town and port, St. George's. His maternal grandmother had been an Africa-born slave. His Gold Coast-born wife, Annie Florence Grant, was the daughter of another Scottish trader, John C. Grant and Ama Egyiriba, a Fante royal of the Stool family of Ekumfie. The Fante were Akan speakers who lived along the coast of West Africa from the area of Sekondi eastwards towards Accra. The geographical references in the genealogy of Wharton were, therefore, those destinations of the triangular slave-trade: Britain, West Africa and the Caribbean.

He left the small southern Caribbean island, one hundred and sixty-two miles south-west of Barbados, to be educated in Glasgow at eight years of age. He may have sailed with his father 'who was for some time master of a vessel trading between Europe and the West Indies'.[517] Six years of cultural and meteorological acclimatisation was passed studying in the city. Biographer William Moister, cleric and mentor of the Grenadan, suggests the education had been worthwhile. Indeed, Wharton later schooled his children in Britain, including his daughter. One of his sons, Arthur, achieved fame as world sprint champion and first man of colour to work as a professional footballer.[518]

Returning to Grenada during Emancipation, he explored the pleasures and experiences that characterise adolescence before committing, vocationally, to the Methodist church. Moister describes the aspiring missionary as 'tall, thin, active; with bronze complexion, dark eyes, black curly hair; sharp European features, prominent nose, and an intelligent cast of countenance'.[519] While he suggests Wharton had visible African antecedence by virtue of skin colour and other physical attributes, his Celtic – European – heritage was revealed by his 'intelligent cast of countenance'.

On the premise that missionaries who were men of colour would have a higher life-expectancy in the Tropics than White Europeans – most of whom did not survive – the London-based Wesleyan Missionary Society (WMS) posted Wharton to West Africa. Making his way to the missionary station at the capital of Asante, Kumase, at the settlement of Dumpoassi he was welcomed *makio brunie! makio brunie!* (Good morning White man.) The young minister was not slow in discerning the cultural

517 Reverend William Moister, *Memoir of the Rev. H. Wharton,* (London 1875), p.12.
518 Vasili, (1998).
519 Ibid., pp21-22.

nuance this greeting revealed.

I would just observe here, that it matters not with the people what a man's colour may be, if he is from England, and wears European clothing, though he is as black as your coat, it is quite enough; he is a 'white man.' [520]

Through his mixed heritage and cosmopolitan experience, Wharton felt affinity with European, African and Caribbean cultures. Yet to those Europeans and Africans who were significant, who had the power to influence and determine events in his life – the Grant family in Accra, his WMS employers, his host the Asantehene and royal family, and his target population the ethnic Africans of the coastal zone – he had no universally agreed identity.

The variation of Anglo-Saxon cultural attitudes and practices towards ethnicity and 'race' experienced by the cosmopolitan Euro-African travelling between the metropolitan centre of empire and peripheral colonies, created a limbo world of moving and changing reference points: in the Africa of the African cultural distinctions were more important than an individual's colour; in the Africa of the European, colour and culture in that order become significant as determinants of social status; in the Europe of the European class – in terms of one's social relation to the means of production – was the primary determinant of political power and social status; in the Europe of the Black, colour was all. There were few distinctions made between different ethnic groups of colour. They were all literally tarred with the same brush as 'darkies', 'niggers' and if the categoriser was feeling benevolent 'noble savages.' [521]

Jean Tull-Warnock stated her father identified as a Scot, an identity undergoing constant and consistent reconfiguration. (The Walter Scott monument in Princes Park, Edinburgh is testimony to perhaps its greatest cultural reincarnation through the pen of that writer.) Irredeemably a part of Edward was his skin colour, the cultural perception of which also went through numerous metamorphoses. The year of his birth, 1886, marked the creation of the Royal Niger Company. Its reason for

520 Letter to Moister in Moister (1875), p.102.
521 Vasili, (London, 1998), p.178.

being was to continue British capitalism's extraction of West Africa's natural resources with greater efficiency and assure the ascendancy of the Crown's political power on that part of the continent. In competition with other European ruling classes with imperial ambitions, such as those of Germany and France, it concentrated on colonising territory that is now Nigeria. In the nineteen thirties, job done, the company was subsumed into Unilever.

CREATION THEORY

From the moment of birth imperial trends, developments and narratives impacted upon Edward's life. In his lifetime he represented and embodied, to those susceptible to these concoctions, the savage, the alien and the immigrant. That is, of course, until you knew him, a White journalist's comment in 1888 when interviewing Henry Wharton's mixed-heritage son, Arthur. 'Arthur is a most sociable fellow when you know him, 'but you have to get to know him first'... taken all-round he is a straightforward good natured chap'.[522]

To use a favourite of Edward's, the football analogy, he and other people of colour living in Britain began every game one-nil down. While settling into the orphanage with Walter – singing, playing sport, making friends, dealing with enemies – the British government was preparing for a second war with the descendants of Dutch settlers, the Boer's, in the self-governing republics of the Transvaal and Orange Free State, South Africa. The latter's increasing amity with Bismarck's regime in Germany caused anxiety in Whitehall where ministers became daily more anxious over the Boer threat to the UK's neighbouring possessions of Cape Colony and Natal. At the heart of the conflict was the yellow treasure underground. The Witwatersrand goldfields were the world's largest. Hostilities broke out in October 1899 with Lord Kitchener in charge of British policy and troops on the ground. He adopted a scorched earth approach creating Concentration Camps and imprisoning and starving captured Boers. Mercilessly brutal, it caused Cornish feminist and pacifist, Emily Hobhouse, to form the Relief Fund for South African Women and Children.

After the war a report concluded that 27,927 Boers had died of starvation, disease and exposure in the concentration camps. In all, about one in four of the Boer inmates, mostly children, died. However, the

522 *Athletic News*, 26 June, 1888.

South African historian, Stephen Burridge Spies argues in 'Methods of Barbarism: Roberts and Kitchener and Civilians in the Boer Republics' (1977) that this is an under-estimate of those who died in the camps.[523]

The wishes of the vast majority of people living in a war zone, the indigenous Africans, were not considered.

A few weeks before the outbreak of the war a team of footballers from Basutoland (now Lesotho), sandwiched between the Orange Free State and Natal, arrived at Southampton. Labelled the 'Kaffirs' they were to play a series of matches arranged and managed by Anglo African officials of the Orange Free State Football Association. Afrikaners – Boers – tended to play rugby. The usual patronising themes of physical strength, animalism and unrepressed sexuality coursed through the reporting of their matches.[524] The unusually sensitive political context, however, produced an ideologically confusing juxtaposition of attitudes.

They were big and strong, handsome yet excrutiatingly naive and honest. However while it would have been simple, literally, to portray the 'Kaffirs' as freak-show footballers for the amusement and entertainment of the Master Race matters became complicated by the unfolding tragedy of the political and military crisis in Southern Africa. A feature of the political debate was the allegiance of the indigenous populations. With whom the Basothos would side was a live question in British newspapers. This political dimension created a dilemma for reporters and editors, some of whom continued to work the tourists as malleable raw material with which to galvanise latent public prejudice. The (Southampton) *Football Echo and Sports Gazette* informed its readers of the 'Kaffirs' arrival via a demeaning cartoon situated centrally on its front page: John Bull echoing Kipling's sentiment of the colonies as the 'White Man's Burden'. The *Athletic News* followed in similar vein. Like the Southampton cartoon it was placed so readers could not miss it. Instead of a group of Africans it had an individual, in football kit, but wearing only one boot. Holding a spear and tomahawk, with a ring through his nose and feathers in his hair, he is kicking a ball. Underneath is the caption: 'Jeeohsmiffikato

523 John Simkin, https://spartacus-educational.com/Whobhouse.htm Accessed 1 January, 2021.
524 *Newcastle Evening Chronicle* 2 September 1899; *Sporting Man* (Newcastle) 5, 6, 7, 8 September 1899; *African Review* 9 September, vol.xx no 355.

the crack Kaffir centre forward thirsting for gore and goals.'[525]

Others were more sensitive – to the political needs of imperial Britain. During war-scare September fears were expressed in the press that 'Boer spies' were inciting the Basothos to rise up against Natal. In light of this should not the tourists be utilised in the anti-Boer propaganda offensive? If so their demeaning image, as portrayed through the press, should be toned down, they and their peoples may well be needed as allies should the emergency escalate. Much of the ambivalent language used in the reporting of the 'Kaffirs' reflected the environment of naked, competing propaganda war scares generate. The zeal with which some scribblers tailored the ideological content of their output to accord with pressing military and political demands and sensitivities sometimes overrode and contradicted 'common-sense' notions previously held. Thus during the War Scare period the Afrikaans became light-skinned savages, a configuration that at one and the same time paved the way for, and justified their imprisonment in, Concentration Camps and negated the rhetorical force of arguments which opposed such inhumane treatment by their British captors. In contrast the anatomy and character of the Basothos was scoured for positive representation. For some newspapers, Boer became Black and Black became something else. This contradictory and confused state of affairs is illustrated by description of other contemporary southern African visitors – human exhibits of the 'Savage South Africa' exhibition at Earls Court – as the 'magnificent men from the Zulu country.' Yet, soon after opening London County Council officials instructed the manager Mr Edwin Cleary to section off the 'native kraals' in order to prevent the public from fraternising with the 'heathen warriors' and their 'ebony babies.' [526]

Edward would have been hardened to the incoherent, nuanced portrayal of people of colour in the media. An avid listener to radio, the BBC's *The Coloured Coons, a children's darkie minstrel show* broadcast in the late nineteen forties was not entertainment conjuring positive self-images with which his grandchildren could identify.[527] It was a theme the Corporation had been developing. During the nineteen-thirties

525 *Athletic News*,18 September 1899.
526 Vasili, (1998), pp140-141.
527 https://genome.ch.bbc.co.uk/schedules/bbchomeservice/basic/ 1947-09-17 Accessed 15 February 2021.

blackface G.H. Elliot, known as the Chocolate Coloured Coon, was aired by the broadcaster. For seventeen years it ran the *Kentucky Minstrels* show, 'harking back to an idealised and sanitised view of plantation life which ignored the harsh realities of slavery'.[528]

The *Daily Herald*, April 1920, published an article by E.D. Morel headlined 'Black Scourge of Europe'. The author freely used racist stereotypes and tropes in condemning France's use of African soldiers to police the Ruhr district of Germany, a condition of the 1919 peace terms. Edward and other people of colour would have known from painful experience the negative repercussions of such imagery. Words could hurt and their social translation result in broken bones. Felt also would have been a similarly symbolic gesture that had lacerating intensity, the decision not to allow Black troops to march in the London victory celebration of July 1919.

CHANGE AND RESISTANCE

Various 'Aliens' acts and orders passed since 1793 restricted the civil liberties of migrants and people of colour. The First World War again changed their social, economic and cultural position in Britain. For these Others life became more precarious. (British women marrying foreign men were also designated 'aliens' by the 1914 Nationality Act.) Economic security became worse with the enactment of legislation that reduced their ability to find work, such as the Aliens Restriction Act, 1919, the Aliens Order, 1920 and the Special Restriction (Coloured Alien Seamen) Order, 1925.

During the war, brown-skinned sailors had been attacked in Canning Town.[529] After, the lives of veterans, seamen and other people of colour were threatened in a number of 'race' riots in port cities including Glasgow. Almost overnight the contribution of these soldiers and

---

528 Peter Astley Grosvenor Waymark, *Television and the Cultural Revolution: the BBC under Hugh Carleton Greene*, Ph.D Dissertation, Department of History, Open University, (2005) p.183.

529 Canning Town had historically one of the largest populations of people of colour in London because of its proximity to the docks. Methodist minister Kamal Chunchie founded the first church in his faith for Black worshippers in Swanscombe Street. Three years later, in 1926, in response to the growing need for a safe public space for working people of colour, he established the Coloured Men's Institute as a religious, social and welfare centre for sailors and local people.

sailors was forgotten, ignored and expunged.

In contrast, half a century earlier during the United States civil war, Lancashire mill workers refused to handle raw cotton grown and forcibly picked with enslaved hands. Thousands of looms became idle and many operatives and their families suffered hunger and deprivation, a distress known as the Lancashire Cotton Famine. As a young Methodist minister in Manchester and Bolton, Reverend Dr Stephenson witnessed the suffering first-hand. President Abraham Lincoln wrote of their 'sublime Christian heroism'. Union-forces ships docked at Liverpool with provisions for the hungry collected in gratitude. Rochdale renamed Catley Road Cotton Famine Road to commemorate this defiant linking of impoverished arms to chained bodies across the Atlantic.

One who had forcibly removed his shackles of enslavement in the US was James Watkins who, during the eighteen-fifties, made Bolton his home.[530] The radicalism of its workers had not gone unnoticed by Marx two decades earlier. 'Of all the towns in England, Bolton is the one in which radicalism is most developed. The Bolton workers are known to be the most radical of all'.[531]

COLOUR, PACIFISM AND POLITICS

Edward's lifetime witnessed increasingly influential political, social and cultural constellations of people of colour. Collectively, the socialist dimension – including Robeson and C.L.R. James – became known as the Black Internationale. Edward's immersion in their political tradition and in the musical genre of the Negro Spiritual brought him firmly within Robeson's orbit. There is an umbilical link between the Spiritual/ Gospel heritage – of which both were excellent practitioners and ambassadors – to the Blues/Rock and Roll/Soul explosion to which Edward witnessed the early beginnings.

His pacifism arose out of the loss of the person most dearest to him in a genocidal carnage whose provenance, even today, some historians

---

530 James Watkins, *Narrative of the Life of James Watkins*, (Bolton, 1852). Another two African American compatriots of Watkins who fled to England because of the passing of the Fugitive Slave Act in 1850 which effectively ended immunity against return for southern runaways, was Ellen and William Craft. See Working Class History, *Working Class History: Everyday Acts of Resistance and Rebellion*, (Oakland, 2020), p.246.
531 Karl Marx, *The Poverty of Philosophy*, (Moscow, 1976), p.155.

claim to be shrouded in mystery.[532] As a resident of Glasgow he was close to numerous and vociferous opponents of war, where Willie Gallacher and John Maclean consistently spoke out. Their influential Clyde Workers Committee, formed in 1915, campaigned not just for better wages and employment conditions but also for peace. Maclean was twice imprisoned on charges of sedition for his opposition to war. From the dock at his second trial in 1918 he defiantly declared

> It was not the workers who instigated the war. The workers have no economic interest to serve as a consequence of the war, and because of that, it is my appeal to my class that makes me a patriot so far as my class is concerned, and when I stand true to my class, the working class, in which I was born, it is because my people were swept out of the Highlands, and it was only because of my own ability that I remained. I have remained true to my class, the working class, and whatever I do I think I am doing in the interest of my class.[533]

Edward's doorstep rejection in Birmingham affirmed society was structured through both class and ethnicity. Though a medical professional, his working class Victorian childhood instructed through experience that poverty and insecurity were always close neighbours. To have a government that, at least in part, was primarily interested in improving the lives of working people, therefore, meant so much. With the introduction of the NHS and a comprehensive welfare state in 1948,

Edward and other members of the SMA may have concluded that their primary goal had been achieved. Personally, he

532 See *The First World War: The Debate*, British Library, 24 February 2014, https://www.youtube.com/watch?v=jvr7UJI47UM; *The Great WW1 Controversy: Who Was to Blame? A Panel Discussion on the Centennial*, Minda de Gunzberg Center for European Studies, Harvard University, 1 December 2014, https://www.youtube.com/watch?v=jvr7UJI47UM Both accessed 15 January 2021.

533 Delivered at the High Court, Edinburgh, 9 May, 1918, https://www.marxists.org/archive/maclean/works/1918-dock.htm Accessed 19 January 2021. Gallacher was imprisoned three times for his political activism, 1916, 1919 and 1925. One action in 1915 saw Gallacher march with thousands to Glasgow Sheriff's Court in support of twenty-thousand rent strikers angry at war profiteering. It led to the introduction of rent controls throughout Britain. See Working Class History (2020), p.225.

could now provide free treatment for all, rather than just a few. Charges for dental work were introduced in 1951 and have risen consistently since. The current condition of the NHS, with its competitive structure and privatise contractor provision, would worry him. From having 299,000 beds in the mid-nineteen eighties this has now more than halved to 141,000 despite a growth in population. The number of acute beds is lower than most other European countries with similar health care systems.[534]

During Edward's years in Kent and London his physical and mental landscape would have been populated with fellow people of colour, albeit sparsely: the mixed-heritage Browns lived some fifty miles from Folkestone at Sheerness; Daniel may well have read and proudly recounted to his children the exploits of late-Victorian sporting celebrity Arthur Wharton; fairs commonly had boxing booths with pugilists of colour; the year he left the orphanage for Glasgow, the first gathering of predominantly Black anti-imperialists convened for the Pan-African Conference at Westminster Town Hall.

In Scotland there has been a consistent presence of people of colour since the sixteenth century comprising enslaved and free, courtiers, and students and graduates of its universities, especially Edinburgh and Glasgow. Glasgow's mixed-heritage nineteenth and early twentieth century residents, the outcome of Black Atlantic relationships, included BEF veteran Arthur Roberts and Queens Park footballers Andrew Watson and Robert Walker.[535] During the First World War, in 1917, the first Black political organisation in Scotland, the African Races Association, formed in the city. Its president shortly after was South African medical student Silas Modiri Molema. Later, he was elected treasurer of the African National Congress (ANC) and arrested in the anti-apartheid Defiance Campaign of 1952.[536] While it is not known if Edward had any involvement with the Association it would be surprising

534 https://www.kingsfund.org.uk/publications/nhs-hospital-bed-numbers Accessed 17 January 2021.

535 Morag Miller, Roy Lacock, John Sadler and Rosie Serdeville, As Good As Any Man. Scotland's Black Tommy, (Stroud, 2014).

536 https://universitystory.gla.ac.uk/biography/?id=WH24165&type =P&o=&start=0&max=20&l= Accessed 19 January 2021. See also Starfield, Jane. 'A Dance with the Empire: Modiri Molema's Glasgow Years, 1914-1921.' *Journal of Southern African Studies*, vol. 27, no. 3, 2001, pp. 479–503. JSTOR, www.jstor.org/stable/823312. Accessed 19 January 2021.

if he was unaware of its existence. He may have been alerted by other African Glasgow University medical graduates who were part of his profession and members of the SMA, such as A.O. Ayose.

In the last decade of his life, with the arrival of Empire Windrush, this development of a confident, heterogeneous, ubiquitous Black Atlantic presence had its momentum propelled forward at pace. Though a longtime coming, the sight of people like his father stepping off the ship – many returning after serving in the armed forces during the Second World War – would have induced both joy and foreboding: joy at the UK government encouraging British citizens from the Caribbean to migrate to, rebuild and replenish a war-torn country; foreboding at the difficulties he knew they would encounter.

Austerity Britain was still under rationing, its cities blotched with destruction and debris. Yet, the creation of the NHS, the Welfare State and the implementation of the 1948 Nationality Act giving colonial subjects British citizenship, were inspirational social and political developments. Even with his developing health problems Edward, metaphorically at least, would have walked with a lighter step.

It was also transparent that in some areas of the world the daily lives of people of colour was getting demonstrably worse. The Malan government of South Africa officially implemented apartheid in 1948. It was not the first country to officially and legally prioritise the rights of one group over another. Colonial powers had done this for centuries. The colony of the Gold Coast (Ghana) had two legal codes.

Fair and just practice was not a quality of government characteristic of British West Africa. Indeed between 1878-82 they had put in place a racist legal system. The new order of wig and gown apartheid reserved local, customary law for Africans and incorporated English law for Europeans. The dual structure not only denied equality before the law for all subjects, but also formally differentiated and categorised the population of the Gold Coast by ethnicity.[537]

The South of the USA had a form of apartheid known as Jim Crow,[538] a social and political response of former Confederate states

537 Vasili, (1998), p.91.
538 'Jim Crow' was the nickname given to the anti-African American laws passed in the South during the nineteenth and twentieth centuries to enforce racial segregation. 'Jim Crow' became synonymous with the institutional

to their civil war defeat: despite the abolition of chattel slavery, African Americans were forced to continue living separate, unequal and inferior lives. Enforcement of Jim Crow was the primary role of the police in these states. Given this context Edward's cousin, Daniel, may have consciously chose the cultural and political capital of African America, Harlem, as home when migrating from the Caribbean in 1924. It was lucky he did. The country outside of this Black enclave of Manhattan was not safe even in the North where Robeson detailed the racism he faced in growing up in New Jersey.

The Greenwood district of Tulsa, Oklahoma had developed a thriving concentration of African American businesses. Known as the Black Wall Street, in late May-early June 1921 rampaging Whites attacked and murdered, setting fire to homes and businesses after stealing what they could carry. Planes dropped petrol bombs. The community was destroyed. At least three hundred were killed and over eight hundred injured. No White attacker was prosecuted. Survivors, incredibly, were detained in holding centres. The Tulsa Massacre stands as a concentrated example of the savage brutality of inter-war racism in the USA. Some historians feel it was an organised response by White capital, envious and jealous of Black economic independence.[539] It is unlikely Edward would have read or heard about the massacre. Like similar others it went unreported. Black lives did not matter.

Apartheid in South Africa, where the state forcibly controlled the economic and geographic circumstance of people of colour and their communities, was a little less hidden. In this re-creation of a society resembling Caribbean slave colonies he identified with their pain. A good friend of Jean and Duncan's, Michael Guthrie Scott, was active in the fight against apartheid while working in the country during the nineteen forties. He was also, like the Finlayson's, a Christian socialist peace activist. He believed in direct action and had served a three month prison sentence. Having in their circle of friends people like Scott they were able to keep in touch with the reality of state racism that was

racism associated with the southern states. The name stuck during the civil rights era and related back to a racist music hall caricature of people of colour.

539 Chris M. Messer, 'The Tulsa Race Riot of 1921: Toward an Integrative Theory of Collective Violence', *Journal of Social History*, Vol. 44, No. 4 (Summer 2011), pp. 1217-1232. A massacre of African Americans for similar reasons had been perpetrated in Slocum, Texas, 29 July, 1910.

largely ignored or positively reconfigured by mainstream press, radio and tv.[540]

In this way also Jean and Duncan remained faithful to Edward's political passions, a family legacy enthusiastically embraced. The geo-political world in which he lived was chaotic and unpredictable, exemplified by that special year of 1948 which saw the introduction of the NHS and the British Nationality Act, the docking of Empire Windrush, the London Olympics and the forced separation of people by colour and ethnicity in South Africa.

CONTINUING EDWARD'S LEGACY

In our 1995 interview, septuagenarian Jean felt the incidence of racism in Scotland had worsened with people of Asian descent having a particularly difficult time. Seven years earlier the racially-motivated murder of Axmed Abuukar Sheekh in Edinburgh heralded a vociferous public debate. This resurgence of racism and fascism provoked a collective response and the formation of the Lothian Black Forum (LBF). Led by people of colour, it comprised activists across all ethnicities.

The man charged with Sheekh's murder was a self-confessed fascist. The all-White jury decided he was guilty of assault and possession of a knife. Now feeling even more insecure and threatened, a sense of outrage spiralled amongst people of colour. They were not mistaken or misguided. In 1998 Surjit Singh Chhokar was killed by three White men in Overtown, Lanarkshire. After their second trial collapsed, Glasgow lawyer Aamer Anwar commented:

> We have two systems of justice at work in this country, one for whites and a very different one for black people and the poor. The Crown Office is a white gentleman's colonial club shrouded in the vanity of wigs and gowns relatively unchanged for 400 years.[541]

540 For more on Scott see: https://www.sahistory.org.za/archive/biography-michael-scott-email-contribution-lorna-richmond-25-november-2015 Accessed 16 June 2021.
541 A. Anwar, 'How racism and police brutality shaped my life', *National*, 07/06/2020 https://www.thenational.scot/news/18501332.aamer-anwar/ in Scottish Critical Heritage, *Fighting Denial: The Lothian Black Forum and Anti-Racist Protests in Edinburgh, 1989-92* https://scottishcriticalheritage.wordpress.com/2020/07/13/fighting-denial-the-lothian-black-forum-and-anti-racist-

Anwar was assaulted by Glasgow Police a couple of years later. It took another four years before they admitted it was racially motivated.

The LBF organised the first anti-racist demonstration in Edinburgh, 3 June 1989. Despite police harassment – confiscating placards, bullying those with megaphones and trying to snatch collection tins – fifteen hundred made it to the Mound. Addressing the crowd, Mukami McCrum could not help but point out the hypocrisy: 'We are so noticeable when we collect money, but [they] don't see us when we are being kicked in the streets'.[542]

The LBF's defiant demand for progressive change was galvanised by alliance with other anti-racist groups, such as Supporters Campaign Against Racism in Football and the Campaign Against Racism and Fascism. Edinburgh's 1990 May Day Rally exemplified this unity. In a symbolically important gesture of international solidarity on the speakers' platform alongside McCrum was Edinburgh University student and leader of the South African Congress of Trade Unions, Eric Mokgathle. His country was still an apartheid state.

Speaking out was problematical for Black South Africans. The apartheid state used smear campaign against its opponents. Its notorious Bureau of State Security (BOSS) was active around the world in taking down its international opponents. In London it framed, in 1975, prominent anti-apartheid activist Peter Hain for armed robbery of Barclays Bank, Putney. Papers released by the CPS in July 2008 revealed Scotland Yard and Hertfordshire Police knew of the plot but did not investigate. He was acquitted after a ten day trial. Secretary of the Anti-Apartheid Movement in Britain, Abdul Minty, was so concerned about the clandestine criminality of BOSS that he wrote to prime minister Harold Wilson asking for an official enquiry.[543]

Forty-six years before Israel prime minister Benjamin Netanyahu effectively declared his country an apartheid state with the announcement that 'Israel is not a state of all its citizens... [it] is the nation state of the Jewish people – and them alone'.[544] It openly supported and collaborated with apartheid South Africa. United Nations General Assembly

protests-in-edinburgh-1989-1992/#_ftnref37 Accessed 22 January 2021.
542 Ibid.
543 Letter 16 March 1976, https://www.aamarchives.org/archive/campaigns/government/gov06-letter-from-abdul-minty-to-harold-wilson/viewdocument.html Accessed 23 January 2021.
544 Ibid.

collusion between Portuguese Colonialism, the apartheid regime and zionism, as exemplified by the political, military and financial aid supplied to each other by Portugal, South Africa and Israel... and condemns in particular, the unholy alliance between Portuguese colonialism, South African racism, zionism and Israeli imperialism.[545]

Just a little under two years later UN General Assembly Resolution 3379 determined 'that Zionism is a form of racism and racial discrimination'.[546] However, this was revoked in 1991, a demand from Israel for participating in the Madrid Peace Conference.

WHY HISTORY MATTERS

Edward saw in his lifetime powerful socio-economic groups, their movements and organisations imposing their will upon the majority through force and undemocratic means. He witnessed and viscerally felt the oppression Paul Robeson faced as an activist for African American rights who recognised that class – a person's social relation to the means of production – was the primary determinant of power, the key component calibrating power relations. Both knew through experience fascism, racism and war were enemies of people of colour in particular and working class people generally.

As the son-in-law of the baillie of Aberdeen, a medical professional, alumnus of Allan Glen's School and friend and associate of influential Glasgow personalities such as James Bowie, he lived with and alongside power. He was at ease in the company of, and friendship with, powerful people. Yet, he retained an affinity, identity and affection for his working-class roots. His embraced his enslaved heritage. In this dimension there existed, pure and naked, a relationship between those with absolute power and those with – ostensibly – no power. He was also aware, through the cultural legacy of his father, that even those in the most

---

545 General Assembly, XXVIII Session, 2201st Plenary Meeting, 14 December 1973, *Policies of Apartheid of the Government of South Africa*, p.33. Portugal was then a fascist dictatorship with colonies in Angola and Mozambique where it was fighting against indigenous liberation movements. 546 United Nations General Assembly Resolution 3379 (XXX) 10 November 1975.

desperate of situations have the ability to resist. Edward's eyes were wide open and his sense acutely aware of the kind of society in which he lived. This drove his passions of family, faith, music, sport and politics. His identity was forged through, and by, the embattled existence of his Black and White predecessors.

The state and media campaigns against Robeson utilised racism and identity politics – the 'uppity Black' – specifically because he encouraged class unity and collective action that cut across divisions of ethnicity, nationality, gender, sexuality and religion. He recognised that the liberation and self-determination of these groups could not be achieved in isolation of one another. This was the message of Toussaint L'Ouverture, Frederick Douglas, William Davidson, Robert Wedderburn, William Cuffay, James Watkins, C.L.R. James, George Padmore Peter Blackman Freddie Hampton, Malcolm X, Muhammad Ali and Martin Luther King.

Alive today Edward would be heartened by the ethnic unity and rainbow complexion of BLM supporters. He would also be disturbed by their necessity.[547] BLM marches in London and other cities in the UK and Europe brought together many who see in the destruction of African Americans lives a foreshadowing of state power that has, with the increasing menace of fascism, the potential to be normalised.

Historically fascism has been imposed by ruling elites when they no longer are willing or able to use the veneer of liberal democracy as a political instrument of wealth accumulation. Its contemporary resurgence, spearheaded globally by the corporatist World Economic Forum (WEF), at a period of systemic neoliberal crisis is a response used in the past by elites in Italy, Germany, Spain, Portugal. Edward would have been under no illusion of the awaiting horror should such a regime take power in the UK.[548]

---

547 https://nicic.gov/sources/international-center-prison-studies-icps-london-england Accessed 26 January, 2021.

548 The World Economic Forum was founded by Klaus Schwab in 1971. Its members and active supporters include multinational corporations, financial institutions, the World Health Organisation, royalty, plutocrats and politicians. Its goal is the Great Reset of the Fourth Industrial Revolution in which WEF members have extensive global political, economic and social power, human rights are 'recalibrated', democracy abolished and populations severely reduced. See https://bit.ly/3wM1ioZ; https://bit.ly/3sWaBjR; https://bit.ly/3Nxy5nl All accessed 25 May 2022;

Injustice and hypocrisy characterise the relationship between the ruling class of the UK and slavery. Ideologically-driven narratives attempt to sustain the enduring myth of their pioneering role in prohibiting the trade in enslaved people in 1807 and ending chattel slavery in 1834. Some mainstream celebrity historians even argue that the creation of the Royal Navy's West Africa Squadron in 1808 was as a protective shield defending the coastline against other countries attempting to continue the trade. In reality, the Slave Trade Act did not abolish the trafficking of enslaved people. People of colour were still bought, sold and transported within the British Empire. And, far from suddenly transforming itself into a benevolent force vigilantly overseeing the welfare of others, the West Africa Squadron and the Royal Navy generally, post-1807, continued its primary role as defender of territory, wealth and possessions of the monarchy, the City of London and British capital.

Evidence suggests that British ships were covertly involved in the slave trade well into the nineteenth century. A Liverpool-registered vessel, the *Douro,* off the isles of Scilly in 1843 was wrecked and sunk. Divers exploring the hulk found large numbers of bronze bracelet-shaped manillas that were commonly used as tokens of exchange for enslaved people in West Africa.[549]

The Slavery Abolition Act did not make illegal enslavement throughout the British Empire. It did not apply to territories captured by the EIC, such as modern-day India, Pakistan and Bangladesh and slavery also continued in Ceylon (Sri Lanka) and St. Helena.

The Apprenticeship system that replaced enslavement was seen and felt as another form of bondage. It ended in Barbados in 1838 and this date marks the moment of emancipation for many.

In *Britain's Black Debt: Reparations for Caribbean Slavery and Native Genocide* (2013), Professor Hilary Beckles makes a politically powerful and morally irrefutable case for reparations. A Reparations Commission has been established by the twenty-member Caribbean Community and Common Market to lobby the UK and other governments that profited. It also demands that families that became wealthy through enslavement

---

549   https://historicengland.org.uk/research/inclusive-heritage/the-slave-trade-and-abolition/sites-of-memory/ending-slavery/1834-the-end-of-slavery/ Accessed 27 January 2021.

pay compensation calling upon, for instance, Conservative MP Richard Drax to return a portion of his inherited wealth to Barbados and Jamaica. The Drax family has been planters in Barbados continuously since the sixteen forties. They still own the Drax Hall plantation. Beckles estimates thirty-thousand people died in Barbados and Jamaica as a result of their captivity on the family estates. Richard (Grovesnor Plunkett Ernle Erie) Drax owns more of Dorset (UK) than any other individual – thirteen thousand, eight hundred and seventy acres – and is reputedly worth one hundred and fifty million pounds.[550]

UK government minster, Lord Ahmad of Wimbledon, reiterated the sentiment of former prime minister David Cameron – whose family received slave compensation – in 2018 when he vehemently rejected reparations. Cameron, visiting Jamaica in 2015, lectured the island should distance itself from its past and move on, offering to build a new prison as a gift from the UK government.

In another more extreme example of governmental refusal to accept any obligation to repair historical damage Home Secretary, Theresa May, in 2012 announced: 'The aim is to create, here in Britain, a really hostile environment for illegal immigrants'.[551] Many asylum seekers and refugees already lived within a climate of fear. May's policy, displayed on the side of advertising vehicles driven around London, was an instrument used specifically against people of colour. Many were deported for not providing paperwork suddenly demanded by police and immigration authorities, including members of the Windrush generation of 1948-71 and their descendants. All those who entered Britain from the Caribbean during this period were UK passport holders or entitled to such under the 1948 Nationality Act. Over time passports and other proofs of residence had been lost, misplaced or binned as no longer needed. On being challenged in the courts over the legality of their deportations the government reluctantly confessed it had discarded evidence that could have been used to prove right of residency, such as landing cards.

Barbados-born Camden resident Michael Braithwaite had his life turned upside down by the policy of hostility. For fifteen years a special needs teaching assistant in a Gospel Oak primary school, his employers became legally obliged to demand from him, as a resident born outside

550 https://caricomreparations.org/?s=drax Accessed 27 January 2021.
551 Joint Council for the Welfare of Immigrants, https://www.jcwi.org.uk/the-hostile-environment-explained Accessed 27 January, 2021.

the UK, paperwork to proving he had the right to live in Britain. Arriving legally in a freezing London as a nine-year old in 1961, in 2017 he had no passport or biometric card. Immediately sacked he found himself in a desperate situation, ineligible for alternative employment, benefits or healthcare.

Brokenhearted and suddenly cash-strapped, he struggled to keep his head above water. Meanwhile the Sisyphean task of winkling papers from the Home Office ground on for two years, leaving him on the edge financially and emotionally... 'it's been three years of hell,' he said. 'I went to Downing Street with Paulette Wilson but she died [in July]. She was just 64 but she was driven to her death.[552]

Braithwaite was not deported but in scenes visually reminiscent of the treatment of their ancestors ripped from family, friends and loved ones, some were shackled and forcibly taken to countries in which they had not lived since early childhood. Despite appeals for meetings from the representatives of the numerous Caribbean-heritage organisations, May and Cameron refused. Eventually, five years after the implementation of the hostile environment the mainstream media finally thought newsworthy the hundreds of Windrush generation deported. Attempting to deny culpability, May – now prime minister – and the Home Office proclaimed the scandal was an administrative accident and commissioned a review. Yet, 2 December 2020, Home Secretary Priti Patel deported thirteen African Caribbean residents arguing they were 'dangerous foreign criminals'.[553]

Virtually all ancestors of those of African descent in the Anglo-phone Caribbean were shipped there as captives. Those who came to Britain entered with rights and freedoms won by these enslaved ancestors. This

---

552 *Camden New Journal*, 'Black History Makers', 22 October 2020, p.3. Other Bajans featured in this pull-out section include: *superb dancer* Jerry Williams, 1924-2017, a shop steward in the National Union of Railwayman and Camden councillor; and youth worker and community activist, Winston Pinder.

553 Home Office tweet, 5.30pm 30 November, 2020. https://www.free-domfromtorture.org/news/windrush-and-the-hostile-environment-all-you-need-to-know Accessed 27 January, 2021. https://www.infomigrants.net/en/post/28845/stoptheflight-public-figures-and-campaigners-urge-uk-government-to-halt-deportation-flight-to-jamaica Accessed 28 January 2021.

included Edward's father, Daniel. Working. They paid taxes a proportion of which, until 2015, was being repaid to the financial institutions that raised the funds for the government in 1834 to pay compensation to slave owners. Daniel, his sons and daughters – William, Cissie, Edward, Walter, Elsie and Miriam – their children, grandchildren and great grandchildren contributed. Beckles describes it as 'the greatest act of political immorality'.[554]

Tired of waiting for justice Barbados in November 2020 made public its intention to terminate membership of the British Commonwealth the following year.

SELF-DETERMINATION

Edward's lifetime coincided with self-determination movements and events that shaped the history of the twentieth century: three Russian revolutions, 1905 and February and October 1917; the 1916 Easter Uprising in Ireland; the 1918-19 mutinies of rank and file troops in the British army; the use of troops and live fire against miners in Wales and dockers in Liverpool, 1911, and Glasgow during the First World War; the 1919 German Revolution; the 1924 Zinoviev letter fabricated by the secret services and published by the Daily Mail, a forgery which largely contributed to the minority Labour government losing the General Election;[555] the 1926 General Strike; the Scottsboro Boys campaign; the fascist insurrection in Spain and civil war; the lie of the Second World War as a fight to destroy fascism; Indian independence; the growth in trade union militancy and membership.

Those who shared Edward's politics were utterly deflated by the defeat of the miners in the General Strike of 1926. It followed the ousting from power of the first Labour government in the Zinoviev Letter election where it took another nineteen years for the party to achieve a majority in the House of Commons. During the strike, with most newspapers not printing, the BBC broadcast government and employers' briefings that workers were giving up and going back to work. The chairman of the Conservative Party, John C. Davidson, personally vetted news

554 Tax Justice Network, https://www.taxjustice.net/2020/06/09/slavery-compensation-uk-questions/ Accessed 27 January, 2021.
555 https://wikispooks.com/wiki/Zinoviev_Letter Accessed 2 February, 2021.

bulletins before airing.[556]

In reality striking workers throughout the country were not returning to work in significant numbers. Aware the miners refusal of accepting a pay cut needed to be defended otherwise they would be next, they remained solidly committed. It was their union leaders – Walter Citrine of the Trades Union Congress (TUC), Ernest Bevin of the Transport & General Workers and Jimmy Thomas of the National Union of Railwaymen – who buckled. They agreed a secret deal with the employers who demanded a return to work.

Always conscious of his worth, it would be interesting to know how Yorkshire Main miner of African-Scottish heritage, Arthur Wharton, felt. It had real and terrible repercussions for the former professional footballer and sprint world champion. He died four years after the strike's end, buried in a paupers grave laying without a headstone, anonymous and forgotten, for over sixty years.

Though a setback for the organised working class, the collapse of the General Strike did not stunt the steady growth in trade union membership. At the beginning of Edward's working life – the period of the Great Unrest 1910-14 – membership rose from two and a half million to four million. At his death in 1950 over nine million workers belonged to trade unions. A generation later membership had risen by another four million.

There is a correlation between working class share of wealth and collective organisation. Working people in the late nineteen seventies took home their greatest ever proportion of GDP. That decade saw the least unequal share of wealth distribution in the UK's industrial history. Punitive anti-union legislation and strategic attacks over the succeeding five decades of neoliberal economic policy has resulted in both union membership and the working class share of national wealth fall dramatically. Britain is now one of the most unequal societies where the employed and self-employed also work on average more hours than their European colleagues.[557]

---

556 https://spartacus-educational.com/ExamIR23.htm Accessed 2 February, 2021. Willie Gallacher commented in 1949: 'The BBC spreads ideas which help the ruling class and not the workers. Whoever heard of the BBC broadcasting the truth, for example, of the working class struggle for better wages'. William Gallacher (1949), p.96.

557   https://www.economicshelp.org/blog/135320/economics/labour-

Resistance was a feature of Edward's life: to preconceived ideas about brown people; to the colour bar and other obstacles preventing him from accessing 'normal' economic, social and cultural life. Bodies such as the Pan-African Congress, Negro Welfare Association, Socialist Medical Association and League of Coloured Peoples represented his political interests as a left-wing man of colour. It is vitally important such collectivities work in the interests of those whom they represent.

Controlling the opposition has been, historically, a strategic chess-game for the ruling class. Charles II had a secret service of at least fifty agents in the sixteen sixties. Edinburgh and Aberdeen educated man of colour William Davidson and his fellow revolutionaries, the Cato Street Conspirators, were betrayed by state spy George Edwards in the early nineteenth century. Former CIA officer Miles Copeland revealed to *The Times* in 1976 that CIA agents were working inside Britain's unions in an effort to shape passivity and conformism.[558] Given the revelations in Italy in the nineteen nineties about the CIA, MI6 and NATO's anti-communist Operation Gladio Copeland's expose, in hindsight, does not seem so surprising. Material detailing the activities of the secret services of the US and UK in the public domain suggests that they have expended greater effort in facilitating, and incubating – encouraging, even – fascism rather than fighting it. Ukraine since the coup of 2014 is an example.[559]

FIGHTING BACK

Edward's enslaved grandparents, Anna and William, experienced first-hand absolute authoritarianism unmediated by the rule of law.

share-of-gdp/ accessed 2 February, 2021.

558 Conservative government minister under Margaret Thatcher, Norman Tebbit, admitted he was given regular Special Branch reports on trade union leaders. Frank Chapple, leader of the EETPU – the electricians' union – was a regular and secret visitor, informing on trade union activists. *Morning Star,* 17 March 2021: https://morningstaronline.co.uk/article/b/tebbit-lifts-lid-government-involvement-spying-trade-unionists Accessed 19 March 2021.
559 https://bit.ly/3ND0t7v; https://bit.ly/3LLafmF Both accessed 26 May 2022.

His father Daniel's birth in 1856 makes him a member of the first generation of African-heritage Bajans to be legally born un-enslaved for over two hundred years. Looking at the workings of civil society through this prism, the necessity in creating grassroots organisations dedicated to resisting social poisons such as fascism, White Supremacy and economic structures such as neoliberal capitalism that systemically produce inequality, is paramount. People of colour are still the most vulnerable and exploited section of the working class. As a consequence, they are often in the vanguard of resistance.

Without his physical legacy of letters, photographs, journals, reminiscences, memorabilia and the wealth of material that constitutes the Finlayson Family Archive this biography could not have been written. Edward, in ensuring their survival – a legacy that continues through Jean and Duncan and now their children – recognised that his mixed-heritage family had a story worth telling.[560] Not from a position of self-aggrandisement but rather as insight into a micro-community of love and tolerance surrounded by stagnant and treacherous swamps that needed careful navigation. His determination to leave a record of his extended family's existence was itself an act of resistance against the dominating, hegemonic narratives that negatively objectified him and other people of colour.[561]

Edward's curatorial diligence facilitated his posthumous 'return' to his paternal roots in 2020, accompanied by other members of his extended family, in an online exhibition hosted by the Barbados Museum and Historical Society. A celebratory portrayal of the historical outcome of

560 In researching and writing both this biography and Walter Tull's I have been fortunate to have the resources of the Finlayson Family Archive made freely available. For this privilege my sincere and grateful thanks go to Pat Justad, Edward, Duncan and Iona Finlayson. I would also like to thank in particular other members of the extended Tull family for their help: Graham Tuthill for his diligence in notifying all of us of new information that surfaces and Mike Gow for providing extensive information about the Warnocks.

561 In contrast on 9 December 1959 the UK government issued a secret memorandum as part of its Operation Legacy programme to destroy official documents of colonial actions and policies that cast a negative light on its imperial history. Ordering the burning of files, it later also allowed incriminating evidence to be buried at sea. See Working Class History (2020), p.240 and Ian Cobain, *The History of Thieves. Secrets, Lies and the Shaping of a Modern Nation*, (London, 2016).

a nineteenth century Bajan migrant's journey, it was a Black Atlantic testimony to the invaluable contribution of African Caribbean people to the UK's social, cultural and economic life.[562]

At the same time as he was starting work as a professional dentist, having already built a reputation as gifted singer and footballer, the *Encyclopaedia Britannica* was asserting 'mentally the Negro is inferior to the white... The mental constitution... is very similar to that of a child'. His story is, in this sense, also a narrative of resistance. Correcting the LCP assertion that Charles Arundel Moody was the first Black British army officer, followed by his determination that the *Glasgow Evening Times* confirm his brother held that distinction, exemplifies a commitment to ensuring an accurate portrayal not only of his family history but also that of people of colour in Britain.

This battle continues. The dominant narrative constructed around Edward's brother by institutions such as the MoD and BBC of a gung-ho war hero ignores Jean's assertion that he *hated* the carnage. The BBC plaque campaign in West Africa that attempts to portray the Royal Navy after 1807 as a benign, protective and benevolent force 'that liberated 150,000 enslaved Africans' ignores its brutal role in colonising vast territories of that same region.[563] This inference that Britain's imperial policy – with the navy as its primary instrument of enforcement – had a predominantly altruistic purpose is completely negated by history as told by the subjects of that policy. West Africa, from the seventeenth century to the present, has been a site of bloodstained plunder by British capital: of bodies and resources.

Despite negotiating this Jekyll and Hyde society characterised by acceptance, tolerance and irrational prejudice and violence, Edward's legacy is characterised by love, humour, compassion, obstinacy, mischievousness, determination, tenacity and the belief in the unity of a common humanity. Most importantly, he knew himself and he knew what he meant to others, whether it be his close and extended family or as an objectified man of colour in the eyes of a stranger. Loved or

562 http://waltertullexhibition.org; For the opening webinar: https://www.youtube.com/watch?v=pkRYIOROJF0 Both accessed 4 February, 2021.

563 https://artsandculture.google.com/asset/plaque-commemorating-the-enslaved-africans-liberated-by-the-west-africa-squadron-bbc/HgEWR293rE4LxA?hl=en Accessed 3 February, 2021.

despised, I am me: *A Man's a Man for a' that.* The defiant mantra *I'm Black and I'm proud* could have been written specifically for him. Emblematic of his upbeat, positive character, he reached out and locked in friendship the hands of all willing to reciprocate.

Appendix 1

LIST OF MEMBERS OF THE GUINEA COMPANY 1618.
Names listed in the patent granted to the Guinea Company on November 16, 1618 by King James I & VI.

1. Robert Rich (earl of Warwick, 1619)
2. Robert Mansell
3. Sir Ferdinando Gorges Knt
4. Sir Warwick Heale Knt
5. Sir Allen Appesley Knt
6. Sir Richard Hawkins Knt
7. Sir Henry Nevill Knt
8. Sir William St. John
9. Sir Thomas Tracy Knt
10. Sir Richard Bingley Knt
11. Sir Giles Mompesson Knt
12. Sir Thomas Dutton Knt
13. Sir Francis Blundell Knt
14. Sir Arnold Herbert Knt
15. Sir John Bingley Knt
16. Sir Henry Williams Knt
17. Abraham Williams Esq.
18. Anthony Bugges Esq.
19. Oliver St. John Esq.
20. Oliver Nicholas Esq.
21. William Herbert/Harbert Esq.
22. Thomas Emerson Esq.
23. Edmund Sadler Esq.
24. Thomas Morgan Esq.
25. Meredith Morgan Esq.
26. Lewis Powell Esq.
27. George Dunscombe Esq.
28. Thomas Love Esq.
29. Phillipp Jones Esq.
30. Samuell Crooke Esq.
31. William Dackombe Esq.
32. John Davies Merchant
33. John Watkins Merchant
34. Michall Best Merchant
35. Richard Salford Merchant
36. William Awdely Merchant

Appendix 2

List of members of the Royal Adventurers trading into Africa on December 18, 1660.

1. Duke of York and Albany, High Admiral of England
2. Maria, Princess Royal
3. Henrietta, Princess
4. Rupert Prince, Count Palatine of the Rhine, Duke of Cumberland
5. George, Duke of Buckingham
6. George, Duke of Albermarle
7. James, Marquess of Ormond,
8. Phillip, Earl of Pembroke and Mountgomery
9. Henry, Earl of St. Albans
10. Edward, Earl of Sandwich
11. John, Earl of Bath
12. Thomas, Earl of Ossery
13. George, Lord Berkley
14. William, Lord Craven
15. John, Lord Berkley
16. Charles, Lord Brandon
17. George Carterett, Sir
18. Charles Howard, Colonel
19. William Coventry Esq
20. Charles Sidely, Sir, Baronet
21. John Warner Sir, Baronet
22. Charles Berkeley, Sir, Knt
23. Henry Jermyn Esq
24. William Legg Esq,
25. John Denham Esq,
26. Anthony de Martes Sir, Knt
27. Ellis Leighton, Sir, Knt
28. Edward Turner, Sir, Knt
29. Edward Gregory Esq
30. Richard Nicholls Esq
31. Cornelius Vermuyden Esq

Appendix 3

List of members of the Royal Adventurers trading into Africa on January 10,1663/4.

1. Katherine, Queen
2. Mary, King's Mother
3. James, Duke of York,
4. Henrietta, Maria Duchess of Orleans
5. Rupert Prince
6. George, Duke of Buckingham
7. Mary, Duchess of Richmond
8. Edward, Earl of Manchester
9. Phillip, Earl of Pembroke
10. Henry Jermyn, Earl of St. Albans
11. John, Earl of Bath
12. Edward, Earl of Sandwich
13. Charles, Earl of Carlisle
14. John Maitland, Earl of Lauderdaile
15. George Lord Berkeley
16. William Lord Craven
17. John, Lord Lucas
18. Charles, Lord Gerrard
19. William, Lord Crofts
20. John, Lord Berkley
21. Thomas Grey Esq
22. George Carterett, Sir, Knt
23. Charles Sidly, Sir, Knt
24. Ellis Leighton, Sir, Knt
25. Edward Gregory Gentl.
26. Edward Turnor, Sir, Knt
27. Anthony de Merces Esq
28. William Legge Esq
29. Richard Nicholls Esq
30. William Davison Sir, Knt
31. William Cutler
32. James Modiford, Sir, Knt
33. Thomas Cullen Gentleman (Gentl.)
34. George Cock Gentl.
35. Charles Porter Gentl.
36. John Colliton, Sir, Knt

37. John Buckworth Gentl.

38. John Robinson, Sir, Knt

39. Nicholas Crispe, Sir, Knt

40. Richard Ford Sir, Knt

41. William Rider, Sir, Knt

42. John Bence

43. George Smith, Sir, Knt

44. John Shaw, Sir, Knt

45. Martin Noell, Sir, Knt

46. Abraham Bigges Gentl.

47. Thomas Povey Esq

48. Edward Blackwell Esq

49. Matthew Wren Gentl.

50. Tobias Rustat Gentl.

51. Martin Noell Gentl. Junior

52. Henry Johnson Gentl.

53. James Congett Gentl.

54. John Ashburnham Gentl.

55. Edward Noell Esq

56. James Noell Esq

57. Francis Meynell Gentl.

58. John Cooper Gentl.

59. Andrew Rickard Sir

60. William Harbert Esq

61. John Jacob, Sir

62. John Harrison, Sir

63. John Wolstenholme Sir

64. William Wake, Sir

65. Sylas Titus

66. Peter Proby

...

Appendix 4

Walter Tull legacy information

compiled and written
by Daniel Morris

How people are learning about Walter Tull.

Manchester United (United Academy) workshopped young people about Walter Tull. Children from St Alphonsus Primary School were invited to participate alongside the under-12 United football team. They took a trip to Northampton to participate in the Walter Tull Memorial Festival, quizzed Walter's biographer, Phil Vasili, about Walter Tull's life and used creative writing in the form of poems and letters which were sent to Walter Tull's relatives in Scotland. It also mentioned that he had shell shock during his time in the war. This occurred in November 2018.

There is an activity pack aimed towards KS2 students that involved learning about different parts of Walter Tull's life, his time at Tottenham Hotspur and the military, the social and political background the early 20th Century and Walter's family. Writing poems, scripts and answers about Walter Tull are part of the activities in the pack.

The website Spartacus Educational has an article about Walter Tull and it goes into detail about his time living at a Methodist orphanage for two years, his brother, his stepmother's struggles, his time playing for Tottenham and Northampton Town, his military career, his family's campaign for him to posthumously receive the Military Cross and a special set of coins made by the Royal Mint that commemorate his life.

Backstone Primary School (in Cumbria) were taught about Walter Tull in 2014 and students wrote about details on Walter's life including a newspaper report by one of the students. The entire class wrote a letter to their M.P, Sir Tony Cunningham, to have Walter posthumously rewarded with the Military Cross. The local newspaper reported on the school's campaign.

There is a video made by the National Army Museum about Walter Tull and there is a downloadable transcript of the video that talks about the 17th Middlesex (1st Football) Battalion, life in the trenches, the first professional footballer in the 17th Middx battalion to die (Cpl Ben Butler of Queen's Park Rangers), the battles he participated in, the 23rd Middlesex (2nd Football)

Battalion, Walter being denied the rank of officer due to his ethnicity, racism in the military and the man who tried to retrieve Walter's body (Private Tom Billingham).

The Guardian posted an article about Walter Tull and it talks about the impact he made on English football. It said that there is a possibility that the first female player of colour may have made her senior debut in 1895 (her name might be Emma Clarke). It also said that his father lived on the Clifton Hall Estate Plantation in Barbados before he moved to England. It stated that he was killed at Favreuil in March 1918.

Tottenham Hotspur had an article about Walter and it said that he did a tour to Argentina and Uruguay during his time with Tottenham, it doesn't mention the incident with him being abused by racist Bristol City fans and the fact he had PTSD during his time in the war. It did however mention that he contracted trench foot. It said Walter was posthumously awarded the British War and Victory Medal.

The KS2 history section on BBC Bitesize has a page about Walter Tull and it says that he was born on 28 April 1888, the orphanage he moved to was in East London, he played a range of sports during his time at the orphanage ranging from cricket to football. He played for Clapton Football Club and his exceptional skills as a player caused him to join Tottenham Hotspur. He was described to be accurate in passing the ball and having a cool demeanor.

There was a TV documentary on ITV called Back to School that explored important but forgotten black people in British history and there was a part that talks about Walter Tull and Allison Hammond, the host of the documentary, met with Walter's great nephew, Ed. The midfielder Dele Alli presented Ed with a signed shirt with Walter's name on the back of it. A 2018 article from the Independent said that the author did not know about Walter Tull until the week he wrote the article. It said that Walter played as an inside-forward during his time as a footballer, he died on 25 March 1918, he had a £4 weekly wage when he played for Tottenham, enlisted in the 17th Battalion of the Middlesex Regiment but doesn't talk about him being transferred to the 23rd Middlesex (2nd Football) Battalion during the first Battle of the Somme. It also doesn't mention he had PTSD.

Archways School, a secondary school in Gloucestershire, have been taught about Walter Tull. It said that he was separated by his siblings, joined the army in 1914, rose through the ranks to become an officer despite his superiors showing prejudice towards him due to his race and class, the men he led admired him to the point where they tried to retrieve his body, died on 25 March

1918 and he was the first officer in the British army to be of mixed-heritage. A primary school in the London borough of Newham called Southern Road Primary school did a project on Walter Tull in 2016 where they did a workshops, hosted by the Walter Tull Heritage and Legacy Project about Walter Tull's life ranging from key points in his childhood, the football clubs he played for and his experience during World War 1. The students created depictions of his life through art.

North Waltham Primary School received a letter from Walter Tull's family and a Tull100 No Barriers medal for removing barriers in their community, read out a diary entry by Walter and held a commemorative football match to remember his life.

Millway Primary, Irthlingborough Junior and Quinton House were schools in Northampton that took part in a workshop about Walter Tull with the first part of the workshop was learning about his life and the second part involved creating poems about Walter or the war.

Leagrave Primary School students in Year 6 worked on a collection of writing from the perspective of Walter Tull by researching about his life, engaged in workshops and role play to help emulate him and his thoughts while writing diary entries. Judging from one of the diary entries, one of the students doesn't know that Walter's mother died before he joined the army.

References:

http://d16nr2hhcygdqc.cloudfront.net/wp-content/uploads/2014/06/Waltertullactivitypack.pdf.

https://www.manutd.com/en/news/detail/united-academy-learn-about-walter-tull#.

https://spartacus-educational.com/FWWtull.htm.

http://www.beckstone.cumbria.sch.uk/curriculum/walter_tull/index.html.

https://www.nam.ac.uk/schools/learning-resources/walter-tull-soldiers-story.

https://www.theguardian.com/football/2019/aug/22/walter-tull-football-hidden-pioneer-first-black-professionals-barbados.

https://www.bbc.co.uk/bitesize/topics/zqhyb9q/articles/zbgxbdm.

https://www.mirror.co.uk/tv/tv-news/alison-hammonds-back-school-leaves-22803974.

https://www.independent.co.uk/sport/football/news/walter-tull-david-

lammy-northampton-tottenham-old-first-division-world-war-one-a8269526.
html.

https://www.archwayschool.net/news/?pid=3&nid=1&storyid=192.

https://southernroad.newham.sch.uk/the-life-of-walter-tull/.

https://www.andoveradvertiser.co.uk/news/regional/basingstoke/16979703.family-walter-tull-praise-schools-work-inclusivity/.

https://www.ntfc.co.uk/news/2019/november2/tull_day/.

https://www.leagraveprimary.co.uk/walter-tull-football-pioneer-and-ww1-hero/.

https://medium.com/@treventour1995/black-soldiers-in-conflict-walter-tull-e5016770977c.

https://www.haringey.gov.uk/libraries-sport-and-leisure/culture-and-entertainment/visiting-haringey/archive-and-local-history/spurs-1909-era-walter-tull.

https://claptonfc.com/wp-content/uploads/2014/04/WalterTTTbooklet.pdf.

https://www.tottenhamhotspur.com/the-club/history/legends/walter-tull/#:~:text=Walter%20Tull%20made%20only%2010,to%20serve%20as%20an%20inspiration.

https://waltertull.org/the-walter-tull-campaign/.

https://www.glasgowlive.co.uk/sport/walter-tull-rangers-army-officer-14455012.

http://www.doverwarmemorialproject.org.uk/Information/Articles/Heroes/Tull.pdf.

https://tommyswar.co.uk/2019/07/29/the-life-of-walter-tull/.

https://nenequirer.com/2018/02/17/the-amazing-adventures-of-walter-tull/.

https://medium.com/lapsed-historian/walter-tull-from-footballer-to-soldier-310e21fb074e.

https://www.geni.com/people/Second-Lieutenant-Walter-Tull/6000000077142786037.

https://100greatblackbritons.com/bios/walter_tull.html.

https://www.bbc.co.uk/sport/football/43504286#:~:text=Walter%20Tull%20%2D%20one%20of%20England's,France%20during%20World%20War%20One.

http://www.doverwarmemorialproject.org.uk/Information/Articles/Heroes/TullWDJ3.htm.

https://www.tottenhamhotspur.com/media/29883/walter-tull-john-fennelly-hotspur-2009.pdf.

https://www.wsc.co.uk/stories/14077-how-everton-and-tottenham-s-pio-neering-tour-gave-walter-tull-his-chance.

https://www.britishnewspaperarchive.co.uk/viewer/bl/0001914/19180302/003/0002.

https://www.britishnewspaperarchive.co.uk/viewer/bl/0002129/19160814/063/0004.

https://www.britishnewspaperarchive.co.uk/viewer/bl/0000317/19180118/040/0004.

https://www.britishnewspaperarchive.co.uk/viewer/bl/0002129/19130407/042/0003.

https://www.britishnewspaperarchive.co.uk/viewer/bl/0002129/19120413/073/0004.

https://www.britishnewspaperarchive.co.uk/viewer/bl/0002129/19120307/086/0004.

https://www.britishnewspaperarchive.co.uk/viewer/bl/0002129/19120830/086/0003.

https://www.britishnewspaperarchive.co.uk/viewer/bl/0002129/19140109/059/0003.

https://www.britishnewspaperarchive.co.uk/viewer/bl/0000893/19090911/099/0007.

https://www.britishnewspaperarchive.co.uk/viewer/bl/0002446/19091009/204/0027.

https://www.britishnewspaperarchive.co.uk/viewer/bl/0003187/19091004/101/0007.

https://www.britishnewspaperarchive.co.uk/viewer/bl/0001716/19091013/078/0004.

https://www.britishnewspaperarchive.co.uk/viewer/bl/0001638/19090918/030/0002.

https://www.britishnewspaperarchive.co.uk/viewer/bl/0000893/19090911/099/0007.

https://www.britishnewspaperarchive.co.uk/viewer/bl/0000986/19090920/081/0005.

https://www.britishnewspaperarchive.co.uk/viewer/bl/0001716/19110301/049/0004.

https://www.britishnewspaperarchive.co.uk/viewer/bl/0000317/19271021/107/0005.

https://www.britishnewspaperarchive.co.uk/viewer/
bl/0000317/19271021/158/0007.

https://www.britishnewspaperarchive.co.uk/viewer/
bl/0000986/19090920/008/0001.

https://www.britishnewspaperarchive.co.uk/viewer/
bl/0001912/19090911/014/0001.

https://www.britishnewspaperarchive.co.uk/viewer/
bl/0003172/19090326/053/0003.

https://www.britishnewspaperarchive.co.uk/viewer/
bl/0000051/19090419/042/0003.

https://www.britishnewspaperarchive.co.uk/viewer/
bl/0001055/19090419/064/0003.

https://www.britishnewspaperarchive.co.uk/viewer/
bl/0001963/19090327/143/0007.

https://www.britishnewspaperarchive.co.uk/viewer/
bl/0003216/19090321/458/0028.

https://www.britishnewspaperarchive.co.uk/viewer/
bl/0000377/19090309/063/0004.

https://www.britishnewspaperarchive.co.uk/viewer/
bl/0002310/19090314/052/0009.

https://www.britishnewspaperarchive.co.uk/viewer/
bl/0000986/19090308/115/0006.

https://www.britishnewspaperarchive.co.uk/viewer/
bl/0000986/19090322/081/0006.

https://www.britishnewspaperarchive.co.uk/viewer/
bl/0001857/19090424/008/0004.

https://www.britishnewspaperarchive.co.uk/viewer/
bl/0001716/19101019/093/0004.

https://www.britishnewspaperarchive.co.uk/viewer/
bl/0000051/19091012/161/0008.

https://www.britishnewspaperarchive.co.uk/viewer/
bl/0001055/19091011/015/0002.

https://www.britishnewspaperarchive.co.uk/viewer/
bl/0002144/19091009/058/0003.

https://www.britishnewspaperarchive.co.uk/viewer/
bl/0002913/19091009/125/0007.

https://www.britishnewspaperarchive.co.uk/viewer/

bl/0000893/19091004/121/0007.

https://www.britishnewspaperarchive.co.uk/viewer/
bl/0001727/19091004/164/0009.

https://www.britishnewspaperarchive.co.uk/viewer/
bl/0000051/19091004/170/0008.

https://www.britishnewspaperarchive.co.uk/viewer/
bl/0000986/19091004/068/0005

Bibliography

Andrews, Kenneth R., *Trade, Plunder and Settlement: Maritime Enterprise and the Genesis of the British Empire 1480-1630* (Cambridge, 1984).

Appiah, Kwame Anthony, Gates Junior, Henry Louis, *Africana: The Encyclopaedia of the African and African American Experience, Volume 3* (Oxford, 2005).

Arbell, Mordehay, *The Jewish Nation of the Caribbean: The Spanish-Portuguese Jewish Settlements in the Caribbean and the Guianas* (Jerusalem, 2002).

Bambery, Chris, A People's History of Scotland, (London, 2014).

Barritt, Gordon E., *Thomas Bowman Stephenson,* (Peterborough, 1996).

Beckett, J.C., *The Making of Modern Ireland 1603-1923,* (London, 1966).

Beckles, Hilary, *A History of Barbados,* (Cambridge, 1990).

Beckles, Hilary, *Black Rebellion in Barbados. The Struggle Against Slavery 1627-1838,* (Bridgetown, 1984).

Beckles, Hilary *Great House Rules. Landless Emancipation and Workers Protest in Barbados 1838-1938,* (Oxford, 2004).

Besson, William W., *Caribbean Reflections. The Life and Times of Trinidad Scholar (1901-1986). An Oral History. Edited and introduced by Jean Besson. Foreward by C.L.R. James,* (London, 1989).

Bicheno, Hugh *Elizabeth's Sea Dogs. How England's Mariners Became the Scourge of the Seas,* (London, 2013).

Bowdich, Thomas *Mission from Cape Coast Castle to Ashantee, &c.,* (London, 1819).

Bradfield, William, *The Life of the Reverend Thomas Bowman Stephenson,* (London, 1913).

Brown, Malcolm, *1918: Year of Victory,* (London, 1998).

Calender of State Papers Treasury Books Volume 1 1660-1667, (London 1904).

Calender of Treasury Books Volume 3 1669-72 Parts1 &2 (London, 1908).

Callow, John, *The Making of King James II. The Formative Years of a Fallen King,* (Stroud, 2000).

Carreta, Vincent *Equiano the African. Biography of a Self-Made Man,* (Georgia, 2005).

Churchill, A. (ed.) *A Collection of Voyages and Travels Volume 6* (London, 1746).

Cobain, Ian, *The History of Thieves. Secrets, Lies and the Shaping of a Modern Nation,* (London, 2016).

Cracknell, M.W. (ed.), *The Barbadian Diary of General Robert Haynes* (Medstead, Hampshire, 1934).

Cundall, Frank, *Jamaica's Part in the Great War 1914-1918,* (London, 1925).

Curtis, Liz et al, *Nothing But the Same Old Story: The Roots of Anti-Irish Rac-*

ism, (London, 1986).

Dabydeen, David, Gilmore, John, Jones, Cecily (eds.), *The Oxford Companion to Black British History*, (Oxford, 2007).

Dalton, Heather, *Merchants and Explorers: Roger Barlow, Sebastian Cabot and Networks of Atlantic Exchange 1500-1560*, (Oxford, 2016).

Davey, Cyril, *A Man for All Children: The Story of Thomas Bowman Stephenson*, (London, 1968).

Devine, T.M. (ed.), *Recovering Scotland's Slavery Past. The Caribbean Connection*, (Edinburgh, 2015).

Donnan, Elizabeth (ed.), *Documents Illustrative of the Slave Trade, Volume 1 1441-1700*, (Washington, 1930).

Edghill, Reverend J.Y. *About Barbados* (London, 1890).

Engels, Frederick, Marx, Karl, *Articles on Britain*, (Moscow, 1971).

Engels, Friedrich, *The Condition of the Working Class in England in 1844*, (London, 1892).

Falconbridge, Alexander, *An Account of the Slave Trade on the Coast of Africa*, (London, 1788).

Fisher, Ruth A. (ed.), *Extracts from the Records of the African Companies* (London,1929)

Fishman, William J., *East End 1888*, (Nottingham, 2009).

Ford, Amos A., *Telling the Truth. The Life and Times of the British Honduran Forestry Unit in Scotland (1941-44)*, (London, 1985).

Fraser, Henry and Hughes, Ronnie *Historic Houses of Barbados* (Barbados, 1986).

Fryer, Peter, *Staying Power. the History of Black People in Britain*, (London, 1991).

Gallacher, William *The Case for Communism*, (London, 1949).

Ganser, Daniele, *'NATO's Secret Armies: Operation GLADIO and Terrorism in Western Europe*, (London, 2004).

Geoffrey of Monmouth, *History of the Kings of Britain*, (Plymouth, 2008 edition).

Hamilton, J. Taylor, *A History of the Church Known as the Moravian Church or the Unitas Fratrum or the Unity of the Brethren During the Eighteenth and Nineteenth Centuries*, (Bethlehem, P.A., 1900).

Hart, John, *A Narrative of the Life and Sufferings of John Hart, a native of Sierra Leone, Africa, from which place he was stolen away by a company of Spaniards, and brought to the town of Charlestown*, (London,1842).

Hart, Richard *Slaves Who Abolished Slavery. Volume 1 Blacks in Bondage* (Kinston, Jamaica,1980).

Haynes, Edmund C. et al *Notes by General Robert Haynes of New Castle and Clifton Hall Plantations, Barbados*, (1910).

Hesse-Lichtenberger, Ulrich, *Tor! The Story of German Football* (London,

2002).Herskovits, Melville J., *The Myth of the Negro Past* (New York, 1941).

Hill, Christopher, *The Century of Revolution 1603-1714* (London, 1974).

Hobsbawm, Eric, *The Age of Empire 1875-1914*, (London, 1995).

Hopper, Andrew, *Turncoats and Renegades: Changing Sides During the English Civil Wars* (Oxford, 2012).

Horne, Gerald, *Paul Robeson. The Artist as Revolutionary*, (London, 2016).

Hotten, John Camden (ed.)*The Original Lists of Persons of Quality; Emigrants; Religious Exiles; Political Rebels; Serving Men Sold for a Term of years; Apprentices; Children Stolen; Maidens Pressed; And Others who went from Great Britain to the American Plantations 1600-1700* (London, 1873).

Hyman, Ronald, *Empire and Sexuality. The British Experience*, (Manchester, 1991).

Inikori, Joseph, *Africans and the Industrial Revolution in England. A Study in International Trade and Economic Development* (Cambridge, 2002).

James, C. L. R., *Beyond a Boundary* (London, 1996).

James, C. L. R., *The Black Jacobins. Toussaint Louverture and the San Domingo Revolution* (London, 1938).

Jobson, Richard, *The Golden Trade or A Discovery of the River Gambra, and the golden Trade of the Aethiopians.* (London, 1968).

Kaufmann, Miranda, *Black Tudors*, (London, 2019).

Kelsey, Harry, *Sir John Hawkins. Queen Elizabeth's Slave Trader* (London, 2003).

Knoller, Freddie, Landaw, John, *Living with the Enemy. My secret life on the run from the Nazis*, (London, 2005).

Lenin, V.I., *On Britain*, (Moscow, 1979).

Levy, Claude, *Emancipation, Sugar, and Federalism. Barbados and the West Indies, 1833-1876* (Gainesville, Florida, 1980).

Lewis, Kingsley *The Moravian Mission in Barbados 1816-1886. A Study of the Historical Context and Theological Significance of a Minority Church Among an Oppressed People*, (Frankfurt am Main, 1985).

Ligon, Richard *A True and Exact History of the Island of Barbados* (London, 1673).

Mangan, J.A. (ed.) *Pleasure, Profit and Proselytism: British Culture and Sport at Home and Abroad, 1700–1914*, (London, 1982).

Manual of Military Law, (London, 1914).

Marx, Karl, *Capital Volume One,* (London, 1970).

Marx, Karl *The Poverty of Philosophy*, (Moscow, 1976).

Maynard, G.G. Oliver *The History of the Moravian Church Eastern West Indies*, (Port of Spain, 1968).

'Meliora' (Pinder, Reverend Edward), *Letters on the Labouring Population of Barbados*, (London, 1858)

Menard, Russell R. *Sweet Negotiations. Sugar, slavery and plantation agriculture in early Barbados* (London, 2006).

Messenger, Charles, *Call to Arms: The British Army 1914–18* (London, 2005).

Miller, Morag, Lacock, Roy, Sadler, John and Serdeville, Rosie, *As Good As Any Man. Scotland's Black Tommy*, (Stroud, 2014).

Moister, Reverend William, *Memoir of the Rev. H. Wharton*, (London 1875).

Moore, Reverend H. and Potter, Mr G.R., *1838-1878 Emancipation Jubilee. Address Delivered in the Moravian Chapel in Demerara*, (1888).

Palmer, Geoff, *The Enlightenment Abolished. Citizens of Britishness*, (Manchester, 2007).

Pennybacker, Susan D., *From Scotsboro to Munich: Race and Political Culture in 1930s Britain*, (Woodstock, 2009).

Pettigrew, William A., *Freedom's Debt: The Royal Africa Company and the Politics of the Atlantic Slave Trade, 1672-1752*, (Virginia, 2013).

Preparata, Guido Giacomo, *Conjuring Hitler. How Britain and America Made the Third Reich*, (London, 2005).

Prince, Mary, *The History of Mary Prince, a West Indian Slave. Related by Herself. With a Supplement by the Editor. To Which is Added, the Narrative of Asa-Asa, a Captured African*, (London, 1831).

Reddington, John (ed), *Calender of Treasury Papers* (London,1868).

Robeson, Eslanda Goode, *Paul Robeson, Negro*, (London, 1930).

Robeson, Paul, *Here I Stand*, (Boston, 1988 edition).

Sainsbury, W. Noel (ed.), *Calender of State Papers, Colonial Series, America and West Indies 1661-1668* (London, 1880).

Samuel, Ralph, *East End Underworld*, (London,1981).

Sancho, Ignatious, *Letters of the Late Ignatious Sancho, An African*, Vol.1, (London, 1782).

Scholes, Theophilus E. Samuel, *Glimpses of the Ages: or the superior and inferior races, so-called discussed in the light of science and history', Volume II* (London, 1908).

Scott, William Robert, *The Constitution and Finance of English, Scottish and Irish Joint Stock Companies to 1720. Volume 2: Companies of Foreign Trade, Colonisation, Fishing and Mining*, (Cambridge, 1912).

Sewell, William G., *The Ordeal of Free Labour in the British West Indies* (London, 1968).

Shepherd, Ben, *A War of Nerves* (London, 2002).

Sherwood, Marika, *Many Struggles. West Indian Workers and Service Personnel in Britain (1939-45)*, (London, 1985).

Simpson, Kevin E., *Soccer Under the Swastika*, (London, 2016).

Smith, Paul, *Aye Ready, Rangers War Heroes*, (Edinburgh, 2011).

Smith, Richard, *Jamaican Volunteers in the First World War*, (Manchester, 2004).

Steel, Peta, *The Battle of Cable Street*, (London, 2018).

Stewart, William, *J. Keir Hardie*, (London, 1925).

Street, John C. *The Genealogy of the Rouses of Devon*, (Wisconson, 2002).

Stuart, Andrea, *Sugar in the Blood. A Family's Story of Slavery and Empire*, (London, 2012).

Talburt, Tony, *Andrew Watson. The World's First Black Football Superstar*, (London, 2017).

Teacher, David, *Rogue Agents. The Cercle and the 6I in the Private Cold War 1951-1991*, (UK, 2013).

The Missionary Manual And Directory Of The Unitas Fratrum Or The Moravian Church (Bethlehem, P.A., 1875).

Thome, J.A. and Kimball, J.H. *Emancipation in the West Indies* (New York, 1936).

Trotsky, Leon, *My Life. An Attempt at an Autobiography*, (London, 1984 edition).

Tryon, Thomas, *Friendly Advice to the Gentleman-Planters of the East and West Indies*, (London,1684).

Vasili, Phil, *The First Black Footballer, Arthur Wharton 1865-1930. An Absence of Memory*, (London, 1998).

Vasili, Phil, *Walter Tull, 1888-1918, Footballer, Officer*, (London, 2018).

Watkins, James, *Narrative of the Life of James Watkins*, (Bolton, 1852).

Watson, Karl, *The Civilised Island of Barbados. A Social History, 1715-1816*, (Barbados, 1979).

Williams, Eric, *Capitalism and Slavery*, (London, 1964).

Working Class History, *Working Class History. Everyday Acts of Resistance and Rebellion*, (Oakland, 2020).

Zahedieh, Nuala, *The Capital and the Colonies: London and the Atlantic Economy, 1660-1700*, (Cambridge, 2010).

Journals, Articles and Pamphlets

African Review, 9 September, Vol. xx No. 355.

An Extract Out of the Report of the Lords Commissioners of Trade, Laid before the House of Commons in 1708-08 setting forth the Fictitious and Real Accounts of the African Company for the 10 per Cent Duty British Library, London.

A Living History of Balloch, (Balloch Village Trust, 2009).

Anonymous, *Thomas Tryon, Sheep, and the Politics of Eden* https://ueae-prints.uea.ac.uk/id/eprint/63014/1/Accepted_manuscript.pdf

Beckles, Hilary, "Plantation Production and White "Proto-Slavery": White Indentured Servants and the Colonization of the English West Indies, 1624-1645" *The Americas* 41.3.

Blakemore, R. J. 'West Africa in the British Atlantic: trade, violence, and empire in the 1640s'. *Itinerario*, 39 (2) (2015).

Blackwood's Edinburgh Magazine, no. 943 (May, 1894), vol. 155.

Brown, Ruth, 'Racism and Immigration Controls', *International Socialism*, Autumn 1995.

B'Tselem. The Israeli Information Center for Human Rights in the Occupied Territories, *A Regime of Jewish Supremacy from the Jordan River to the Mediterranean Sea. This is Apartheid*. January 2021.

Burford, Beverly and Watson, Julian, *Celebrating Black and Asian History in Greenwich*, (London's Museums, Archives and Libraries, undated).

Dawson, Ashley, 'The Rise of the Black Internationale: Anti-imperialist Activism and Aesthetics in Britain during the 1930s', *Atlantic Studies* 6 (2009).

Dietz, Frederick C.'The Receipts and Issues of the Exchequer During the Reign of James 1 and Charles 1' (vol.XIII, 4) in Sidney Brayshaw Fay and Harold Underwoood Faulkner (eds) *Smith College Studies in History Volumes 12-14 1926-29* (Northampton Mass., 1929).

Edwards, Dudley 'The Last Stand of the Levellers' *In Defence of Marxism* 27 October 2009.

Engels, Frederick in Sigismund Borkheim, *In Memory of German Arch-Patriots of 1806-07*, (Gottinggen-Zurich, 1888).

Finayson, Reverend Duncan, *Story of a Family*, (1997).

Finlayson, Jean *Tales of Grandfathers (and Grandmothers)*, (undated).

Ganser, Daniele 'Terrorism in Western Europe: An Approach to NATO's Secret Stay-Behind Armies', *The Whitehead Journal of Diplomacy and International Relations*, Winter-Spring 2005.

Gill, G.E., 'The Silencing of Paul Robeson' in *No Surrender! No Retreat!* (New York, 2000).

Gow, Mike, *Dental History Magazine*, Vol. 1, No. 1, 2007.

Gow, Mike, *Dental History Magazine*, Vol. 5, No. 2, 2011.

Gunkel, A. and Handler, J.S. 'A German Indentured Servant in Barbados in 1652: The Account of Heinrich von Uchteritz' *Journal of the Barbados Museum and Historical Society*, 33 (1970).

Haile-Selassie, Yohannes, Melillo, Stephanie M., Vazzana, Antonio, Benazzi, Stefano and Ryan, Timothy, 'A 3.8-million-year-old cranium from Woranso-Mille, Ethiopia', *Nature*, 12 September, 2019, vol. 573.

Handler, J. 'Slave revolts and conspiracies in seventeenth century Barbados' in *New West Indian Guide/Nieuwe West-Indische Gids* 56 (1982), no: 1/2, Lieden.

Herz, John H. "The Fiasco of Denazification in Germany." *Political Science Quarterly*, vol. 63, no. 4, 1948,

Highways and Hedges, 'The Story of Forty Years, 1869–1909, for the Children of Sorrow', July and August, 1909.

Horsley, David, *Billy Strachan, 1921-1998*, (London, 2019).

Inikori, Joseph, 'Measuring the unmeasured hazards of the Atlantic slave trade: documents relating to the British trade', *Revue française d'histoire d'outre-mer*, tome 83, 312, 3,1996.

Kasrils, Ronnie, 'I fought South African apartheid. I see the same policies in Israel.', *Guardian*, 3 April 2019.

Jenkinson, Hilary, 'The Records of the English African Companies', *Transactions of the Royal Historical Society*, 3, 6 (1912).

Jenkinson, Jacqueline, *Black Sailors on Red Clydeside: rioting, reactionary trade unionism and conflicting notions of 'Britishness' following the First World War*, University of Stirling (undated).

Latrobe, Charles, *Journal written in the year 1788 and beginning 1789.*

Killingray, David, 'All the King's Men? Blacks in the British Army in the First World War' in Rainer Lotz and Ian Pegg (eds.), *Under the Imperial Carpet: Essays in Black British History*, (Crawley, 1986).

Manning, Brian, 'God, Hill and Marx', *International Socialism*, 59, Summer, 1993.

MacKinnon, Dr Iain and Mackillop, Dr Andrew, *Plantation slavery and land-ownership in the west Highlands and Islands: legacies and lessons. A Discussion Paper,* (Scotland, 2020).

Markham, Sir Clements Roger 'The Hawkins' Voyages during the reign of Henry VIII, Queen Elizabeth and James 1' in *Works Issued by the Hakluyt Society No. LVII* (London, 1878).

Maxwell-Stuart, Hamish, 'Transportation from Britain and Ireland, 1615–1875.' *A*
Global History of Convicts and Penal Colonies. Ed. Clare Anderson. (London, 2018).

McCance, Andrew, 'James McFadyen McNeill' *Biographical Memoirs of Fellows of the Royal Society*, Vol.11 (Nov., 1965).

McGeorge, Tristan, *Hacker,* Jamie and Wessely, Simon, 'The MoD PTSD decision: a psychiatric perspective', *Occupational Health Review*, 122. July/August, 2006.

Messer, Chris M., 'The Tulsa Race Riot of 1921: Toward an Integrative Theory of Collective Violence', *Journal of Social History*, Vol. 44, No. 4 (Summer 2011).

Miller, James A., et al. 'Mother Ada Wright and the International Campaign to Free the Scottsboro Boys, 1931-1934.' *The American Historical Review*, vol. 106, no. 2, 2001.

Moore, Katharine,' 'The Warmth of Comradeship', The First British Empire Games and Imperial Solidarity', *International Journal for the History of Sport*, vol.6, September 1989, No2.

Napier, Steven 'The Royal African Company' in Leslie M. Alexander and

Walter C Rucker (eds.) *Encyclopaedia of African-American History, Volume 1* (California, 2010).

Piggott, David, Leslie, Gary & Poller, Greg, *Widening Participation in Golf. Barriers to Participation and Golfmark,* (English Golf Union and University of Lincoln, undated)

Roberts, James ' "The Best Football Team, the Best Platoon": The Role of Football in the Proletarianisation of the British Expeditionary Force, 1914-1918.' *Sport in History,* volume 26, 1, April 2006.

Scottish Critical Heritage, *Fighting Denial: The Lothian Black Forum and Anti-Racist Protests in Edinburgh, 1989-92.*

Sherwood, Marika, 'The Comintern, the CPGB, Colonies and Black Britons, 1920-1938', *Science and Society,* Vol.60, No 2, (Summer, 1996).

Stephenson-Knight, Marilyn, *'Who did He Think He Was?" Walter Tull's Family History in Dover and Folkestone,* (Dover War Memorial Project, undated).

The Several Declarations of the Company of Royal Adventurers of England trading into Africa.

Thurlow, Richard C. "The Guardian of the 'Sacred Flame': The Failed Political Resurrection of Sir Oswald Mosley after 1945." *Journal of Contemporary History* 33, no. 2 (1998).

Toye, Richard, 'Winston Churchill's "Crazy Broadcast": Party, Nation and the 1945 Gestapo Speech', *Journal of British Studies* 49 (July 2010).

Transactions of the Aborigenes Protection Society 1890-96, 4, 1.

Tull, Daniel, *A Short Journal* (Commenced 1877).

Tull-Warnock, Edward, *Paul Robeson,* (undated).

Tull-Warnock, Edward, *The Film That Will Never Be Screened,* (undated).

Tull-Warnock, Edward, *Types of Humanity to be Seen in a Dentists Chair,* (undated).

Weissbourd, Emily. "'Those in Their Possession': Race, Slavery, and Queen Elizabeth's 'Edicts of Expulsion.'" *Huntington Library Quarterly,* vol. 78, no. 1, 2015,.

Newspapers

Aberdeen Press and Journal
Ayr Advertiser.Ayrshire Post
Barbadian
Buenos Aires Herald
Carrick Herald
Camden New Journal
Daily Chronicle (London)
Daily News (London)

Daily Worker
Dover Express
East London Observer
Folkestone Herald
Glasgow Evening Times
Glasgow Herald
Guardian
Inverness Courier
Irish Post
Milngavie and Bearsden Herald
Morning Star
Negro Worker
Newcastle Evening Chronicle
Scottish Referee
Sporting Man (Newcastle)
The People's Paper
Tottenham and Wood Green AdvertiserWeekly Herald (Tottenham and Edmonton)

Archives

Action for Children Archive, Watford, Hertfordshire. *Tull* file.
Barbados Archives, Black Rock, Barbados
Lunatic Asylum Records
Births, Deaths, Marriages, Registers
Finlayson Family Archive (incorporating The Walter Tull Archive), Strathpeffer, Scotland.
Finlayson, Jean *Tales of Grandfathers (and Grandmothers),* (undated).
Tull-Warnock, Edward, *Paul Robeson,* (undated).
Tull-Warnock, Edward, *The Film That Will Never Be Screened,* (undated).
Tull-Warnock, Edward, *Types of Humanity to be Seen in a Dentists Chair,* (undated).
Hull History Centre
Socialist Medical Association
Imperial War Museum
Floyer-Acland, Arthur Nugent, *The Journal of Arthur Nugent Acland.*
John Rylands Library, Manchester.
Christian L.G. Latrobe *Journal written in the year 1788 and beginning 1789.*
Results of the Synod of the Brethren Church held in Herrnhut in 1836.
Kent History and Library Centre, Maidstone.
Elham (Poor Law) Union Minute Book.
Grace Hill Wesleyan Chapel, Folkestone.
Moravian Archives, Muswell Hill, London.

Barbados Letters from 1768-1813 'A' Book.
Periodical Accounts.
Moore, Reverend H. and Potter, Mr G.R., 1838-1878 *Emancipation Jubilee. Address Delivered in the Moravian Chapel in Demerara*, (1888).
National Archives, Kew, London.
Slave Registers
Colonial Office Papers

Dissertations

Aitchison, Jean, *A Study of the Servant Class in South Ayrshire. 1750-1914*, M. Phil dissertation (1998) University of Glasgow.
Corpuz, Jose Rowell Tapac *Essays on the Royal Africa Company and the Slave Trade* Ph.D dissertation (2019), University of Warwick.
Evans, June, *African/Caribbean in Scotland. A Socio-Geographical Study*, Ph.D dissertation (1995), University of Edinburgh.
Gray, Audrey, *The 'Happiest Corner' of London: Bethnal Green 1881-1951*, M.A. dissertation (2012), Louisiana State University.
McNaught, Lilian, *The 1816 Barbados Slave Revolt*, M.A. dissertation (2017) University of Exeter.
Newton, Melanie, *"The Children of Africa in the Colonies": Free People of Colour in Barbados During the Emancipation Era, 1816-1854*, Ph.D dissertation (2001), University of Oxford.
Ross, Rufus Myer *The development of dentistry: a Scottish perspective circa 1800-1921*. Ph. D dissertation (1994), University of Glasgow.
Senior, Clive Malcom, *An Investigation of the Activities and Importance of English Pirates 1603-40* , Ph.D dissertation (1972), University of Bristol.
Svalastog, J.M. *Mastering the worst of trades: England's early Africa companies and their traders, 1618-1672* Ph.D dissertation (2018), University of Leiden.
Waymark, Peter Astley Grosvenor, *Television and the Cultural Revolution: the BBC under Hugh Carleton Greene*, Ph.D Dissertation (2005), Open University.
Zook, George Frederick, *The Company of Royal Adventurers Trading into Africa*, Ph.D dissertation (1919), Cornell University.

Websites

Barbados Planters, Eminent 1673 — https://www.geni.com/projects/Barbados-Eminent-Planters-1673/3290
Barbados Slave Code 1661 — http://pryan2.kingsfaculty.ca/pryan/assets/File/Barbados%20Slave%20Code%201688%20(repealed%20the%201661%20code).pdf

Barbados Slave Revolts — http://jeromehandler.org/wp-content/up-loads/2009/07/Revolts-82.pdf

British Social and Political History — https://spartacus-educational.com

Dall, William, dentist — http://www.historyofdentistry.group/index_htm_files/1998Oct4.pdf

Dictionary of Scots Language — https://www.dsl.ac.uk/entry/snd/dinger

Education, Elementary in England, 1861 — http://www.educationengland.org.uk/history/chapter06.html

Finlayson, Duncan — https://blantyreproject.com/2017/08/rev-duncan-finlayson-1917-2012/

Glasgow and slave trade — https://it.wisnae.us/glasgow-and-the-slave-trade/

Infant Mortality, 1880 — https://www.open.edu/openlearn/ocw/mod/oucontentview.phpid=28151&section=2.2

Infant Mortality, 2020 — http://www.geoba.se/country.php?cc=GB&year=2020

Legacies of British Slave Ownership — https://www.ucl.ac.uk/lbs/

Levellers - https://www.marxist.com/last-stand-of-the-levellers.htm

Marxism - https://www.marxists.org

Moody, Harold — https://www.encyclopedia.com/history/encyclope-dias-almanacs-transcripts-and-maps/moody-harold-arundel

Obeah - http://www.people.vcu.edu/~wchan/poco/624/harris_south/Obeah%20and%20Myal.htm

Palestine/Israel — https://electronicintifada.net

Polgreen, Rachel Pringle — https://www.blackpast.org/global-african-history/polgreen-rachel-pringle-1753-1791/

Pulmonary Arterial Hypertension — https://www.webmd.com/lung/pulmonary-arterial-hypertension

Reparations — https://caricomreparations.org

Robeson, Paul — https://nsarchive2.gwu.edu/coldwar/interviews/epi-sode-6/robeson1.html

Seaview Hospital — https://forgotten-ny.com/2000/03/hospital-of-the-damned/

Slavery, Scotland and Highlands — https://www.spanglefish.com/slavesandhighlanders/index.asp?pageid=222591

Tull, Walter — www.vasili.co.uk

Tull-Warnock, Edward,

https://www.bda.org/library/history/bame-in-dental-history

https://www.britishnewspaperarchive.co.uk/viewer/bl/0000578/19950109/776/0012

https://www.firstworldwarglasgow.co.uk/CHttpHandler.ashx-

?id=25685&p=0

https://www.firstworldwarglasgow.co.uk/index.aspx?articleid=11636.

https://www.britishnewspaperarchive.co.uk/viewer/
bl/0000573/19431021/077/0004

Wage Rates, Agricultural Labourers — http://www.geoba.se/country.
php?cc=GB&year=2020

Index

Northampton Town FC 252, 254, 268, 273, 276, 334
Obeah 65
Palmer, Stephen 131, 135
Pepys, Samuel 99
Philip II 87
Pigmentocracy 15, 31, 40
Pitt, William. 19
Planters 16-19, 21, 28-29, 40, 42, 48-49, 51, 53-56, 58-60, 62-67, 97, 102, 105-108, 116-120, 124, 128-129, 173, 322
Plantocracy 21-22, 31, 34, 41, 44, 47-48, 51-52, 63-64, 68, 117
Praedials 58
Quakers 15-17, 105, 117, 126
Queen's Park FC 199, 204, 334
Racism 59, 67, 132, 231-234, 276, 278, 289, 318
Raleigh, Sir Walter 88
Rangers FC 175, 193-194, 199, 204-205, 208-209, 249, 252, 259, 272-273, 302, 334
Reid, Fred 175, 204, 206, 217
Reid, Jimmy 285
Restoration 55, 75, 97, 99, 100, 104, 107, 171, 195
Robeson, Paul 26, 182, 243, 278-283, 285, 293, 295, 297-298, 301, 319
Royal Adventurers 60, 64, 74, 98-104, 106-109, 123, 171, 195, 331-332
Scientific Racism 67, 231-232, 234
Scottish Guinea Company 95
Sectarianism 188, 289
Senegal Adventurers 90
Sharon 17, 18, 20-21, 38, 47
Sierra Leone 20, 49, 70-71, 75, 77, 86, 91, 110, 172
Simmons, Henry 15, 17, 23-25, 50
Slave Code 60
Slave Register 17, 21, 25, 38-39, 196
Slavery 15-21, 23-25, 28, 31-32, 34-48, 50-56, 58, 60-72, 74-82, 86-91, 94-96, 98, 102, 107, 109-110, 112-113, 117, 118-124, 127-128, 132, 161, 165, 171-172, 186, 195-197, 208, 212-213, 226, 230, 234-236, 272, 279, 312, 314, 320-321, 324, 327-328
Socialist Medical Association 181-183, 242, 314-315, 326
Spain 17, 83, 88-91, 94, 121, 181, 242, 280, 299, 320, 324
St Vincent Street 166, 170, 172, 176, 187-188, 206, 246, 248, 250-251, 291
St. Lucia 32
Stephenson, Thomas Bowman 135, 144-145, 147-150, 156, 164-166, 176, 239, 312
Struth, Bill 204-205
Stuarts, the 35-36, 55, 60, 64, 73, 97, 101, 103, 107-108, 110-111, 117, 171, 195, 222-223

Acknowledgements

Throughout the research and writing the support of the extended family of Edward has been consistent and much appreciated. The Finlayson and Justad families have given their time and patience in responding to my frequent requests for help, guidance and material from their archive. Mike Gow has provided invaluable information about his Warnock antecedents. The Humphreys in Kent, descendants of Edward's brother William, as always have been willing to assist whenever called upon. Another member of the Kent clan from Edward's maternal lineage, Graham Tuthill, as a vigilant observer of mainstream and social media, has regularly alerted me with his emails to topics of relevance. I am deeply in your debt.

The ability to research the Barbados Archives came from a generous grant from the Lipman-Miliband Trust for socialist writers. Thank you. Whilst there I received generous support and kind hospitality from the wonderful staff at the Archives: Timothy Sealy, Ingrid Thompson, Stacia Adams, Charmaine Payne, Jennifer Brady and Kerri Yarde. Harriet Pearce, librarian of Shilstone Memorial Library, Barbados Museum and Historical Society, kindly arranged and hosted a meeting with Dr Patricia Stafford. Both provided an excellent overview of the island's resources relevant to this research. Rene Delmas of Barbados Spurs gave his time and energy in seeking out Tull and Lashly graves under the merciless heat at Westbury Cemetery, Bridgetown. He also provided a welcome change of topic with his prescient comments about Mourinho's regime at White Hart Lane. Frank Forde, who provided my accommodation, was an amiable, understanding and tolerant host. He even drove me to the airport on my departure after I'd accidentally broken his tv and carelessly lost his keys! I'm grateful to you all for making my stay on the island comfortable, pleasant and productive.

The writing was funded by a Kickstarter crowdfunding campaign and the Society of Authors John C. Laurence Award which assists projects seeking to improve understanding between ethnicities. The full list of subscribers is elsewhere but special mention should be of John McCartney, Leon Mann, Irene Turner, Martin Borgars and Paul Renny for their generosity.

Special thanks to Elaine Taylor who managed with warmth, sensitivity and understanding the Walter Tull Heritage and Legacy Project Twitter account. An invaluable researcher, she provided great insights into the inter-connectedness of material.

The staff at the British Library, National Archives, Moravian

Archives, John Rylands Library, Cambridge University Library, Kent Archives and Local History Centre, Hull History Centre, British Dental Association Library, Strathclyde University Archives, Allan Glen School archives went out of their way to help. Particular thanks to Mike McCreery, Dr Anne Cameron, Lorraine Parsons and Helen Nield.

Immense gratitude to Ritchie and Lorna Conaghan of the Girvan and District Great War Project for unearthing the treasured photo of Girvan Athletic FC featuring Edward.

Curator of the Tull exhibition at Folkestone Museum, Sally Hough, was a valued source of Tull genealogy upon which I've relied.

I'm indebted to Dr Richard Smith of Goldsmiths College, University of London for his invaluable comments and suggestions.

I benefitted greatly from talking over the project with Professor David Killingray and Marika Sherwood. Both were inspirational with their input and primary source contributions.

I burdened my multi-talented and pregnant daughter Louisa and longtime friend and confidante John McCartney with a request to proof-read the manuscript which both did with incredible patience and diligence. Many, many, thanks and to Louisa, much love.

I'm really appreciative of publisher and author Ian Spring of Rymour Books for his belief and providing the platform for the public to access Edward and his families' achievements. It is fitting that Ian and Rymour are based in a part of the world Edward loved and adored.

The positive qualities of this project have been immeasurably enhanced by the support of you all. I alone am responsible for any failure to do justice to its subject.

The following kindly agreed to subscribe to this book before publication:

Ruth Appleton, Debbie Auld, Daniel Bagley, Megan Bird, Peter Bond, Martin Borgars, Sarah Chrisp, Elizabeth Coombe, Peter Crella, Francesca Day, Una Doyl, Harriet Evans, Leah Fenner, Emily Ferrufino-Coqueugniot, Iona Finlayso, Ed Finlayso, Simon Gibbons, Jan Jackson, Pat Justad, Tor Justa, Andreas Kaluza, Mindie Kapla, Richard Kerridge, David Killingay, Richard Kuper, Adrian Mallory, Leon Mann, Annu Mayor, Andrew McAnulty, John A McCartney, Debra McCulloug, Andrew Merriman, Robert Monroe, Jr, Ian Moore, Tanya Moti, Jayasri Narasimha, Wolf Owczarek,

Stephen Press, Paul Renny, Abhilash Lal Sarhadi, Gill Scott, Marika Sherwood, Mark Smith, Michael Streissguth, Elaine Taylor, Irene Turner, Lauren Morris Turner, Esq, Louisa Anna-Maria Zinzi Vasili, Walter Tull Heritage and Legacy Project, Nigel Warburton, Martin Warne, Joyce Watkinson, Peter Wickenden, Shelley Williams, Nicholas Wilson, Colin Yates, Joanna Yeung

RYMOUR